Excel with

INFORMATION AND COMMUNICATIONS TECHNOLOGY

Excel with

INFORMATION AND COMMUNICATIONS TECHNOLOGY

J.B. Dixit
Saurabh Gupta

FIREWAL MEDIA

(An Imprint of Laxmi Publications Pvt. Ltd.)

BANGALORE • CHENNAI • COCHIN • GUWAHATI • HYDERABAD
JALANDHAR • KOLKATA • LUCKNOW • MUMBAI • RANCHI
NEW DELHI

Published by :
FIREWAL MEDIA
(*An Imprint of Laxmi Publications Pvt. Ltd.*)
113, Golden House, Daryaganj,
New Delhi-110002

Phone : 011-43 53 25 00
Fax : 011-43 53 25 28

www.laxmipublications.com
info@laxmipublications.com

Price : **Rs. 495.00** *Only.*

First Edition : 2010

OFFICES

© **Bangalore**	080-26 61 15 61	© **Chennai**	044-24 34 47 26
© **Cochin**	0484-237 70 04, 405 13 03	© **Guwahati**	0361-254 36 69, 251 38 81
© **Hyderabad**	040-24 65 23 33	© **Jalandhar**	0181-222 12 72
© **Kolkata**	033-22 27 43 84	© **Lucknow**	0522-220 95 78
© **Mumbai**	022-24 91 54 15, 24 92 78 69	© **Ranchi**	0651-221 47 64

FIN-3022-495-INFO & COMM TECHNOLOGY
Typeset at : **Alankar Graphics (P) Ltd.**, New Delhi

C— 438/09/08
Printed at : *Repro India Ltd.*

CONTENTS

TERM ONE

TERM TWO

TERM THREE

PREFACE

Information and Communications Technology (ICT) is so important in the world today that it makes it imperative for every young person to be competent in the use of ICT for the many tasks that one will have to accomplish. This book is written to provide all the important skills in ICT for the students of all levels. It is expected that the knowledge and skills gained through this book will help the students to use ICT in almost all their courses at school and college. The book covers selected basic topics in ICT which offer hands-on activities to help students in acquiring the required ICT skills.

The key features of this book will help the students to:

- acquire basic ICT literacy.
- develop interest and use ICT for learning in other subjects.
- acquire the knowledge for application of ICT in education and business.
- use the Internet to communicate effectively.
- access and share information through the Internet.
- follow basic ethics in the use of ICT.
- maintain high level speed in typing.

The text has been designed in a simple and user friendly way. This text focuses on the fundamentals of ICT, which change slowly. This not only makes the information remain useful to a student when one graduates, but it also allows the author to focus on the foundation concepts on which everything else rests. This book also provides the latest developments from the rapidly changing world of ICT. Abundance of review questions have been given at the end of each unit.

AUTHORS

SECTION
ONE

TERM-ONE

BASIC ICT CONCEPTS

UNIT 1: Information and Communications Technology (ICT)

UNIT 2: Introduction to Computers

General Objectives

After reading this section, the student will be able to:

1. understand the basic concepts of ICT and information processing.
2. appreciate the impact of ICT on everyday life.

UNIT 1 INFORMATION AND COMMUNICATIONS TECHNOLOGY (ICT)

Specific Objectives

After reading this unit, the student will be able to:

1.1.1 explain the concept of ICT and its related terminologies.

1.1.2 describe the information processing cycle.

1.1.3 outline the uses of ICT for educational/social/economic purposes.

1.1.4 analyse the impact of ICT on educational, social and economic development.

1.1.5 identify career opportunities in ICT education.

1.1.0 Introduction

Information Technology (IT), is "the study, design, development, implementation, support or management of computer-based information systems particularly software applications and computer hardware". IT deals with the use of electronic computers and computer software to convert, store, protect, process, transmit and retrieve information, securely.

Recently it has become popular to broaden the term to explicitly include the field of *electronic communication* so that people tend to use the abbreviation ICT (Information and Communications Technology), it is common for this to be referred to as IT & T in the Australasia region, standing for Information Technology and Telecommunications.

1.1.1 Definition of ICT, Related Basic Concepts and Terminologies

When computer and communications technologies are combined, the result is **Information** and **Communications Technology.**

- **Information and Communications Technology (ICT)**

ICT is a general term that describes any technology that helps to produce, manipulate, store, communicate, and/or disseminate information. *ICT* merges computing with high-speed communications links carrying data, sound, and video. Examples of Information and Communications Technology include not only personal computers but also new forms of telephones, televisions, appliances, and various hand held devices.

- **Information and Communications Technologies (ICTs)**

  Note that there are two important parts of ICT—computers and communications:

Computer Technology

I am sure that you have seen, and probably used, a computer. Nevertheless, let us define what it is. *A computer is a programmable, multiuse machine that accepts data—raw facts and figures—and processes, or manipulates, it into information that we can use,* such as summaries, totals, or reports. Its purpose is to speed up problem solving and increase productivity. As mentioned earlier, Information Technology deals with computer-based information systems.

Communications Technology

Unquestionably you have been using communications technology for years. *Communications technology, also called telecommunications technology, consists of electromagnetic devices and systems for communicating over long distances.* For example, telephone, mobile, radio, broadcast, television and cable TV. More recently there has been the addition of communication among computers—which is what happens when people "go online" on the Internet. The term *'online' means using a computer or some other information device, connected through a network, to access information and services from another computer or information device.* Internet is the world wide computer network that connects hundreds of thousands of smaller networks linking computers at academic, scientific, and commercial institutions, as well as individuals.

- **Data**

  Data consists of the raw facts and figures that are processed into information—for example, the marks of different subjects for students to compute result.

Why it is important: Users need data to create useful information.

As mentioned earlier, data are the raw materials of information processing. Some of the most commonly types of processed data are given in table 1.1.

Table 1.1 Most Common Types of Data

Data Type	Description
847 637 645 574 337 645 123 987 565 234 574 324 231 334 567 337 345 111 129 342 637 789 245 807 777	Numeric data, first for the military and then for corporations, was the first data to be widely processed on computers. Currently, data such as inventory, sales, and payrolls are still processed in basically the same way.
Enjoy	Words are processed into memos, letters, reports, articles, books, and scripts. You can even format them into final form—a process called *desktop publishing*.

$\sqrt{295}$ $\frac{5}{8}$ 89%	Numbers are used by almost everyone at some time to make calculations. They might be as simple as calculating an annual budget for a year at school/college or as complex as the budget used to operate the national government.
	Charts that plot numbers can be used to illustrate and inform more effectively than tables of numbers.
	Photographs and other graphics can be stored, edited, and inserted into other applications to illustrate documents or become part of a multimedia presentation.
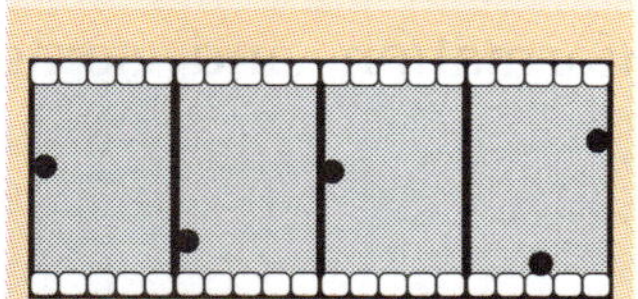	Animated characters and objects move about on the screen to entertain and inform.
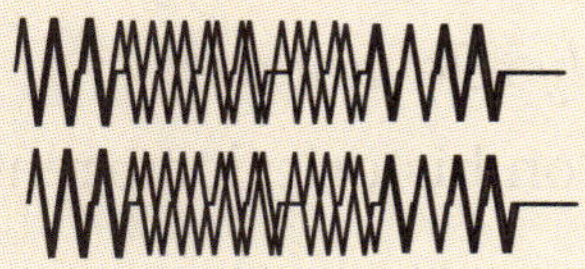	Sounds, such as music, speech, or sound effects, can be stored, edited and played back.
	Videos, such as interviews or movies, are stored as data so they can be edited or played back.

Data is not what it used to be

Not too long ago, the vast majority of information was just lists, integers, times, and characters. Although not at all simple to collect, analyse and distribute, these kind of data are known as simple data (or primitive) because they are relatively simple when compared to some of the other types of computer data now being used.

Over the past few years there has been an explosion of other types of data, complex data, that is much more than just integers and characters. For example, videoconferencing, phone calls, movies, sounds, and animations are routinely used both in business and on the Internet. Handling this diverse information has been made possible by the tremendous increases in computing power over the past decade.

- **Information**

Information is data that have been summarised or otherwise manipulated for use in decision making—for example, the total marks for each student, which are used to decide who is the topper.

Why it is important: The whole purpose of a computer (and communications) system is to produce (and transmit) usable information.

Types of Information

The types of information are: **structured**, **unstructured** and **semistructured**.

Structured information is detailed, current, and non-subjective; concerned with past events, it records a narrow range of facts, and covers an organisation's internal activities.

Unstructured information is summarised, less current, and highly subjective; concerned with future events, it records a broad range of facts, and covers activities outside as well as inside the organisation.

Semistructured information includes some structured information and some unstructured information.

In general, all information must be

Correct (accurate) and ***verifiable*** (checkable).

Complete, including *all* relevant data, yet *concise*, including *only* relevant data.

Cost effective, meaning timely, yet also time sensitive, based on historical, current, or future information tools.

Accessible, means quickly and easily obtainable.

Figure 1.1 illustrates the processing of raw data into useful information, its recycling and its packaging in a new form so that it is easier to understand, more attractive, or more useful.

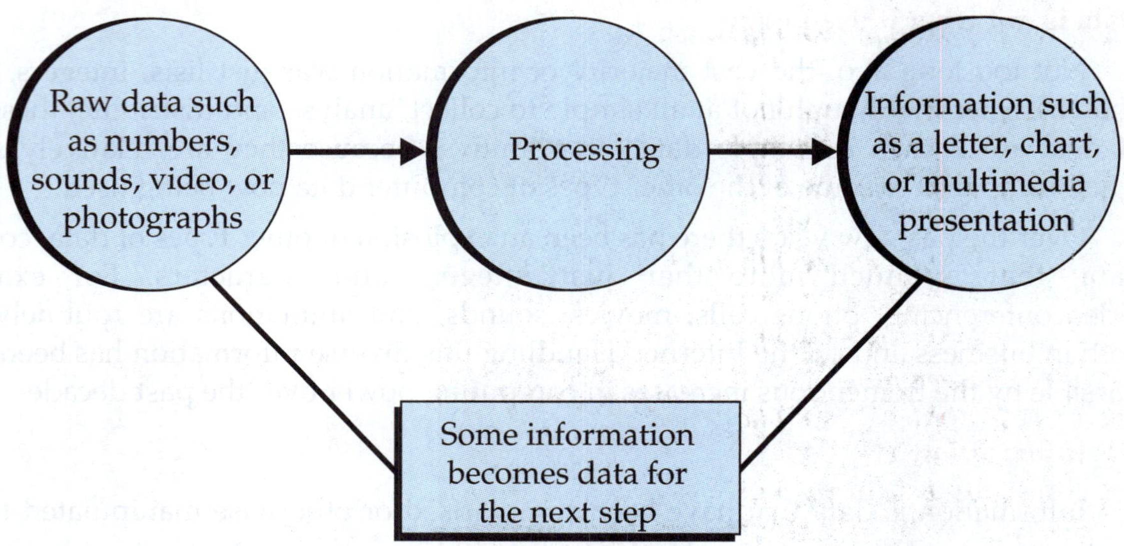

Figure 1.1 Data versus information

Table 1.2 gives the differences between data and information.

Table 1.2 Differences Between Data and Information

Data	Information
It is a collection of facts and figures.	It is collection of final results.
It is in unorganised (raw) form.	It is in organised form.
It is not in directly useful form.	It is in directly useful form.
It needs processing.	It does not need any processing.
It is also termed as input.	It is also termed as output.

- **e-learning: What is e-learning?**

Learning is the process of acquiring knowledge or skills by instruction or study. Traditionally, learning has been imparted using static content, which does not change for the duration of a semester or a training session. However, with an increase in the use of the Internet, the focus is now shifting to Web-based Training (WBT). In WBT, content is placed on a Web site and learners can gain access to it.

The world's Information and Communications Technology (ICT) education and training market is growing rapidly all over the world. The growth rates are higher in the Asia-Pacific region. The ICT training markets in India, China, and Korea are expected to grow at over 25 percent each. The West African region is also coming up in this field.

Skilled jobs will constitute 85 percent of all jobs in the new economy. Individuals, therefore, need to continuously upgrade their skills. The average age of an e-learner is 40. This goes to show that lifelong learning is the emerging trend in the knowledge economy.

Consequently, there is a huge demand for customised learning solutions, anytime and anywhere. e-learning is emerging as the most significant response to the demands of individual learning.

Advantages of e-learning

The main advantages of e-learning are given below:

1. First-in Market

The e-learning model enables the placement of content on the Web as soon as it is ready without having to wait for packaging and shipping through distribution channels. This results in cutting down the lead-time between the development of a course and its availability to learners. The early availability of content gives the learner a headstart over others.

2. Learner Control

You can learn at any time and at any place. All you need for e-learning is a Web connection. You can limit the duration of an e-learning session to study only the volume of content that you can fully absorb.

3. Enhanced Retention

Since you follow a learning style that suits you, e-learning enhances your retention. Also, the e-learning material is delivered in small logical modules known as skillets. This results in better retention and recall for a learner.

4. Timely and Easy Access

e-learning is available 24 hours a day, seven days a week. Therefore, e-learning enables you to learn at the time that is convenient to you. The timely retrieval of the learning material enables you to practise what you have learned. You can gain access to the e-learning material from any location that has a computer and an Internet access.

5. Interactive Mode

As an e-learner, you have access to a Web tutor at all times. Experts are also available for you to resolve content-related queries.

e-learning also allows you to chat with co-learners on different topics related to their subject and participate in discussion forums. *Chat is the typed discussion among participants who are online at the same time; it is just like telephone conversation, except that messages are typed rather than spoken.*

6. Assessment and Feedback

e-learning provides you with assessment exercises that test you on the course that you are learning. Online tests are typically an optional self-initiated test. You get a dynamic set of questions to answer. Unlike tests in CBT (Computer-based Training), these tests give you a feedback comparing your performance with that of other learners who have attempted the test.

7. Up-to-date Content

The e-learning technology allows the dynamic updation of information on courses. Therefore, unlike CBT or books, the content in an e-learning course is updated regularly. This enables you to gain access to the latest information on the course.

8. State-of-the-art Environment

The future of all activities in educational and commercial spheres is on the Internet. Therefore, most of the new development in educational technologies is Web-based. Most transactions are changing from physical to virtual, and the Internet is at the core of everything. Therefore, with e-learning, you work in a state-of-the-art environment that is going to be the environment of the future.

1.1.2 Information Processing Cycle

Processing information is only one stage in a larger process called the information processing cycle. This cycle has five stages:

Stage 1 — Receiving data

Stage 2 — Processing data

Stage 3 — Display result

Stage 4 — Storing information

Stage 5 — Distribution of information

Computer hardware and software are used at each stage. Let us look at each stage and the hardware and software that applies to it, as illustrated in figure 1.2.

Stage 1—Receiving data (Input devices)

The user input **data** into the computer using a keyboard, mouse or other device (such as scanner, microphone, still camera or video camera). The input may be text, numbers, images or sounds.

Stage 2—Processing data (Processing device)

Once in the computer, data can be processed (numbers added or sorted, text formatted, images or sounds edited). Processing devices are CPUs such as Celeron, Pentiums, AMD, MC 68040 etc.

Stage 3—Display result (information) (Output devices)

To see (or hear) what the computer has processed, it has to be output on a monitor, printer, speakers or LCD Projector. It might also be transferred to another device that processes the data further. For example, edited sound or video output may become input for a multimedia presentation.

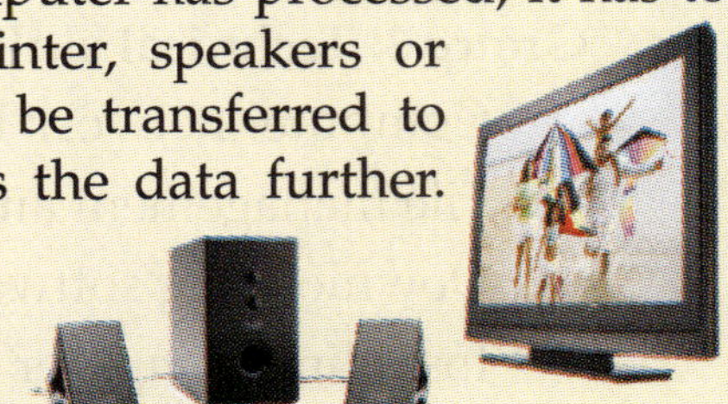

Stage 4—Storing information (Storage devices)

Data and programs not currently being used are held in storage. Primary storage is computer circuitry. Secondary storage is usually some kind of disk (such as floppy disk, hard disk, pendrive, CDs, DVD) or tape.

Stage 5—Distribution of information (human being, e-mail, fax etc.)

Data or information can be printed and distributed or directly distributed from one computer to other computers. Two popular ways to do so are to send documents as attachments to e-mail or to post them on a Web site. Human beings can also be helpful or fax can be used.

Figure 1.2 The information processing cycle

1.1.3 Uses of ICT Tool

There is a wide range of ICT tools e.g., portable and wireless technologies, tablet PCs, IWBs (Interactive White boards), digital cameras/recorders, data capture hardware and software. The use of these and other ICT tools, especially the use of software can create and manipulate 3D images and ICT. Visualisation and modelling in 3D is fundamental to a wide variety of disciplines—and to science, technology, engineering and mathematics in particular.

The major ICT skills can be divided into three groups. These are given below:

Group 1: Presenting Information in a range of formats

Word processing
Spreadsheets
Databases
Electronic presentations
Use of digital cameras

Group 2: Using e-Communication tools

Web navigation and appreciation
VoIP
Email management
Videoconferencing
Online blogs and forums
Online banking

Group 3: Technical skills related to School Systems

Computer network knowledge
File management and Windows Explorer
Downloading software and resources from the Web
Installing computer software onto a computer system
Computer-related storage devices
Use of scanners
Familiarity with PDAs
Familiarity with Internet safety issues
Understanding educational copyright
Knowledge of computer security
Submitting e-returns

Let us discuss the uses of ICT tools for educational/social/economic purposes:

The Uses of ICTs for Educational Purposes

Education policymakers and planners must first of all be clear about what educational outcomes are being targeted. These broad goals should guide the choice of technologies to be used and their modalities of use.

The potential of each technology varies according to how it is used. There are at least five levels of technology use in education: *presentation, demonstration, drill and practice, interaction,* and *collaboration.*

Each of the different ICTs—print, audio/video cassettes, radio and TV broadcasts, computers or the Internet—may be used for presentation and demonstration, the most basic of the five levels. Except for video technologies, drill and practice may likewise be performed using the whole range of technologies. On the other hand, networked computers and the Internet are the ICTs that enable interactive and collaborative learning the best; their full potential as educational tools will remain unrealised if they are used merely for presentation or demonstration.

The Uses of ICTs for Social Purposes

We can reach marginalised sectors of society through ICTs. It has been claimed that ICTs have the potential to impact the livelihood strategies of small-scale and local commercial enterprises.

When applied to disease prevention and epidemic response efforts, ICT can provide considerable benefits and capabilities. Public broadcast media such as radio and television have a long history of effectively facilitating the dissemination of public health messages and disease prevention techniques in developing countries. The Internet can also be utilised to improve disease prevention by enabling more effective monitoring and response mechanisms.

The Uses of ICTs for Economic Purposes

ICTs are everywhere and business and industry are using them in new ways. Without ICTs, the modern corporations could not even exist. ICTs have become so important that almost no activity would be possible without them. Some of the important uses are in the following fields:

- Transaction processing
- Home-based workers
- Desktop publishing
- Financial analysis
- Product design
- Factories
- Architectural walk-throughs

The e-commerce is spreading most quickly among developing countries. M-commerce, defined as the buying and selling of goods and services using wireless handheld devices such as mobile telephones or personal data assistants (PDAs), is likewise growing at a rapid rate.

Businesses clearly see the Internet as a way to enhance productivity and competitiveness. Text messaging has been the most successful m-commerce application in developing countries, where rates of low fixed-line connectivity and Internet access have made it an e-mail substitute.

1.1.4 Impact of ICT on Educational, Social and Economic Development

The most effective route to achieving substantial benefit with ICTs in development programmes is to concentrate on re-thinking development activities by analysing current problems and associated contextual conditions, and considering ICT as just one ingredient of the solution. This implies an approach to developing strategies for information systems and technology that are derived from and integrated with other components of the overall development strategy. This approach is shown in figure 1.3.

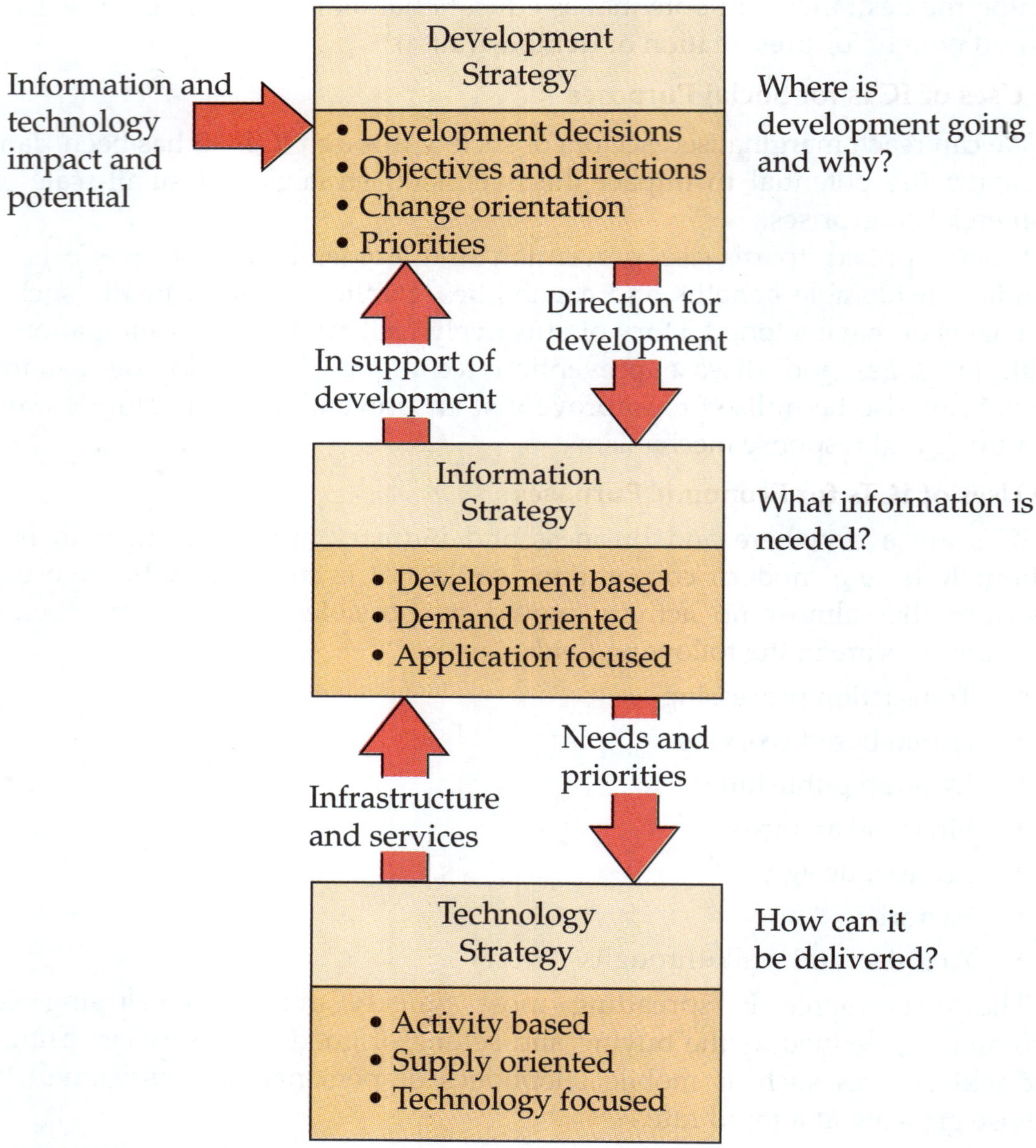

Figure 1.3 The relationship between development, information and ICTs

The model was developed to facilitate a grass-roots implementation targeting community development where heavy emphasis was laid on empowering the community to construct their own agenda for ICT-assisted development, prior to introducing the technology.

Let us see the impacts of ICT on educational, social and economic development.

Impact on Educational Development

The growth of distance education is being fuelled by the urgent need to close the education gap between poor and rich nations. According to the United Nations Educational, Scientific and Cultural Organisation (UNESCO), only about three percent of young people in sub-Saharan Africa and seven percent in Asia attend some form of postsecondary education. This compares with 58 percent in industrialised countries as a whole, and 81 percent in the United States.

Developing countries see investing in distance education programmes as a way to educate more people for less money. UNESCO and the World Bank have reported that in the world's 10 biggest distance education institutions, the majority of which are in the Third World, the cost of education per student is on average about one third the cost at traditional institutions in the same country.

On-line distance education is better suited to adult learners and there are now many organisations opening virtual universities to cater for them. The element of flexible timing for learning appeals to adults who are employed and who realise the value of life-long learning in a changing work environment.

Most development in e-learning benefits the already privileged. Nevertheless, examples of pro-poor learning indicate the possibilities for the less privileged. It is almost a universally observable phenomenon that children seem to take to computers naturally.

The **International Society for Technology in Education (ISTE)** has established standards for students, teachers and administrators about the use of technology in the classrooms. This professional organisation is a leader in helping teachers become more effective users of technology in their teaching. ISTE gives support to the following principle. The effective use of technology can help change the current educational paradigm in the following ways:

OLD PARADIGM	NEW PARADIGM
Teacher-centred instruction	Student-centred learning
Single sensory stimulation	Multi-sensory stimulation
Single path progression	Multi-path progression
Single media	Multimedia
Isolated work	Collaborative work
Information delivery	Information exchange
Passive, receptive learning	Active, inquiry-based learning
Factual, knowledge-based	Critical thinking, informed decision making

Reactive response	Proactive, planned
Isolated, artificial context	Authentic, real-world context

Impact on Social Development

Some impacts of ICTs on social development are given below:

1. Targeting Disadvantaged and Marginalised Groups

Within populations of poor people, disadvantaged and marginalised sections of society usually face impediments to using, and making good use of ICTs in much the same way that they might face impediments in using other resources. Women in developing countries in particular face difficulties in using ICTs, as they tend to be poorer, face greater social constraints, and are less likely to be educated or literate than men. Moreover, they are likely to use ICTs in different ways, and have different information requirements than men. Women are also less likely to be able to pay for access to ICTs, either because of an absolute lack of funds or because they lack control of household expenditure. Constraints on women's time or their movement outside the home can also reduce their ability to access technologies. Such groups usually require special assistance and attention in order to benefit from programmes that are targeted at poor people.

People who do not understand the English language are also a marginalised section of society on the Internet. Such people include the majority populations of French-speaking Africa, the Middle East, Eastern Europe and Latin America. Even when users have basic English proficiency, they are discouraged from using Websites that are only in English.

The selling of handicrafts on the Internet by local artisans (an artisan is skilled workman or craftsman), a form of e-commerce, also provides buyers with the historical and cultural background of indigenous products.

Nearly 80 percent of the world's disabled population of 500 million people lives in developing countries. Efforts to enable access to ICTs by disabled people are under way. One such effort relates to the development of adaptive technology, which is a major prerequisite for many people with disabilities to use computer technology. These are modifications or upgrades to a computer's hardware and software to provide alternative methods of entering and receiving data. Many of the modifications can be made relatively inexpensively.

2. Promoting Local Commercial Activities

ICTs are used by marginalised sectors to promote their goods over the Internet, through chat-rooms and mail lists. They work from a computer, either at home or in a cyber cafe, and draw commissions on the sales that they achieve. Indeed, small scale entrepreneurs in developing countries, especially women, have shown the ability to harness ICTs for developing their enterprises.

ICT and e-commerce are attractive to women entrepreneurs (who in many developing countries account for the majority of small and medium size enterprise owners), as it allows them to save time and money while trying to reach out to new clients in domestic and foreign markets. There are many success stories in business-to-consumer (B2C) retailing or e-tailing from all developing-country regions, demonstrating how women have used the Internet to expand their customer base in foreign markets while at the same time being able to combine family responsibilities with lucrative work.

3. Improving Poor People's Health

Health care is one of the most promising areas for poverty alleviation with ICTs, based largely as it is on information resources and knowledge. There are many ways in which ICTs can be applied to achieve desirable health outcomes. ICTs are being used in developing countries to facilitate remote consultation, diagnosis, and treatment. Thus, physicians in remote locations can take advantage of the professional skills and experiences of colleagues and collaborating institutions. Health workers in developing countries are accessing relevant medical training through ICT-enabled delivery mechanisms. Several new malaria Internet sites for health professionals include innovative "teach-and-test" self-assessment modules. In addition, centralised data repositories connected to ICT networks enable remote health care professionals well-informed about the rapidly evolving stock of medical knowledge.

Impact on Economic Development

ICTs have a great impact on economic development throughout the world. It is in the Asia Pacific region that e-commerce is spreading most quickly among the developing countries. The region's enterprises, particularly in manufacturing, are exposed to pressure from customers in developed countries to adopt e-business methods and are investing to be able to do so. China's population of Internet users is already the world's third largest.

M-commerce, defined as the buying and selling of goods and services using wireless handheld devices such as mobile telephones or personal data assistants (PDAs), is likewise growing at a rapid pace. In the last four years, growth in the number of mobile telephone users worldwide has exceeded fixed lines. The introduction of wireless communications has also brought wireless data services, which are essential to conducting m-commerce, to many developing countries. If the convergence of mobile and fixed Internet and ICTs continues, first access to the Internet for a significant part of the world will be achieved using mobile handsets and networks. Wireless technologies have made inroads even in relatively low-income areas, where prepaid cards allow access to people who cannot take out a subscription because of billing or creditworthiness problems. Developing Asia is the leader in this area.

Tourism and e-commerce are natural partners. Tourism is highly information-intensive. PEOPLink is a non-profit organisation that has been equipping and training grass-roots artisan organisations all over the world to use digital cameras and the Internet to market their wares while showcasing their cultural richness.

1.1.5 Career Opportunities

When it comes to ICTs at work, you can run but you cannot hide. No matter what firm you might work for, or what your position might be in the firm, the chances are that a computer will be involved in some aspect of your work. Regardless of where you are in the corporate hierarchy, you will be expected to know how to perform a core of activities with computers. If you do not do this common core, you will not be able to do your job.

Since ICTs are so widely used in business, most jobs require computer skills specific to the field and an understanding of the ICT tools used to enhance performance. In these jobs computer is not only absolutely essential but also central and very useful.

All the ICT services within an organisation are supported and maintained by a highly trained staff. Here are some of the important positions:

1. Computer Operators
2. Internet Cafe Operators
3. Programmers
4. Database Administrators
5. Network Administrators
6. System Analysts
7. Information and Communications Systems Managers
8. Webmasters, etc.

The World Wide Web is full of employment services and company listings of job openings. You can search for specific company listings, openings in specific fields e.g., ICT.

Almost all positions have career opportunities that allow you to move up the career ladder to positions with more responsibility and higher pay. Secretaries can become supervisors, programmers can become department managers, and sales people can become marketing or sales managers. Some employees who gain extensive experience within a large firm become entrepreneurs and start their own businesses. Many word processing operators have started small firms that do word processing for professionals and other people who do not have their own full-time staff to do work of this kind.

When it comes to career opportunities in ICT education, the Internet has it all. There is more information on Internet, about ICT, than you could ever possibly digest. The great thing about the Web is that you can use it to keep in touch with changes in the fields and groups that make these changes happen. For example, you can keep up with the latest research in ICT at IBM's research site.

Let us discuss some of the important career opportunities in ICT education:

- **Internet Cafe Operator**

The Internet Cafe operators operate and teach people how to use computers and the Internet. They load programs and data, back up files, run jobs and print reports for the users. They help Internet users coming to Internet Cafe in all respects so that the users can work with ease.

Figure 1.4 Internet Cafe

- **Programmer**

To know about programmer, we must understand what constitutes a program. A **program** is a list of instructions that the computer must follow in order to process data into information. The instructions consist of statements used in a programming language, such as C++. Examples are programs that do word processing, desktop publishing, or payroll processing.

The decision whether to buy or create a program depends on the organisation's need and urgency.

Programmers write programs that are used to process the company's information. They convert specifications (precise descriptions) of business or scientific problems into sequences of detailed instructions to solve the problems by computer. The programmer describes how data is to be structured in the computer and specifies the precise steps and processing logic which cause the program to produce the desired result.

Programmers do not just write programs; they test and correct them and also prepare instructions for those who will use their finished programs. They modify programs to increase their operating efficiency or to respond to change in work processes and maintain records that document the programs development and revisions.

In software companies that specialise in writing computer software, programmers are the computer equivalent of writers, authors, and film producers. Using nothing more than a keyboard, they create programs that pull together text, graphics, sounds, movies, and animations that perform useful work, inform, educate, entertain or that are tools used in turn to create other such programs. All the software programs that you purchase have been created by professional programmers.

Figure 1.5 Programmer

- **Database Administrator**

A database is a collection of interrelated files in a computer system. These computer-based files are organised according to their common elements, so that they can be retrieved easily. Sometimes called a *database manager* or Database Management System (DBMS), database software is a program that sets up and controls the structure of a database and access to the data.

Large databases are designed by a **data administrator (DA)** and managed by a specialist called a **database administrator**. **The database administrator (DBA) coordinates all related activities and needs for an organisation's database.** To manage the database, companies hire a DBA to protect and manage the database on a regular basis.

The DBA determines user access privileges; sets standards, guidelines, and control procedures; assists in establishing priorities for requests; prioritises conflicting user needs; and develops user documentation and input procedures. DBA is also concerned with security—setting up and monitoring a system for preventing unauthorized access and making sure that the system is regularly backed up and that data can be recovered should a failure or disaster occur. Finally, the DBA establishes and enforces policies about privacy.

The DBA has a full-time, highly responsible job. In addition to a managerial background, the DBA needs technical knowledge to deal with database designers. For example, the DBA needs to maintain the data dictionary and evaluate new database features and their implementation. The combination of technical and managerial backgrounds makes the job of the DBA unique.

- **Network Administrator**

Systems organised into a network are supervised by a network manager or administrator. This person can be a member of either the department the network is located in or the corporate computing department. The network manager is responsible for setting up or enforcing network procedures. For example, one user may be authorised access to correspondence files but denied access to financial analysis files. Some users can be given just read-only access, whereas others can be allowed to enter and update the files. This security prevents unauthorised users from altering files. The network administrator is responsible for troubleshooting problems should they arise and assisting both new and experienced users with problems.

Figure 1.6 LAN administrator

SUMMARY

- When computer and communications technologies are combined, the result is Information and Communications Technology.
- **ICT** is a general term that describes any technology that helps to produce, manipulate, store, communicate, and/or disseminate information.
- Data consists of raw facts and figures that are processed into information. Users need data to create information.
- Date has many types e.g., numeric, words, charts, photographs, animated, sounds, videos.
- Data used these days is much more than just integers and characters. For example, videoconferencing, phone calls, movies, sounds and animations.
- Information is data that has been summarised or otherwise manipulated for use in decision making.
- The whole purpose of a computer (and communications) system is to produce (and transmit) usable information.
- The types of information are: *structured*, *unstructured* and *semistructured*.
- e-learning is emerging as the most significant response to the demands of individual learning.
- There are many advantages of e-learning.
- Processing information is only one stage in a large process called the information processing cycle.
- There is a wide range of ICT tools.
- ICT is used mainly for educational/social/economic purposes.

- There are great impacts of ICT on educational, social and economic development.
- The most effective route to achieving substantial benefit with ICTs in development programs is to concentrate on re-thinking development activities by analysing current problems and associated contextual conditions, and considering ICT as just one ingredient of the solution.
- When it comes to ICTs at work, you can run but you cannot hide.
- Since ICTs are so widely used in business, most jobs require computer skills specific to the field and an understanding of the ICT tools used to enhance performance.
- Some of the important career opportunities in ICT education are: Internet Cafe Operator, Programmer, Database Administrator and Network Administrator.
- The Internet Cafe Operators operate and teach people how to use computers and the Internet.
- Programmers write programs that are used to process the company's information.
- The Database Administrator (DBA) coordinates all related activities and needs for an organisation's database.
- The Network Administrator is responsible for setting up or enforcing network procedures.

REVIEW QUESTIONS

STATE WHETHER TRUE OR FALSE

1. ICT is "the study of International Crime Topology".
2. When computer and communications are combined, the result is Information and Communications Technology.
3. Information is data that has been summarised or otherwise manipulated for use in decision making.
4. e-learning does not enhance the user's retention.
5. The e-learning technology allows the dynamic updation of information.
6. Tablet PCs are not ICT tools.
7. There is no impact of ICT on educational, social and economic development.
8. ICTs are used by marginalised sectors to promote their goods over the Internet.
9. ICTs are being used in developing countries to facilitate remote consultation, diagnosis, and treatment.
10. The Network Administrator is also known as network manager.

FILL IN THE BLANKS

1. ICT stands for ....
2. .... consists of raw facts and figures that are processed into information.
3. The types of information are : structured, unstructured and ....
4. Processing information is only one stage in a larger process called ....
5. .... enables you to learn at the time that is convenient to you.
6. As an e-learner, you have access to a .... at all times.
7. When it comes to .... at work, you can run but you cannot hide.
8. .... do not just write programs; they test and correct them and also prepare instructions for those who will use their finished programs.
9. To manage the database, companies hire a .... to protect and manage the database on a regular basis.
10. The .... is responsible for troubleshooting problems on the network, should they arise and assisting both new and experienced users with problems.

MULTIPLE CHOICE QUESTIONS

1. When computers and communications technologies are combined the result is ....

   (a) Computer　　*(b)* ICT
   (c) Internet　　*(d)* None of these

2. .... consists of facts and figures that are processed into information.

   (a) Data　　*(b)* Machine
   (c) Numbers　　*(d)* IT

3. Information Processing Cycle has .... stages.

   (a) Three　　*(b)* Four
   (c) Five　　*(d)* Six

4. Career Opportunities in ICTs are ....

   (a) Programmers　　*(b)* DBAs
   (c) Network Administrators　　*(d)* All of these

ANSWER THE FOLLOWING

1. Explain the concept of ICT.
2. Write short notes on the following:

   (i) Data　　*(ii)* Information

3. What is e-learning? Give its advantages.
4. Describe the information processing cycle.
5. Differentiate between the following:
   (i) ICT and ICTs *(ii)* Data and Information
6. Use a simple diagram to illustrate how data is processed into information stored and distributed using the various devices.
7. List the devices used in the stages of information processing cycle and describe the process.
8. Outline the uses of ICT for educational/social/economic purposes.
9. Discuss the impact of ICT on educational, social and economic development
10. Discuss the various career opportunities in ICT education.

FIELD TRIP

Visit some big educational organisation and report on:

(a) basic concepts of ICT and Information Processing.

(b) impact of ICT on everyday life.

ASSIGNMENT

Students should select an ICT career of their choice and find out the requirements and job description, and present to the class.

UNIT 2 INTRODUCTION TO COMPUTERS

Specific Objectives

After reading this unit, the student will be able to:

1.2.1 identify types of computers.

1.2.2 state the uses of computers.

1.2.3 boot, reboot and shut down computer correctly.

1.2.4 identify possible threats to computers and users.

1.2.5 demonstrate the responsible use of computers.

1.2.0 Introduction

Computer is perhaps the most powerful and versatile tool ever created by human being. In today's world, the use of computers has increased so rapidly that we can no longer ignore them. Computers influence our lives in one way or the other. These days we see computers being used to perform several functions that have made our life easy. The list of services for which computers are used is a long one.

What is a Computer?

Computer is an electronic device that can accept, store and process data under the control of a set of instructions. The instructions, called a program, are stored in the computer when in use, so they can be executed automatically.

A computer appears to be far more intelligent and informed than human beings but the fact is, it cannot perform any task on its own. We need to give the computer instructions on exactly what it has to do.

If an unanticipated situation arises, computers will either produce wrong results or abandon the task altogether. They do not have the potential to work out alternative solutions.

Figure 2.1 shows some of the physical components of a computer:

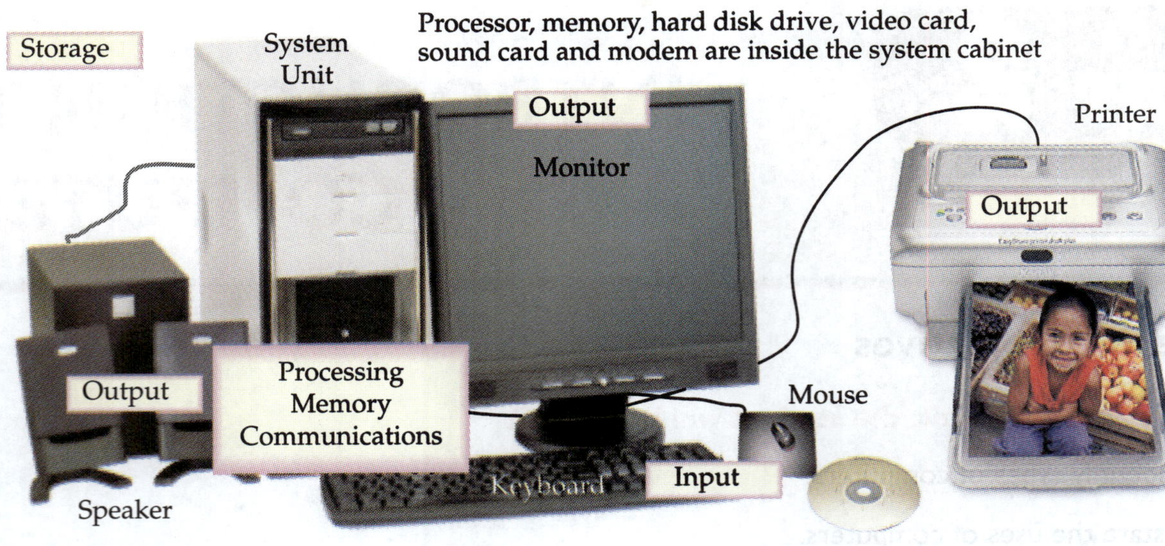

Figure 2.1 Physical components of a computer

History of the Development of Computers

Necessity is the mother of invention. The saying holds true for computers too. Computers were invented because of human beings' search for fast and accurate calculating devices.

Abacus

Abacus (Figure 2.2) is considered to be the first computer and was invented nearly 5,000 years ago by the Chinese in 3000 BC.

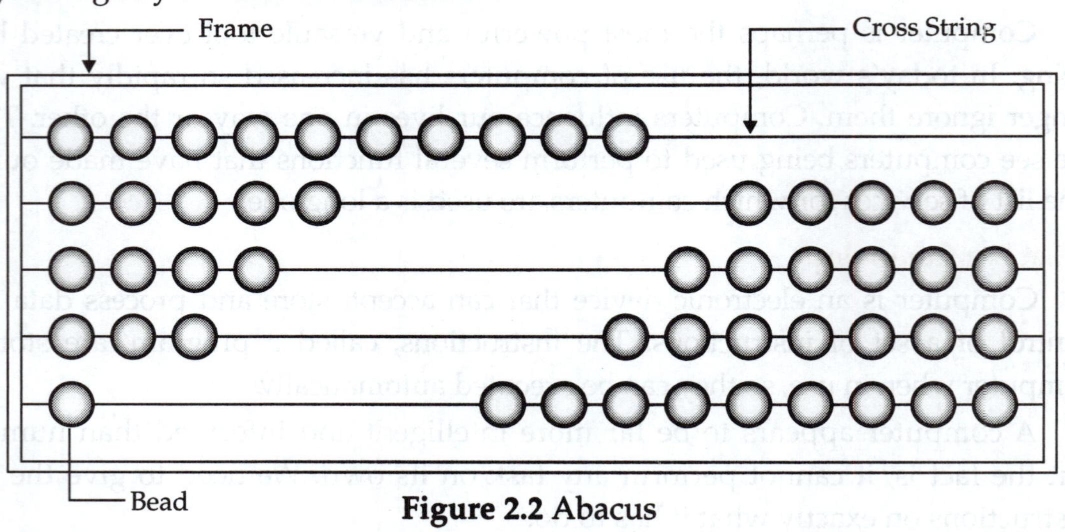

Figure 2.2 Abacus

The basic purpose of the device is to make calculations. It consists of a rectangular frame with a number of strings attached. Each string has a collection of beads. These beads are used to perform calculations. Abacus is used even today to teach small children how to count. A skilled Abacus operator can be as fast as a hand held calculator.

Pascal's Mechanical Calculator

The French Mathematician Blaise Pascal used this adding machine (1662) simply for addition and subtraction. The machine consisted of gears, wheels and dials. With this, calculation could be performed by dialling these series of wheels carrying the number 0 to 9 around their circumference. The wheels were arranged in such a manner that each wheel had 10 segments and when a wheel completed one rotation the next wheel would move by one segment. The machine was later improved by Gottfried (Germany) to perform multiplication and division.

Babbage's Mechanical Computer

Charles Babbage invented the first mechanical computer during the period 1830 to 1850. This computer performed basic arithmetic functions. It had the following five components:

1. A storage unit that held the numbers.
2. An arithmetic unit, called Mill, to perform the arithmetic calculations.
3. A control unit that controlled the activities of the computer.
4. An input device that gave the numbers and instructions to the computer.
5. An output device that displayed the result.

Figure 2.3 shows the components of Babbage's computer:

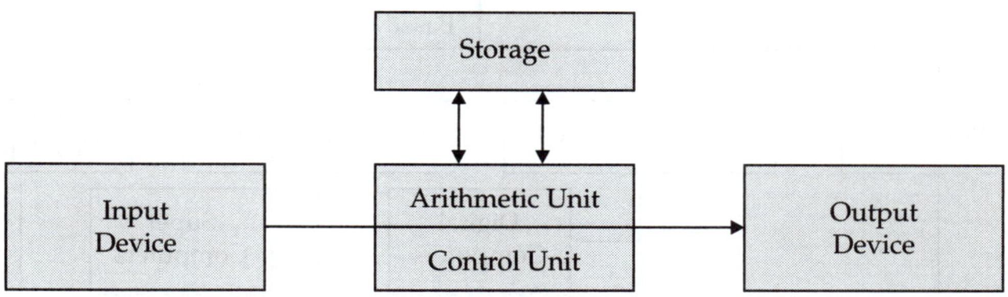

Figure 2.3 Components of Babbage's computer

Note

Charles Babbage is known as the 'Father of Modern Digital Computers' due to his pioneering work.

Mark I

In 1934, Harvard professor H. Eiken developed an automatic calculating machine which was called Mark-I digital computer. Its internal operation was automatically controlled.

Electronic Numeric Integrator And Calculator (ENIAC)

While Mark–I was the first electromechanical computer, the first electronic general purpose computer called ENIAC was built in 1946 by a team of professors at Moore School of University of Pennsylvania. It was a heavy machine consisting of 18,000 vacuum tubes, 70,000 resistors, 10,000 capacitors, 60,000 switches and having a large size occupying 1500 square feet of space. It was a very fast machine as compared to its ancestors and could perform 5000 additions or 350 simple multiplications in just one second.

Universal Automatic Computer (UNIVAC)

UNIVAC was the first computer made by a private company, IBM. It was followed by EDVAC (Electronic Discrete Variable Automatic Computer) which had a storage capacity of 1024 words of 44 bits each.

The computer's memory was stored on magnetic storage devices—primarily magnetic tapes and magnetic drums. Most of the data were entered into the computer on punched cards. Output consisted of punched cards on paper, and machine and assembly languages were used to program the computers. However, a human operator physically had to reset relay switches and wiring before a program could be run.

1.2.1 Types of Computers

Computers are classified into various types based on historical development (computer generations), purpose, technology used, size and storage capacity. Figure 2.4 illustrates the classification of computers based on different criteria.

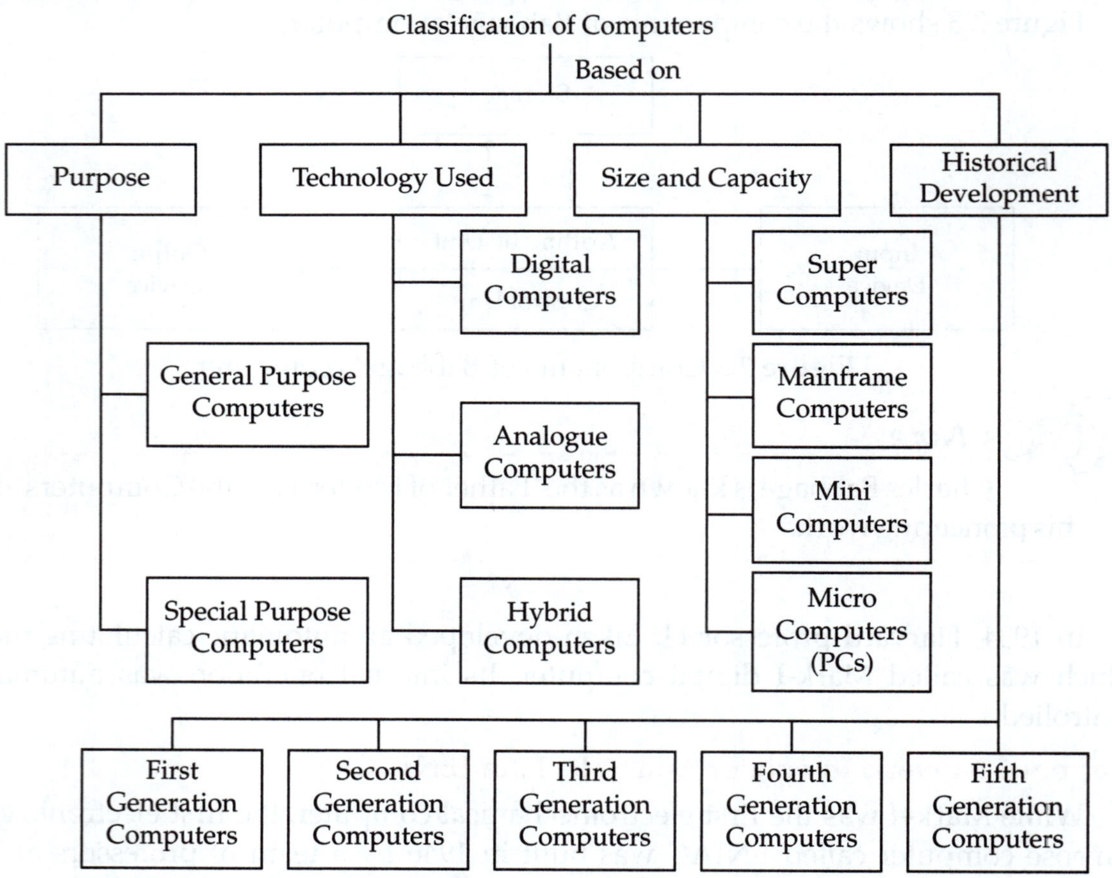

Figure 2.4 Classification of computers based on different criteria

According to the technology used, computers are of the following three types:

(i) Digital computers

(ii) Analogue computers

(iii) Hybrid computers.

Let us discuss these three types:

- **Digital Computers**

Digital computers are mainly general-purpose computers that represent and store data in discrete quantities or numbers. In these computers, all processing is done in terms of numeric representation (binary digits) of data and information. Although the user enters data in decimal or character form, it is converted into binary digits (0s and 1s). Almost all the computers used these days are digital computers. For example, PC, Laptop etc.

PCs (Microcomputers) are of several types: desktop PCs, tower PCs, laptops (or notebooks) and personal digital assistants—handheld computers or palmtops.

Desktop PCs are those in which the case or main housing sits on a desk, with keyboard in front and screen (monitor) often on top.

Tower PCs are those in which the case sits as a "tower," often on the floor beside a desk, thus freeing up desk surface space.

Desktop microcomputer

Tower microcomputer

Figure 2.5 Two microcomputers

Notebook computers, also called laptop computers, are lightweight portable computers with built-in-monitor, keyboard, hard disk drive, battery, and AC adapter that can be plugged into an electrical outlet. They weigh anywhere from 720 gms to 3.6 kgs.

Notebook

PDA

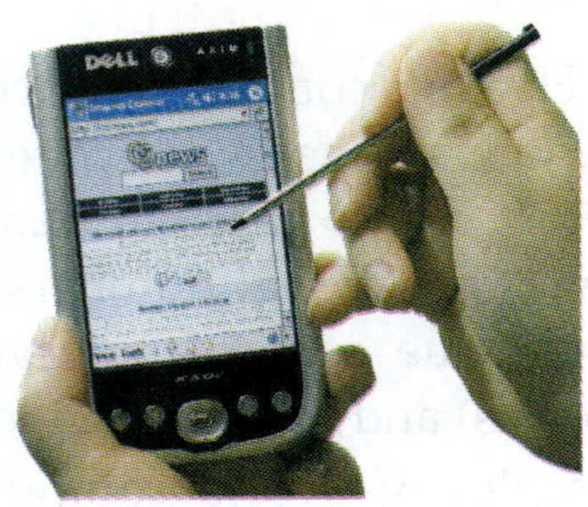

Figure 2.6 A Notebook and a PDA

Personal Digital Assistants (PDAs), also called handheld computers or palmtops, combine personal organisation tools—schedule planners, address books, to-do lists—with the ability in some cases to send e-mail and faxes. Some PDAs have touchsensitive screens. Some also connect to desktop computers for sending or receiving information.

- **Analogue Computers**

Analogue computers are special purpose computers that represent and store data in continuously varying physical quantities such as current, voltage or frequency. These computers are programmed for measuring physical quantities like pressure, temperature, speed, etc., and to perform computations on these measurements. Analogue computers are mainly used for scientific and engineering applications.

Some of the examples of analogue computers are given below:

Thermometer. It is a simple analogue computer used to measure temperature. In thermometer, the mercury moves up or down as the temperature varies.

Speedometer. Car's speedometer is another example of analogue computer where the position of the needle on dial represents the speed of the car.

Thermometer

Speedometer

Figure 2.7 Analogue computers

Limitations of Analogue Computers

1. These do not have logical facilities afforded by programming.
2. They do not have the ability to store data in large quantities.
3. Cost of implementation of computation is very high.

- **Hybrid Computers**

Hybrid computers incorporate the technology of both analogue and digital computers. These computers store and process analogue signals which have been converted into discrete numbers using analogue-to-digital converters. They can also convert the digital numbers into analogue signals or physical properties using digital-to-analogue converters. Hybrid computers are mainly used in artificial intelligence (robotics) and computer aided manufacturing (e.g., process control).

Examples of hybrid computers are: money counting machine and Automated Teller Machine (ATM).

The money counting machine is used in banks for counting the currency.

The ATM is a self-service banking machine that is connected through a telephone network to a central computer.

Figure 2.8 ATM

1.2.2 Uses of Computers

Computers have a significant impact on modern society. Nearly every profession uses computers to a certain extent. Major uses of computers are given below:

- **Process and Store of Data and Information**

Users need data to create useful information. The whole purpose of a computer (and communications) system is to produce (and transmit) usable information. Computers have become so deeply embedded in information processing and communications systems that almost no activity would be possible without them.

Processing is the manipulation the computer does to transform data into information. Processing is the essence of any computer, and the processor is the computer's "brain".

Secondary storage, also called storage, are devices and media that store data and programs permanently—such as disks and drive, tape and tape drives, CDs and CD drives. Without storing of data and information, users would not be able to store their work. Storage also holds the computer's software.

- **To Enhance Teaching/Learning**

Computers have been used in schools since the first Apple computers were introduced in the 1970s. However, their impact was limited. As technology has advanced, educational software has become a major influence at all levels from elementary schools to universities.

In educational institutions computers are used as teaching aid, information source and computing and research tool. When computer is used as a teaching aid it is referred to as Computer Assisted Instruction (CAI).

The ability to connect computers and students together over a network such as the Internet opens up fantastic educational opportunities.

At schools computers are increasingly being used to teach courses like the ones you are taking. For example, this text has a computer application integrated into it, i.e., Word Processing.

Elementary and secondary schools are using computers to play multimedia educational programs and to teach kids to explore the Web for information.

Computers are especially valuable for students with special needs. A computer's voice recognition capabilities and its connection to the Internet make it possible for special education users to participate in learning experiences from which they may have previously been excluded.

- **Produce Documents**

Important work performed in daily functioning of various offices are: preparation of letters, reports, memorandum, copy of advertisement, publicity, contracts, forms, and notes. Today these tasks are efficiently performed by computers.

We use computers for preparing manuscripts of books. The word processing package is used for preparing text, typing thesis, office and administrative work, preparation of test questions etc. Teachers can use computers to maintain student grades, to analyse student performance, grade students, and to give home assignments.

1.2.3 Booting, Rebooting and Shutting Down of Computer

Windows is a special kind of software known as the operating system, OS in short. Operating system is a software that must always be running when the computer is on.

- **Booting**

The work of the operating system begins as soon as you turn on, or "boot", the computer. Booting is the process of loading an operating system into a computer's main memory. The loading is accomplished by programs stored permanently in the computer's electronic circuitry (called Read Only Memory, or ROM).

What happens when you turn on the Computer?

When you turn on the computer the processor (CPU) automatically begins executing the part of the operating system's start-up system (BIOS) located in ROM. These instructions help load the operating system from the hard disk into the computer's main memory i.e., RAM (Random Access Memory), and then they pass control to the OS. The OS remains in RAM until you turn the computer off. When you power up a computer by turning on the power switch, this is called a **cold boot.**

Windows provides a Graphical User Interface (GUI). A graphical user interface is simple to use because any action that is performed is in the form of button clicks or selection of commands, and is user-friendly.

Figure 2.9 The desktop of Windows XP

The large area on the screen that can be seen immediately after Windows gets loaded is called the **desktop**. The small pictures on the desktop are called **icons.** These small images can represent a file, a folder or a program. The text below each icon is the icon name.

To open a file, folder or program on the desktop, you need to double-click on its icon. When the mouse is placed over the icon, a text appears identifying its contents. This is called the tool tip.

The applications in Windows can be started using the Start menu, click the Start button present in the taskbar. A pop-up menu appears. Select the desired application, which you want to open and press the mouse button on the particular application. The application opens in a window.

Note

Window Vista is the newest Microsoft Windows operating system.

- **Rebooting**

If your computer is already on and you restart it, this is called **rebooting** (i.e., a **warm boot** or a **warm start** which is done by simultaneously pressing the **Ctrl + Alt+ Del** keys or pressing the Reset button on your computer).

Normally, your computer would boot from the hard drive, but if that drive is damaged, you can use a floppy disk called a boot disk to start up your computer. (If your computer does not come with a boot disk, create your own by copying your operating system onto one or more floppy disks or a CD).

Rebooting is necessary when your computer hangs.

- **Shutting Down**

Shutting down means turning off the computer. The correct procedure must be followed i.e., close all the running applications and use the Start menu button to shut down.

To turn off the computer:

1. Click the **Start** button. The Start menu appears.
2. Click the **Turn Off Computer** option. (See figure 2.10)

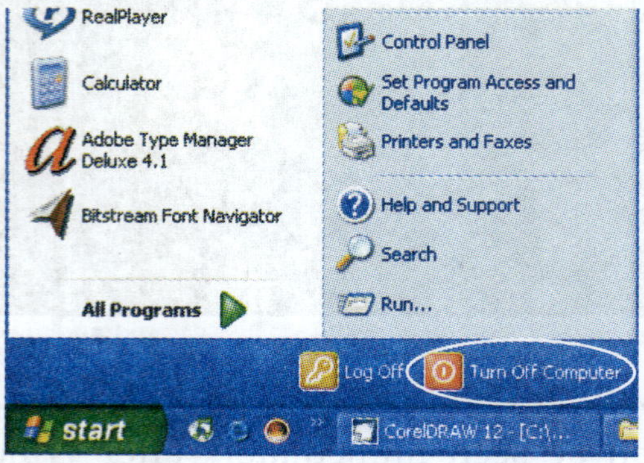

Figure 2.10 The 'Turn Off Computer' button

Figure 2.11 The 'Turn Off' button

3. In the **Turn off computer** dialog box, click the **Turn Off** option. (See figure 2.11)
4. The computer shuts down.

1.2.4 Threats to Computers and Users

Computers have invaluable uses for specialised work but many users are hypnotised by the computer's power to threat the computers and the users.

Security issues go right to the heart of the workability of computer and communications systems. Table 2.1 presents the threats to computers and communications.

Table 2.1 Threats to Computers and Communications Systems

Threat Category	Types of Threats
Errors and accidents	• Human errors • Procedural errors • Software errors • Electromagnetic problems • "Dirty data" problems

Natural hazards Civil unrest and terrorism Crimes against computers and communications	• Theft of hardware • Theft of software and data • Theft of time and services • Theft of information • Crimes of malice and destruction
Crimes using computers and communications Worms and viruses Computer criminals	• Hackers and crackers • Employees • Outside users • Professional criminals

For computer users, the medical and physical effects of working long hours on computers are not fully known. However, muscle and eye strain are common complaints.

Let us discuss the threats to computers and users mentioned in this course:

- **Threats to Computers**

The possible threats to computers are given below:

Viruses

Viruses are forms of high-tech maliciousness. There are many viruses that could afflict your computer in the future.

A virus is a "deviant" program, stored on a computer floppy drive, hard drive, or CD, that can cause unexpected and often undersirable effects, such as destroying or corrupting data. There are various types of viruses. For example:

Boot-sector virus
File virus
Multipartite virus
Macro virus
Logic bomb
Trojan horse

You get viruses in two ways:

1. **By floppy disk:** The first way is via an infected diskette, perhaps obtained from a friend or a repair person.
2. **By the Internet or some other network:** The second way is via a network such as the Internet, as from e-mail or a downloaded file. This is why, when taking advantage of all the freebie games and other software available online, you should use virus-scanning software to check downloaded files.

The virus usually attaches itself to your hard disk. What happens next depends on the intent of the person who created the virus.

***Antivirus software* scans a computer's hard disk, floppy disks, and main memory to detect viruses and, sometimes, to destroy them.** Examples of antivirus programs are Symantec's Norton Anti Virus, McAfee VirusScan, Panda Antivirus Platinum, and Computer Associates' eTrust EZ Antivirus for Windows, and Virex for Macs. Figure 2.12 shows Norton Antivirus.

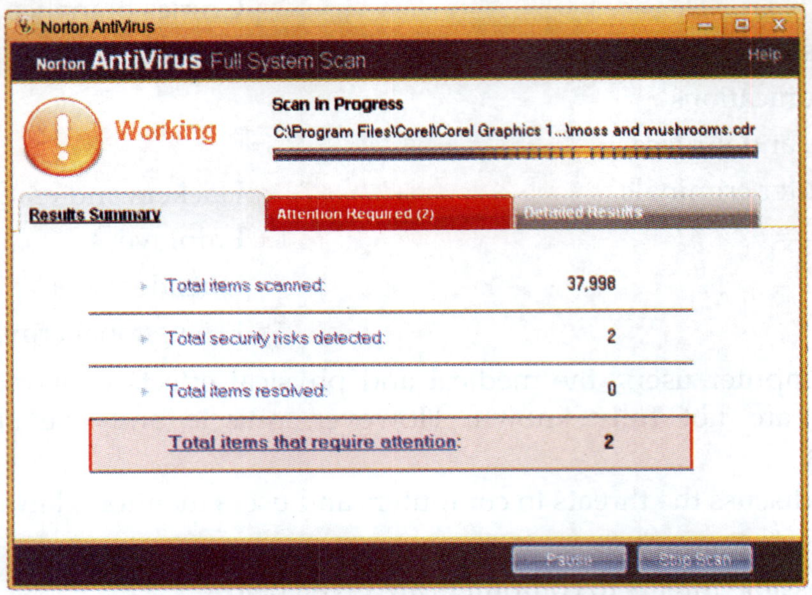

Figure 2.12 Norton Antivirus

Useful Tip

Keep Antivirus Software Updated

The antivirus software that comes with your computer would not protect you forever. To guard against new worms and viruses, visit the antivirus software maker's Website frequently.

Dust

In order to ensure trouble free, prolonged life and smooth working of computer, you must take into consideration that dust free environment is maintained for it. You must take care of the following:

1. Keep the computer in a cool, dry and dust-free environment.
2. Clean the work area of the computer everyday; cover your system at the end of the day.
3. Use a vacuum cleaner to clean keyboards as it can extract the dust collected.
4. Vacuum cleaner must be used at regular intervals to clean your computer.
5. Do not allow eating or drinking near the computer.

6. Do not run any electric equipment like a vacuum cleaner in the vicinity of the computer when it is on.
7. Excessive dust or paper scrap should not be allowed to remain in the close proximity of your computer.

Power Fluctuation

To keep your computer in proper working condition, it is necessary to protect the hardware from environmental hazards, unreliable power supply and natural calamities.

Following points should be borne in mind about power fluctuations while using your computer:

1. Proper and sufficient number of power controlling equipments such as UPS (Uninterrupted Power Supply), Constant Voltage Stabilisers must be pooled to regulate the power supply for the computer.
2. In order to avoid any mishap, the plug sockets and cables must be covered properly.
3. Ensure that the power switch on the system unit, monitor and printer are in the OFF position before switching off the mains.

Rodents

Rodents present a serious threat to human health and safety. They are involved in the transmission of many serious diseases. In addition, their constant gnawing causes structural damage to buildings, creates a risk of fires when rodents gnaw through the power cables, and hamper the proper functioning of computers and data networks when they gnaw through communication cables.

House mice cause structural damage, and create a fire hazard through their gnawing.

Norway rats have adapted to living in and around building occupied by humans, where they present serious safety risks to computers.

Roof rats have adapted to living in buildings occupied by humans. Like other commensal rodents, roof rats also present a threat to computer safety through their capacity to destructive gnawing.

The comprehensive rodent control programmes begin with exclusion, or the sealing off holes, cracks and other openings that rodents use to gain access to a building. These include:

1. Garage doors
2. Water pipes
3. Exterior doors
4. Holes in structure
5. Dryer vents and other entry points.

Exclusion minimizes the need for trapping and chemical control, and provides a more permanent solution to rodent problems.

- **Threats to Users**

Egronomics is the study of the interaction between people and machines. As a user, you should be aware of the things which are quite useful in avoiding problems that arise from working on computers.

The medical and physical effects of working long hours on computers are not fully known. Some problems, however have become common place. Complaints generally concern vision problems and muscle strain. You can avoid most, if not all, of these problems.

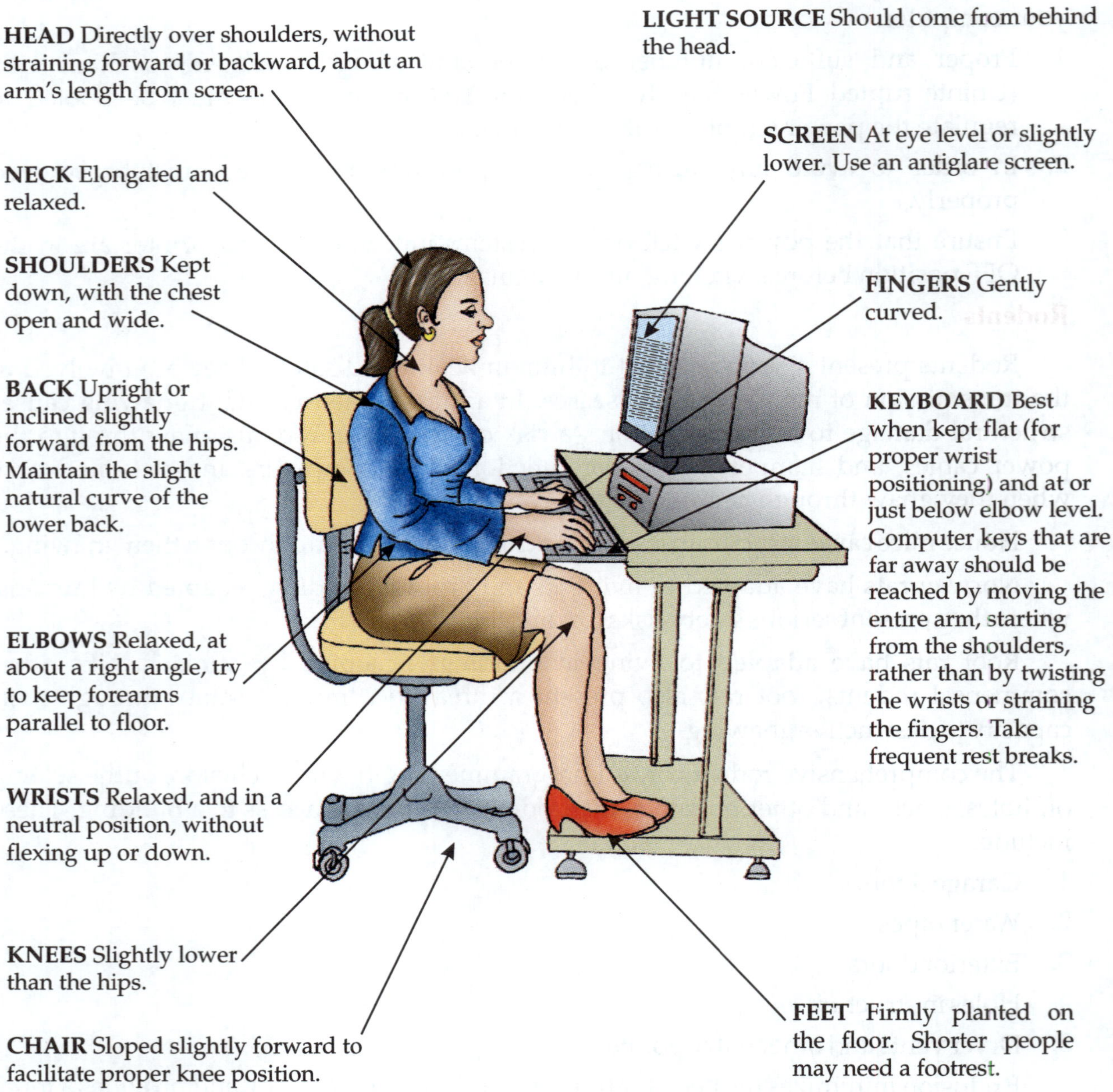

Figure 2.13 Correct sitting posture to avoid threats to computer user

Posture

For using your computer properly take care of the following:

1. Use an adjustable chair, which can be a vision aid by enabling you to sit at a proper angle to the display screen. Generally, the top of the display screen should be 10 degrees above, and the centre of the screen 20 degrees below, your straight-ahead seeing position. The distance from your eyes to the screen should be 14 to 20 inches.
2. Place your reference material as close as possible to the display screen to avoid frequent large eye and head movements. It should also be placed at the same distance from your eyes as the display screen so that you do not have to continually adjust focus as you look back and forth between them. A copy stand is very useful for this.

Vision

As a user, you should be aware of some of the things that researchers in this field recommend to avoid problems that arise from working on computers. Follow the recommendations given below for your workplace and vision care.

1. Screen should be at the eye level or slightly lower. It should be at a safe distance from the eyes to avoid straining in your eyes.
2. Reference material should be placed near the screen.
3. Reference material and screen should be at the same distance from eyes.
4. Screen brightness should be properly adjusted.
5. There should be proper overall room lighting.
6. Windows and other sources of bright light must be shielded.
7. Proper light for reading the reference material should be there.
8. Sources of screen reflection should be eliminated.
9. Fifteen minute breaks should be taken every two hours for moderate users.
10. Fifteen minute breaks should be taken every hour for frequent users.

Wrist pain

In addition to vision problems, anyone who has worked on a computer for long hours can tell stories about aches and pains. To avoid wrist and forearm injuries, you should keep your wrists straight and hands relaxed as you type. Instead of putting the keyboard on top of a desk, you should put it on a low table or in a keyboard drawer under the desk. Otherwise the nerves in your wrists will rub against the sheaths surrounding them, possibly leading to some pains. Some experts also suggest using a padded, adjustable wrist rest, attached to the keyboard, or a hand brace. You may also try setting an hourly alarm on your watch or on an alarm clock; when the alarm goes off, take a short break and rotate your wrist and hand a bit.

Ergonomic keyboards designed to reduce or eliminate repetitive stress injuries to the wrists and arms have gentle slopes and shapes to remove the stress put on the wrists and arms by the normal flat keyboard.

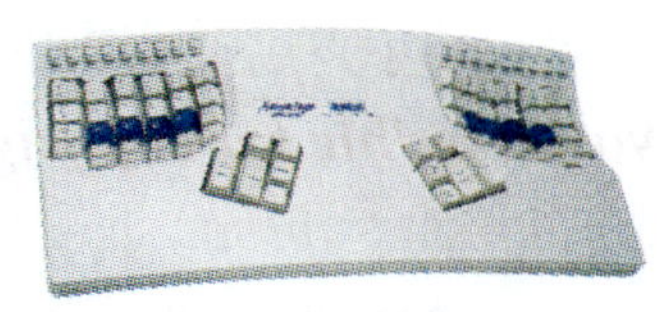

Figure 2.14 Ergonomic keyboard, courtesy of Microsoft

1.2.5 Responsible Use of Computers

Every computer user will have to wrestle with ethical issues related to the use of information technology. **Ethics** is defined as a set of moral values or principles that govern the conduct of an individual or a group. Ethical questions arise often in connection with ICT.

- **Computer Ethics**

Computer ethics are nothing but a standard of behaviour regarding use of computers for individuals and organisations. It may not be immediately apparent that computers pose any particular ethical problems. Computer ethics are but needed in addition to any laws that exist, for example, copyright and privacy concerns.

The observance of ethics is a way of self-regulating conduct when law or situation does not indicate a clear course of action.

Here are some commandments of computer ethics:

1. Never use a computer to harm other people.
2. Never interfere with other people's computer work.
3. Never snoop around in other people's computer files.
4. Never use a computer to steal.
5. Never use a computer to bear false witness.
6. Never copy or use proprietary software for which you have not paid.
7. Never use other people's computer resources without authorisation or proper compensation.
8. Never use other people's intellectual output.
9. Always think about the social consequences of the program you are writing or the system you are designing.
10. Always use a computer in ways that demonstrate consideration and respect for your fellow humans.

- **Copyright**

Copyright acts have been enacted by governments in many countries. Copyright laws are quite similar in most of the cases. Main motive of these laws is to protect literary works, computer software programmes and other similar works constituting intellectual property from being pirated and sold commercially without giving due credit or royalties to the original creator of such works. Following are excerpts of a typical Copyright Act from a country in Africa.

Work eligible for copyright

1. *(1) An author, co-author or joint author of the literary and the computer software or programmes is entitled to the copyright and protection afforded to that work under this Act.*

(2) *Despite subsection (1), a work is not eligible for copyright unless*

(a) *it is original in character,*

(b) *it has been fixed in any definite medium of expression now known or later to be developed with the result that the work can either directly or with the aid of any machine or device be perceived, reproduced or otherwise communicated, and*

(c) *it is*

(i) *created by a citizen or a person who is ordinarily a resident,*

(ii) *first published in the country and in the case of a work first published outside the country is subsequently published in the country within thirty days of its publication outside the country, or*

(iii) *a work in respect of which the country has an obligation under an international treaty to grant protection.*

(3) *The eligibility of a work for copyright is not affected by its artistic quality, the purpose of the author in creating it or by the manner or form of its expression.*

(4) *For the purposes of this section a work is original if it is the product of the independent effort of the author.*

Ideas, concepts excluded from copyright

2. *Copyright shall not extend to ideas, concepts, procedures, methods or other things of a similar nature.*

Government and international body copyright

3. *The copyright of work shall vest in*

(a) *the Head of the State on behalf of and in trust for the people of the country; or*

(b) *an international body*

Figure 2.15 Copyright symbol

if the work is made by or under the direction or control of the Head of the State on behalf of and in trust for the people of the country or a specified international body.

Almost any material that you find in print or electronic form is copyrighted, the rights to use it belonging solely to the owner of that copyright. Even uncopyrighted materials are protected. Using the materials without written permission violates the owner's rights and subjects you and your organisation to penalties and embarrassment.

The only way software developers can recover their expenses in developing programs and make a profit is to sell the program in large numbers. Naturally, each pirated copy sold reduces the number developers can sell. The pirates have to pay only the copying costs.

To discourage unauthorised copying, software developers use such methods as:

1. Licensing one or several developers to produce the programs and pay developer a royalty fee on each program produced.
2. Putting a seal on the software package and stating that when the seal is broken, the buyers are automatically agreeing that only they will use the software.
3. Building locks into the programs to prevent them from being copied or permitting only a limited number of backup copies to be made.

Privacy Concerns

In general, computer security, privacy and integrity are used interchangeably whereas all of these address different aspects.

Privacy is a concept applied to an individual and it is the right of an individual to decide what information one wishes to share with others or is willing to accept from others.

Privacy is the right of people not to reveal information about themselves. Many people are worried about the loss of their right to privacy, fearing they will lose all control of the personal information being collected and tracked by computers. There are good reasons for this concern:

1. Name migration.
2. Identity theft.
3. Resumé resulting and online snooping.
4. Government prying and spying.
5. A national ID card.

Over the years, concerns about privacy have led to the enactment of a number of laws to protect individuals from invasions of privacy. Different countries have their own privacy laws. Still, the tension between security and privacy worries many observers.

SUMMARY

- Computer is an electronic device that can accept, store and process data under the control of a set of instructions.
- Computers are inflexible and cannot work out alternative solutions, besides being incapable of performing on their own.
- Abacus is considered to be the first computer.
- Charles Babbage is known as the 'Father of Modern Digital Computers' due to his pioneering work.
- The types of computers are digital (e.g., PC, Laptop), analogue (e.g., thermometer, speedometer) and hybrid (e.g., money counting machine, Automated Teller Machine (ATM).

- Uses of computers include processing and storage of data and information, enhancing teaching/learning, producing documents etc.
- Windows is a special kind of software known as the operating system (OS) that must always be running when the computer is on.
- Booting is the process of loading an operating system into a computer's main memory.
- Windows provides a Graphical User Interface (GUI).
- The large area on the screen that can be seen immediately after Windows gets loaded is called the desktop.
- The small pictures on the desktop are called icons. These small images can represent a file, a folder or a program.
- Windows Vista is the newest Microsoft operating system.
- If your computer is already on and you restart it, this is called rebooting.
- Shutting down means turning off the computer.
- The correct procedure of shutting down is to close all running applications and use the Start menu button to shut down.
- Possible threats to computers are viruses, dust, power fluctuation, rodents etc.
- Possible threats to users are posture, vision, wrist pain etc.
- Responsible use of the computers requires computer ethics e.g., copyright, privacy concerns etc.

REVIEW QUESTIONS

STATE WHETHER TRUE OR FALSE

1. Computer is an electronic device.
2. Digital computers process all data as binary 0s and 1s.
3. Random Access Memory (RAM) is where the computer stores the programs and data that you are working on.
4. Read Only Memory (ROM) is where the computer stores the programs and data that you are working on.

5. Windows XP is an Operating System.
6. Automated Teller Machine (ATM) is an example of analogue computers.
7. Computers can be used to enhance teaching and learning.
8. The user should not close the running applications and not use the Start menu button to shut down the computer.
9. Possible threats to computers are viruses, dust, power fluctuation and rodents.
10. Identity theft is related to privacy concerns.

FILL IN THE BLANKS

1. .... is perhaps the most powerful and versatile tool ever created by human being.
2. Charles Babbage is known as the .... due to his pioneering work.
3. Windows is a special kind of software known as ....
4. .... is the process of loading an operating system into a computer's main memory.
5. The small pictures on the desktop are called ....
6. If your computer is already on and you restart it, this is called ....
7. .... are forms of high-tech maliciousness.
8. .... is the study of the interaction between people and machines.
9. .... is defined as a set of moral values or principles that govern the conduct of an individual or a group.
10. .... is the right of people not to reveal information about themselves.

MULTIPLE CHOICE QUESTIONS

1. A personal computer can ....

   (*a*) add numbers (*b*) sort lists

   (*c*) display graphs (*d*) do all of the above

2. The software that must be loaded into the computer before you load any other program is ....

   (*a*) a programming language (*b*) the operating system

   (*c*) a utility program (*d*) all of the above

3. Which of the following is the newest Microsoft Windows operating system?
   (a) Windows Vista (b) Windows NT
   (c) Windows 2000 (d) Windows XP
4. Rodents gain access to a building via ....
   (a) Garage doors (b) Water pipes
   (c) Exterior doors (d) All of these
5. Ergonomics is the study of ....
   (a) cost reductions in manufacturing
   (b) the interaction between people and machines
   (c) artificial intelligence
   (d) making computers faster
6. The centre of the display screen should be .... your straight-ahead seeing position.
   (a) 10 degrees above (b) 20 degrees below
   (c) 10 degrees below (d) 20 degrees above
7. Which of the following is not an appropriate term about computers?
   (a) Booting (b) Hooting
   (c) Rebooting (d) Shutting down

ANSWER THE FOLLOWING

1. What is a computer? Give its types.
2. Discuss the history of the development of computers.
3. Discuss the types of computers by giving suitable examples.
4. Discuss in brief the uses of computers.
5. Discuss the following:
   (i) Booting (ii) Rebooting (iii) Shutting down a computer
6. Give the correct procedure for shutting down a computer.
7. Explain when reboot is necessary.
8. Discuss the possible threats to computers and their users.
9. Discuss the responsible use of the computers.

FIELD TRIP

Organise a field trip to various places to find out and report on:

(a) **Different types of computers and their uses.**

(b) **Threats to computers and their users.**

ASSIGNMENT

1. **Collect the pictures of different types of computers and identify these.**
2. **Write the procedure for booting, rebooting and shutting down a computer.**
3. **Students should come out with their own rules and regulations for the responsible use of computers.**

SECTION TWO

TERM-ONE

HARDWARE AND SOFTWARE

UNIT 1: Hardware

UNIT 2: Software

General Objective

After reading this section, the student will be able to:

1. recognize the different types of Hardware and Software, and their uses.

UNIT 1 HARDWARE

Specific Objectives

After reading this unit, the student will be able to:

2.1.1 describe the categories of Computer Hardware.

2.1.2 identify the vital components of the System Unit.

2.1.3 describe commonly used Input/Output devices and their functions.

2.1.4 identify the main types of storage devices.

2.1.5 identify devices which serve as both input and output.

2.1.0 Introduction

A system is a group of various components that work together to achieve a specific goal or target. For example, in your school, teachers and administrative members work together for the success of students. A school may therefore be called a system of students, teachers and administrators working together so that students can clear examination after attaining the knowledge. Similarly, various components of a computer work together to achieve a single target *i.e.*, to process data. That is why a computer is called as a system.

The computer mainly consists of hardware and software. Both of these components work together to process data. Figure 1.1 illustrates these two components.

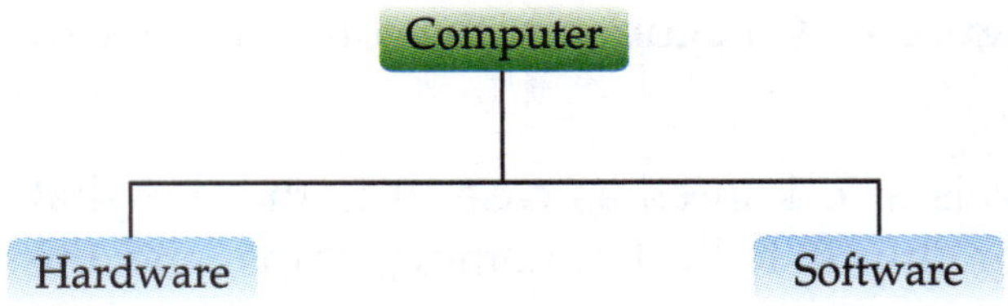

Figure 1.1 Hardware and software

The parts of computer that can be touched and have some weight are called as hardware. The term hardware is used to refer to all the components inside or outside the computer. In addition to this, components used to interconnect two or more components, for example, wires, are also regarded as hardware. We have several hardware devices that are used at various phases of data processing cycle. The hardware that are used to supply input to computer are called as *input devices*. The hardware that are used to process the data, are called as *processing devices* and the devices that are used to present output of computer, are called as *output devices*. Each of these categories has a broad variety of devices of various brands and qualities. In this unit, we will study the hardware.

2.1.1 Categories of the Computer Hardware

Hardware consists of all the machinery and equipment in a computer system. The hardware includes, among other devices, the keyboard, the monitor, the printer, and the "box" — the computer or processing device itself. Figure 1.2 illustrates hardware of a computer.

Figure 1.2 Hardware of a computer

The categories of the computer hardware are given in figure 1.3.

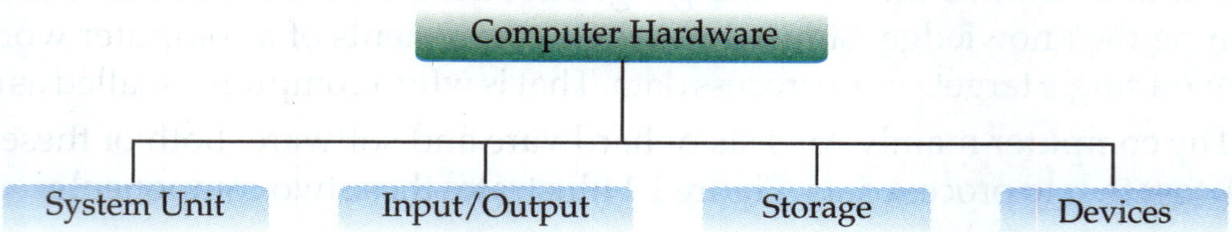

Figure 1.3 Categories of the computer hardware

System Unit

The system unit is also known as case. It is the box that houses the processor chip (CPU), the memory chips, and the motherboard with power supply, as well as some secondary storage devices — floppy-disk drive, hard-disk drive, and CD or DVD drive. The case comes in desktop or tower models. It includes a power supply unit and a fan to keep the circuitry from overheating.

Figure 1.4 Case or system cabinet

Input/Output

Input hardware consists of devices that allow people to put data into the computer in a form that the computer can use, for example, keyboard and mouse.

Figure 1.5 Input hardware

Output hardware consists of devices that translate information processed by the computer into a form that humans can understand—print, sound, graphics, or video, for example.

Figure 1.6 Output hardware

Storage

Within the motherboard in the system cabinet, the memory chips are installed and secondary storage devices are connected to it. The memory chips deal only with temporary storage. Secondary storage or permanent storage stores your data as long as you want.

For today's student purposes, you will need at the minimum a floppy-disk drive, a hard disk drive, and a CD/DVD drive. If you work with large files, you will also require a Zip-disk drive. These storage devices slide into the system cabinet from the front and are secured with screws. Each drive is attached to the motherboard by a flat cable (called a ribbon cable). Also, each drive must be hooked up to a plug extending from the power supply.

Figure 1.7 Memory chip

Devices

You must be familiar with the term *peripheral device*. A peripheral device is any component or piece of equipment that expands a computer's input, storage, and output capabilities. In other words, a peripheral device is not part of the essential computer. Peripheral devices can be inside the computer or connected to it from the outside, for example, printers and disk drives.

2.1.2 The Vital Components of the System Unit

As mentioned earlier, the *System Unit* is also called a *case*. It is a box that houses the processor chip (CPU), the memory chips, and the motherboard with power supply, as well as secondary storage devices—floppy-disk drive, hard-disk drive, and CD or DVD drive. The case comes in desktop or tower models. It includes a power supply unit and a fan to keep the circuitry from overheating. The number of buttons on the outside of the computer case will vary, but the on/off power switch will appear somewhere, either front or back. Let us discuss the vital components of the system unit.

- **Front Side**

Figure 1.8 illustrates the front side of the system unit. It includes the following components:

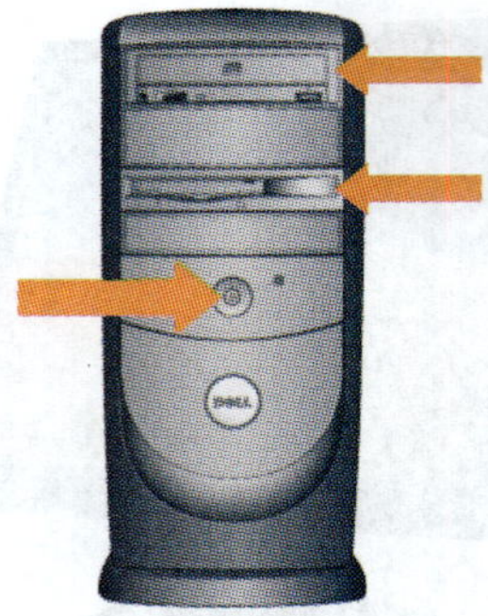

Figure 1.8 Front side of the System Unit

Mains or Power ON/OFF Switch

Depending on the model, this switch is located either in the front or at the side of the system unit and it is used to switch the system ON or OFF.

Reset Button

This is a press switch which can be used to restart the PC without switching off the mains power supply. Use this switch as a last resort when the PC hangs and does not accept a command from the keyboard. When you restart the PC, it will lose all the information currently stored in its memory.

Key Lock

You can lock the computer by inserting and turning clockwise a special key in the key lock. Once locked, the computer cannot be switched on and thus you can prevent unauthorised access to your machine. To unlock the PC, you need to insert the special key in the key lock and turn it anticlock-wise.

Turbo Switch

If you are using a PC that has two different speeds of operation, then you will find a turbo switch on the front side of your PC. This switch changes the speed from a low value to a high value and hence the name *turbo*. Pressing this switch ON will result in running the computer at its highest speed.

Indicator Lights

Your unit may have coloured lights to indicate the working of the PC. These lights also glow whenever data is recorded on to or read from the floppy or hard disk. The wires for these lights are attached to the motherboard.

Floppy Drive

A floppy-disk drive is a storage device that stores data on removable 3.5-inch-diameter disks. These diskettes do not seem to be "floppy", because they are encased in hard plastic, but the mylar disk inside is indeed flexible or floppy. Each can store 1.44 MB or more data. Using the floppy-disk drive you can insert a diskette through a slot in the front and remove it by pushing the eject button.

Figure 1.9 Floppy drive and floppy

> **Note**
>
> You must not remove the diskette from floppy-disk drive until its light goes off, or else you risk damage to both the disk and the drive.

CD ROM Drive

A CD (Compact Disk) drive, or its more recent variant, a DVD (Digital Video Disk) drive, is a storage device that uses laser technology to read data from optical disks. (Some companies call a DVD a "Digital Versatile Disk".) These days new software is generally supplied on CDs rather than on floppy disks.

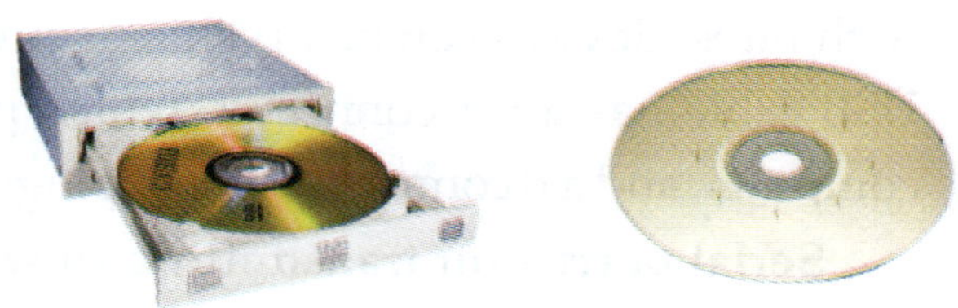

Figure 1.10 CD/DVD drive and a CD

- **Back Side**

The back side of a PC contains various ports and sockets. Figure 1.11 illustrates the back side of a PC.

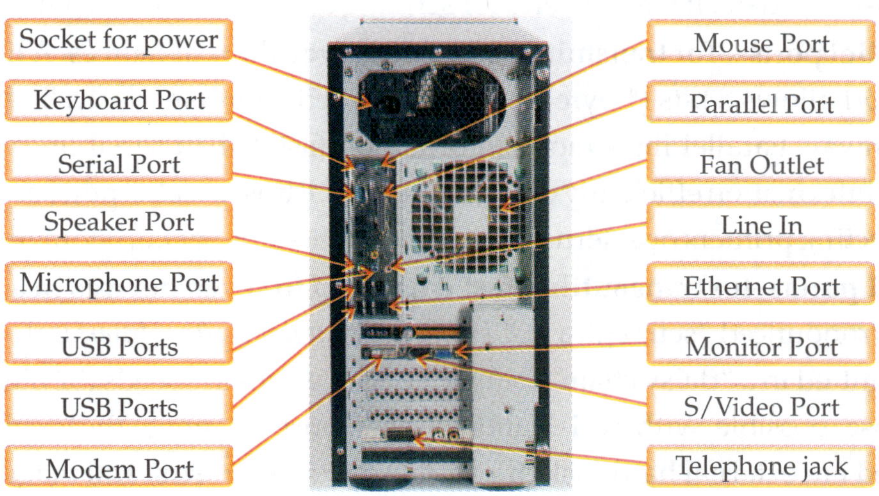

Figure 1.11 Backside of the system unit

A port is a connecting socket or jack on the outside of the system unit into which different kinds of cables can be plugged. (See figure 1.11)

A port allows you to plug in a cable to connect a peripheral device such as a monitor, printer, or modem, so that it can communicate with the computer system.

Ports are of several types. Following are the important ones:

USB ports—for transmitting data to up to 127 devices in a daisy chain (in a series). A *USB (Universal Serial Bus) port* can theoretically connect up to 127 peripheral devices daisy-chained to one general-purpose port. USB ports are useful for all kinds of peripherals. USB is "hot swappable," or "hot pluggable"—it allows USB devices to be connected or disconnected even while the PC is running.

In addition, USB permits *plug and play,* which allows peripheral devices and expansion cards to be automatically configured while they are being installed. This avoids the hassle of setting switches and creating special files, which plagued the earlier users.

Figure 1.12 USB hub

Individual USB cables can run as long as 5 metres; with hubs, devices can be up to 30 metres away. Each USB cable has an A connector, which plugs into the computer, and a B connector, which plugs into the peripheral USB device.

Serial ports—for transmitting slow data over long distances. A line connected to a *serial port* will send bits one at a time, one after another, like cars on a one-lane highway. Because individual bits must follow each other, a serial port is usually used to connect devices such as keyboard, mouse, monitors, and modems, that do not require fast transmission of data. It is also useful for sending data over a long distance.

Parallel ports—for transmitting fast data over short distances. A line connected to a *parallel port* allows 8 bits (1 byte) to be transmitted simultaneously, like cars on an eight-lane highway. Parallel lines move information faster than serial lines do, but they can transmit information efficiently only up to 15 feet. Thus, parallel ports are used principally for connecting printers or external disk or magnetic-tape backup storage devices.

SCSI ports—for transmitting fast data to up to seven devices in a daisy chain (in a series). Pronounced "scuzzy," a *SCSI (Small Computer System Interface) port* allows data to be transmitted in a "daisy chain" to up to seven devices at speeds (32 bits at a time) higher than those possible with serial and parallel ports. Among the devices that may be connected are external hard disk drives, CD drives, scanners, and magnetic-tape backup units. Figure 1.13 illustrates an internal daisy chain.

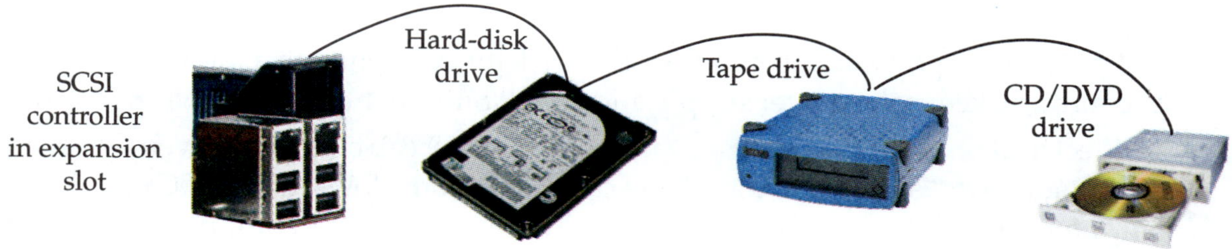

Figure 1.13 Internal daisy chain (Inside computer)

Power socket—for connecting power to power supply. The computer cannot function without power, so power socket is very important for supplying power to your computer from external source.

- **Inside**

Inside the system unit are motherboard, CPU, power supply, memory, hard disk and cards (for example, sound and network cards).

Motherboard

The *motherboard,* or *system board,* is the main circuit board in the system unit. The motherboard consists of a flat board that fills one side of the case. It contains both soldered, non-removable components and sockets or slots for components that can be removed—microprocessor chip, RAM chips, and various expansion cards.

Figure 1.14 Motherboard

CPU

The most fundamental part of the motherboard is the microprocessor chip or the Central Processing Unit (CPU). A *microprocessor* is the miniaturised circuitry of a computer processor. It consists of mainly an integrated circuit of semiconductor devices and other electronic components manufactured on a thin sheet of semiconductor material. CPU executes and stores program instructions that process or manipulate data into information. The CPU is often referred to as the "brain" of the computer.

Figure 1.15 Microprocessor chip

CPUs have to communicate with the rest of the PC. This is accomplished through a collection of interconnected chips on the motherboard called a *chipset.* Chipsets determine what types of processors, memory, and video card ports will work on the same motherboard.

Power Supply

The electricity available from a standard wall outlet is alternating current (AC), but a computer runs on direct current (DC). The *power supply* is a device that converts AC to DC to run the computer. The on/off switch in your computer turns on or shuts off the electricity to the power supply. Because electricity can generate a lot of heat, a fan inside the computer keeps the power supply and other components from becoming too hot.

Electrical power drawn from a standard AC outlet can be quite uneven. For example, a sudden surge, or "spike," in AC voltage can burn out the low-voltage DC circuitry in your computer ("fry the motherboard"). Instead of plugging your computer directly into the wall electrical outlet, it is a good idea to plug it into a power protection device. One of the principal types is UPS.

UPS: A *UPS (Uninterruptible Power Supply)* is a battery-operated device that provides a computer with electricity if there is a power failure. The UPS will keep a computer going for 5 to 30 minutes or more. It goes into operation as soon as the power to your computer fails. It also stabilizes any sudden fluctuation in the power supply.

Memory

So far we have described only the kinds of chips known as microprocessors. But other silicon chips called *memory chips* are attached to the motherboard. There are two types of storage, primary and secondary. Primary storage is temporary or working storage and is often called the *memory* or the *main memory*; secondary storage, usually called just *storage*, is relatively a permanent storage. *Memory* refers to storage media in the form of chips, and *storage* refers to media such as disks and tape. The two principal types of memory chips are *RAM* and *ROM*.

RAM chips—to temporarily store program instructions and data: ***RAM (Random Access Memory) chips*** temporarily hold (1) software instructions and (2) data before and after it is processed by the CPU. You can think of memory (RAM) chips as a collection of boxes, each of which, holds a single byte of data.

Because its contents are temporary, RAM is said to be ***volatile*—the contents are lost when the power goes off or is turned off**. This is why you should *frequently*—say, every 5 minutes, save your work to a secondary storage medium such as your hard disk, in case the electricity goes off while you are working.

RAM allows the stored data to be accessed in any order, that is, at *random*.

Figure 1.16 Random Access Memory (RAM) chips

ROM chips—to store fixed start-up instructions. Unlike RAM, to which data is constantly being added and removed, ***ROM (read-only memory)*** **cannot be written upon or erased by the computer user. ROM chips contain fixed start-up instructions.**

That is, ROM chips are loaded, at the factory, with programs containing special instructions for basic computer operations, such as those that start the computer (BIOS) or put characters on the screen. These chips are nonvolatile; their contents are not lost when power to the computer is turned off.

In computer terminology, *read* means to transfer data from an input source into the computer's memory or CPU. The opposite is *write*—to transfer data from the computer's CPU or memory to an output device. Thus, with a ROM chip, *read-only* means that the CPU can retrieve programs from the ROM chip but cannot modify or add to those programs. A variation is *PROM (Programmable Read Only Memory),* which is a ROM chip that allows you, the user, to load read-only programs and data. However, this can be done only once.

Hard Disks

Floppy disks use flexible plastic, but hard disks are rigid. *Hard disks* are thin but rigid metal, glass, or ceramic platters covered with a substance that allows data to be held in the form of magnetised spots. Most hard disk drives have at least two platters; the greater the number of platters, the larger the capacity of the drive. The platters in the drive are separated by spaces and are clamped to a rotating spindle that turns all the platters in unison. Hard disks are tightly scaled within an enclosed hard disk drive unit to prevent any foreign matter from getting inside. Data may be recorded on both sides of the disk platters. (See figure 1.17). In a microcomputer, the hard disk is enclosed within the system unit. Unlike a floppy disk, it is not accessible.

Figure 1.17 Hard disk

Cards

Today many new microcomputer systems can be expanded. *Expansion* is a way of increasing a computer's *capabilities* by adding hardware to perform tasks that are not part of the basic system. *Upgrading* means changing to a newer, usually more powerful or sophisticated version.

The types of expansion cards are graphics, sound, modem, and network interface cards. A special kind of card is the PC card.

- **Graphics cards—for monitors.** Graphics cards are included in all PCs. Also, called a *video card* or *video adapter,* a *graphics card* converts signals from the computer into video signals that can be displayed as images on a monitor. Each graphics card has its own memory chips, a graphics BIOS ROM chip, and a dedicated processor. The processor is designed specifically to handle the intense computational requirements of displaying graphics.
- **Sound cards—for speakers and audio output.** A *sound card* is used to convert and transmit digital sounds through analogue speakers, microphones, and headsets. Sound cards come installed on most new PCs.
- **Modem cards—for remote communication via phone lines.** Occasionally you may still see a modem that is outside the computer. Most new PCs, however, come with internal modems—modems installed inside as circuit cards. The modem not only sends and receives digital data over telephone lines to and from other computers but can also transmit voice and fax signals.

- **Network interface cards—for remote communication via cable.** A *Network Interface Card (NIC)* allows the transmission of data over a cable network, which connects various computers and other devices such as printers.
- **PC cards—for laptop computers.** Originally called *PCMCIA cards* (for the Personal Computer Memory Card International Association), PC *cards* are thin, credit card-size (2.1 by 3.4 inches) devices used principally on notebook computers to expand their capabilities.

Figure 1.18 shows the inside of the system unit.

Figure 1.18 Inside of the system unit

(The arrangement of the components varies among models)

2.1.3 Input and Output Devices

Input refers to data entered into a computer for processing— for example, from a keyboard or from a file stored on disk. Input includes program instructions that the CPU receives after commands are issued by the user. *Output* refers to the results of processing—that is, information sent to the screen or the printer or to be stored on disk or sent to another computer in a network. Figure 1.19 illustrates the common input and output devices used with a computer.

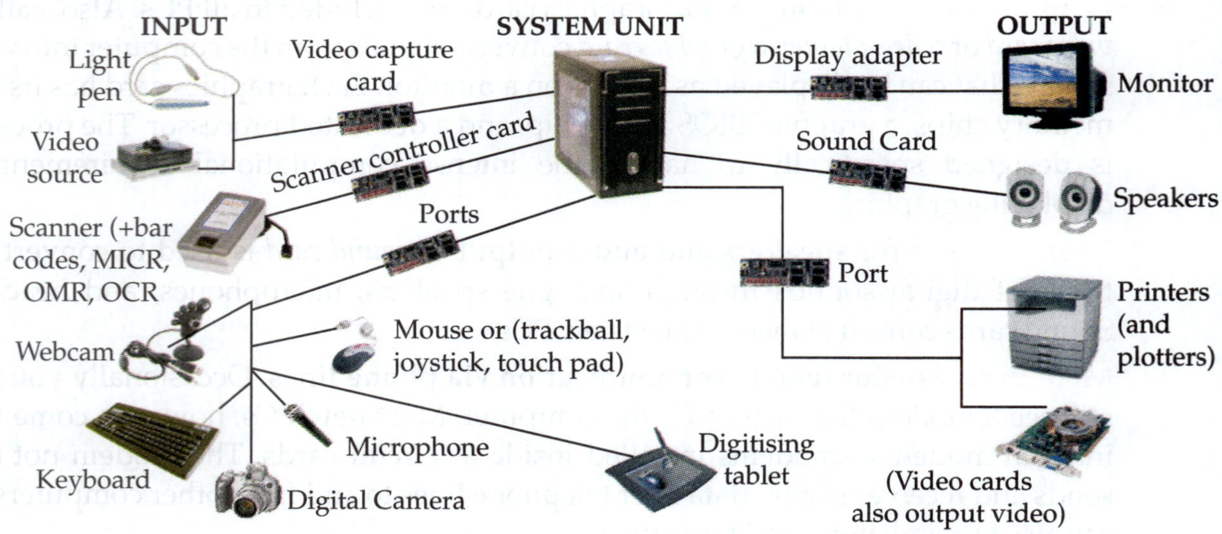

Figure 1.19 Common input and output devices

- **Input Devices**

Any device that allows information from outside the computer to be communicated to the computer is considered an input device. Since, the Central Processing Unit (CPU) of a digital computer can understand only discrete binary information, all computer input devices and circuitry must eventually communicate with the computer in this form. Many devices are capable of performing this task. Some common computer input devices are:

1. Keyboard
2. Mouse
3. Light Pen
4. Touch Screens
5. Graphics Tablets (Digitisers)
6. Joystick
7. Trackball
8. MICR
9. OCR
10. Scanner
11. Smart Card Reader
12. Barcode Reader
13. Biometric Sensor
14. Web Camera
15. Digital Camera

Let us discuss some of the input devices and their functions:

Keyboard

Keyboard is perhaps the most popular and widely used device for entering data and instructions in a computer system (See figure 1.20). A keyboard is similar to the keyboard of a typewriter. It contains alphabets, digits, special characters and some control keys. A general purpose keyboard normally contains cursor control keys and function keys. Function keys allow user to enter frequently used operations in a single keystroke, and cursor-control keys can be used to select displayed objects or co-ordinate positions by positioning the cursor on the screen.

Figure 1.20 A Keyboard

Some of the special keys on a keyboard are given in table 1.1.

Table 1.1 Special Keys on a Keyboard and their Purpose

Special Key	Purpose
Arrow Key	To move the cursor in the top, down, left and right directions in a document.
Backspace Key	To delete the character on the left of the cursor.
Caps Lock	To capitalise letters.
Del	To delete the character from the current position of the cursor.
End	To move the cursor to the end of the line.
Enter	To start a new paragraph in a document.
Esc	To cancel a command.

Home	To move the cursor to the beginning of the line.
Ins	To insert characters.
Shift	To type the special characters above the numeric keys. If you press this key along with a number key, the special character above that number will be typed. For example: To type "#", you have to press the shift key and the number key 3.
Space Bar	To enter a space.
Tab	To enter multiple spaces between two words in a document.

Mouse

A mouse is a pointing device (See figure 1.21). It is a small hand held box and it is used to position the cursor on the screen. The amount and the direction of movement can be detected by the wheels or the rollers on the bottom of the mouse. The wheels have their axes at right angles. Each wheel is connected to a shaft encoder and whenever the wheel moves this shaft encoder emits electrical pulses. The distance moved is determined by the number of pulses emitted by the mouse.

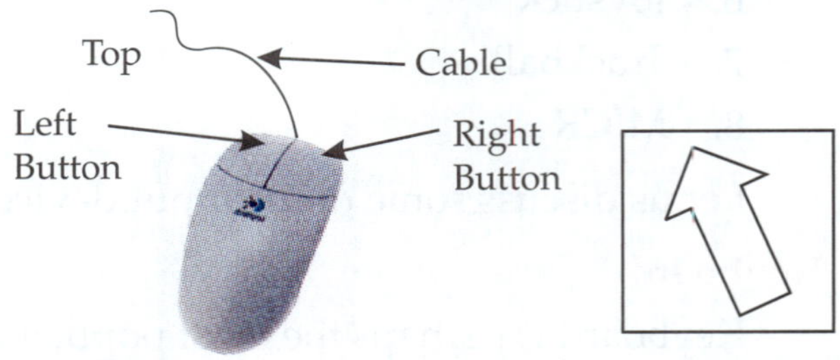

Figure 1.21 A mouse and standard mouse pointer

The movements of the mouse cursor always match that of the mouse. There are three kinds of clicks. They are left-click, right-click and double click. The mouse can be used to drag and drop objects on the screen. Cordless mice are also available.

Advantages

1. It is a simple device and very easy to use.
2. It is not very expensive.
3. It moves the cursor faster than the arrow keys of the keyboard.

Disadvantages

1. The movement of the cursor is not very sensitive to the movement of mouse.
2. If the contact between wheels and mouse pad is lost, the cursor does not move.

Note

It is a good practice to use the mouse pad instead of just any flat surface for movement of the mouse.

Scanner

Scanners, or *optical scanners*, use light-sensing (optical) equipment to translate images of text, drawings, photos, and the like into digital form (See figure 1.22).

The images can then be processed by a computer, displayed on a monitor, stored on a storage device, or transmitted to another computer. Scanners are similar to photocopy machines except they create electronic files of scanned items instead of paper copies.

Figure 1.22 A desktop scanner

Scanners vary in resolution. *Resolution,* refers to the clarity and sharpness of an image and is measured in *dots per inch (dpi)*—the number of columns and rows of dots per inch. The higher the number of dots, the clearer and sharper the image.

One of the most popular types of scanners is the *flatbed scanner,* or *desktop scanner,* which works much like a photocopier—the image being scanned is placed on a glass surface, where it remains stationary, and the scanning beam moves across it. Three other types of scanners are *sheet-fed, handheld* and *drum.*

Joystick

A joystick is also a pointing device (See figure 1.23). It consists of a small, vertical lever fitted on a base. This lever is used to move the cursor on the screen. The screen-cursor movement in any particular direction is measured by the distance that the stick is shifted or moved from its centre position. The amount of movement is measured by the potentiometers that are plugged at the base of the joystick. When the stick is released, a spring brings it back to its centre position. The joystick can move right or left, forward or backward.

Figure 1.23 A joystick

Trackball

The *trackball* is a movable ball, mounted on top of a stationary device, that can be rotated using your fingers or palm (See figure 1.24). In fact, the trackball looks like the mouse turned upside down. Instead of moving the mouse around on the desktop, you move the trackball with the tips of your fingers. A trackball is not as accurate as a mouse, and it requires more frequent cleaning, but it is a good alternative when desktop space is limited. Trackballs come in wired and wireless versions, and newer optical trackballs use laser technology.

Figure 1.24 Trackball

Bar code Reader

Bar codes are the vertical, zebra-striped marks you see on most manufactured retail products–everything from candy to cosmetics to books.

Figure 1.25 Bar codes and bar code reader

Bar code readers are photoelectric (optical) scanners that translate the symbols in the bar code into digital code (See figure 1.25). In this system, the price of a particular item is set within the store's computer. Once the bar code has been scanned, the corresponding price appears on the sales clerk's point-of-sale terminal and on your receipt. Records of sales from the bar code readers are input to the store's computer and used for accounting, restocking store inventory, and weeding out products that do not sell well.

- **Output Devices**

An output device is a device which accepts results from the computer and displays them to the user. The output device also converts the binary code obtained from the computer into human readable form. The principal kinds of output are hardcopy and softcopy. Table 1.2 illustrates the types of output devices.

Table 1.2 Types of Output Devices

Type	Example
Soft copy Devices	CRT display screens, Flat-panel display screen (*e.g.*, liquid crystal display)
Hard copy Devices	Impact printers: dot-matrix printer Non impact printers: laser, ink-jet, thermal
Other Devices	Sound output, Voice output, Video output

Let us discuss some of the output devices and their functions:

Monitors

These are also known as **Visual Display Unit (VDU)** or simply screens. They are output devices that show programming instructions and data as they are being input and information after it is processed. The size of a computer screen is measured diagonally from corner to corner in inches. For desktop microcomputers, the most common sizes are 13, 15, 17, 19, 21 and 24 inches; for laptop computers, 12.1, 13.3, 14.1 and 15.1 inches. Figure 1.26 illustrates some sizes of computer screen.

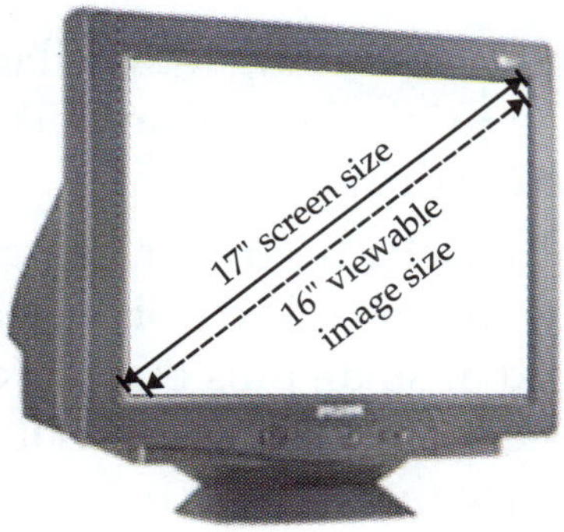

Monitor screen size	Viewable image area
15 inches	14 inches
17 inches	16 inches
21 inches	20 inches
24 inches	23 inches

Figure 1.26 Illustrating sizes of computer screen

Type of Monitors

The two types of monitors are CRT and flat-panel.

CRT

A CRT, for cathode-ray tube, is a vacuum tube used as a display screen in a computer or video display terminal. These are the most common type of computer display, at least for desktop systems. Figure 1.27 illustrates CRT display.

Figure 1.27 CRT display

Flat-panel Displays

Compared to CRTs, flat-panel displays are much thinner, weigh less and consume less power. Thus, they are better for portable computers, although they are available for desktop computers as well. Figure 1.28 illustrates a flat-panel display.

Flat-panel displays are made up of two plates of glass separated by a layer of a liquid crystal display in which light is manipulated.

Figure 1.28 A flat-panel display

Advantages

1. Lower power consumption.
2. Cover less space than conventional monitors.
3. Reduction in cooling load (as these radiate less heat).
4. High performance monitors.
5. Flexibility of usage.
6. More viewing area.

Printers

A *printer* is an output device that prints characters, symbols, and perhaps graphics on paper or another hardcopy medium. The resolution, or quality of sharpness, of the printed image is indicated by *dpi (dots per inch)*, which is a measure of the number of rows and columns of dots that are printed in a square inch. For microcomputer printers, the resolution is in the range of 60–1,500 dpi.

Printers can be separated into two categories, according to whether or not the image produced is formed by physical contact of the print mechanism with the paper. *Impact printers* have contact with paper; *nonimpact printers* do not.

Impact printers: An *impact printer* forms characters or images by striking a mechanism such as a print hammer or wheel against an inked ribbon, leaving an image on paper. A *dot-matrix printer* contains a print head of small pins that strike an inked ribbon against paper, to form characters or images (See figure 1.29). Now-a-days impact printers are more commonly used with mainframes than with personal computers. Note that dot matrix printers are the only desktop printers that can use multilayered forms to print "carbon copies."

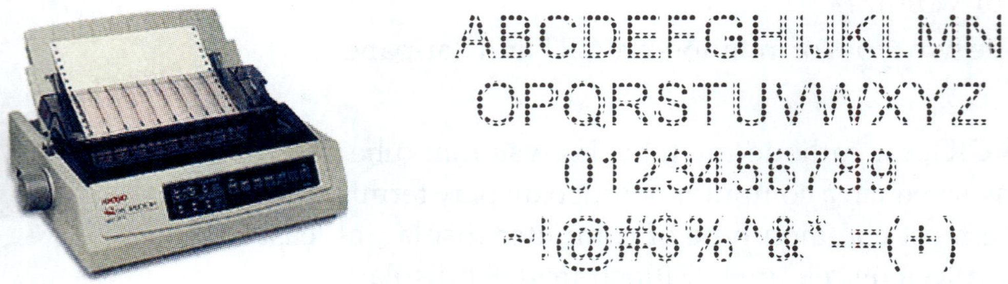

Figure 1.29 A dot-matrix printer and its character pattern

Advantages

1. They are inexpensive and are used widely.
2. Other language characters can also be printed.
3. The width of characters can be doubled to get bolder characters for headings.

Disadvantages

1. The speed of these printers is slow.
2. The quality of the printing is not so good.

Nonimpact printers: Nonimpact printers are faster and quieter than impact printers because no print head strikes paper. *Nonimpact printers* form characters and images without direct physical contact between the printing mechanism and the paper. Two types of nonimpact printers often used with microcomputers are *laser printers* (See figure 1.30) and *ink-jet printers* (also called desk-jet printers). A third kind, the *thermal printer,* is seen less frequently.

Figure 1.30 A laser printer

Unlike a dot-matrix printer, a *laser printer* creates images and characters completely. As in a photocopying machine, these images are produced on a drum, treated with a magnetically charged ink-like toner (powder), and then transferred from drum to paper.

Advantages

1. Very high speed.
2. Low noise level.

3. Low maintenance requirements.
4. Very high image quality.
5. Excellent graphics capabilities.
6. A variety of type sizes and styles.

Ink-jet printers spray on to the paper small, electrically charged droplets of ink from four nozzles through holes in a matrix at high speed. Figure 1.31 shows an ink-jet printer.

Figure 1.31 An ink-jet printer

Speakers

Speakers are the devices that play sounds transmitted as electrical signals from the sound card (See figure 1.32). Most PCs are now multimedia computers, capable of outputting not only text and graphics but also sound, voice, and video.

Sound output devices produce digitised sounds, ranging from beeps and chirps to music. To use sound output, you need appropriate software and a sound card. The sound card plugs into an expansion slot in your computer; on newer computers, it is integrated with the motherboard. Most computers have simple internal speakers. Many users hook up external speakers for high-quality sound. These are similar to the ones connected to a stereo but are smaller in size and have their own small amplifier.

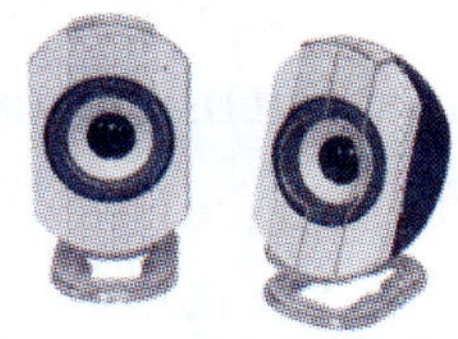

Figure 1.32 Speakers

Speakers receive the sound in form of constantly changing electric current from the sound card and then using a magnet convert it to sound format, which pushes the speaker core back and forth. Sound is created when pressure vibrations are generated.

LCD Projectors

Screen image projector is an output device used to project information from a computer on a large screen (such as a cloth, screen or wall) so that a group of people can view it simultaneously (See figure 1.33). It is very useful for making presentations to a group of people with direct use of a computer.

Figure 1.33 A screen image projector

A screen image projector can be plugged to a computer system directly, and a presenter can make a presentation to a group of people by projecting the presentation material one after the other on a large screen with the help of computer's keyboard or mouse.

Screen image projectors have become common presentation equipment today. These are used commonly with portable notebook computers to set up a modern presentation facility quickly at any place with great ease. Like monitors, screen image projectors provide a temporary softcopy output.

2.1.4 Types of Storage Devices

Let us consider more traditional forms of *secondary storage hardware*, devices that permanently hold data and information as well as programs. Figure 1.34 illustrates commonly used secondary storage devices.

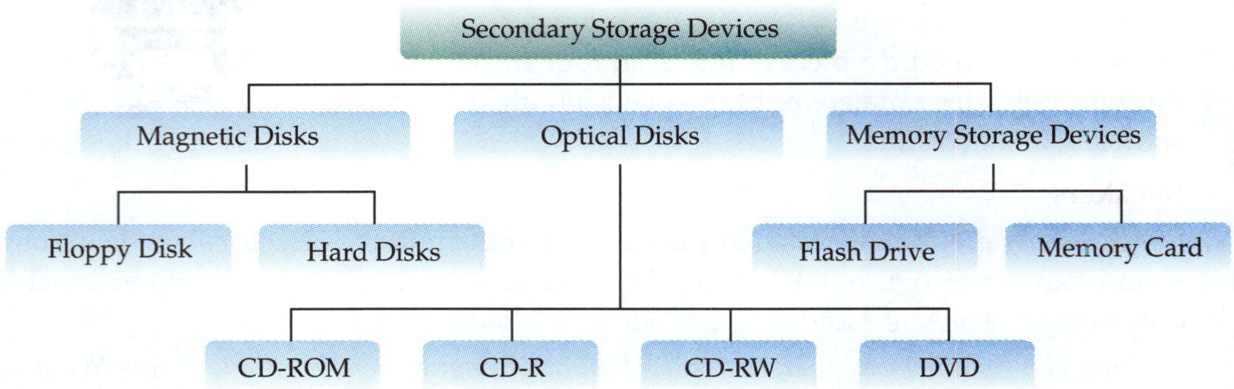

Figure 1.34 Commonly used secondary storage devices and their classification

Let us discuss some commonly used storage devices:

Compact Disk (Optical Disk)

Everyone who has ever played an audio CD is familiar with optical disks. An *optical disk is a removable disk, usually 4.75 inches in diameter and less than one-twentieth of an inch thick, on which data are written and read through the use of laser beams.* An audio CD holds upto 74 minutes of high-fidelity stereo sound. Some optical disks are used strictly for digital data storage, but many are used to distribute multimedia programs that combine text, visuals and sound.

The storage density of optical disks is enormous, the storage cost is extremely low and the access time is relatively fast. An optical disk can hold over 4.7 gigabytes of data, the equivalent of 1 million typewritten pages.

Nearly every PC marketed today contains a CD or DVD drive, which can also read audio CDs. These, along with their recordable and rewritable variations, are the two principal types of optical-disk technology used with computers. Figure 1.35 shows how to use a CD/DVD disk.

Figure 1.35 How to use a CD/DVD disk

The types of optical disks are:

(*i*) CD-ROM — Compact Disk Read Only Memory

(*ii*) CD-R (Compact Disk Recordable)

(*iii*) CD-RW (Compact Disk Rewritable)

(*iv*) DVD-ROM (Digital Versatile or Digital Video Disk, with Read Only Memory)

(*i*) **CD-ROM – for reading only.** For PC users, the best known type of optical disk is the CD-ROM. *CD-ROM (Compact Disk Read Only Memory) is an optical-disk format that is used to hold prerecorded text, graphics and sound.*

(*ii*) **CD-R—for recording on once.** *CD-R (Compact Disk Recordable) disks can be written to only once but can be read many times.* You can view the disk on any personal computer with a CD-ROM drive and the right software. Many new computers come equipped with CD-R drives.

(*iii*) **CD-RW—for rewriting many times.** *A CD-RW (Compact Disk Rewritable) disk, also known as an erasable optical disk, allows users to record and erase data, so the disk can be used over and over again.* CD-RW drives are becoming more common on microcomputers. CD-RW disks are useful for archiving and backing up large amounts of data or work in multimedia production or desktop publishing. CD-RW disks cannot be read by CD-ROM drives. CD-RW disks have a capacity of 650-700 megabytes.

(*iv*) **DVD-ROM—the versatile video disk.** *A DVD-ROM (Digital Versatile Disk or Digital Video Disk, with Read Only Memory) is a CD-style disk with extremely high capacity, able to store 4.7 or more gigabytes.*

Many new computer systems now come with a DVD drive as standard equipment. A great advantage is that these drives can also take standard CD-ROM disks, so now you can watch DVD movies and play CD-ROMs using just one drive. DVDs have enormous potential to replace CDs far archival storage, mass distribution of software, and entertainment.

Not all the optical-disk drives and different types of optical media (read-only, rewritable, and so on) are mutually compatible. You should check product information before buying to make sure you get what you require.

Magnetic Tape

Magnetic tape is a secondary storage device which can hold large volumes of data on it. The tape is a sequential access media and data on it can be accessed sequentially. Large files are stored on them. Due to their sequential access nature, they are not suitable for storage of data that are accessed randomly.

Similar to the tape used on an audio tape recorder (but of higher density), *magnetic tape* is a thin plastic tape coated with a substance that can be magnetised. Data are represented by magnetised spots (representing 1s) or non-magnetised spots (representing 0s). Today, "mag tape" is used mainly for backup and archiving—that is, for maintaining historical records—where there is no need for quick access.

On large computers, tapes are used on magnetic-tape units or reels and in special cartridges. These tapes store up to 160 gigabytes each. On microcomputers, tape is used in the form of *tape cartridges*, modules resembling audio cassettes that contain tape in rectangular, plastic housings (See figure 1.36). An internal or external tape drive is required to use tape media.

Figure 1.36 Magnetic tape cartridge and tape

Flash Drive (Pen Drive)

Flash drive is a compact device of the size of a pen, comes in various shapes and stylish designs (such as pen shape, wallet shape etc.), and may have different added features (such as with a camera, with a built-in MP3/WMA/FM Radio play back for music on the go, etc.). It enables easy transport of data from one computer to another.

It is a plug-and-play device that simply plugs into a USB (Universal Serial Bus) port of a computer. The computer detects it automatically as removable drive. A flash drive does not require any battery, cable, or software, and is compatible with most PCs, desktop, and laptop computers with USB port. All these features make it ideal external data storage for mobile people to carry or transfer data from one computer to another. It has the data retention capability of more than 10 years.

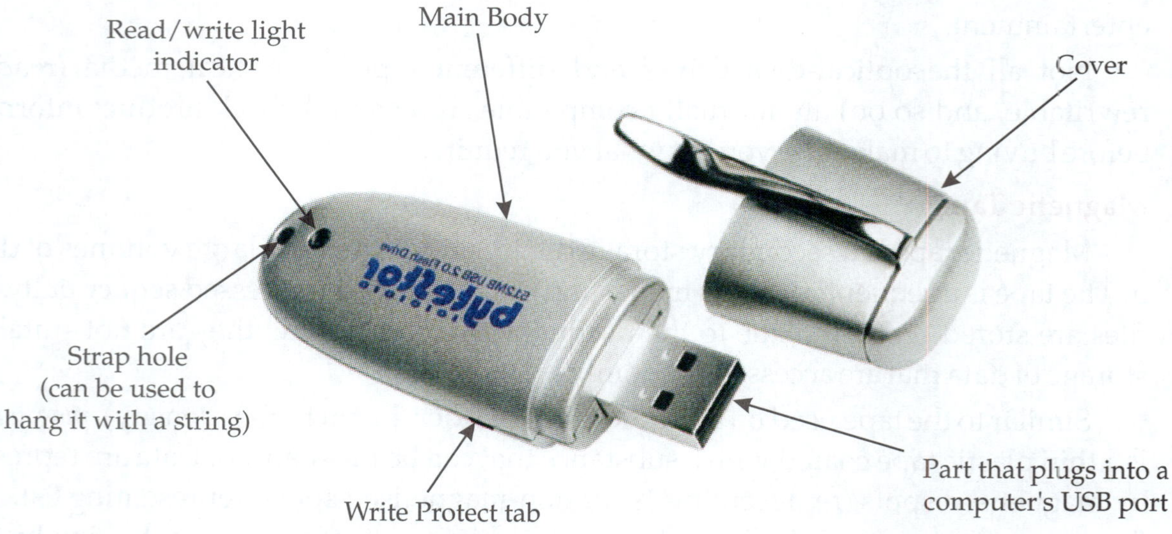

Figure 1.37 A flash drive (pen drive)

Available storage capacities are 8MB, 16MB, 64MB, 128MB, 256MB, 512MB, 1GB, 2GB, 4GB, and 8GB. A pen drive of 16MB capacity has 5600 times more storage capacity than a 1.44MB floppy disk.

Figure 1.37 shows a flash drive. It has a main body and usually a port connector cover. The cover is removed or port connector is pushed out when the drive is to be plugged into the USB port of a computer. The main body usually has a write protect tab, a read/write LED (Light Emitting Diode) indicator, and a strap hole. Some manufacturers also provide software to be used with the drive.

Floppy Diskette

A floppy disk is a very popular direct access secondary storage medium for micro and mini computers. A floppy disk, often called a diskette or simply a disk, is a removable flat piece of mylar plastic packaged in a 3.5-inch plastic case. Data and programs are stored on the disk's coating by means of magnetised spots. The plastic case protects the mylar disk from being touched by human hands.

Floppy disks are inserted into a floppy-disk drive, a device that holds, spins, reads data from, and writes data to a floppy disk. *Read* means taking data from secondary storage (converted to electronic signals) to the computer's memory (RAM). *Write* means copying the electronic information processed by the computer to secondary storage.

On the diskette, data is recorded in concentric circles called **tracks.** On a formatted disk each track is divided into sectors, invisible wedge-shaped sections used for storage and reference purpose. The read/write head is used to transfer data between the computer and the disk. Figure 1.38 illustrates a 3½ inch floppy disk.

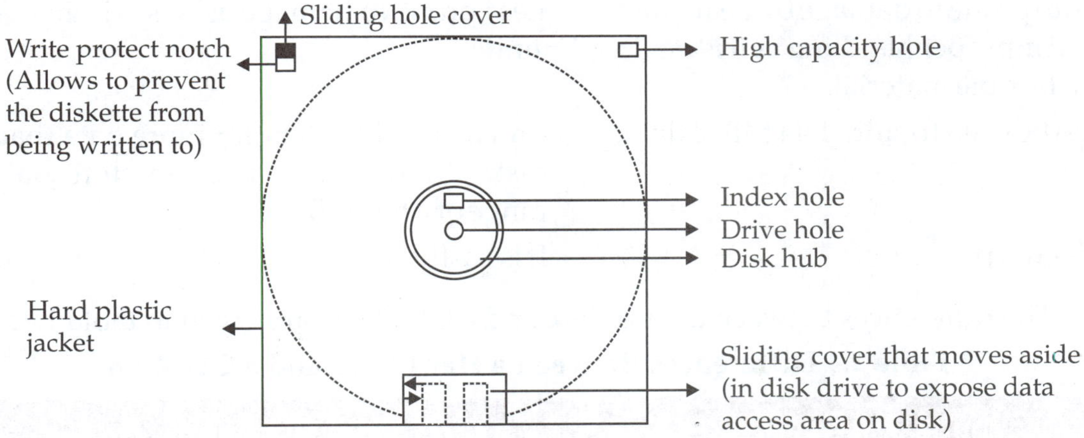

Figure 1.38 3½ inch floppy disk

The Floppy Drive is of a moving head variety and therefore, the floppy can be removed and replaced by another. The head actually contacts the surface during reading/writing, though in other times it is lifted up from the surface. The hole at the centre is to allow a spindle to lock the floppy so that it can rotate. The Index hole is used to recognise the starting sector of any track. The purpose of write permit notch is to protect valuable information recorded on the floppy from accidental damage. If this notch is covered, writing is not allowed on the floppy, only reading is possible. If the notch is not covered reading as well as writing is possible.

Floppies offer a number of advantages. They are exchangeable. The storage capacity is high as compared to its size and weight. These are portable. Floppies are inexpensive also as compared to hard disks. The most common uses of floppy disks are as follows:

(*i*) Moving files between computers that are not connected through communication channel.

(*ii*) Loading new programs on to a system.

(*iii*) Backing up data or programs, the primary copy of which is stored on hard disk.

Useful Tip

Do not remove the disk when the access light is on or while working on a file open from that disk. Save and close the file before removing the disk.

The differences between a floppy disk and a hard disk are given in table 1.3.

Table 1.3 Differences Between a Floppy Disk and a Hard Disk

Floppy Disk	Hard Disk
Floppy disks are also known as floppies or microdisks.	Hard disks are also known as fixed disks.
The computer takes more time to read from a floppy disk.	The computer takes less time to read from hard disk.
More prone to damage by heat, dust and improper handling as it is made of a flexible material.	Less prone to damage as it is within the system unit.
Can be used to store 1.44 MB of data.	Can be used to store far more data than floppy disks. They can be used to store data in the range of a few GBs.
It is cheap.	It is costly.

The differences between a hard disk and a CD-ROM are given in table 1.4.

Table 1.4 Differences Between a Hard Disk and a CD-Rom

Hard Disk	CD-ROM
Hard disks are also known as fixed disks. Data is stored in the form of concentric circles.	CD-ROMs are also known as optical disks. Data is stored in the form of a single spiral track.
The computer takes less time to read from hard disk. It is in the range of 10 to 30 milliseconds.	The computer takes more time to read from CD-ROM. It is in the range of 100 to 300 milliseconds.
Hard disks are not portable.	CD-ROMs are portable.

Data can be read or written as and when required. These can be reused.	It is a permanent storage medium. Data once recorded, cannot be erased and hence, the CD-ROMs cannot be reused.
Hard disks require a less complicated drive mechanism.	CD-ROMs require a more complicated drive mechanism.
Hard disks have a very large storage capacity (Disk packs have virtually unlimited storage capacity).	It has a storage capacity of about 650 Megabytes.
It is costly.	It is cheap.
Not a better storage medium for data archiving as compared to CD-ROMs.	CD-ROMs have a data storage life in excess of 30 years. These are a better storage medium for data archiving as compared to Hard disks.

2.1.5 Devices which Serve as Both Input and Output

So far we have studied input and output devices which can be used specifically for input and output purposes respectively. There are devices which serve as both input and output. Some of these are computer, head set and modem.

- **Computer**

A computer is a programmable, multiuse machine that accepts data—raw facts and figures—and processes, or manipulates it into information we can use, such as summaries, totals, or reports. Its purpose is to speed up problem solving and increase productivity.

We can use computer for communications. It happens when people "go online" on the Internet. Here, online means using a computer or some other information device, connected through a network, to access information and services from other computer or information device.

One of the first things new computer users learn is how to send and receive *e-mail*—"electronic mail", messages transmitted over a computer network, most often the Internet. A network is a communications system connecting two or more computers; the Internet is the largest such network.

When you send some data or information from your computer, it acts as an input device. In case you receive some data or information from some other source then your computer acts as an output device.

- **Head Set**

It is a device that serves as both input and output. It can be connected to a computer whenever required. Two of its major parts are microphone and speakers. Microphone is used for input purpose and speakers are used for output.

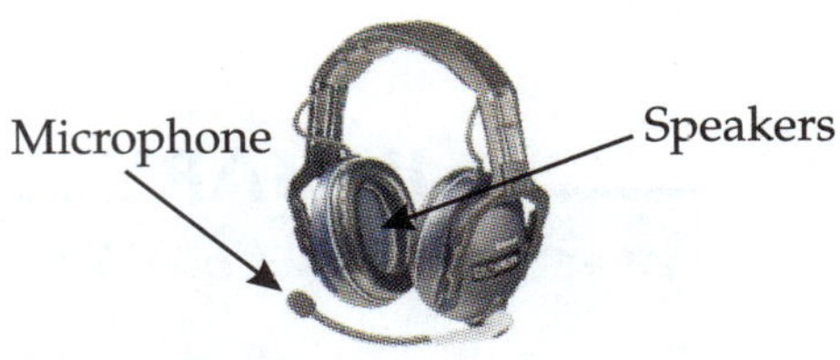

Figure 1.39 Head set

- **Modem**

Computers can be stand-alone machines, unconnected to anything else. If all you are doing is word processing to write documents, a stand-alone system may be fine for you. The communications component of the computer system vastly extends the range of a PC. This piece of hardware is called modem.

A standard modem is a device that sends and receives data over telephone lines to and from computers. The modem is mounted on an expansion card, which is fitted into an expansion slot on the motherboard. This type of modem uses a ***dial-up connection***. There are also external modems. Figure 1.40 illustrates the modem connection.

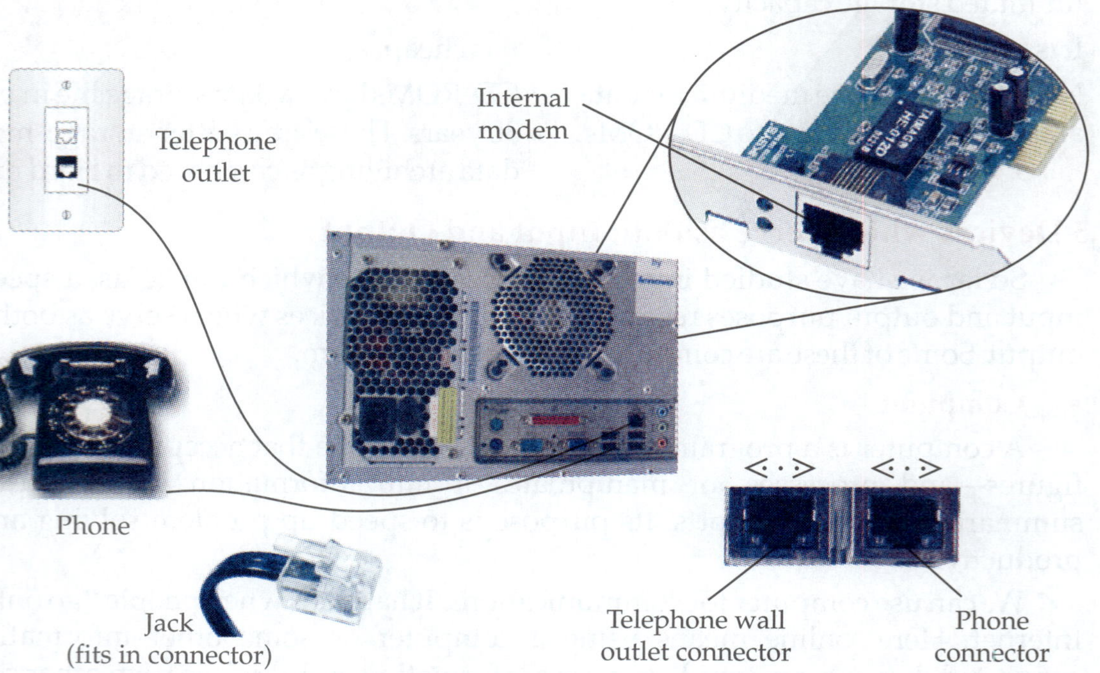

Figure 1.40 The modem connection

You connect the modem inside your computer from a port (socket) in the back of your computer to a line that is then connected to a wall jack. Your telephone is also connected to your computer so that you can make voice calls.

One disadvantage of a telephone modem is that while you are online you cannot use that phone to make voice calls unless you have installed special equipment. In addition, people who try to call you while you are using the modem will get a busy signal. Some modems can handle call waiting.

SUMMARY

- Hardware consists of all the machinery and equipment in a computer system.
- The system unit houses the motherboard (including the processor chip and memory chips), the power supply, and storage devices.
- The number of buttons on the outside of the computer case will vary, but the on/off power switch will appear somewhere, either front or back.

- Output hardware are hardware devices that convert machine-readable information, obtained as the result of processing, into people-readable form. The principal kinds of output are softcopy and hardcopy.
- Floppy-disk drive is a storage device that stores data on removable 3.5-inch-diameter flexible diskettes encased in hard plastic.
- CD-ROM drive is a storage device that uses laser technology to read data from optical disks. Now, software is generally supplied on CDs rather than diskettes.
- USB (Universal Serial Bus) port is a port that can theoretically connect up to 127 peripheral devices daisy-chained to one general-purpose port.
- Serial port is a connector for a line that sends bits one after another, like cars on a one-lane highway.
- Motherboard is the main circuit board in the computer.
- CPU (Central Processing Unit) is the processor. It follows the instructions of the software (program) to manipulate data into information. The CPU is the "brain" of the computer.
- Power supply is a device that converts A.C. to D.C. to run the computer.
- RAM (Random Access Memory) chips are also called *primary storage* and *main memory*, chips that temporarily hold software instructions and data before and after it is processed by the CPU. RAM is a volatile form of storage.
- ROM (Read Only Memory) is a memory chip that cannot be written upon or erased by the computer user without special equipment.
- Hard disk is a secondary storage medium; thin but rigid metal, glass, or ceramic platter covered with a substance that allows data to be stored in the form of magnetised spots.
- Sound card is an expansion card used to convert and transmit digital sounds through analogue speakers, microphones, and headsets.
- Network interface cards are for remote communication via cable.
- Keyboard is an input device that converts letters, numbers, and other characters into electrical signals that can be read by the computer's processor. Keyboards are the most popular kind of input device.
- Mouse is a pointing device that is rolled about on a desktop mouse pad and directs a pointer on the computer's display screen.
- Scanner is a source-data-input device that uses light-sensing (optical) equipment to translate images of text, drawings, photos, and the like into digital form.
- Trackball is a movable ball, mounted on top of a stationary device, that can be rotated by the user's fingers or palm.
- Joystick is a pointing device that works on the same principle as a trackball.

- Bar code reader is a photoelectric (optical) scanner that translates bar codes into digital codes.
- Bar codes are vertical, zebra-striped marks imprinted on most manufactured retail products.
- Display screen is also called monitor, CRT, or simply screen is an output device that shows programming instructions and data as they are being input and information after it is processed. Screens are needed to display softcopy output.
- Flat-panel is a display screen that is much thinner, weighs less, and consumes less power than a CRT.
- Hard copy is printed output.
- Printer is an output device that prints characters, symbols, and perhaps graphics on paper or another hard copy medium.
- Impact printer is a printer that forms characters or images by striking a mechanism such as a print hammer or wheel against an inked ribbon, leaving an image on paper.
- Nonimpact printer is a printer that forms characters and images without direct physical contact between the printing mechanism and paper.
- Laser printer is a nonimpact printer.
- Ink-jet printer is a printer that sprays on to paper small, electrically charged droplets of ink from four nozzles through holes in a matrix at high speed.
- Speaker is an output device used to create sound. It plays sound transmitted as electrical signals from the sound card.
- LCD projector is an output device used to project information from a computer on a large screen (such as a cloth screen or wall) so that a group of people can view it simultaneously.
- Secondary storage hardware are devices that permanently hold data and information as well as programs.
- CD-R (Compact Disk-Recordable) disk is an optical-disk form of secondary storage that can be written to only once but can be read many times.
- CD-ROM (Compact Disk Read Only Memory) is an optical-disk form of secondary storage that is used to hold prerecorded text, graphics, and sound.
- CD-RW (Compact Disk-Rewritable) disk is also known as erasable optical disk; optical-disk form of secondary storage that allows users to record and erase data, so that the disk can be used over and over again.
- DVD-R (DVD-Recordable) disks are the DVD disks that allow one-time recording by the user.

- DVD-ROM (Digital Versatile Disk or Digital Video Disk, with Read Only Memory) is a CD-type disk with extremely high capacity, able to store 4.7 or more gigabytes. It is a powerful and versatile secondary storage medium.
- Magnetic tape is a thin plastic tape coated with a substance that can be magnetised. Today, "mag tape" is used mainly for backup and archiving—that is, for maintaining historical records—where there is no need for quick access.
- Pen drive (Flash drive) is a compact device of size of a pen, comes in various shapes and stylish designs, and may have different added features. It enables easy transport of data from one computer to another.
- Floppy disk is often called *diskette or simply disk;* removable flat piece of mylar plastic packaged in a 3.5-inch plastic case.
- Tracks are the rings on a diskette along which data is recorded.
- Headset is a device that serves as both input and output.
- Modem is a device that sends and receives data over telephone lines to and from computers.

REVIEW QUESTIONS

STATE WHETHER TRUE OR FALSE

1. Hardware refers to all the physical components inside or outside the computer.
2. USB can theoretically connect up to 127 peripheral devices.
3. The power supply is a device that converts DC to AC to run the computer.
4. Main memory is nonvolatile.
5. A mouse is a pointing device.
6. Magnetic tape is now used mainly for maintaining historical records.
7. The principal kinds of output are hard copy and soft copy.
8. CRTs consume more power than flat-panel displays.

FILL IN THE BLANKS

1. The .... is often referred to as the "brain" of a computer.
2. .... are used to enter data into the computer so it can be processed. .... are used to get it out so we can see it or distribute it to others.
3. The two main categories of printer are .... and ....
4. .... displays are the most common type of desktop computer display.
5. A printer that forms characters or images by striking a mechanism such as a print hammer of wheel against an inked ribbon, leaving images on a paper, is called a (n) .... printer.

MULTIPLE CHOICE QUESTIONS

1. Which of the following is used to temporarily store program instructions and data?
   (a) ROM (b) RAM
   (c) CPU (d) CD-R
2. Which of the following is not included on a computer's motherboard?
   (a) Microprocessor (b) RAM chips
   (c) Keyboard (d) ROM chips
3. On the keyboard, the key you press to finalize a command or entry, is ....
   (a) Enter (b) Escape
   (c) Control (d) All of these
4. Data on a tape is stored so you access it ....
   (a) Randomly (b) Sequentially
   (c) Optically (d) Manually.
5. Which of the following device(s) serve as both input and output?
   (a) Computer (b) Headset
   (c) Modem (d) All of these

ANSWER THE FOLLOWING

1. What are the categories of the computer hardware?
2. Describe the vital components of the system unit.
3. Write a short note on the following:
   (i) Floppy drive (ii) CD-ROM drive
   (iii) USB ports (iv) Serial port
4. Discuss the most fundamental part of the motherboard.
5. Write a short note on the following:
   (i) CPU (ii) Power supply
   (iii) Memory (iv) Hard disk
   (v) Cards (sound and network)
6. What are RAM and ROM?
7. Discuss the commonly used input and output devices and their functions.
8. Write a short note on the following:
   (i) Keyboard (ii) Mouse
   (iii) Scanner (iv) Joystick
   (v) Trackball (vi) Bar Code Reader

9. Write a short note on the following:
   (i) Monitors (ii) Printers
   (iii) Speakers (iv) LCD projectors
10. What is the difference between impact and nonimpact printers?
11. Discuss the types of the main storage devices.
12. Explain the various types of optical disks.
13. How is magnetic tape used?
14. Write a short note on the following:
   (i) CD (ii) DVD
   (iii) Tape (iv) Pen drive
   (v) Floppy diskette
15. Differentiate the following :
   (i) Floppy disk and Hard disk (ii) Hard disk and CD-ROM
16. Discuss the devices which serve as both input and output.

FIELD TRIP

1. Cut out an advertisement from a newspaper or a magazine that features a new microcomputer system. Circle all the terms that are familiar to you. Define these terms on a separate sheet of paper. Is this computer expandable? How much does it cost? Is the monitor included in the price? A printer?
2. Consider the secondary storage components for a new system you are planning to buy. Using the advertisements in a computer magazine, pick out particular examples of each of the following devices and write a brief description of why you would want them and how much they would cost. Keep in mind that many of these components are already part of many systems, so you will concern yourself with adding them only after the system has been purchased.
   (i) Hard disk drive (ii) Floppy disk drive
   (iii) Floppy disks (iv) Removable disks
   (v) CD-ROM drive (vi) DVD drive

ASSIGNMENT

1. Prepare a chart showing the classification of fixed and removable data storage devices.
2. Show the correct procedure for attaching and removing removable data storage device.

UNIT 2 SOFTWARE

Specific Objectives

After reading this unit, the student will be able to:

2.2.1 identify types of Software Packages.

2.2.2 distinguish between Open Source and Proprietary Software.

2.2.3 identify different types, examples and uses of Application Software.

2.2.4 launch some Application Software.

2.2.0 Introduction

Software is an internal set of programs that is designed to perform a well defined function. The software is created by grouping various related programs. A program is a sequence of instructions written to solve a particular problem. The programs are created in computer programming languages. These software are created by programmers and distributed by using disks or the Internet.

Software is the deriving force behind the working of computer. Without the presence of software, the computer is as good as a piece of plastic and metal. Hardware can be considered as organs and the software is life that moves inside these organs. Both of them cannot perform their function without the presence of each other.

Types of Software

Software is generally divided into two main categories: System Software and Application Software. The system software are generally concerned with the various operations of a computer system and the application software are concerned with providing various services to the users. Figure 2.1 shows the two types of software.

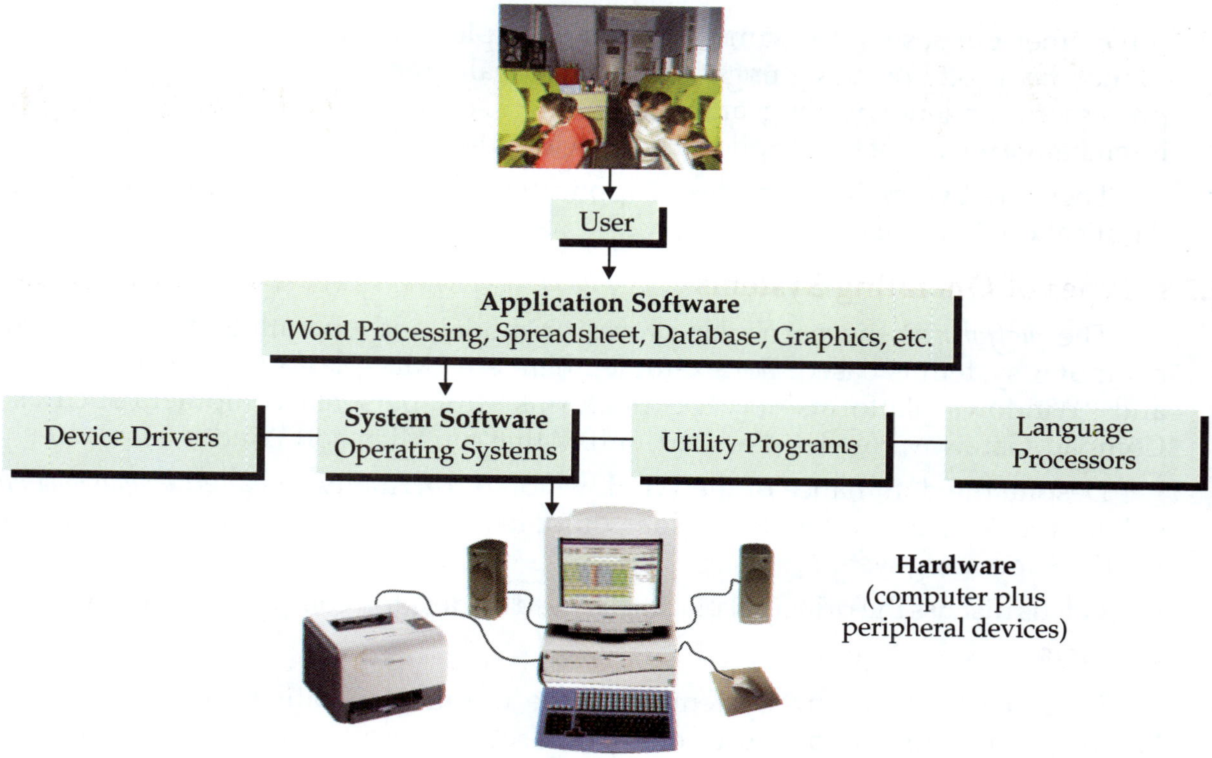

Figure 2.1 Types of software

System Software

System software is a set of master programs that is designed to control various system activities. System software check for the availability of different devices, scan input devices for input and sends output to output devices. In case of systems that allow multiple applications to run simultaneously, system software keep track of utilization of CPU time and memory by different running applications. System software also convert the instruction from user understandable language to computer understandable language.

The four basic components of system software are given below:

1. **Operating Systems.** An Operating System is the principal component of system software in any computing system. Booting is the process of loading an operating system into a computer's main memory. There are different types of Operating Systems.
2. **Device Drivers.** Device drivers help the computer control peripheral devices.
3. **Utility Programs.** Utility programs are generally used to support, enhance, or expand existing programs in a computer system.
4. **Language Processors.** Language processors are the types of system software that are used to convert the instructions written in one type of language into the other type.

Application Software

Application software are designed to satisfy a particular need of a particular environment. An application software, designed to satisfy one purpose may not be able to solve other purpose of the same user. For example, software for financial management cannot be used for designing two-dimensional graphics. Similarly, we have word processors for letter writing and presentation software for presentations. We cannot interchange the use of two application software with each other.

There are two main categories of application software: Pre-Written and Customised Applications Software.

2.2.1 Types of Operating Systems

The *platform* is the particular processor model and operating system on which a computer system is based. For example, there are "Mac platforms" (Apple Macintosh) and "Windows platforms" or "PC platforms" (for personal computers such as Dell, Compaq, Gateway, Hewlett-Packard, or IBM that run Microsoft Windows).

Despite the dominance of the Windows platform, many so-called *legacy systems* are still in use. A legacy system is an older, outdated, yet still functional technology, such as the DOS operating system.

Let us discuss the principal platforms used on desktop computers and servers:

- **DOS**

DOS (Disk Operating System) was the original operating system produced by Microsoft and had a hard-to-use command driven user interface. Its initial 1982 version was designed to run on the IBM PC as PC-DOS. Later Microsoft licensed the same system to other computer makers as MS-DOS. With the growing popularity of cheaper PCs produced by these companies, MS-DOS came to dominate the industry. Two years before the advent of Windows 95, which eventually grew out of DOS, there were reportedly more than 100 million users of DOS, which at that time made it the most popular software ever adopted—of any sort.

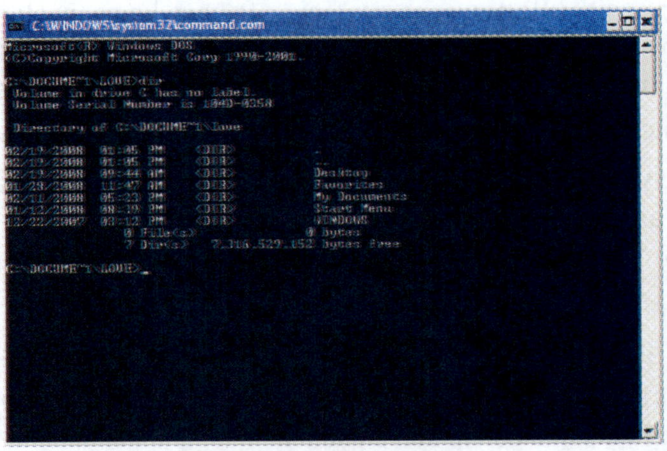

Figure 2.2 DOS screen

- **Windows**

Microsoft Windows 98: *Microsoft Windows 98* is still a popular operating system for desktop and portable microcomputers, supporting the most hardware and the most application software. Among other improvements over its predecessors, Windows 98 gives support to a standard called Universal Plug and Play, which is supposed to let a variety of electronics seamlessly network with each other. *Plug and play* is defined as the ability of a computer to automatically configure a new hardware component that is added to it. In reality, Plug and Play did not perform as smoothly as promised. This feature has been improved in newer Windows versions.

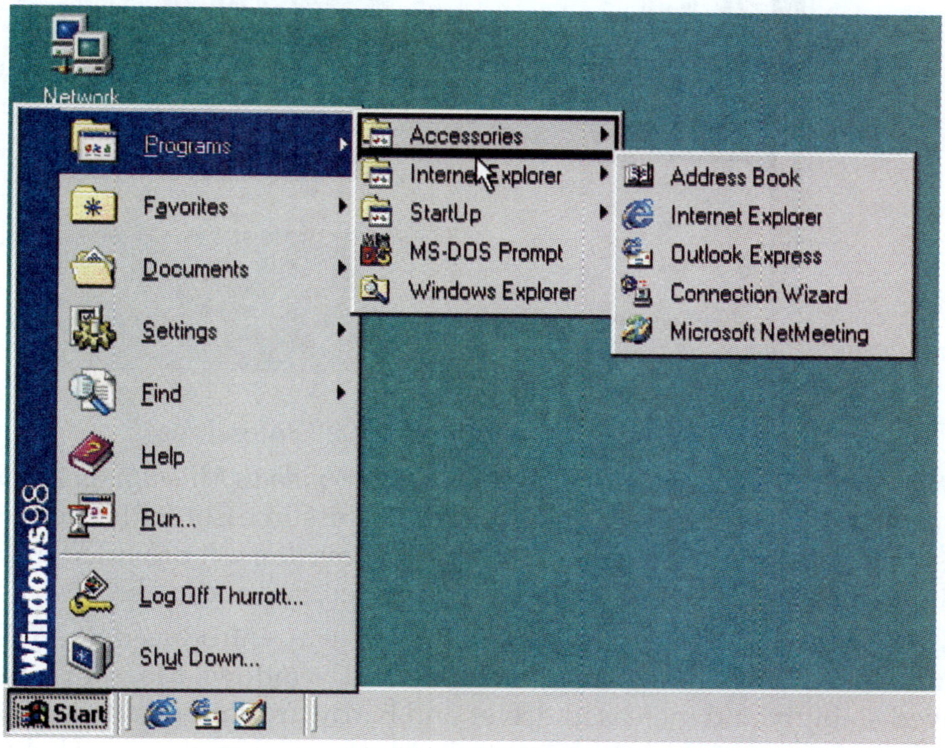

Figure 2.3 Windows 98

Windows NT and 2000/2003—the challenge from Microsoft: Windows desktop operating systems (98/Me/XP) can be used to link PCs in small networks in homes and offices. However, something more powerful was needed to run the huge networks linking a variety of computers—PCs, workstations, mainframes—used by many companies, universities, and other organisations, which previously were served principally by Unix and NetWare operating systems. *Microsoft Windows NT* (the NT stands for "New Technology"), later upgraded to *Windows 2000,* is the company's multitasking operating system designed to run on network servers in businesses of all sizes. It allows multiple users to share resources such as data, programs, and printers and to build Web applications and connect to the Internet.

Windows 2000 includes the Windows 2000 server family, for various levels of network servers: Windows 2000 Professional, Windows 2000 Server, Windows 2000 Advanced Server, and Windows 2000 Datacenter Server. In 2003, Microsoft introduced a new version of Windows 2000 called the Windows *Server 2003* family. This version enhances security, reliability, and manageability, among other things, and includes the Microsoft .NET Framework, a means for building, distributing, and maintaining Web services and applications.

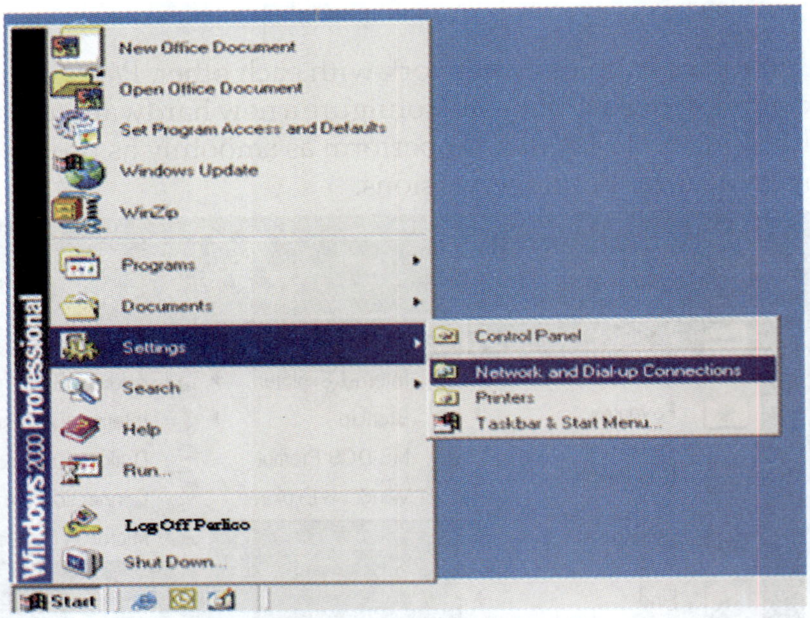

Figure 2.4 Windows 2000 Professional

Microsoft Windows Millennium: *Microsoft Windows Millennium Edition*, or *Windows Me* (the *Me* stands for "Millennium Edition"), is the successor for home users to Windows 98, designed to support desktop and portable computers. It provided improved support of multimedia features—still pictures, digital video, and audio files.

Microsoft Windows XP: *Windows XP* OS was introduced in 2001; it combines elements of Windows networking software and Windows Me with a new GUI. It has improved stability and increased driver and hardware support. It also has new features such as built-in instant messaging, centralised shopping managers to help you keep track of your favourite online stores and products, and music, video, and photography managers. Windows XP Home Edition is for typical home users. Windows XP Professional Edition is for businesses of all sizes and for home users who need to do more than get e-mail, browse the Internet, and do word processing. Windows XP Tablet PC Edition is for business notebook computers that support data entry via a special pen used to write on the display screen.

Figure 2.5 The look of Windows XP

Microsoft Windows Vista: Windows Vista is the company's newest version of ever popular operating system called Windows. It is an enhancement of the different releases till now, *i.e.*, Windows 95, Windows 98, Windows NT, Windows 2000, Windows ME and Windows XP.

Windows Vista comes in five different versions: Home Basic, Home Premium, Business Enterprise and Ultimate.

In Windows Vista, you explore new features for searching, staying connected, networking, sync-ing devices, and managing files on your computer—find things fast, get down to business, and focus on what matters to you. Figure 2.6 shows the Windows Vista Screen.

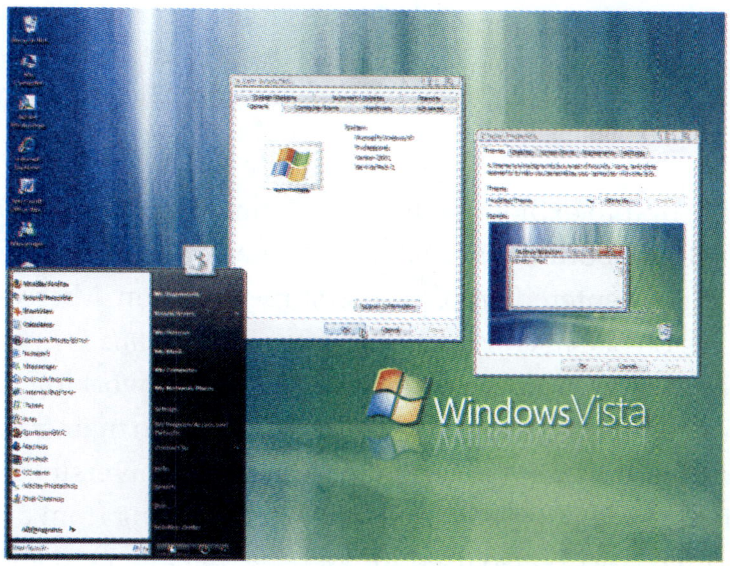

Figure 2.6 Windows Vista

Note

All Microsoft Windows OSs are proprietary.

- **Linux**

Linux is the software built by a community. It began in 1991 when programmer Linus Torvalds, a graduate student in Finland, posted his free Linux operating system on the Internet. Linux (pronounced "*linn*-uks") is the rising star of network software. *Linux* is a free (nonproprietary) version of Unix, and its continual improvements result from the efforts of tens of thousands of volunteer programmers. Whereas Windows is Microsoft's proprietary product, Linux is *open-source software*—meaning any programmer can download it from the Internet for free and modify it with suggested improvements. The only qualification is that changes cannot be copyrighted; they must be made available to all and remain in the public domain.

Linux Logo:
Tux, the Linux Penguin

Because it was originally built for use on the Internet, Linux is more reliable than Windows for online applications. Hence, it is better suited to run Websites and e-commerce software. Its real growth, however, may come as it reaches outward to other applications and, possibly, replaces Windows in many situations. Figure 2.7 shows the Linux screen.

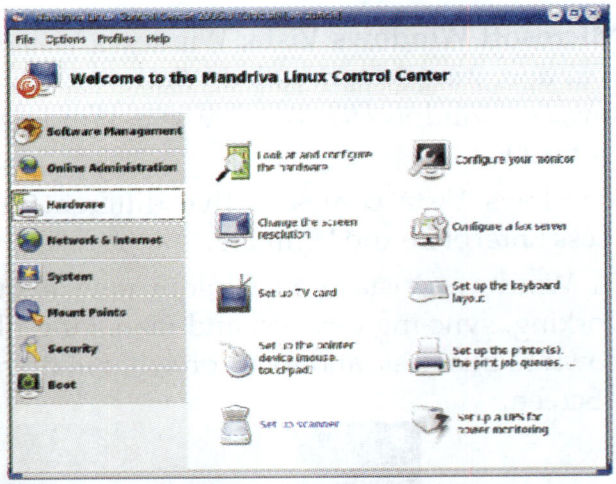

Figure 2.7 Linux screen

- **Unix**

Unix was the first to exploit the Internet. Unix (pronounced "*you*-nicks") was developed at AT&T's Bell Laboratories, USA in 1969 as an operating system for minicomputers. By the 1980s, AT&T entered into partnership with Sun Micro-systems to develop a standardised version of Unix for sale to industry. Today *Unix* is a proprietary multitasking operating system for multiple users that has built-in networking capability and versions that can run on all kinds of computers. It is used mostly on mainframes, workstations, and servers, rather than on PCs. Government agencies, universities, research institutions, large corporations, and banks—all use Unix for everything from designing airplane parts to currency trading. Unix is also used for Website management and runs the backbone of the Internet. The developers of the Internet built their communications system around Unix because it has the ability to keep large systems (with hundreds of processors) churning out transactions day in and day out for years without fail.

Like MS-DOS, Unix uses a command-line interface. Figure 2.8 illustrates a list of files/directories using Unix.

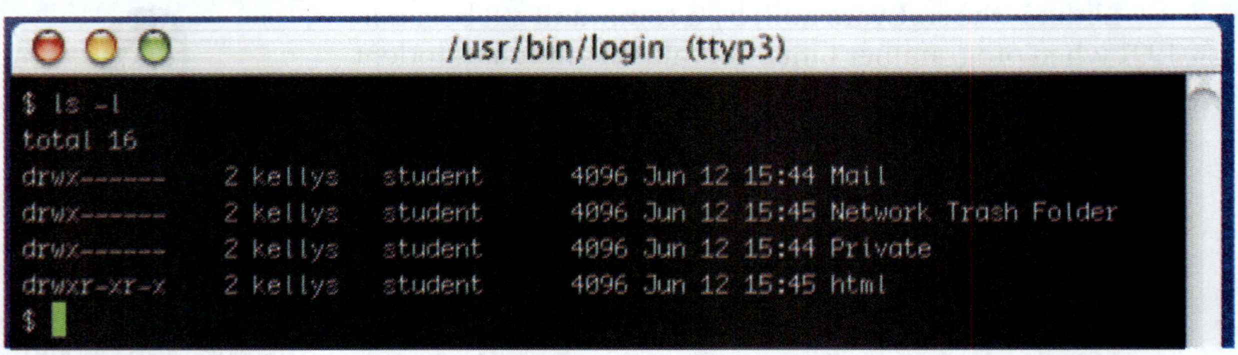

Figure 2.8 Unix screen

• Macintosh

The Macintosh operating system is for love of Mac. The Macintosh *operating system (Mac OS),* which runs only on Apple Macintosh computers, set the standard for icon-oriented, easy-to-use graphical user interfaces. The software generated a strong legion of fans shortly after its launch in 1984 and inspired rival Microsoft to upgrade DOS to the more user-friendly Windows operating systems. Much later, in 1998, Apple introduced its iMac computer (the "i" stands for "internet"), which added capabilities such as small-scale networking.

The Mac OS is *proprietary*, meaning that it is privately owned and controlled by a company. Most Mac users still use System 9, introduced in October 1999. The newest version of the operating system, Mac OS X (called "ten"), broke with 15 years of Mac software to use Unix to offer a dramatic new look and feel. Figure 2.9 shows the Mac OS X.

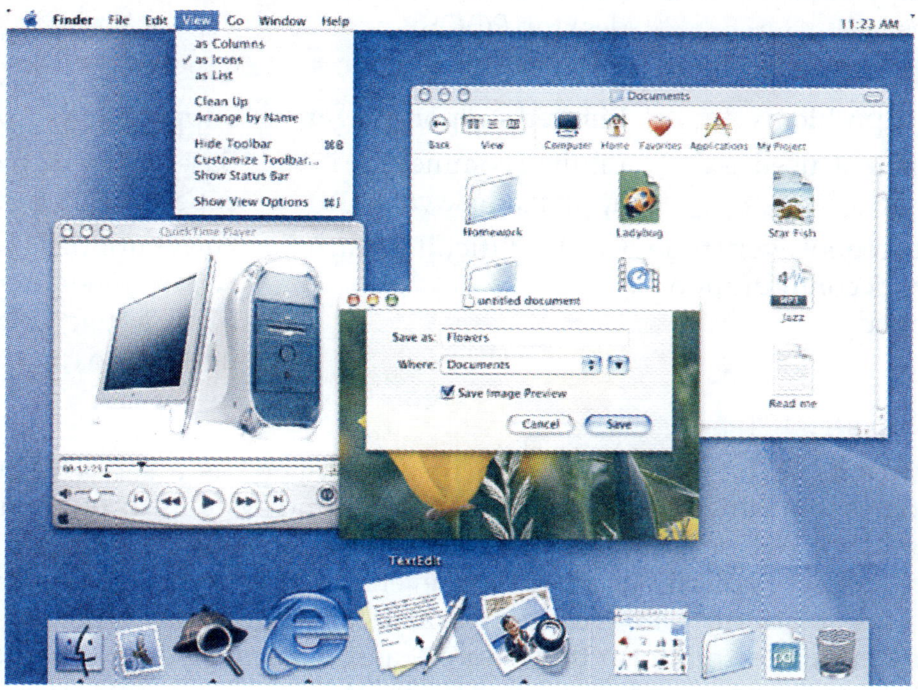

Figure 2.9 Mac OS X

The new user interface, *Aqua,* has Hollywood-like tricks. Many Apple users claim that OS X would not allow software conflicts, a frequent headache with Microsoft's Windows operating systems.

Mac OS X also offers free universal e-mail services, improved graphics and printing, CD burning capability, DVD player, easier ways to find files (using Dock), and support for building and storing Web pages. There are still more System 9-compatible applications available than there are for Mac OS X, but the situation is improving rapidly.

Macintosh is still considered king in areas such as desktop publishing, and Macs are still favoured in many educational settings. For very specialised applications, most programs are written for the Windows platform. However, programs for games and for common business uses such as word processing and spreadsheets are also widely available for the Mac.

The three major microcomputer operating systems are compared in table 2.1.

Table 2.1 Comparison of Windows XP, Linux and Mac OS

Windows XP	Linux	Mac OS X
Pros:	*Pros:*	*Pros:*
Runs on a wide range of hardware	Runs on a wide range of hardware	Easy to install
Has largest market share	Has largest number of user interface types	Best GUI
Has many built-in utilities	Can be used as server or desktop PC OS	Secure and stable
Cons:	*Cons:*	*Cons:*
Security problems	Limited support for games	Supports only Apple computers
Not efficient, used as a server OS	Limited commercial applications available	Base hardware more expensive than other platforms
Have to reboot every time a network configuration is changed	Can be difficult to learn	Fewer utilities available, Fewer games than for Windows, Many applications still being updated to run with OS X

- **Microsoft .NET**

Microsoft .NET (pronounced "Microsoft dot-net") is a set of Microsoft software technologies for connecting information, people, and systems through the use of special building-block Web service programs. These programs are complicated to explain, but basically they let applications share data, even across networks, and enable applications to run cross-platform and cross-network regardless of how they were built, what operating system or platform they run on, and what devices are used to access them. These Web service programs are created using *XML*, or *eXtensible Markup language*, a Web-document-tagging format and program writing language that represents an advance over HTML. The programs remain independent of one another but can loosely link themselves into a collaborating group that performs a particular task.

- **Novell's NetWare**

Novell's NetWare is PC networking software. *NetWare* has long been a popular network operating system for coordinating microcomputer-based local area networks (LANs) throughout a company or a campus.

LANs allow PCs to share programs, data files, and printers and other devices. Novell, the maker of NetWare, thrived as corporate data managers realised that networks of PCs could exchange information more cheaply than the previous generation of mainframes and midrange computers. The biggest challenge to NetWare has been Windows NT,

Windows 2000/2003, and Windows XP. However, Novell is continuing to improve its networking OS with its new version, 6.5.

2.2.2 Differences Between Open Source and Proprietary Software

Software, or *programs,* consist of all the instructions that tell the computer how to perform a task. These instructions come from a software developer in a form (such as a CD, or compact disk) that will be accepted by the computer.

Open source software is a software that any programmer can download from the Internet free and modify with suggested improvements. The only qualification is that changes cannot be copyrighted; they must be made available to all and remain in the public domain. Because this software is not proprietary, any programmer can make improvements, which can result in a better-quality software. Many open source applications run on multiple platforms including Windows and Linux.

Open source software has become mainstream. Applications such as the Firefox Web browser and Linux operating system are available to aid in all areas of operation, including teaching and learning.

Proprietary software also called *commercial software* or *packaged software,* is a software that is offered for sale, such as Microsoft Word, Microsoft Office XP, or Adobe Photoshop.

Although such software may not show upon the bill of sale when you buy a new PC, you have paid for some of it as part of the purchase. And, most likely, whenever you order a new game or other commercial program, you will have to pay for it. This software is copyrighted. A *copyright* is the exclusive legal right that prohibits copying of intellectual property such as a software without the permission of the copyright holder.

Software manufacturers do not sell you their software, rather they sell you a license to become an authorised user of it. What is the difference? In paying for a ***software license,*** you sign a contract in which you agree not to make copies of the software to give away or resell. That is, you have bought only the company's permission to use the software and not the software itself. This legal nicety allows the company to retain its rights to the program and limits the way its customers can use it. The small print in the licensing agreement usually allows you to make one copy *(backup copy* or *archival copy*) for your own use. (Each software company has a different license; there is no industry standard.)

Open source software has become a strong contender in online training and e-learning sectors. As technology continues to evolve, more open source offerings will continue to emerge in the area of e-learning, continuously changing the landscape of online teaching and learning, both in academia and business fields.

The main difference between commercial support for proprietary software and commercial support for open source software is that the proprietary software is obligatory and the open source software is optional. If you opt out of paying for support for proprietary software, you lose the right to use it in most cases. The costs incidentally tend to be quite high for proprietary software.

The *advantages of proprietary software* are:

1. Reliable, professional support and training available.

2. Packaged, comprehensive, modular formats.
3. Regularly and easily updated.

The *disadvantages of proprietary software* are:

1. Costly
2. Has closed standards that hinder further development.

The *advantages of open source software* are:

1. Low cost and no license fees.
2. Open standards that facilitate integration with other systems.
3. It is easily customisable.

The *disadvantages of open source software* are:

1. Lack of professional support.
2. Evolving developer communities.
3. Lack of release co-ordination.
4. Erratic updates.

So what is the right solution for you and your organisation? Generally, for smaller organisations and projects, open source solutions seem to suffice. The difference in cost more than makes up for the perceived disadvantages mentioned above. Larger organisations seem to require more robust, high-quality product with high levels of service and support. They want responsibility, reliable assistance, and support from their suppliers. With rapid developments in technology, chances are that you can find tools to meet your training needs in either the open source or commercial sector. But open source provides unique advantages which include filling the low-cost high-control niche that are difficult, if not impossible, to achieve through commercial proprietary avenues.

At one time, just about everyone paid for microcomputer application software. You bought it as part of the computer or in a software store, or you downloaded it online with a credit card charge. Now, other ways exist to obtain software. Table 2.2 gives the choices among Application Software.

Table 2.2 Choices among Application Software

Type	Definition
Proprietary software or commercial software or packaged software	Copyrighted. If you do not pay for it, you can be prosecuted.
Public-domain software	Not copyrighted. You can copy it for free without fear of prosecution.
Shareware	Copyrighted. Available free, but you should pay to continue using it.
Freeware	Copyrighted. Available free.
Rentalware	Copyrighted. Lease for a fee.

Occasionally, companies or individuals need software written specifically for them, to meet unique needs. This software is called *Customised Software*, and it is created by software engineers and programmers.

2.2.3 Types, Examples and Uses of Application Software

Application software can be classified in many ways—for productivity, speciality education/reference, entertainment, and personal uses. Figure 2.10 illustrates the types of application software.

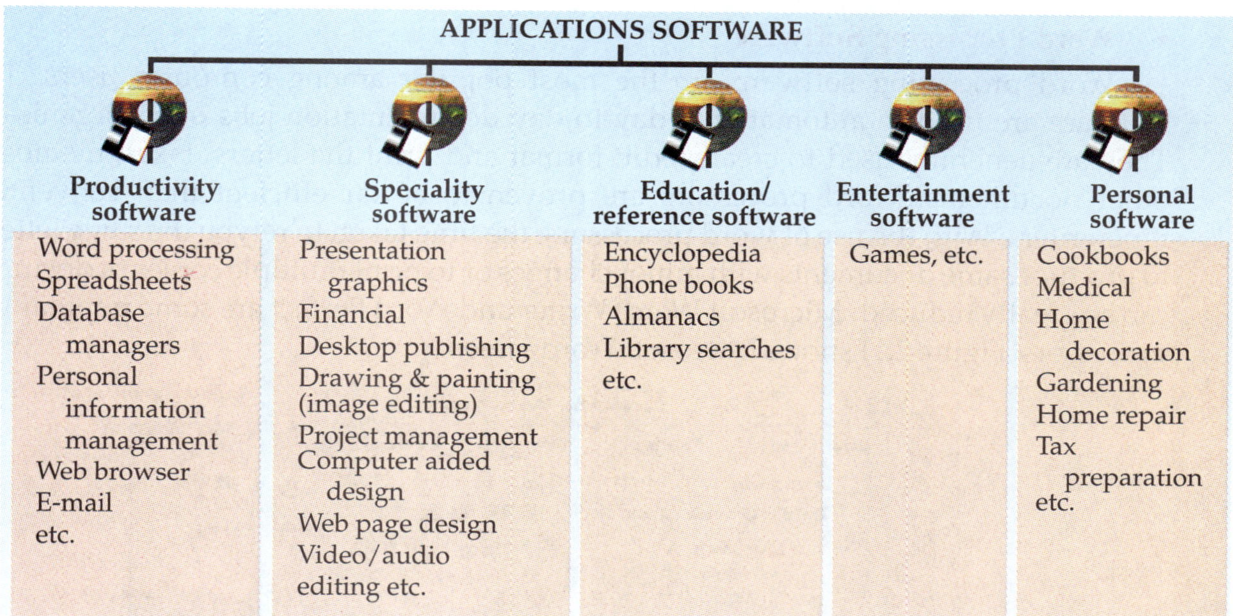

Figure 2.10 Types of application software

Let us discuss the two main categories of software:

1. Pre-Written Application Software

Pre-written application software are designed to satisfy common needs of various businesses. For example, every business uses computers for letter writing and mailing purposes. These application software are developed by leading companies and sold as a product in the market. The cost of these software depends upon the functionality provided by the software, area of use and expected number of users. These software can be suitable for an individual or for a group of individuals. These software are helpful in controlling the general activities of organisations. For example, all organisations need software for word processing. It does not mean that the organisation should create a software of their own. They can purchase a company built software like MS-Word. Some of the most common categories of software that are available in the market are given below:

- Word Processing Software
- Electronic Spreadsheets
- Database Management Systems
- Presentation Software

- Educational Software
- Games Software
- Browsers
- Authoring Software
- Graphics Software
- Communication Software
- Desktop Publishing Software

- **Word Processing Software**

Word processing software are the most popular among computer users. These software are used to automate the day-to-day documentation jobs of an organisation. They are generally used to create, edit, format and print the letters, faxes, memos and other documents. Word processors are proven to be far efficient than conventional typewriters. With the use of word processors, the time taken to retype the same letters or to produce same documents with minor changes or to print multiple copies of documents can be greatly reduced. Microsoft Word, Writer and Word Perfect are some popular word processors. Figure 2.11 shows Microsoft Word screen.

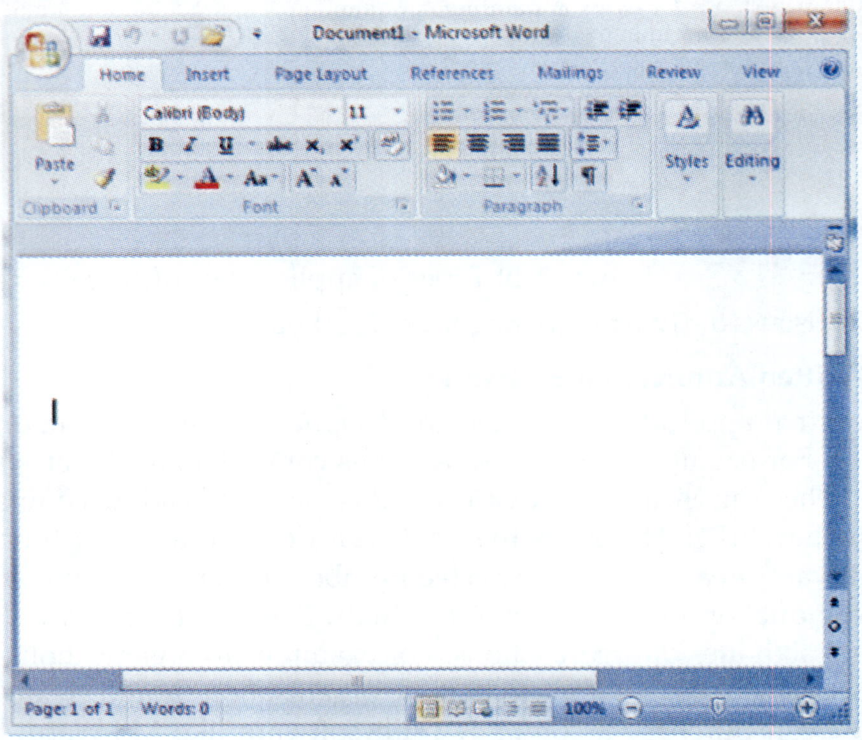

Figure 2.11 Microsoft Word

- **Electronic Spreadsheets**

Electronic spreadsheets are used for mathematical and financial calculations. These software have worksheets made up of rows and columns. Each of such sheets is capable of storing and manipulating numbers, characters, formulae and all other types of data such as graphs and pictures. These software have capabilities of automatically calculating the results, generating graphs and producing sub-totals.

Electronic spreadsheets are very popular as they:

1. are very easy to operate.
2. recalculate results automatically on changing data.
3. contain several in-built functions to automate calculations.
4. can handle large volumes of data.

Microsoft Excel, Quatropro, and Lotus 123 are some of the popular electronic spread-sheet packages. Figure 2.12 shows the Microsoft Excel screen.

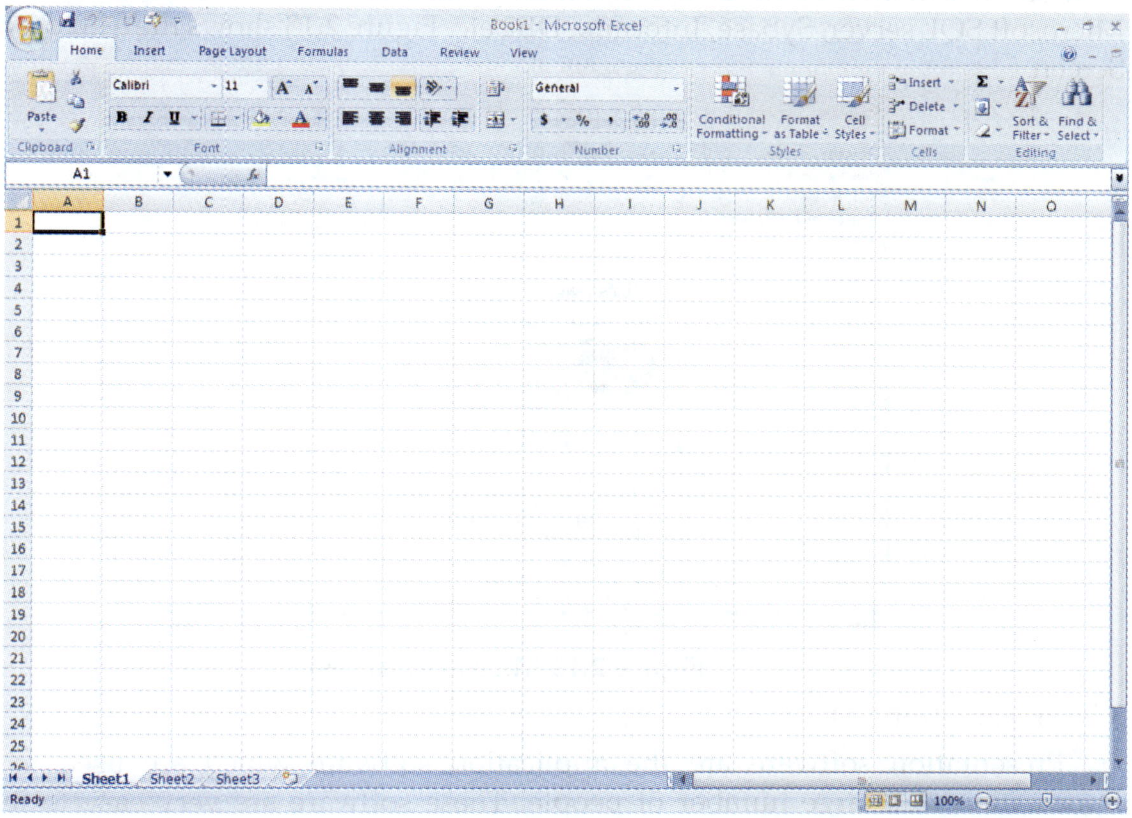

Figure 2.12 Microsoft Excel

- **Database Management Systems**

Database Management Systems are the application software, which are designed to create and edit databases and query data from the database, as required by the users. A database is an organised collection of related data.

Database Management Systems are widely used in the field of ICT. Every organisation produces huge volumes of data every year. These huge volumes of data are stored in the form of tables that are generally related to each other. The data are stored in a way that it is easier to retrieve data based on a condition. DBMS provides commands for creation, updation and deletion of data that are stored in tables. They also provide commands to create procedures, functions, packages and other database objects. The user types their requests or questions called "queries" that are processed by DBMS and the result is displayed back to them. Examples are Access, Base.

Database Management Systems have seen many development in past few years. These developments have resulted into the evolution of new types of systems called "Relational Database Management Systems" (RDBMS) and "Object Relational Database Management Systems" (ORDBMS).

Modern Database Management Systems can be operated on a local area network as well as on Internet. Some of the commonly used RDBMS and ORDBMS are Oracle, Microsoft SQL server, Sybase, Informix, DB2 etc. Figure 2.13 shows the Microsoft Access Screen.

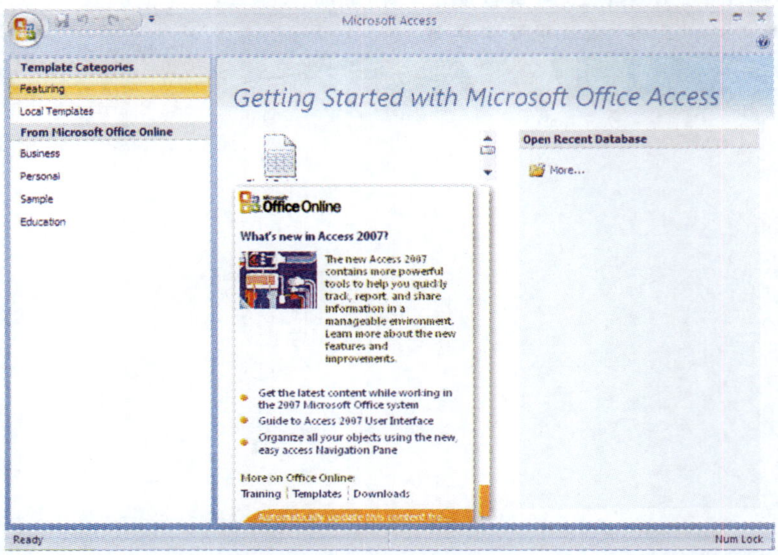

Figure 2.13 Microsoft Access

- **Presentation Software**

Presentation software are the application software which are used to present information to a large number of people. These software are very easy to learn and operate. Presentation software are widely used by executives of companies in advertisement campaigns of their new products, distributing financial information, communicating ideas and discussing marketing plans. These presentations have been proven to be very efficient in day-to-day needs of organisations.

Presentation software are equipped with designing and animating tools that help in making the presentation more effective. The information is formulated in different types of slides. These slides are animated to run with particular visual and sound effects. Then the slides are displayed in a particular sequence. Examples include PowerPoint and Impress. Microsoft PowerPoint is one of the most popular presentation software. Figure 2.14 shows the Microsoft PowerPoint screen.

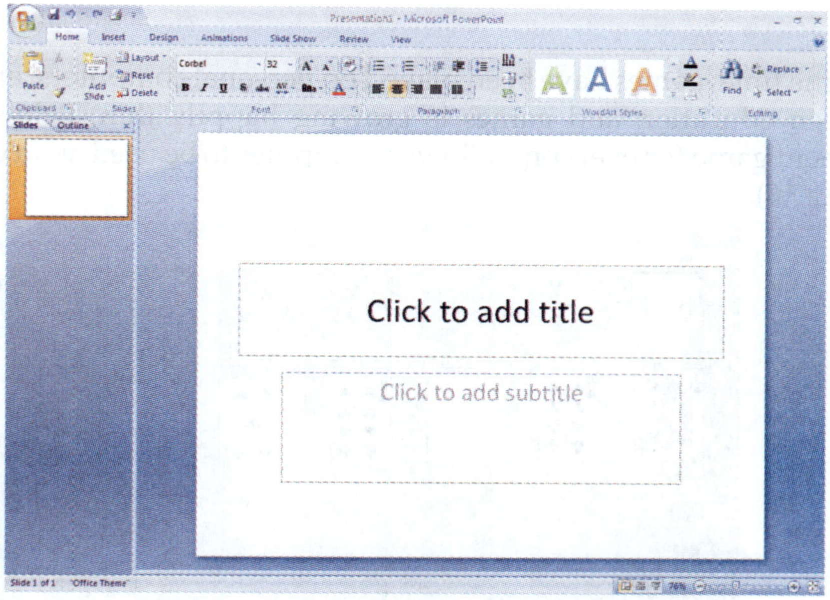

Figure 2.14 Microsoft PowerPoint

- **Educational Software**

Educational software allows a computer to be used as a teaching and learning tool. As technology has advanced, educational software has become a major influence at all levels from elementary schools to universities. The ability to connect computers and students together over a network such as the Internet opens up fantastic educational opportunities.

Elementary and Secondary Schools are using computers to play multimedia educational programs and to teach kids to explore the Web for information. A few examples of educational software include those used for teaching mathematics, grammar language, or any other subject. Microsoft Encarta and Mavis Beacon are the two very useful educational software. Figure 2.15 shows the Microsoft Encarta screen.

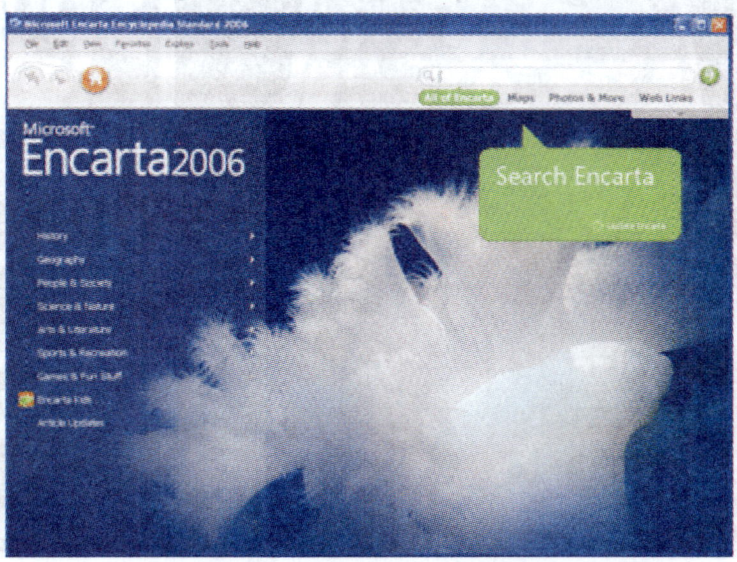

Figure 2.15 Microsoft Encarta

- ## Games Software

For some time, games have been played on personal computers, and increasingly the line between education and games is growing happily thin. Below, the Solitaire, an entertainment game for everyone, allows a computer to be used as an entertainment tool. (See figure 2.16)

Figure 2.16 Solitaire

Computer can add some fun to the learning process. Below, Pinball allows both children and adults to experience fun. (See figure 2.17)

Figure 2.17 Pinball

- **Browsers**

To use the Web, the software you use is a browser. This is an intensely competitive field right now and browsers are undergoing very rapid change. Some are independent software programs such as those developed by Microsoft Mozilla and Netscape. Others are integrated into application programs such as word processing program, spreadsheets, and databases. A browser provides a number of useful functions:

1. It allows you to enter the address of the site you want to jump to (called a URL- or Uniform Resource Locator) or to jump there by clicking hotspot, highlighted word, buttons, pictures or icon called hyperlinks, on your screen.
2. It formats Web documents for display on your screen.
3. It allows you to back up and go forward through pages you have already visited.
4. It allows you to copy text from the screen and paste it into a word processing program.
5. It allows you to print the document you see on the screen.
6. It makes it possible to transfer files—text, graphics, movies , animations, sounds, and programs—from other computers to your computer (called downloading).
7. It allows you to send and receive e-mail and other Internet Services such as FTP (File Transfer Protocol), Gopher, and Usenet newsgroups.

Examples of browsers are Opera, Internet Explorer and Mozilla Firefox. Figure 2.18 shows Opera and 2.19 shows Mozilla Firefox.

Figure 2.18 Opera

Figure 2.19 Mozilla Firefox

- **Authoring Software**

Professional multimedia development programs called authoring software give you total control over an interactive presentation. In addition to allowing you to give the viewer interactive control over the sequence and timing of sounds, videos, graphics and animations, they provide a scripting language (also called a programming, macro, or authoring language) in which you write programs to control the action. Examples of authoring software are Macromedia Dreamweaver and Microsoft FrontPage. Figure 2.20 shows the Microsoft FrontPage.

Figure 2.20 Microsoft FrontPage

- **Graphics Software**

Graphics software enable us to use a computer for creating, editing, viewing, storing, retrieving, and printing of designs, drawings, pictures, graphs, and various kinds of graphics.

Today's graphics packages normally support the following features:

1. Draw designs
2. Paint drawing and pictures
3. Present graphs
4. Drag-and drop objects
5. Import objects
6. Screen capture

An example of graphics software is CorelDraw. Figure 2.21 shows CorelDraw.

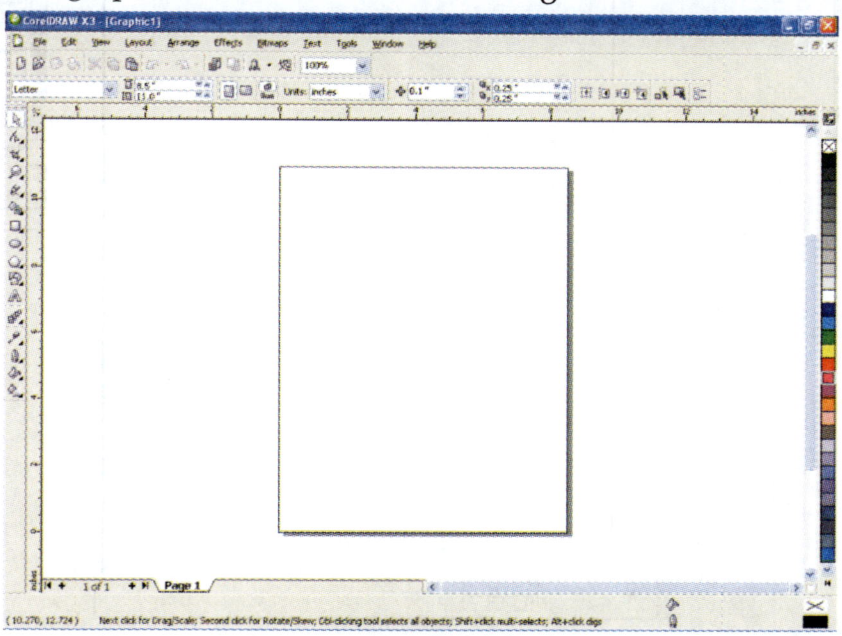

Figure 2.21 CorelDraw

- **Communication Software**

With the evolution of Internet, the communication has acquired new meanings and standards. Computers offer faster and reliable forms of communication through networks. Now, organisations are no longer using conventional letters to communicate with their clients; rather they use electronic modes of communication. We have sophisticated software that are used for sending and receiving data in the electronic form. E-mail is the electronic form of letter that can reach to any location from any location within seconds. E-mail has become an integral part of the daily life of the people where they rapidly communicate ideas with each other.

Communication software are specially designed to send and receive data through e-mails. Microsoft Outlook is a widely used e-mail assistant that keeps track of sent and received mails for an individual or an organisation.

- ## Desktop Publishing Software

Desktop publishing software are used for typesetting and designing purposes. The book you are studying, the calendars you see, the diaries, book titles, newspapers and magazines etc., all are designed by using desktop publishing software. These software are capable of drawing high level graphical shapes, can include various fills and textures, and generally support various types of image formats. CorelDraw, Publisher, and PageMaker are well known desktop publishing software. Figure 2.22 shows Adobe PageMaker.

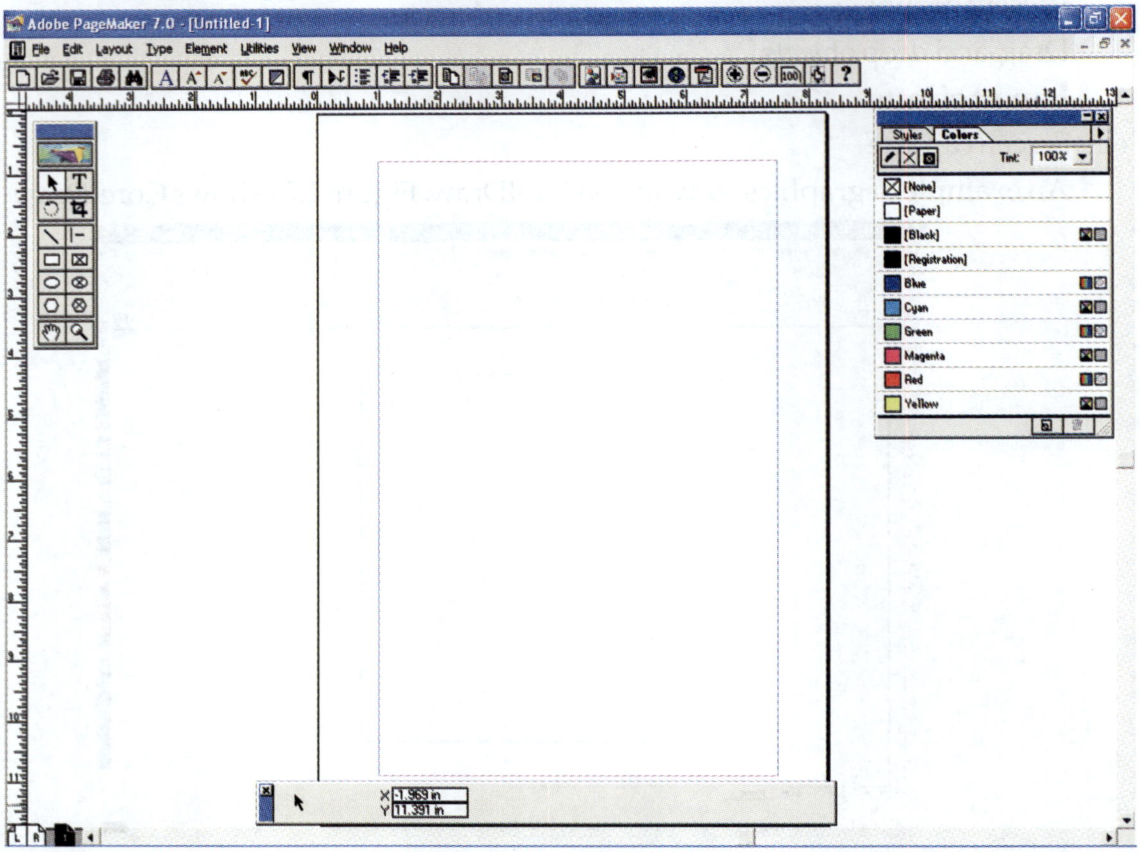

Figure 2.22 Adobe PageMaker

2. Customised Application Software

Customised application software are the application software that are created to satisfy specific needs of an organisation. For example, software required to manage a computer assembling house may contain features to keep track of stock of different devices of different companies, records of different computers sold to different customers and the data about the warranty period of a particular device, etc. This type of software may not be required by a computer stationery dealer as it is not dealing in the items having warranty period.

Computer software engineers are hired to create such software. The cost of such software depends upon the extent of work automated through software. Different computer languages are used to create these software.

2.2.4 Launching Application Software

Launching application software means loading it into the memory of computer. You can launch various types of application software; for example, Word Processor, Spreadsheet, Browser and Internet Explorer. Let us see how these application software can be launched:

- **Word Processor**

MS-Word 2007 is a member of the MS-Office family provided by Microsoft. It is a Windows based application. Let us assume that your computer has MS-Word installed on it.

Starting Microsoft Word 2007

To start MS-Word or Word:

1. Click the *Start* button on the task bar.
2. Choose the *All Programs* option in the Start menu.
3. Click the *Microsoft Office* option.
4. Click the *Microsoft Office Word 2007* option. (See figure 2.23)

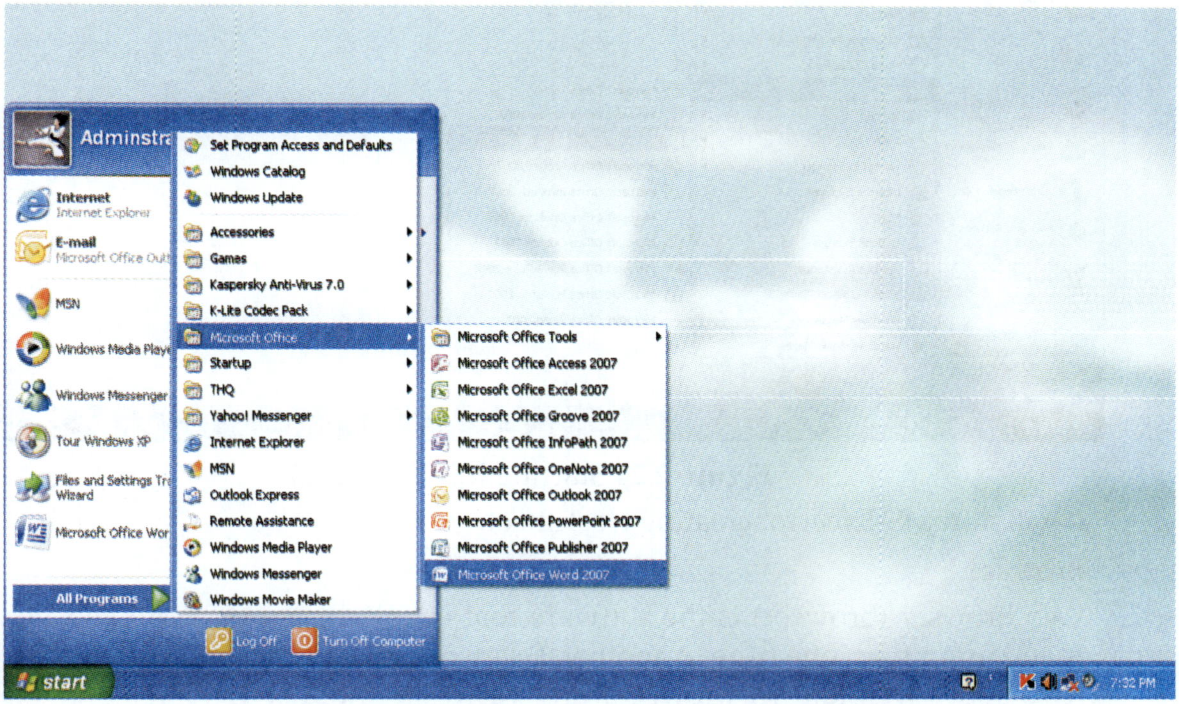

Figure 2.23 Starting MS-Word 2007

It will start MS-Word for word processing.

- **Spreadsheet**

MS-Excel 2007 is a member of the MS-office family provided by Microsoft. It is a Windows based application. Let us assume that your computer has MS-Excel installed on it.

Starting MS-Excel 2007

To start MS-Excel,

Double-click on the MS-Excel 2007 icon on the desktop.

OR

1. Click the *Start* button.
2. Choose *All Programs* option in the Start menu.
3. Click the *Microsoft Office* option.
4. Click the *Microsoft Office Excel 2007* option. (See figure 2.24)

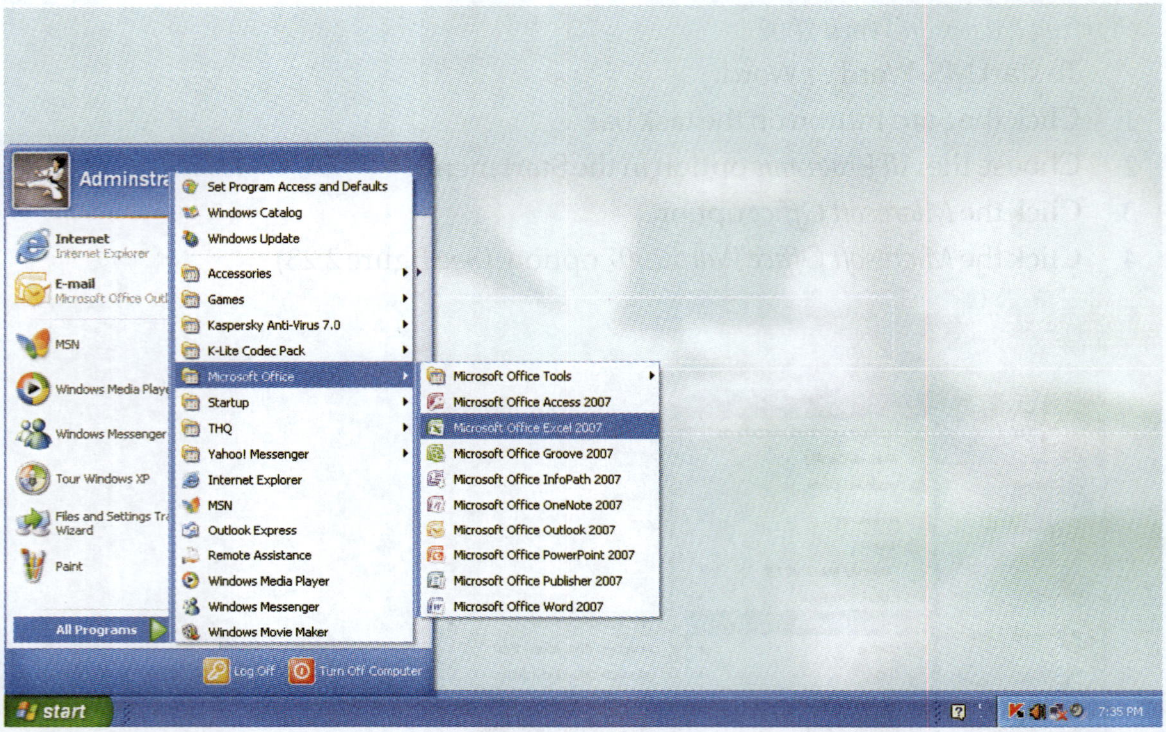

Figure 2.24 Starting MS-Excel 2007

It will start MS-Excel for creating worksheet.

- **Browser**

Web browser (browser) is the software that enables users to locate and view Web pages and jump from one page to another. Users cannot surf the Web without a browser. The two most well-known browsers are Microsoft Internet Explorer and Netscape Navigator.

Starting Netscape Navigator

To start Netscape Navigator:

1. Click the *Start* button.
2. Choose *All Programs*.
3. Click the *Netscape* option. This opens the Netscape browser. (See figure 2.25)

Figure 2.25 Netscape Browser

Now you can search information from the Internet.

- **Internet Explorer**

  It is one of the best known browsers.

Starting Internet Explorer

To start Internet Explorer,

Double-click the Internet Explorer symbol displayed on the screen.

Figure 2.26 Launching Internet Explorer

OR

1. Click the *Start* button.
2. Choose *All Programs*.
3. Click the *Internet Explorer* option.

   The Internet Explorer splash screen is displayed for a few seconds (See figure 2.27),

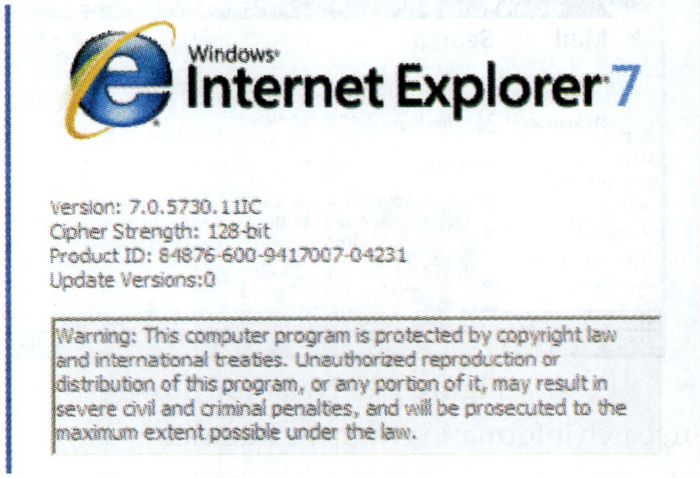

Figure 2.27 Internet Explorer Splash Screen

and then the Internet Explorer opening screen is displayed. (See figure 2.28)

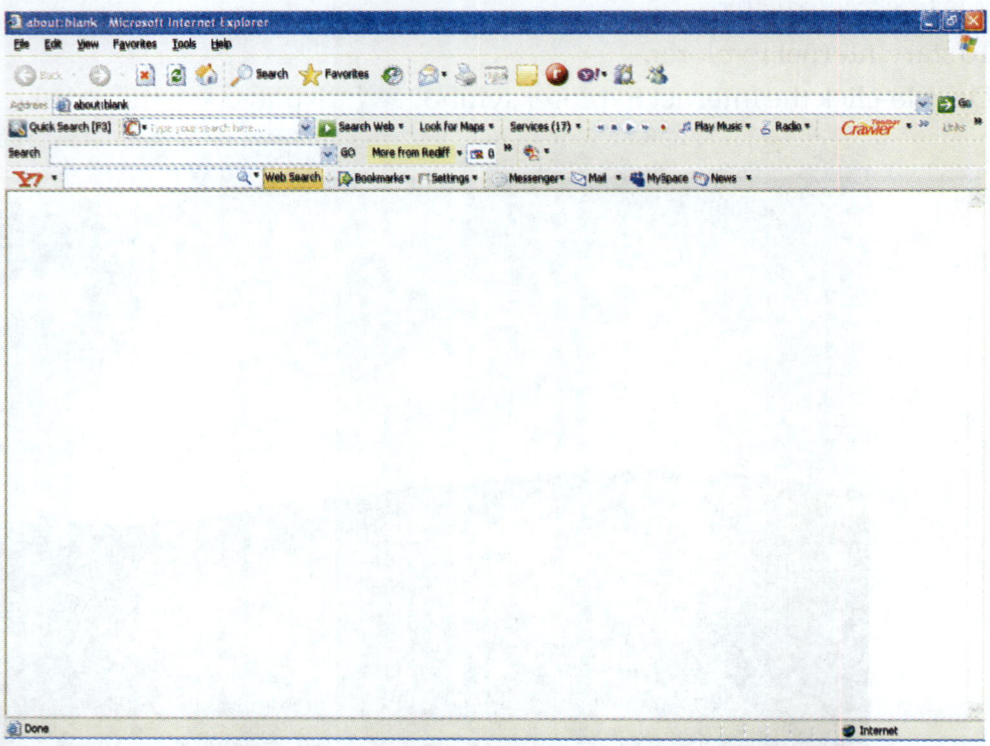

Figure 2.28 Microsoft Internet Explorer

Now you can search information from the Internet.

SUMMARY

- Software is a set of programs, which is designed to perform a well defined function.
- Software and hardware cannot work without the presence of each other.
- System software are the software used for controlling the internal working of the computer.
- Application software is software that has been developed to solve a particular problem for users—to perform useful work on specific tasks or to provide entertainment.
- A computer cannot run without the presence of operating system (OS).
- DOS (Disk Operating System) is the original operating system produced by Microsoft, with a hard-to-use command-driven user interface.
- Microsoft Windows 98 is the operating system for desktop and portable microcomputers that supports the most hardware and the most application software. Windows has become the most common system software used on microcomputers.
- Microsoft Windows NT/2000 is multitasking operating system designed to run on network servers.
- Microsoft Windows Millennium Edition (Windows Me) is successor to Windows 95 and 98 operating system designed to support desktop and portable computers.
- Microsoft Windows XP OS was introduced in 2001; it combines elements of Windows networking software and Windows Me and has a new GUI.
- Microsoft Windows Vista is Microsoft's newest OS.
- Linux is free version of Unix, supported by efforts of thousands of volunteer programmers.
- Unix is multitasking operating system for multiple users that has built-in networking capability and versions that can run on all kinds of computers.
- Macintosh operating system (Mac OS) is system software that runs only on Apple Macintosh computers.
- Open-source software is a software that any programmer can download from the Internet free and modify with suggested improvements.
- Properietary software also called commercial software or packaged software, is software that is offered for sale, such as Microsoft Word, Microsoft Office XP, or Adobe Photoshop.
- Word Processing application software are designed for document creation. For example, Microsoft Word, Star Word and Writer.
- Electronic Spreadsheets are mainly used for mathematical and financial calculations. For example, Microsoft Excel, Quatropro, Lotus 123.

- Database Management Systems are designed to create and maintain the information in databases. For example, Access, Base.
- Presentation Software are the application software, which are used to present information to a large number of people. For example, PowerPoint, Impress.
- Customised application software are created for a specific application of a specific environment.
- Educational software are the application software, which are used for educational purpose. For example, Microsoft Encarta, Mavis Beacon.
- Games software are the application software, which are used for entertainment purpose. For example, Solitarie, Pinball.
- Browsers are the application software that enable the users to locate and view Web pages and jump from one page to another. Users cannot surf the Web without a browser. For example, Opera, Internet Explorer, Mozilla Firefox.
- Authoring software are the application software, which are used for writing books. For example, Dreamweaver, FrontPage.
- Graphics software are the application software, which are used for designing. For example, Corel Draw.
- Desktop publisher are the application software, which are used for publication. For example, PageMaker, Publisher.
- Launching application software means loading it into the memory of computer. You can launch various types of application software; *e.g.*, Word Processor, Spreadsheet, Browser and Internet Explorer etc.

REVIEW QUESTIONS

STATE WHETHER TRUE OR FALSE

1. A software is a set of programs which is designed to perform a well-defined function.
2. The two types of software are system software and application software.
3. System software includes the operating system that manages your system.
4. Application software are not designed to satisfy common needs of various business.
5. A Web browser cannot be used to use the Web.
6. Unix crashes often and thus is not normally used for running important large systems.

FILL IN THE BLANKS

1. .... enables the computer to control various system activities.
2. Unix is a .... software.
3. .... is the Microsoft's newest version of OS.

4. Software that is .... means that it is privately owned and controlled by a company.
5. Linux is ...., meaning that any programmer can download it from the Internet for free and modify it with suggested improvements.
6. The operating system serves as a link between user and the ....

MULTIPLE CHOICE QUESTIONS

1. The software that must be loaded into the computer before you load a word processing program is ....
   (*a*) a programming language (*b*) the operating system
   (*c*) a utility program (*d*) All of these
2. The software that has no restrictions regarding its use is ....
   (*a*) Freeware (*b*) Shareware
   (*c*) Public domain (*d*) All of these
3. The most widely used operating system is ....
   (*a*) UNIX (*b*) DOS
   (*c*) Windows (*d*) Windows NT
4. An operating system owned by a single company is called ....
   (*a*) Public (*b*) Portable
   (*c*) Proprietary (*d*) Multiuser
5. Which of the following is not an operating system?
   (*a*) Windows (*b*) Unix
   (*c*) Macintosh (*d*) Opera
6. Which of the following is the newest Microsoft Windows operating system?
   (*a*) Windows Me (*b*) Windows XP
   (*c*) Windows 2000 (*d*) Windows Vista

ANSWER THE FOLLOWING

1. What are the main types of software?
2. Discuss the types of software packages.
3. What is system software?
4. Name the main types of system software.
5. What is an operating system? Give examples.
6. Write a short note on the following:
   (*a*) DOS (*b*) Windows 98
   (*c*) Windows 2000 (*d*) Windows ME

(e) Windows XP
(f) Windows Vista
(g) Linux
(h) Unix
(i) Macintosh

7. Differentiate between Open Source and Proprietary software.
8. Discuss types, examples, and uses of application software.
9. Write a short note on the following application software:
    (a) Word Processing
    (b) Spreadsheets
    (c) Databases
    (d) Presentation
    (e) Educational
    (f) Games
    (g) Browsers
    (h) Authoring
    (i) Graphics
    (j) Desktop Publisher
10. What is the difference between application software and system software?
11. How will you launch application software? Describe the same for the following:
    (a) Word Processer
    (b) Spreadsheet
    (c) Browser
    (d) Internet Explorer

FIELD TRIP

The new computer you are going to purchase comes with a choice of Windows XP Windows Vista. Using computer magazines or the Internet, try to find out the pluses and minuses of each. Based on your analysis, explain which one did you choose and why you did so?

ASSIGNMENT

State the principles underlying Open Source and Proprietary Software.

SECTION THREE

TERM-ONE

TYPING SPEED DEVELOPMENT

UNIT 1: Keyboarding and Mouse Skills Review

General Objective

After reading this section, the student will be able to:

1. improve typing speed.

UNIT 1 KEYBOARDING AND MOUSE SKILLS REVIEW

Specific Objectives

After reading this unit, the student will be able to:

3.1.1 type 30-35 words per minute.

3.1.2 use mouse skills in document creation.

3.1.3 use the numeric keypad.

3.1.0 Introduction

The first thing you look at when you call up any application software on the screen is the *user interface—the user-controllable display screen that allows you to communicate, or interact, with the computer.*

You can interact with the display screen using the keys on your keyboard. You will also frequently use your mouse to interact with the user interface. The keyboard and mouse skills play an important role in typing speed development. In this unit, you will learn about improving the typing speed.

3.1.1 Improving Speed in Typing Using a Typing Software

You can improve your speed in typing using a typing software: for example, Typing Tutor or Mavis Beacon. Use of the nine fingers in typing is very important for it. You should be able to type 30-35 words per minute after some practice.

Learning Tips

Keep your Eyes on the Monitor

You will learn the key position faster if you do not peek (look quickly and often secretively) at the keyboard while training. If you cannot remember where a key is located, check the keyboard picture on the screen to find it.

Keep Wrists UP

Keep your wrists up and straight when typing. Resting your wrists on the wrist rest or the desk will create an uncomfortable angle making it more difficult to move your fingers.

This may cause errors and slow you down. Holding your wrist too high has the same effect and may increase the tension in the shoulders.

Focus on Accuracy

It is believed that good accuracy is the building block of fluent typing. This is why you will have an accuracy target throughout the course. Your speed will develop over time as you continue to train and start using your typing skills on a daily basis.

Relaxed Posture

Sit up straight, elbows close to the body. Try to keep shoulders, arms and hands relaxed to avoid tension and discomfort.

Typing Tutor

To launch Typing Tutor:

1. Click on the icon of *Typing Tutor*. (See figure 1.1)

Figure 1.1 Launching Typing Tutor

2. On clicking the Typing Tutor icon, you are asked to enter your name in the *Enter Your Name* text box (See figure 1.2). After entering your name, press the Enter key.

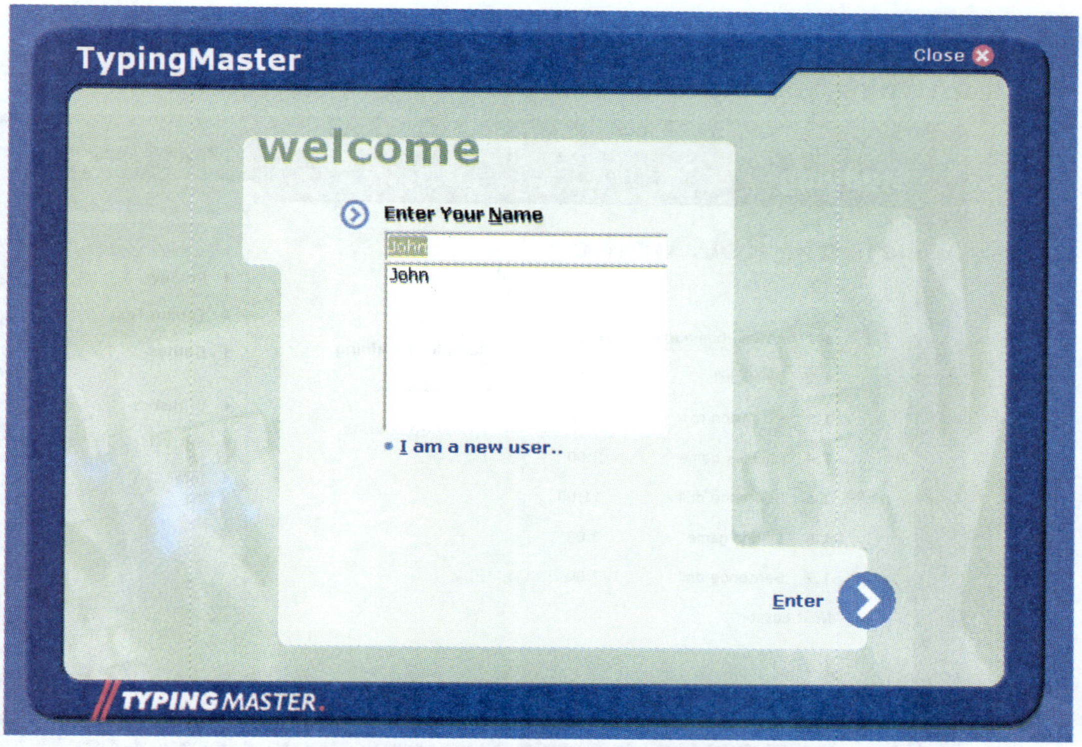

Figure 1.2 Entering User Name

3. Now select any course which you want to practise (See figure 1.3). Here, we select *Complete Training*.

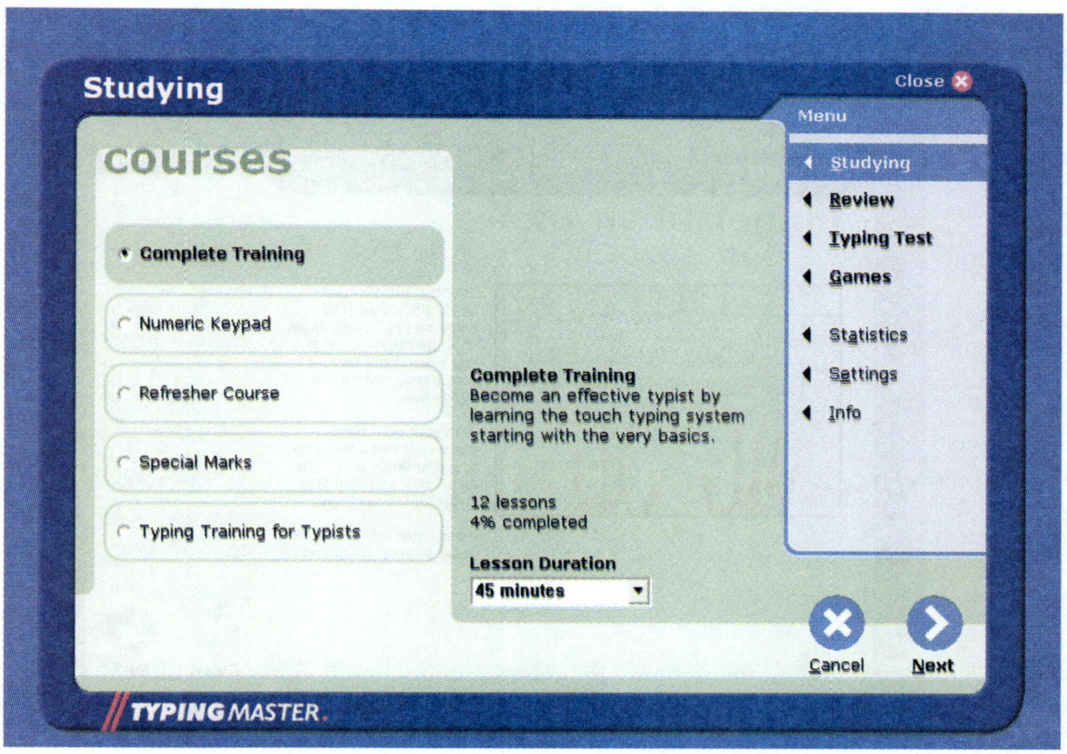

Figure 1.3 Selecting a course

Basics, home row

To learn typing, you must start with *Basics, home row* (See figure 1.4).

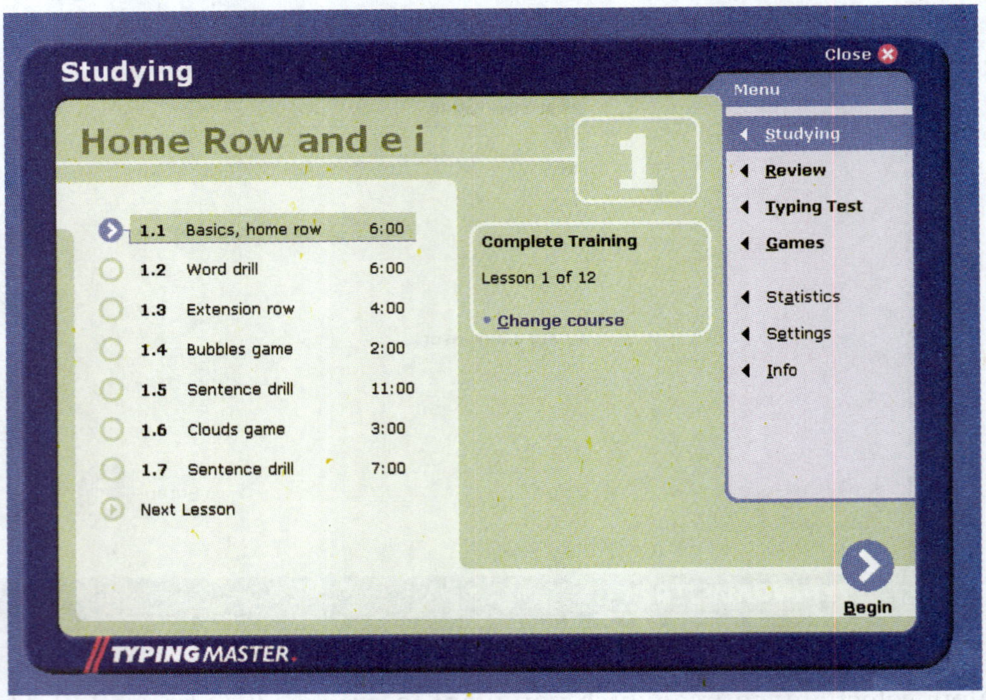

Figure 1.4 Selecting *Basics, home row*

About Finger Position: In their basic position, your fingers rest on the middle row of the keyboard—called the "Home Row" (See figure 1.5). The home row is the base from which all other keys can be reached.

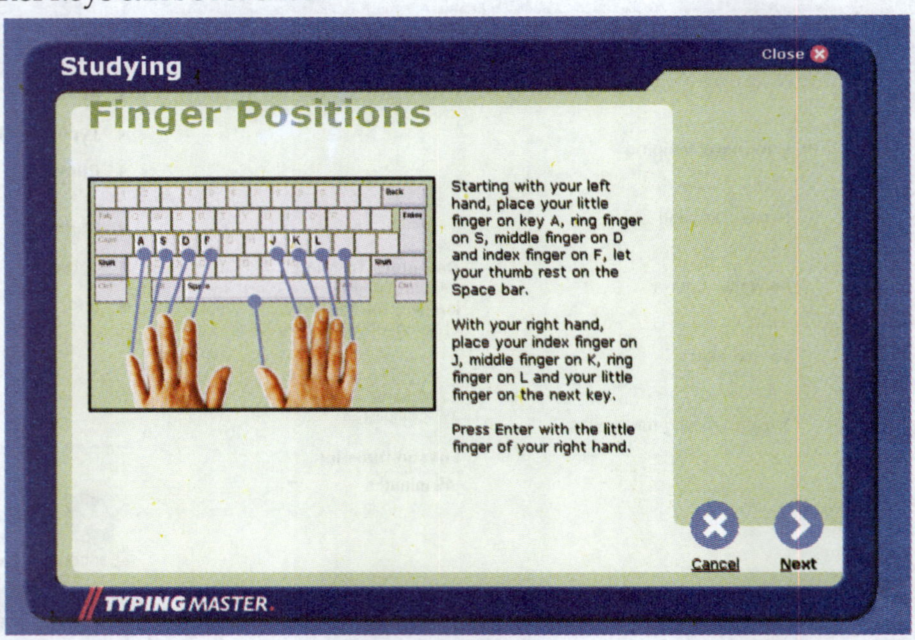

Figure 1.5 Finger Positions on the Home Row

Position of Fingers on the Home Row

(*i*) Put your left hand fingers on keys A S D F. (See figure 1.5)

(*ii*) Put your right hand fingers on keys J K L;

(*iii*) Put your thumb lightly on the Space bar.

(*iv*) Keep your wrists straight and fingers lightly curled.

Note

You feel small bumps on the F and J keys. They are there to help you find the home row keys without looking at your hands.

Use of Keyboard

Pressing Keys

Each key is pressed by the finger on the home row that is closest. After reaching a key away from the home row, the finger needs to return to its home row key. The next key to be typed is always highlighted.

Example: How to type letter U

(*i*) Make sure that your fingers are on their home row keys.

(*ii*) Move your right index finger from J upwards to U. Your hand may move slightly to make it easier to reach U.

(*iii*) Press U with a quick and light touch keeping your hand relaxed.

(*iv*) Move the index finger back to its home key J.

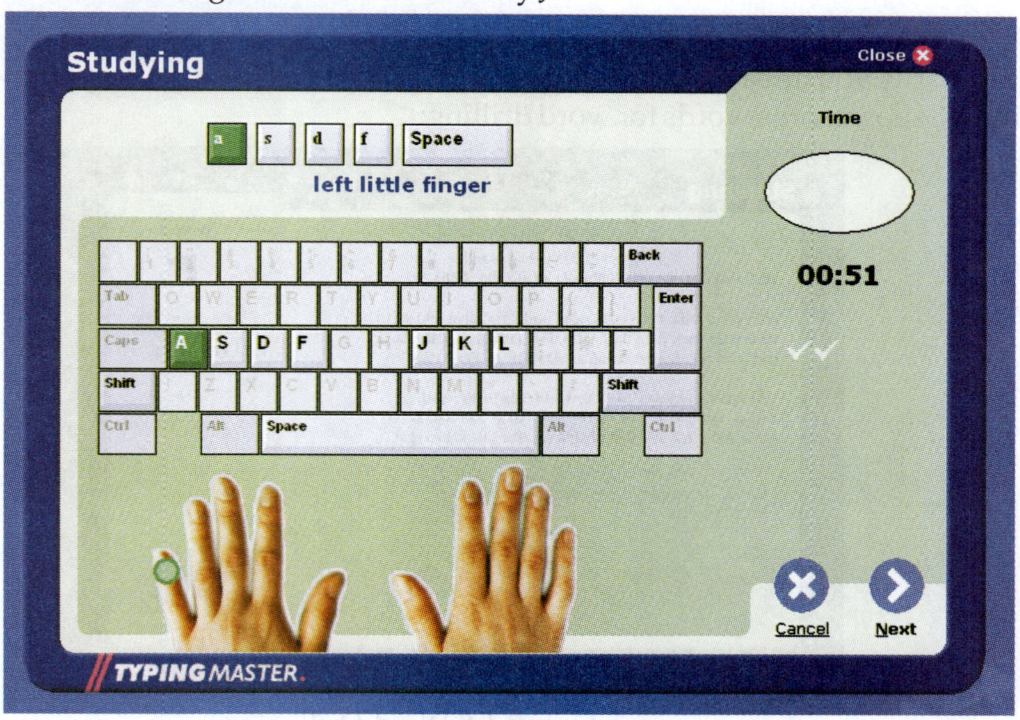

Figure 1.6 Pressing Keys

The Space Bar

Most people use their right thumb for the Space Bar. Left-handed people may find it easier to use their left thumb. Whichever thumb you decide to use, stick with it. Never use both thumbs.

Pressing the Wrong Key

If wrong button is pressed then a cross mark will be displayed. (See figure 1.7)

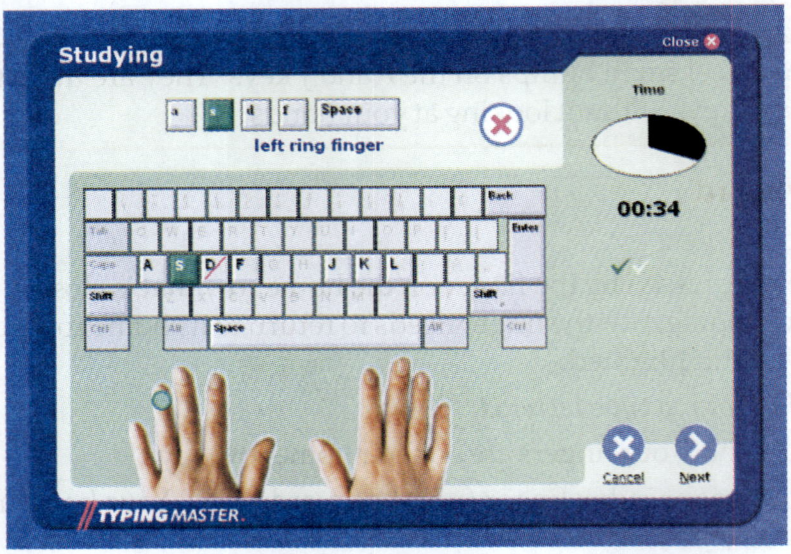

Figure 1.7 On Pressing the Wrong Key

Once you have mastered a course, you can change to another course as per your need.

Word Drill

Primarily you must have enough practice in word drill to improve your typing speed. Figure 1.8 shows some words for word drilling:

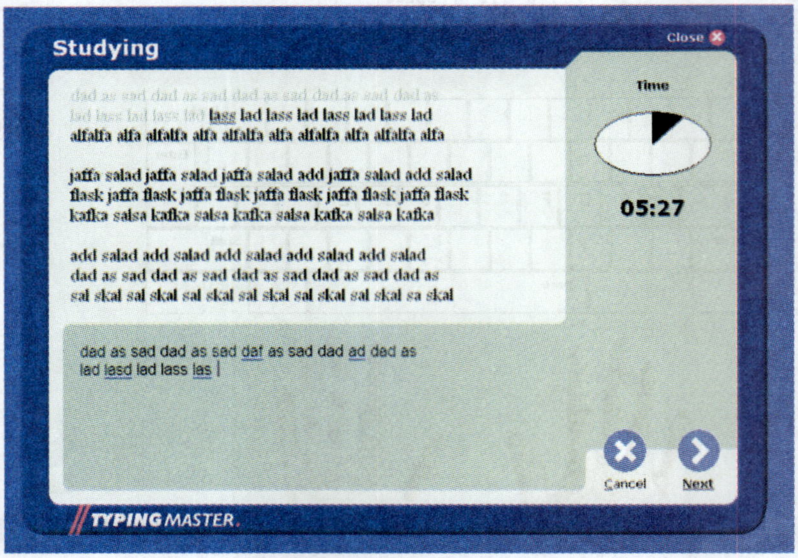

Figure 1.8 Word Drill

Writing Paragraph

After enough practice in word drilling, you can switch on to paragraph writing.

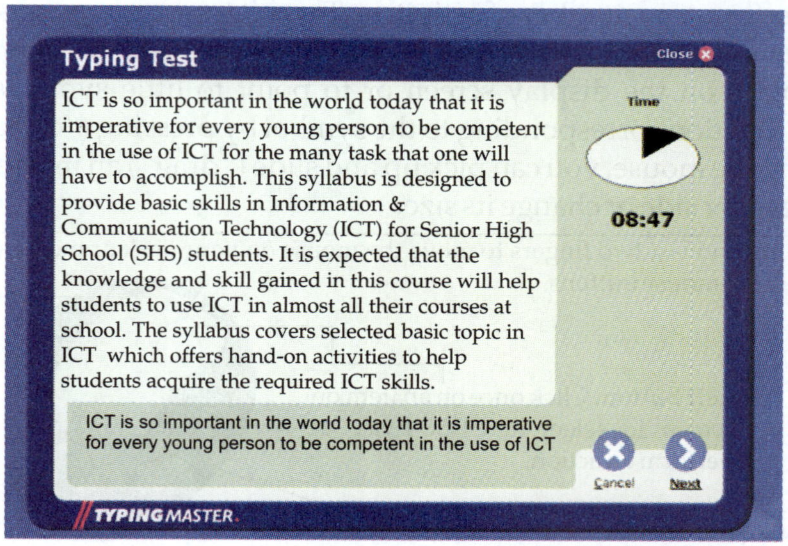

Figure 1.9 Writing a Paragraph

Result

Typing Tutor shows the results of a specific test. WPM on the Report refers to words-per-minute, where a word consists of five characters including spaces. Typing Tutor reports *accuracy* as the percentage of characters correctly typed. An accuracy rate of 96% indicates an average of approximately three mistakes per line on a test. As you gain experience, you should aim for an accuracy rate of 96% or higher, and you may practise using the backspace key to attain an accuracy rate of 100%.

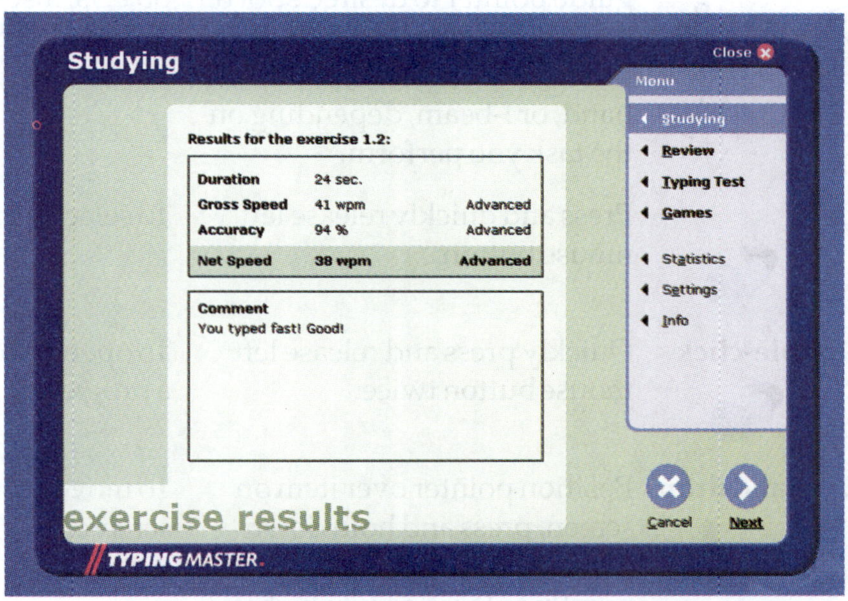

Figure 1.10 Exercise Results

3.1.2 Using Mouse Skills in Document Creation

You use your mouse more frequently. The mouse allows you to direct an on-screen pointer to perform any number of activities. *The pointer usually appears as an arrow, although it changes shape depending on the application.* The mouse is used to move the pointer to a particular place on the display screen or to point to little symbols, or icons. You can activate the function corresponding to the symbol by pressing ("clicking") buttons on the mouse. Using the mouse, you can pick up and slide ("drag") an image from one side of the screen to the other side or change its size.

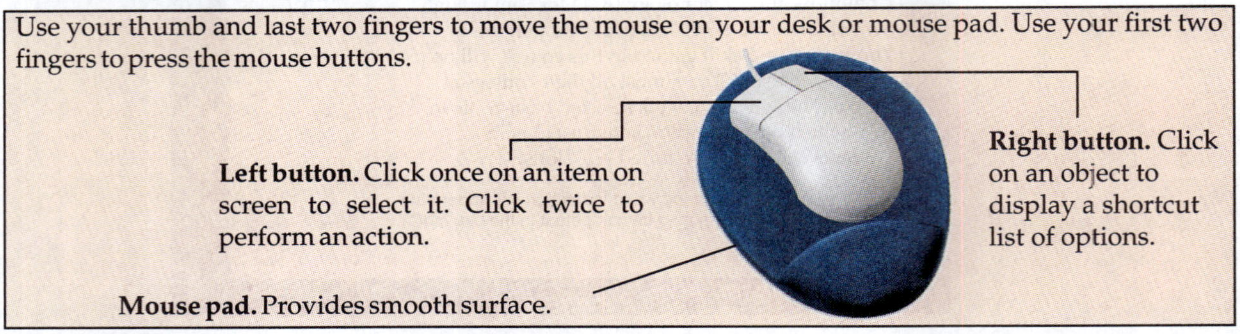

Figure 1.11 Using the Mouse

You can use mouse skills in document creation. The mouse skills are Single clicking, Double clicking, Right click, Drag hold and drop in document creation. Table 1.1 shows useful terms associated with mouse.

Table 1.1 Terms Associated with Mouse

S.No.	Term	Action	Purpose
1	**Point** 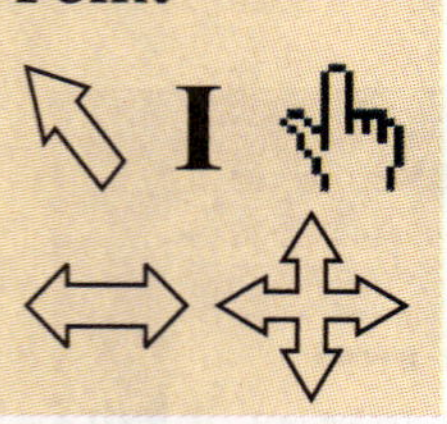	Move mouse across desk to guide pointer to desired spot on screen. The pointer assumes different shapes, such as arrow, hand, or I-beam, depending on the task you perform.	To execute commands, move objects, insert data, or similar actions on screen.
2.	**Click** Click 	Press and quickly release left mouse button.	To select an item on the screen.
3.	**Double-click** Click Click 	Quickly press and release left mouse button twice.	To open a document or start a program.
4.	**Drag and drop** 	Position pointer over item on screen, press and hold down left mouse button while moving pointer to location in which you want to place item, then release.	To move an item on the screen.

5.	**Right-click** Click	Press and release right mouse button.	To display a shortcut list of commands, such as a pop-up menu of options.

3.1.3 Using the Numeric Keypad

You can interact with the display screen using the keys on your keyboard. Besides the letter, number, and punctuation keys and often a calculator-style numeric keypad, computer keyboards have special-purpose and function keys.

Numeric Keypad on Keyboard

When the *Num Lock* light is on, you can use the number keys (0 through 9) to enter numbers. When the *Num Lock* light is off, you can use these keys to move the cursor around the screen. To turn the light **on** or **off**, press *Num Lock*. You can use the numeric keypad of Typing Tutor to do more practice on the numeric keypad.

Selecting course of numeric keypad: Select the **Numeric Keypad** option to become an effective numeric keypad user.

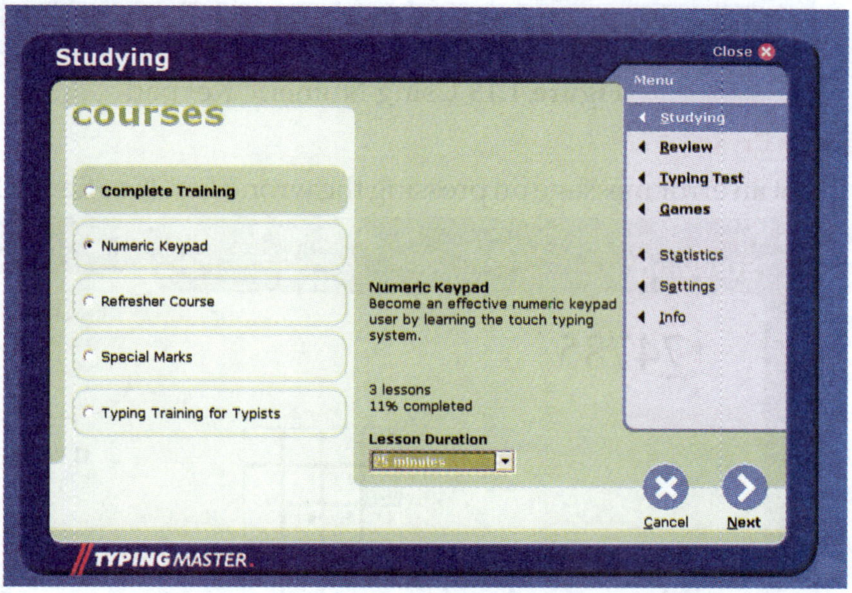

Figure 1.12 Selecting Numeric Keypad

Finger Position on Numeric Keypad and Num Lock

The numeric keypad, which is usually located in the right hand side of the keyboard, is a very effective and fast way to enter a long series of numbers.

Put your hands on the numeric keypad in the following way:

- Right index finger on the "4" key
- Right middle finger on the "5" key
- Right ring finger on the "6 " key
- Right thumb on the "0" key

Exercise on Numeric Keypad

You can use the drills in Typing Tutor to do more practice on the numeric keypad.

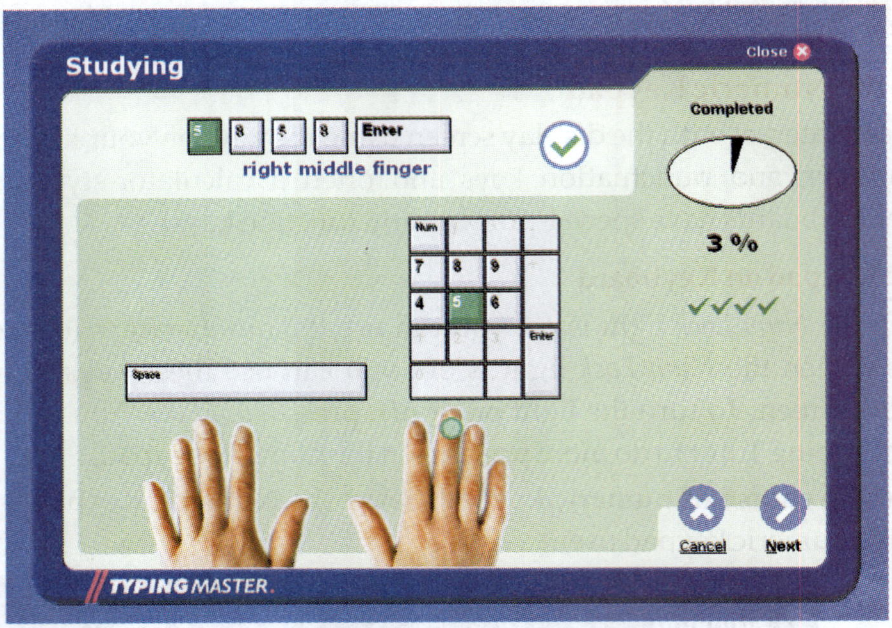

Figure 1.13 Using Numeric Keypad

For Wrong Key Press

You will get an error message on pressing the wrong key. (See figure 1.14)

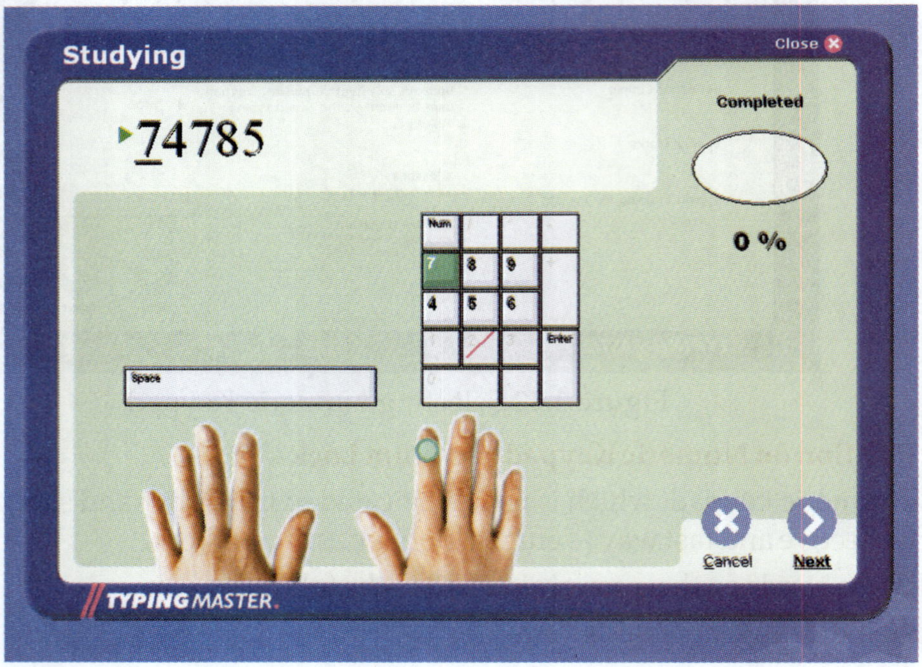

Figure 1.14 On pressing the wrong key on Numeric Keypad

Practice leads to perfection. So use the numeric keypad in Typing Tutor or Mavis Beacon to do more practice on it.

SUMMARY

- User interface is the display screen that allows users to communicate, or interact, with the computer.
- You can improve your speed in typing using a typing software: for example, Typing Tutor or Mavis Beacon.
- After some practice you should be able to type 30-35 words per minute.
- You can use mouse skills in document creation.
- The mouse skills are Single clicking, Double clicking, Right click, Drag hold and drop in document creation.
- Use of numeric keypad plays an important role in improving the typing speed.

REVIEW QUESTIONS

STATE WHETHER TRUE OR FALSE

1. Typing 15-20 words per minute is a very good typing speed.
2. Using mouse skills in document creation is very important.
3. Using the numeric keypad properly does not help in improving typing speed.

FILL IN THE BLANKS

1. .... is the display screen that allows users to communicate, or interact, with the computer.
2. You can improve your typing speed using a ....

MULTIPLE CHOICE QUESTIONS

1. Example(s) of typing software is/are ....
   (*a*) Keyboard (*b*) Typing Tutor
   (*c*) Mouse (*d*) All of these
2. Which of the following is not a mouse skill?
   (*a*) Single clicking (*b*) Double clicking
   (*c*) Right click (*d*) Function keys

ANSWER THE FOLLOWING

1. How will you improve speed in typing using a typing software?
2. Using mouse skills in document creation is very important. Discuss.
3. Using the numeric keypad is quite useful in creating a given document. Comment.

ASSIGNMENT

1. Create and reproduce a given document involving alpha and numeric keypad, in the typing software.
2. Type the following document using a typing software:

Denographics of a nation in West Africa

Population:

21,029,853 (July 2005 estimate)

Estimates for this country explicitly take into account the effects of excess mortality due to AIDS; this can result in lower life expectancy, higher infant mortality and death rates, lower population and growth rates, and changes in the distribution of population by age and sex than would otherwise be expected.

Age structure:

0-14 years: 37.1% (male: 3,946, 326; female: 3,862, 390)
15-64 years: 59.1% (male: 6,203,035; female: 6,235, 107)
65 years and over: 3.7% (male: 366, 472; female: 416, 523) (2005)

Median age:

Total: 20.45 years
Male: 20.2 years
Female: 20.7 years (2005)

Population growth rate:

1.25% (2005 estimate)

Birth rate:

23.97 births/ 1,000 population (2005 estimate)

SECTION ONE

TERM-TWO

WORD PROCESSING APPLICATION

General Objective

After reading this section, the student will be able to:

1. acquire basic skills in creating document in Word Processing.

UNIT 1 WORD PROCESSING

Specific Objectives

After reading this unit, the student will be able to:

1.1.1 identify Word Processing package.

1.1.2 state the importance and use of Word Processing.

1.1.3 create a document using the Word Processor.

1.1.4 save a document using the 'Save As' command.

1.1.0 Introduction

After a long and productive life, the typewriter has almost departed. Indeed, it is practically as difficult today to get a manual typewriter repaired as to find a blacksmith. Word processing software offers a much-improved way of dealing with documents.

What is so unique about word processing programs is the way they separate the process of entering and editing text from the process of printing it. With a word processing program, the text has a more malleable existence on the computer screen. It is easy to change an electronic page. Text can be quickly copied, moved, deleted, or typed over. If you insert new text, any text below it moves down automatically. When people first did word processing, it seemed like a magic. In this unit we look at Microsoft Word 2007, which is an important Word Processing application.

1.1.1 Word Processing Packages and their Uses

Word processing software allows you to create, edit, format, print, and store text material, among other things. Word processing is the most common software application. The well known word processing programs are:

- Microsoft Word
- Writer
- Wordpad
- Text Editor
- Star Word

Word processing software allows users to work through a document and *delete*, *insert* and *replace* text, the principal editing and correction activities. It also offers such additional features as *creating, formatting, printing* and *saving* documents such as letters memos, reports, manuscripts and contracts.

The advantages of using word processor to type documents over hand written documents are given in table 1.1.

Table 1.1 Advantages of Word Processor

Hand Written or Typed Documents	Documents Created Using Word Processors
Slow creating process	Can be created quickly and easily
Difficulty in inserting pictures and images	Pictures and images can be inserted easily
Looks messy after making corrections	Error correction is simple and neat.

Microsoft Word—An Example of a Word Processing Package

Microsoft Word (MS-Word) is the most popularly used word processing application software that provides you with a number of useful and fabulous features to process the text. A word processor, in general, can be used to manipulate the text in a variety of ways. In addition to it, you can save your documents in a word processor and use them according to the need, whenever required.

The features that are provided by any word processor (as editing, formatting text) are available in MS-Word, which also supports some additional and special features (as mail merge).

MS-Word is a member of the MS-Office family provided by Microsoft, used explicitly for WINDOWS (*i.e.*, it is a Windows based application). This means, in order to work with MS-WORD, you need to install WINDOWS in your PC and get it running.

1.1.2 Importance of Word Processing

Word processing is by far the most widely used computer application because it is used for communication, our most common activity. Word processing is used to write, edit, and format memos, letters, reports, manuscripts, contracts, and every imaginable type of document. No matter what the information is, or what form it takes, the chances are it was initially composed and written using a word processing program.

A word processor is software which provides a graphical user interface with better capabilities than a text editor does. The main advantage of a word processor is that it provides WYSIWYG (What You See Is What You Get) interface which helps you make changes quickly and easily. The main features of today's word-processing packages are:

Creating Documents

It means entering text using the keyboard. Word processing software has three features that affect this process—the *cursor, scrolling* and *word wrap*.

1. **Cursor:** The cursor is the movable symbol on the display screen (monitor) that shows us where we may next enter data or commands. It is often a blinking rectangle or an I-beam. We can move the cursor by using the keyboard's directional arrow keys or a mouse. The point where the cursor lies at a particular instant is known as the *insertion point*.
2. **Scrolling:** Scrolling means moving quickly upward, downward or sideways through the text or other screen display. A standard computer monitor displays only 20–22 lines of standard-size text at a time. Generally, the documents are longer than that. Using the directional arrow keys, or the mouse and a scroll bar located at the side of the screen, we can move or "scroll" through the display screen and into the text above and below it.

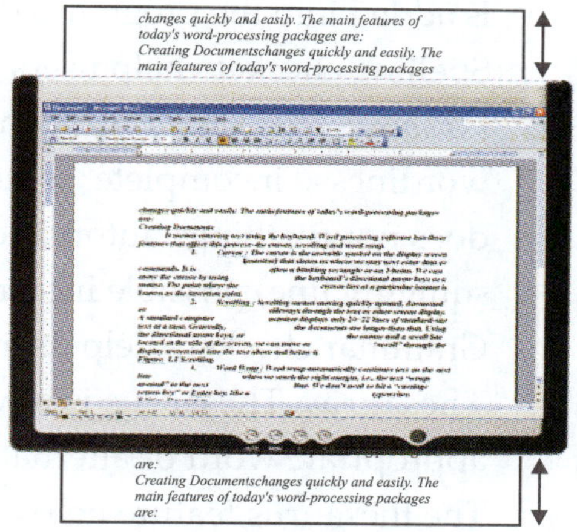

Figure 1.1 Scrolling

3. **Word Wrap:** *Word wrap* automatically continues text on to the next line when we reach the right margin, *i.e.*, the text "wraps around" to the next line. We do not need to hit a "carriage return key" or Enter key, like in a typewriter.

Editing Documents

When editing a document to correct mistakes, we can move the insertion point where we wish to enter new text and then just type it in. To *delete* characters, we press *Backspace* or *Delete key*. Pressing Backspace key deletes characters to the left of the insertion point and pressing delete key deletes those to the right. We can also drag the mouse to highlight any section of the text and then *copy* it to another file, *move* it to some other place in the document being used, give it a new format, or delete it all at once.

The *Undo command* allows us to change our mind and restore text that we have just deleted. *Inserting* is the act of adding to the document. The *Insert key* plays an important role in the replacement of text and exiting from Insert mode.

In addition to the **insert and delete, cut/copy and paste** features of editing explained above, some other features of editing are:

1. **Find and replace:** The *Find* or *Search,* command allows us to find any word, phrase or number that exists in our document being edited. It can be replaced automatically with something else with the help of *Replace command*.

2. **Spelling checkers:** *Spelling checkers* compare all words in a document with a list of words in the program's dictionary. Words not available in the dictionary are highlighted and we can then decide whether to change them, leave them as such or add them to the dictionary. We must note that a highlighted word is not necessarily misspelled. It just means that the word is not available in the dictionary. Any word that is added into the program's dictionary is not highlighted again (if found next time).
   Spelling checkers help users prepare accurate documents.
3. **Grammar checkers:** Grammar checkers are programs that check the grammar wordiness, incomplete sentences and awkward phrases. The grammar checker does not fix things automatically, but it will flag (perhaps with a different colour of squiggly line) possible incorrect word usage and sentence structure.
   Grammar checkers help users produce better-written documents.
4. **Thesaurus:** Thesaurus is a word processing feature that presents the user with the appropriate word or alternative words.
   The thesaurus feature helps users prepare well-written documents.

Useful Tip

Short Cut Keys

You do not always need to use the mouse to pull down menus to perform functions. These menus provide information about which short cut keys serve the same mouse-click function. Most commands have a short cut key, and common functions usually have the same short cut command in different programs.

Formatting Documents with the Help of Templates and Wizards

Formats are used to make a document both more attractive and easier to read. All word processing programs have built-in format settings known as defaults, which are designed so we can easily override them.

Templates: These are preformatted documents that provide basic tools for shaping a final document—the text, layout and style for a letter, for example.

Wizards and helpers: These answer the user questions and use the answers to lay out and format a document. In Word, we can use the Memo Wizard to create professional-looking memos or the Resumé Wizard to create a resumé.

Among the many aspects of formatting are the following:

1. **Margins:** These are the white spaces on all four sides of the text block. They set off the text and make it more attractive visually.
2. **Headers and footers:** These can be entered at the top or bottom of pages to identify sections or provide other useful information.

3. **Numbers:** These can be used to set off lists so when you insert or delete items, the numbers adjust automatically.
4. **Bullets:** We can use bullets to set off lists where the order is not important.
5. **Fonts:** These can be changed by selecting a new one from a list of those available on the system. We can then use *bold, italic, underline formats* to provide emphasis on the text.
6. **Tables:** These are used to present tabular materials.
7. **Indents:** These specify how much space the paragraph should be indented from the left and right margins.
8. **Page numbers:** These can be positioned almost anywhere on the page and printed in either Roman numerals (*i, ii, iii* etc.) or Arabic numbers (1, 2, 3 etc.).

Printing, Faxing or E-Mailing Documents

We have several options for printing in most of the word processing software. *For example*, we can print *several copies* of a document, *individual pages* or a range of pages can also be printed. We can even preview a document before taking its hard copy or print out. *Previewing* (*print previewing*) means viewing a document on the screen to see what it will look like in the printed form before printing it. Whole pages are shown in reduced size.

We can also send out a document off to someone else by fax or as an e-mail attachment, if the computer has the appropriate communication link.

Saving Documents

It means storing, or preserving, a document as an electronic file permanently—on floppy disk or hard disk (say). This feature is available in nearly all application softwares. The saved document can be retrieved and used when needed.

1.1.3 Creating Document Using a Word Processor

As mentioned earlier MS-Word is a member of the MS-Office family provided by Microsoft. It is a Windows based application. Let us assume that your computer has MS-Word 2007 installed on it. Remember that there are differences in MS-Word 2003 and MS-Word 2007.

Starting Microsoft Word 2007

To start MS-Word or Word:

1. Click the *Start* button on the task bar.
2. Choose the *All Programs* option in the Start menu (See figure 1.2).
3. Click the *Microsoft Office* option from the All Programs menu.
4. Click the *Microsoft Office Word 2007* option.

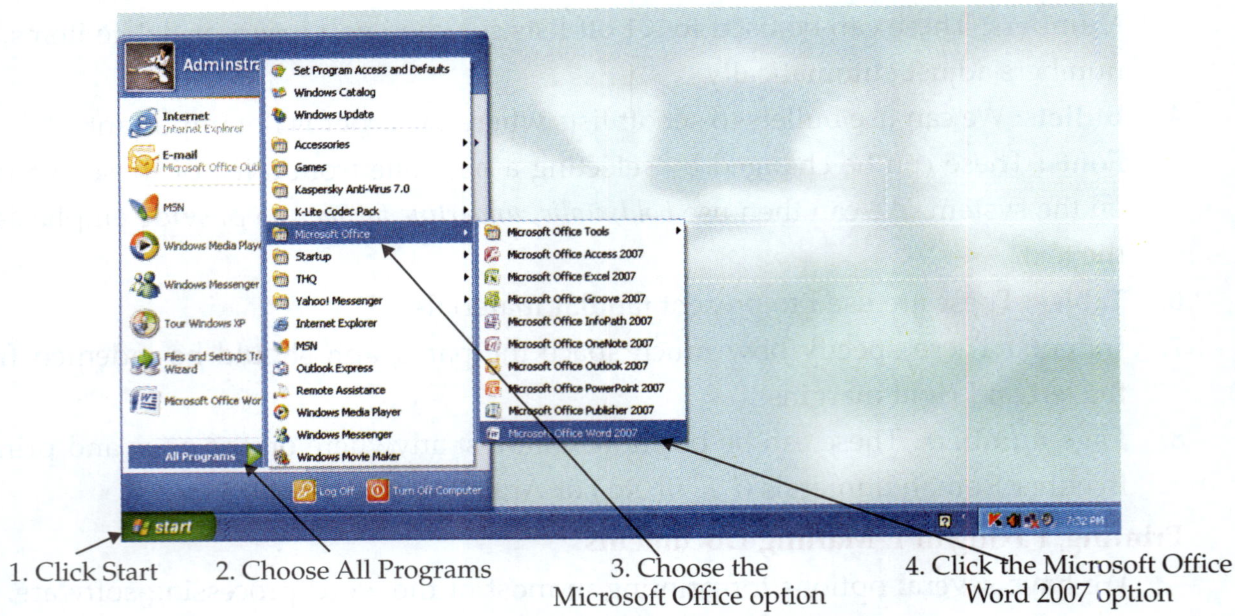

Figure 1.2 Starting MS-Word 2007

This opens a blank new document. (See figure 1.3)

Creating Document

When you start MS-Word, a blank document window appears. MS-Word, by convention, names newly created documents as DOCUMENT1, DOCUMENT2, DOCUMENT3, ... and so on. Thus each new document, when created, is given a name DOCUMENT <serial number>. The various parts of that window are shown in figure 1.3.

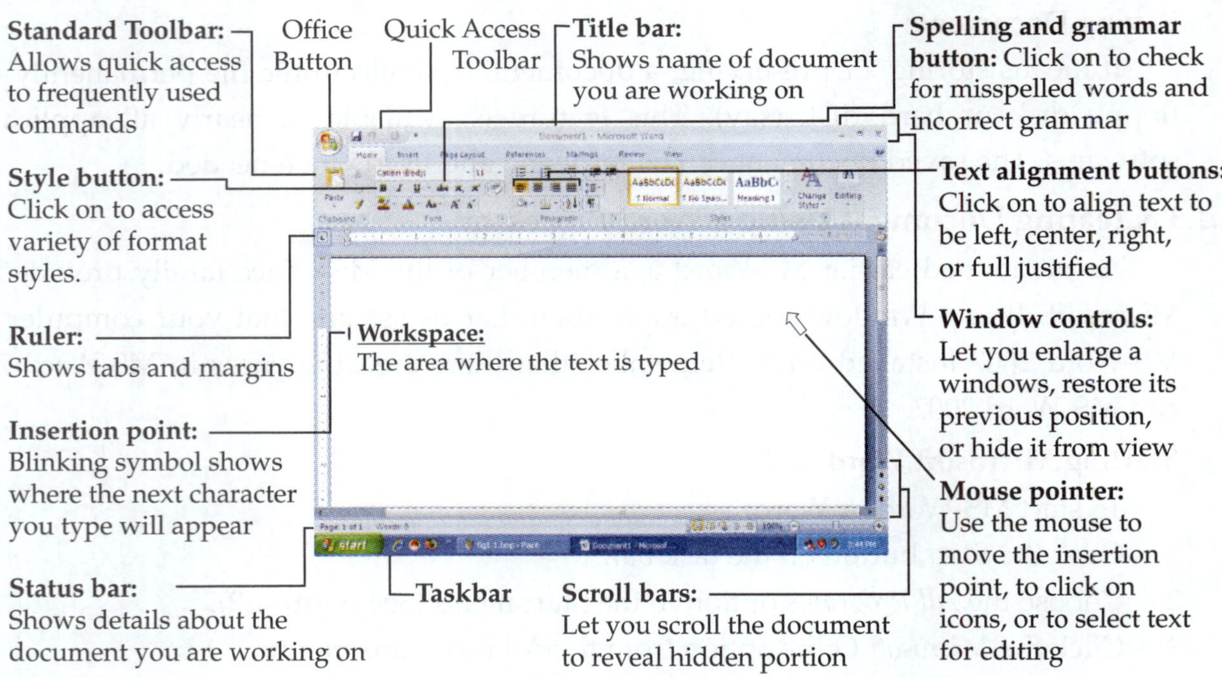

Figure 1.3 Components of a Document Window

The important features of MS-Word are:

- **Outline features:** It enables you to view headings in your document.
- **Cut-and-paste feature:** It enables you to move blocks of text.
- **Formatting feature:** It enables you to change type font and size.

These features are discussed in detail later on in this section.

Note

Toolbar is a collection of buttons, which are used to perform actions, similar to those performed using the menu items.

Creating a New Document

If you are already working in MS-Word and you want to create a new document, then:

1. Click the *Office Button*. (See figure 1.4)

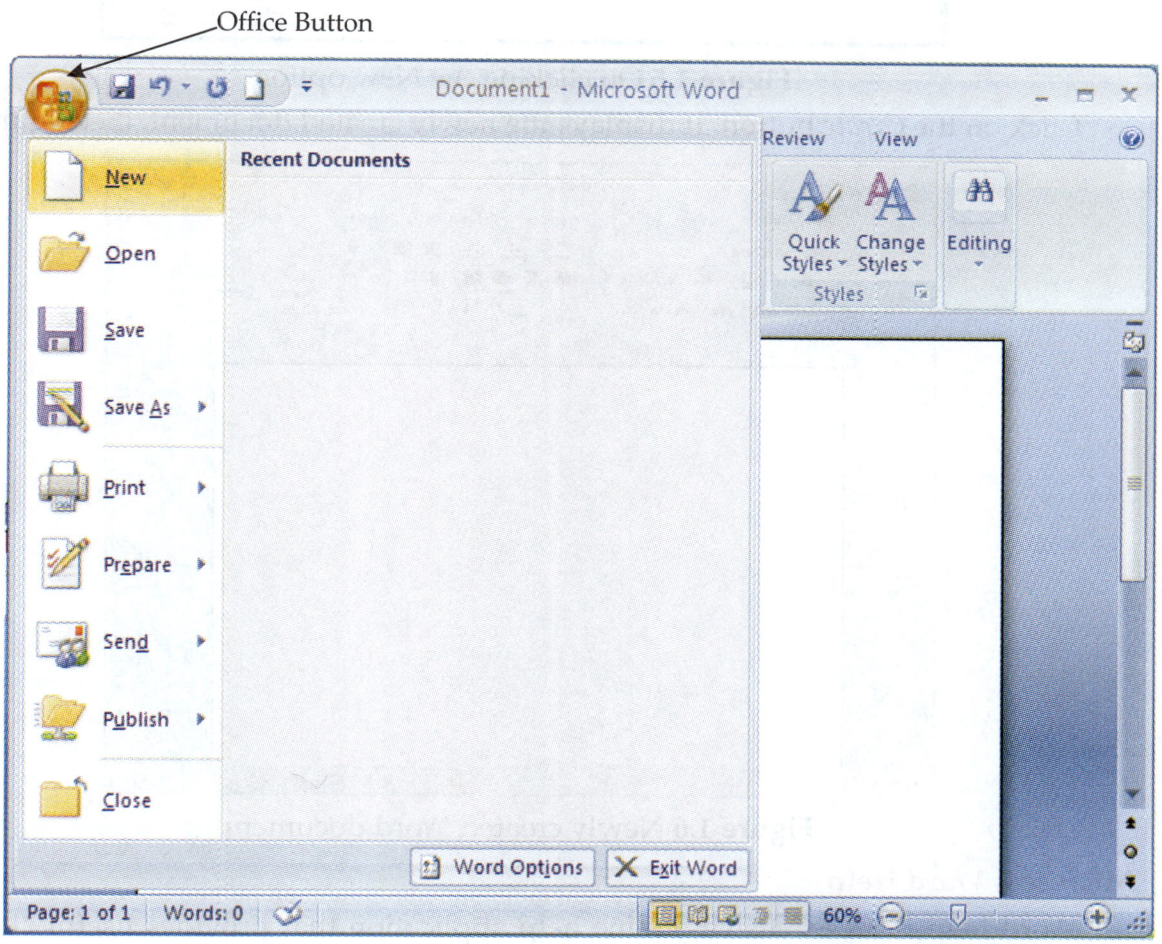

Figure 1.4 Creating a new document

2. Click on the *New* option. It displays the following window. (See figure 1.5)

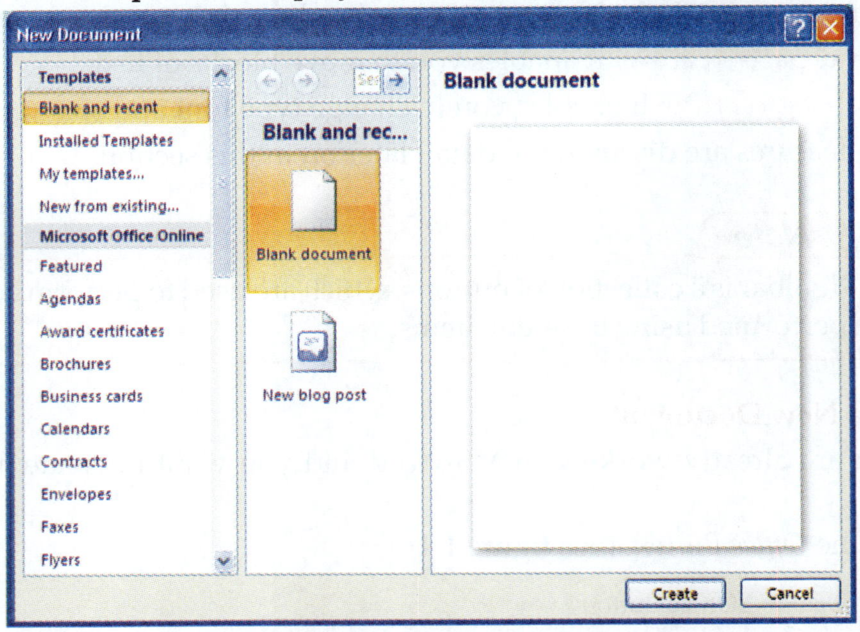

Figure 1.5 On clicking the New option

3. Click on the *Create* button. It displays the newly created document. (See figure 1.6)

Figure 1.6 Newly created Word document

Microsoft Word Help

Word help is an extensive on-line help application that provides useful "how to" and "what is" information on every aspect of the Word program. Word help can be easily accessed as follows:

1. Click on ? sign on Standard Toolbar or press *F1* for getting help. (See figure 1.7)

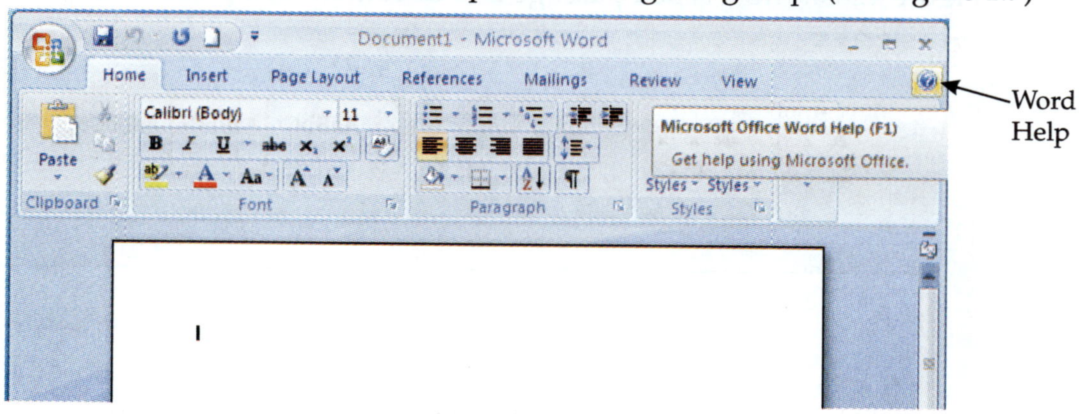

Figure 1.7 Getting Word Help

2. On clicking, you will get the Word Help. (See figure 1.8)

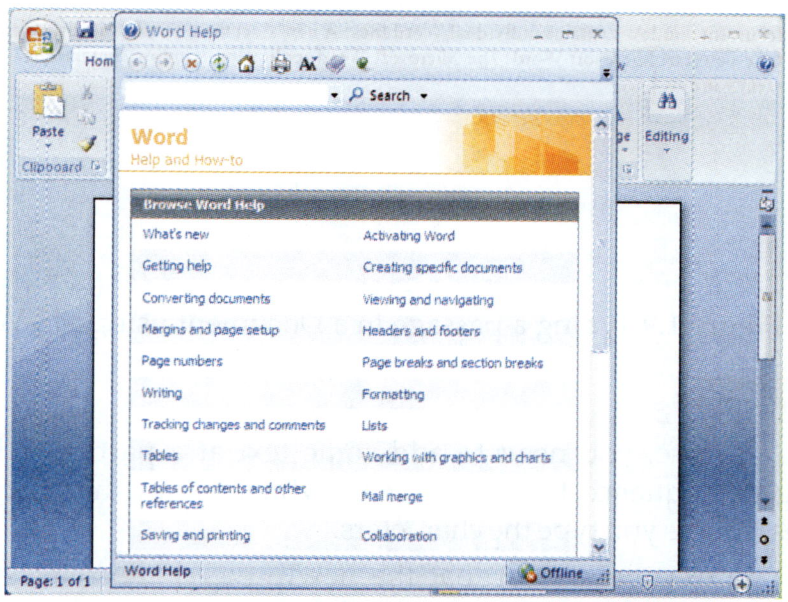

Figure 1.8 Word Help

3. Type your question that you want to ask.
4. Click on *Search* button.
5. A help on related topic will appear.
6. For closing Word Help, click on × in upper right corner of Word Help.

Typing a Passage Using MS-Word

To insert text in your document, place the cursor at the position where you want to enter the text and start typing.

To insert a paragraph you have to press the enter key and start typing.

When you type text in a document, MS-Word automatically inserts the text in the document area.

Figure 1.9 shows a typed passage in a document using MS-Word 2007.

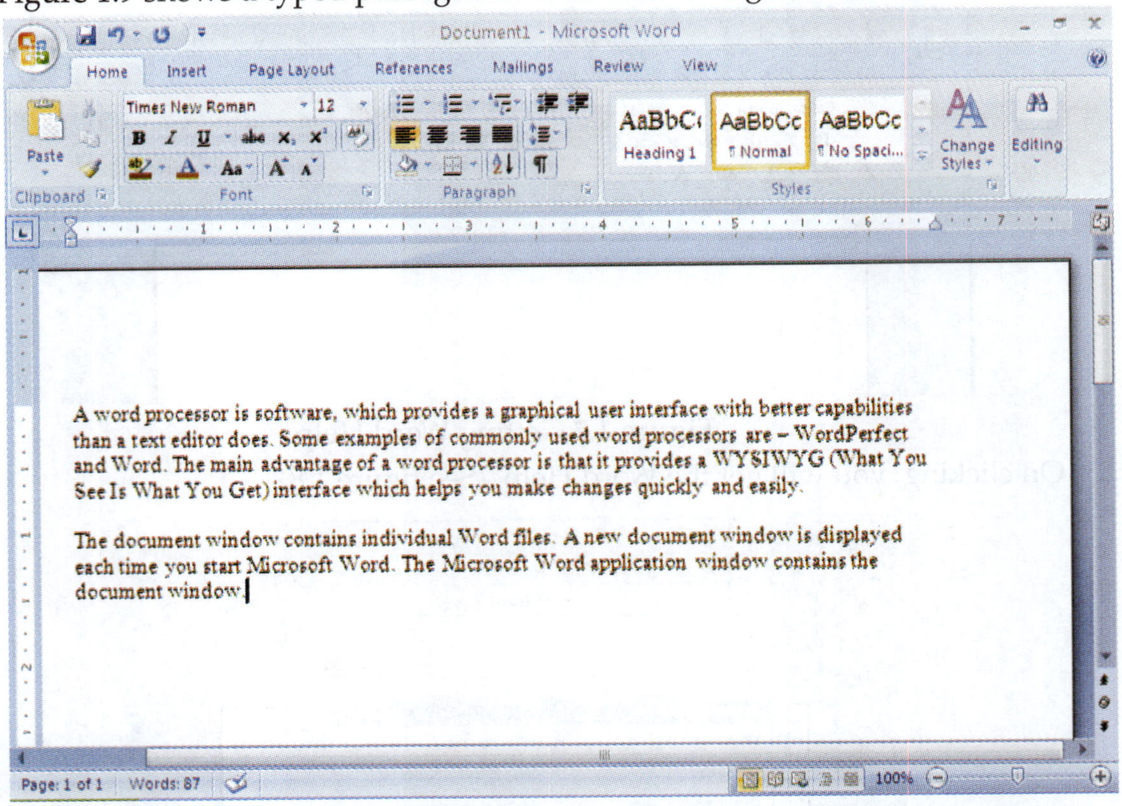

Figure 1.9 Typing a passage in a Document using MS-Word

Note

1. In case, you need to add some text at a particular location, before an existing text sequence, the text sequence which follows the insertion point is shifted towards right as you type the characters.

2. In case, you wish that the newly typed characters should replace the existing text, before starting typing the characters, press the key **'Insert'**. Now whatever you will type will overwrite the characters. To return to the normal mode of typing (i.e., to cancel the overtype feature) press the **'Insert'** key again.

1.1.4 Saving Document Using the 'Save As' Command

When you type in a document, the document is stored in the internal memory of the computer.

Once you have created a document, you have to save it for future use and you must save it on a disk. To save means to preserve the document safely for further use.

To save a word document:

1. Click the *Office Button*.
2. Click the *Save* option. (See figure 1.10)

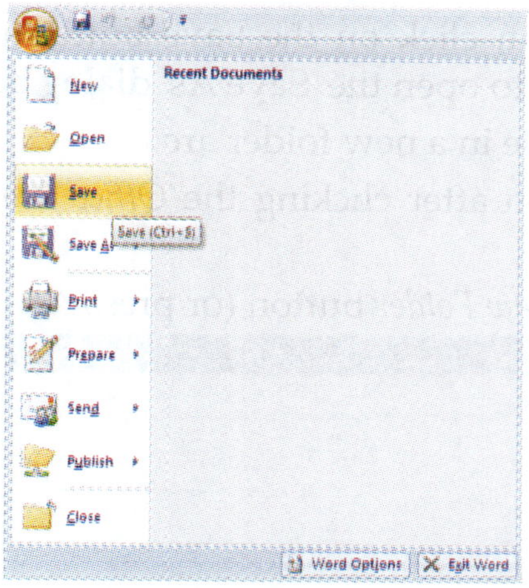

Figure 1.10 Selecting the Save option

3. The *'Save As'* dialog box is displayed as shown in figure 1.11.

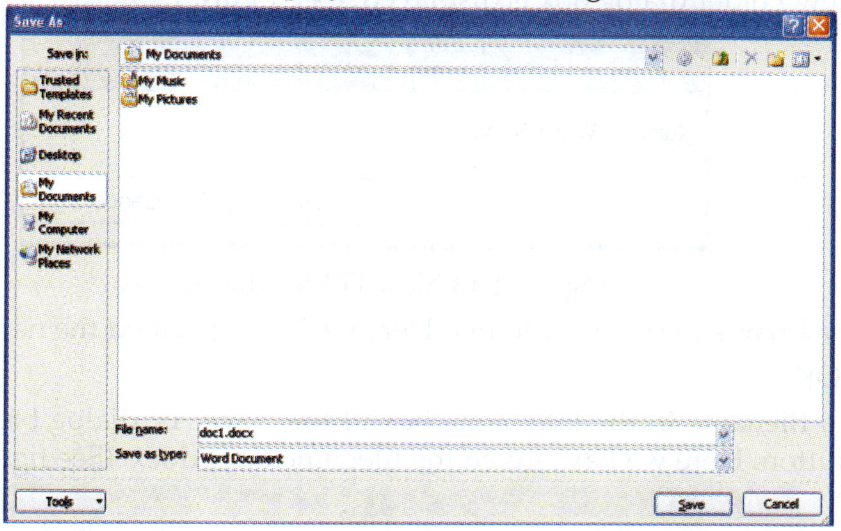

Figure 1.11 The 'Save As' dialog box

The 'Save As' dialog box is displayed only under the following circumstances:

(i) When you have clicked 'Save As'.

(ii) If you have clicked Save and you are saving the document for the first time.

4. You must enter the name by which you want to save the document. Here we have given the name doc1.docx.
5. Click the *Save* button.

Note

MS-Word, by default, saves all the documents in the folder 'My Documents' with extensions.docx. However, you can save them elsewhere by selecting the desired location, from the **'Save in:'** drop-down list provided in the 'Save As' dialog box.

Alternatively, you can click on the Save button on the Quick Access Toolbar or press the Ctrl and S keys to open the 'Save As' dialog box.

The steps to save a file in a new folder are:

1. Select the *Save* option after clicking the *Office Button*. The 'Save As' dialog box is displayed.
2. Click on the *Create New Folder* button (or press Alt+4). (See figure 1.12)

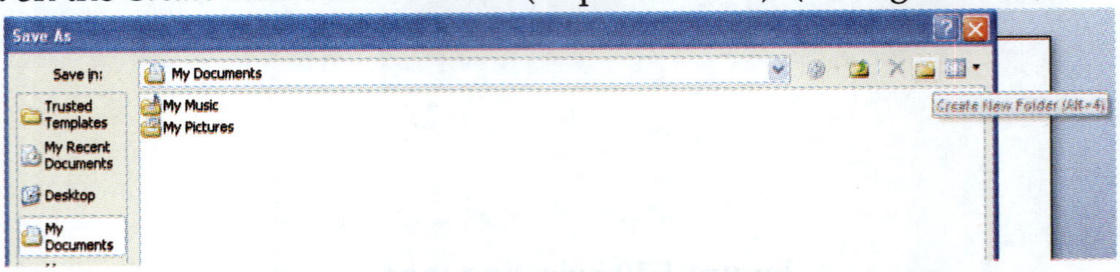

Figure 1.12 Creating New Folder for Saving a file

3. The New Folder dialog box is displayed. (See figure 1.13)

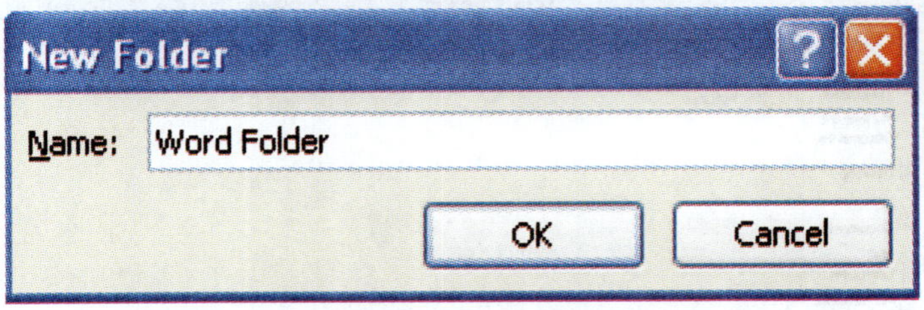

Figure 1.13 New Folder dialog box

4. Specify a name for the new folder. Here we have specified the name Word Folder.
5. Click OK.
6. Enter a filename in the File name box of the 'Save As' dialog box and click on the *Save* button. Here we have given the filename doc1.docx. (See figure 1.14)

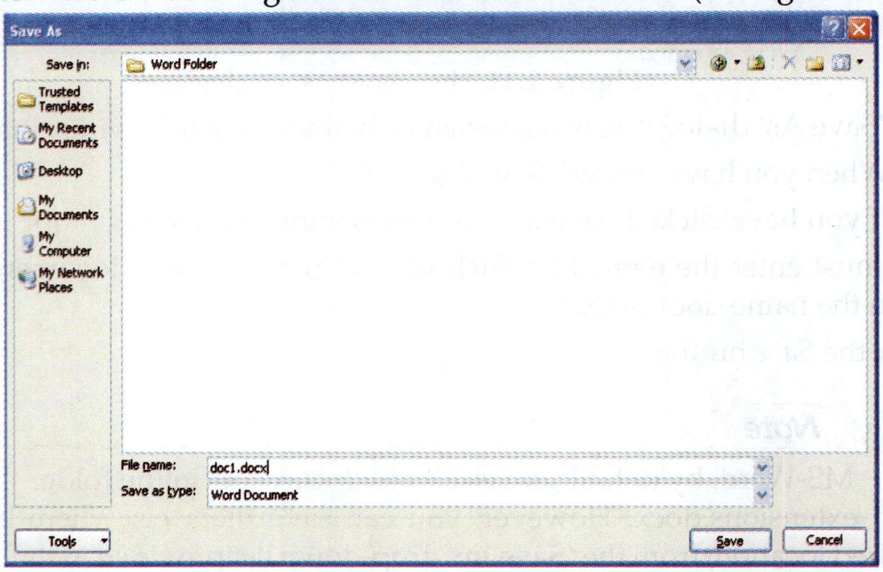

Figure 1.14 Saving a document in a folder

Caution: When you are using the 'Save As' option, make sure that you do not overwrite the existing copy of the file.

Closing a Document

After your work is complete you need to close the document without exiting from the MS-Word.

To close a document without exiting the MS-Word,

1. Click the *Office Button*.
2. Click the *Close* option.

If you have not saved the document before closing, MS-Word gives you warning asking to save the document. (See figure 1.15)

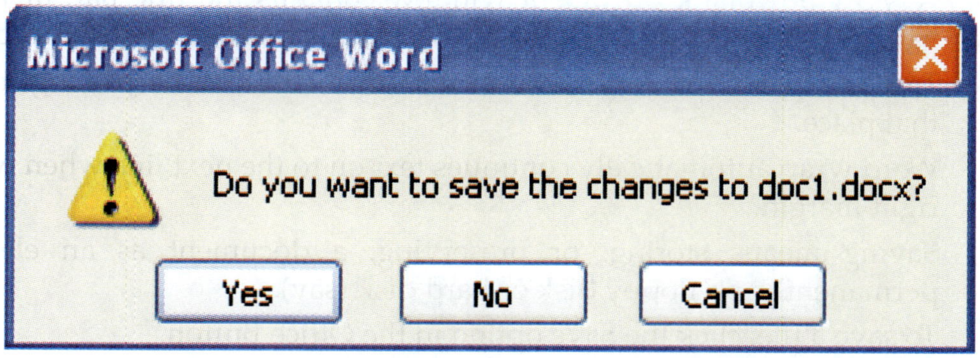

Figure 1.15 The warning dialog box

From the above shown dialog box:

If you want to *Save* the document, click the *Yes* button.

If you do not want to *Save* the document, click the *No* button.

If you want to remove the message box, click the *Cancel* button.

Exiting Microsoft Word

When the Word Processing work is over, you must exit properly from MS-Word.

To exit MS-Word:

1. Click the *Office Button*.
2. Click the *Exit Word* button.

If you have not saved the document, Word prompts you to save changes before closing the application. (See figure 1.15)

Useful Tip

You can close the document using Close button available in the Title bar.

SUMMARY

- Word processing is by far the most widely used computer application.
- A Word Processor is a software that helps you to create, edit and save documents.
- The main advantage of a Word processor is that it provides a WYSIWYG (What You See Is What You Get) interface which helps you make changes quickly and easily.
- A file created in word processor is called the document.
- Microsoft Word is a Windows based application.
- For creating a new document, you use New option in Office Button.
- A MS-Word blank document window contains the title bar, menu bar, tool bars, rulers, document area, insertion point, scroll bars and status bar.
- Text can be entered anywhere in the document area by placing the cursor at that place.
- Word wrap automatically continues text on to the next line when we reach the right margin.
- Saving means storing, or preserving, a document as an electronic file permanently–on floppy disk or hard disk (say).
- To save a file, click the Save option in the Office Button.
- To close a file, click the Close option in the Office Button.
- To open an existing file, click the Open option in the Office Button.
- There are differences in MS-Word 2003 and MS-Word 2007.
- When you are using the 'Save As' option, make sure that you do not overwrite the existing copy of the file.
- If you have not saved the document, Word prompts you to save changes before closing the application.

REVIEW QUESTIONS

STATE WHETHER TRUE OR FALSE

1. In word processing, you manipulate text.
2. MS-Word is not a member of the MS-Office family provided by Microsoft.
3. MS-Word is not a Windows based application.
4. Microsoft Word is a database program.
5. You can start Microsoft Word by using Start button.
6. For creating a document, you use New option in Office Button.
7. For saving a document, you need to have a name for it.

8. When you are using the 'Save As' option, make sure that you do not overwrite the existing copy of the file.
9. There are no differences in the MS-Word 2003 and MS-Word 2007.
10. Using Word Processors error correction is simple and neat.

FILL IN THE BLANKS

1. Word processing is the most common software ....
2. Word processing is used to write, edit, and format memos, letters and ....
3. .... automatically continues text on to the next line when we reach the right margin.
4. .... is the activity of moving upward or downward through the text or other screen display.
5. For creating a new document, you use .... option in *Office Button*.
6. For saving a document, you need to have a .... for it.
7. For opening an existing document, you need to click .... in *Office Button*.
8. The well known word processing programs are Microsoft Word, Writer, WordPad and ....
9. .... means storing, or preserving, a document as an electronic file permanently.
10. .... is the area, in a document, where the text is typed.

MULTIPLE CHOICE QUESTIONS

1. Word processing program(s) is/are
   (a) Microsoft Word (b) Writer
   (c) WordPad (d) All of these.
2. Microsoft Word is ....
   (a) an application software (b) a spreadsheet
   (c) an operating system (d) a database.
3. You can start Microsoft Word by .... button.
   (a) New (b) Start
   (c) Program (d) Exit
4. For creating a document, you use .... Button.
   (a) Office (b) Open
   (c) Document (d) Save As
5. For saving a document, you need to have a .... for it.
   (a) Name (b) Surname
   (c) Father's name (d) None of these

ANSWER THE FOLLOWING

1. What can you do with word processing package that you cannot do with pencil and paper?
2. Discuss Word Processing Packages and their uses.
3. Discuss the role of the cursor, scrolling, and word wrap in creating documents.
4. What Word Processing features are available to help edit documents?
5. What is the importance of Word Processing? Discuss.
6. How will you create a document using a Word Processor? Explain.
7. How will you save a document using the 'Save As' command? Explain.

FIELD TRIP

Using computer magazines or the Web, do the following:

Find out what are the latest versions of Microsoft Word and Corel Word Perfect. Are there any features you like that one has and the other does not?

ASSIGNMENT

1. Students to type a letter using name and save it in a folder.
2. Perform the following:

   (i) Create a MS-Word document and type the following text:

   Importance of Trees

   Do you know how important trees are?

   They are one of the major constituents of the earth's ecosystem. Without their presence it is difficult for us to survive. They share important relationship with the human beings as well as the animals. Most important feature is that they take carbon dioxide gas and release oxygen gas in the air, and as you know we need oxygen to breathe in and to live. They also prevent soil erosion by holding soil with their roots. Their valuable wood is used to make furniture and also in cooking food. Trees provide us fruits also like Mango. Some find use for medicinal purposes.

   So, you should never think of cutting trees nor allow others to do so. Always treat trees as your best friend and plant trees.

   (ii) Save the document as Trees.docx.

   (iii) Exit from MS-Word.

UNIT 2 EDITING TEXT IN WORD PROCESSING DOCUMENT

Specific Objective

After reading this unit, the student will be able to:

1.2.1 edit, and save Word document using editing tools.

1.2.0 Introduction

Editing is the act of altering your document. Some Edit features are *insert* and *delete, undelete, find and replace, cut/copy and paste, spelling checker, grammar checker*, and *thesaurus*. All of these commands are in the Home tab shown as icons.

1.2.1 Editing and Saving Word Document Using Editing Tools

When you edit text, you change text by either inserting text, deleting text or replacing text. To edit text, place the cursor at the required position and either insert, delete or replace text. Table 2.1 shows how to move around a document using the keyboard. You can also use the mouse to change the position of the cursor.

Table 2.1 Moving Around a Document Using the Keyboard

Keys	Functions
<UP> arrow, <Down> arrow	One character up, down
<Left> arrow, <Right> arrow	One character left, right
<Ctrl> + <Right> arrow	Next word
<Ctrl> + <Left> arrow	Previous word
<Home>	Beginning of the line
<End>	End of the line
<Ctrl> + <Home>	Beginning of the document
<Ctrl> + <End>	End of the document
<Ctrl> + <Page Up>	Previous page
<Ctrl> + <Page Down>	Next Page

To delete a character, you can use the backspace key or the delete key.

The delete key removes the character to the immediate right of the cursor.

The backspace key removes the character to the immediate left of the cursor.

You can also delete words, sentences or paragraphs by selecting them and pressing the delete or the backspace key.

Useful Tip

You must keep on saving document when working to avoid losing document when power goes off.

You can edit a Word document using the following editing tools:

- Spell check functions
- Copy/cut and paste facilities
- OVR
- Undo and redo keys
- Search and replace

Spell Check Functions

Spell checking is a very big plus point while talking about word processing. You can spell check your document for wrong spellings and even wrong grammar too.

Let us type some text in a document to use the above mentioned tools. (See figure 2.1)

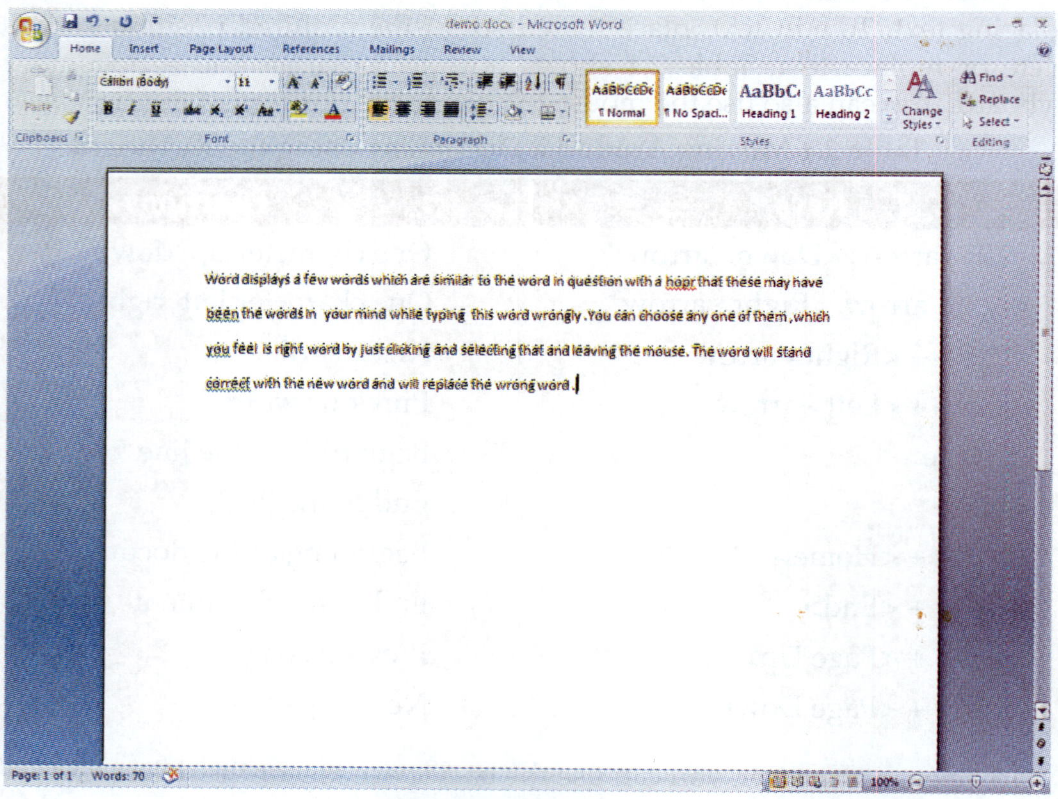

Figure 2.1 A Word document

While typing the above document, you must have noticed that some words are underlined by wavy red lines and some with green lines. Well, the red lines show that the word is wrongly spelled whereas the grammatical mistakes are pointed out by the green lines.

There are two methods of correcting these errors. One method is to correct these errors one by one, picking them up. Secondly, you can spell check the whole document. First let us take up the option of correcting the misspelled words one by one.

For correcting the misspelled words one by one do the following:

1. Click with the mouse at any place within the word to be corrected, say "hopr".
2. Now right click the mouse button.
3. A pop-menu will pop-up as shown in figure 2.2.

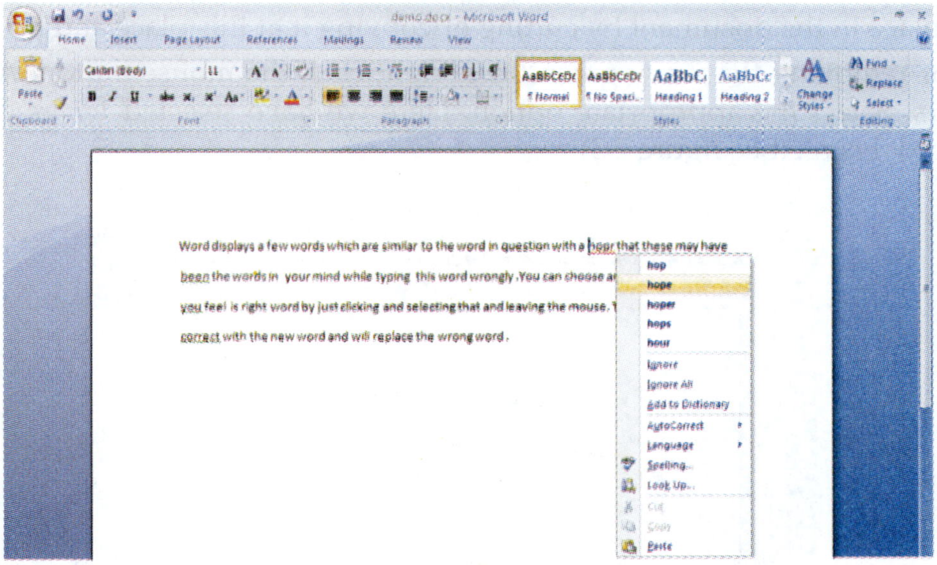

Figure 2.2 Correcting the misspelled words one by one

4. Among the various options available are:

Alternative words: Word 2007 displays a few words which are similar to the word in question with a hope that these may have been the words in your mind while typing this word wrongly. You can choose any one of them, which you feel is the right word by just clicking and selecting that and leaving the mouse. The word will stand corrected with the new word and will replace the wrong word.

In our case we select "hopr" and the word changes from "hopr" to "hope"–red line disappears.

Ignore: It is like over ruling the dictionary and saying that whatever you have typed is right and would like the dictionary to ignore this not only at this place but also at all other places within the document.

Ignore All: This will allow you to ignore this error throughout the document.

Add to Dictionary: If you feel that this word is right and would like this word to be added to the dictionary so that it is not shown as an error in the future.

Auto Correct: This is another option of Microsoft Word 2007 where you define the words which are most likely to be spelled wrong by you and their alternative words. These words when typed wrongly are corrected automatically.

Language: You feel that this particular word which has been pointed as wrong by the current dictionary would be available in other language dictionary. So mention here the name of the other dictionary where this word could be found. If you do not have a second dictionary loaded, just ignore this.

Spelling...: By clicking at this, you can start the spell checking of the whole document from this point onward.

Look Up...: It looks for an alternative word in the thesaurus.

Cut, Copy and Paste: These can be used for transferring the selected word to some other place in the document by cutting or copying it at this place and pasting it there.

For removing the wavy green lines, right click the mouse button. A pop-up menu appears. Select the appropriate option. Here we have selected *Ignore Once* option for the word 'been'. (See figure 2.3)

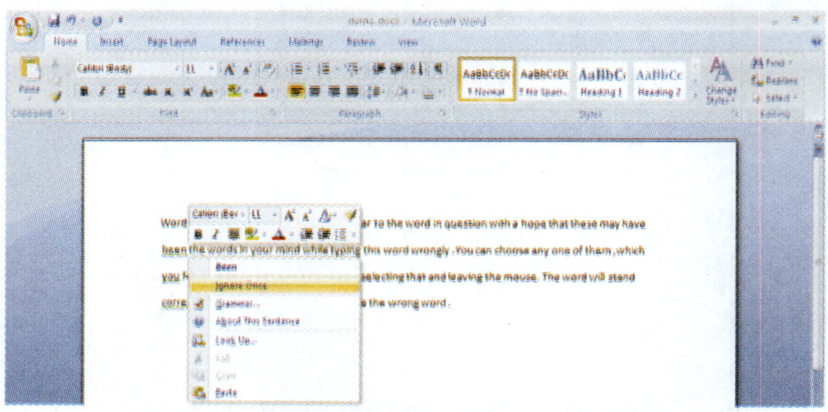

Figure 2.3 Removing wavy green lines

Repeat the above process for the whole document.

5. After spell checking the document word by word, you will get the corrected document. (See figure 2.4)

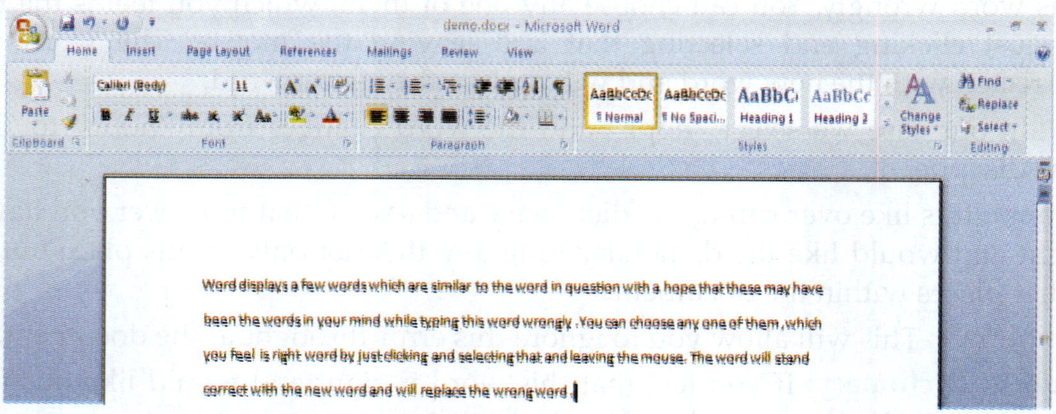

Figure 2.4 Document after applying the corrections

6. Save and close the document.

For spell checking the whole document do the following:

As mentioned above you can correct all the misspelled words one by one. This method is little tedious since, you have to pick up word by word. On the other hand, if you have a long document, then the other method of spell checking is more appropriate. This is discussed below.

1. Place the cursor at the beginning of the text in the document (See figure 2.5)

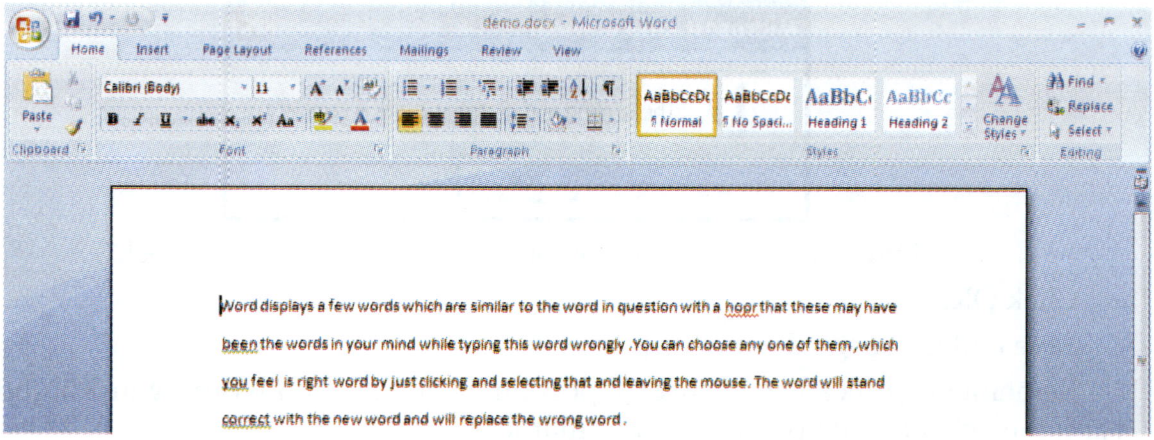

Figure 2.5 Spell checking the whole document

2. Select *Spelling & Grammar* from the Review tab.

OR

Press F7

OR

Click at *Spelling & Grammar* in Proofing Panel of Review.

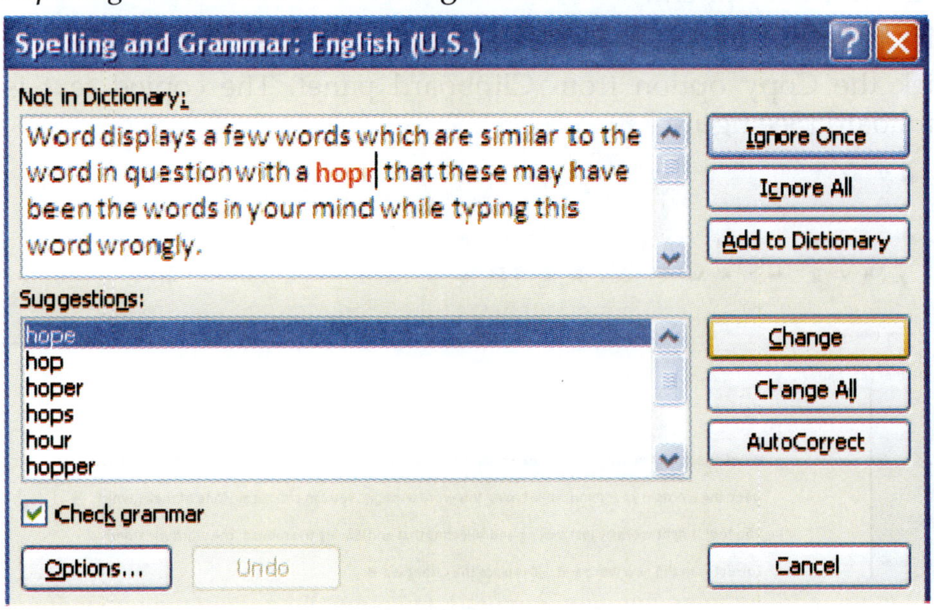

Figure 2.6 Spelling and Grammar check

This will initiate the spell checking process and will start the spell checking of the document with each word of the document being searched with the similar words available in the dictionary. If not found, it will point it out to you. Select the appropriate word from the suggestions box. Here we have selected 'hope'. For green wavy lines select *Ignore Once*.

3. After checking the spelling of the whole document, if there is no word left for checking, you will get the message shown in figure 2.7.

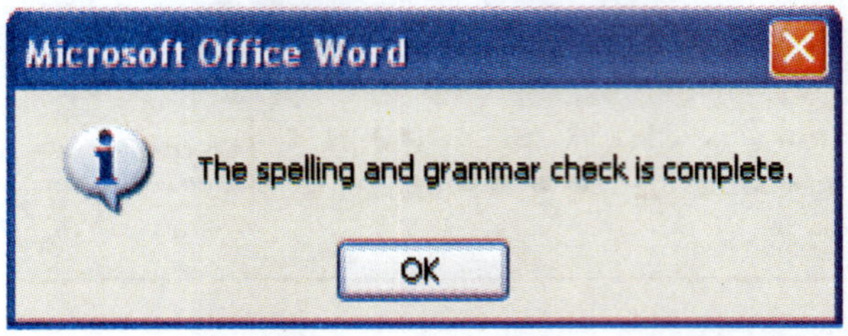

Figure 2.7 On completion of spelling and grammar check

4. Click OK.
5. Save and Close the document.

Remember, you can spell check a portion of the text or a word by just highlighting it and then clicking at Spelling & Grammar icon.

Copy/Cut and Paste Facilities

You can copy text from one place in a document to another place.

When you copy text, you duplicate the text.

To copy text:

1. Open a document and select the text you want to copy. Here we have opened the demo. docx document.
2. Click the Home tab.
3. Click the Copy option from Clipboard panel. The copied text is placed in the Clipboard (See figure 2.8).

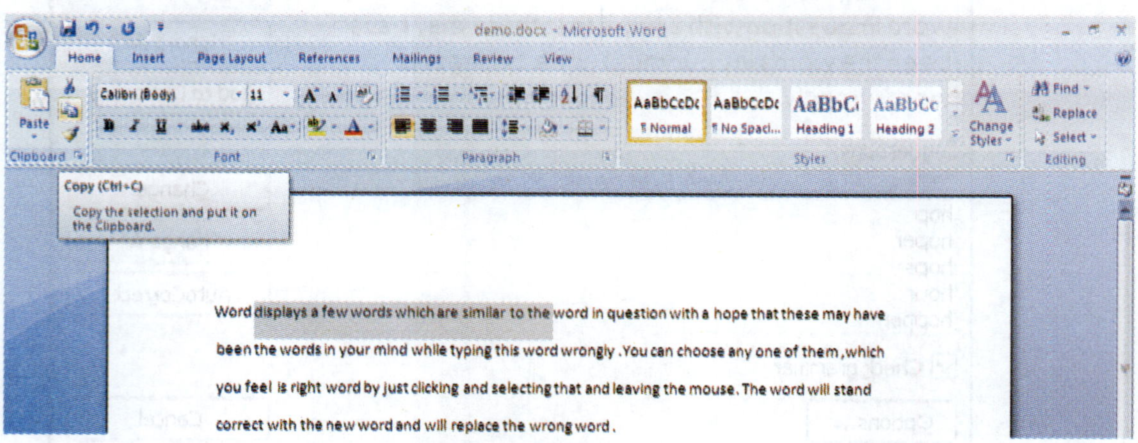

Figure 2.8 The Copy option

4. Place the cursor at the place where you want to paste the text. (See figure 2.9)

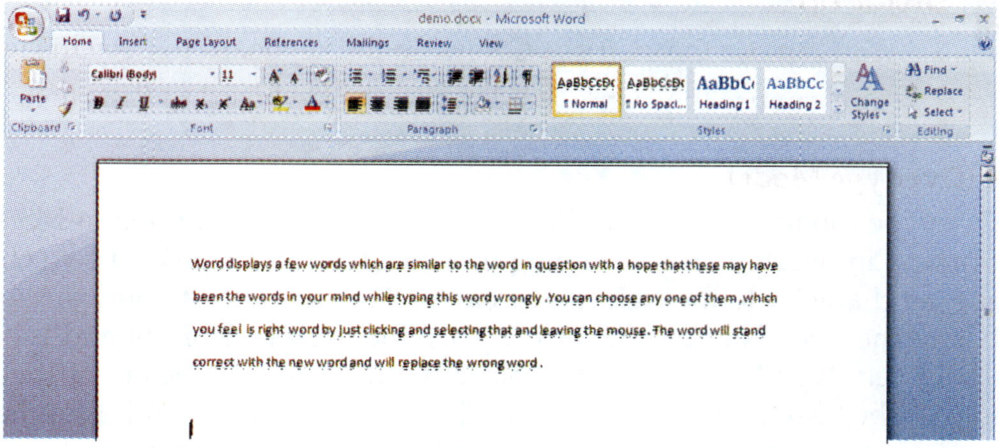

Figure 2.9 Cursor position for pasting the text.

5. Click the Paste option from the Clipboard panel. (See figure 2.10)

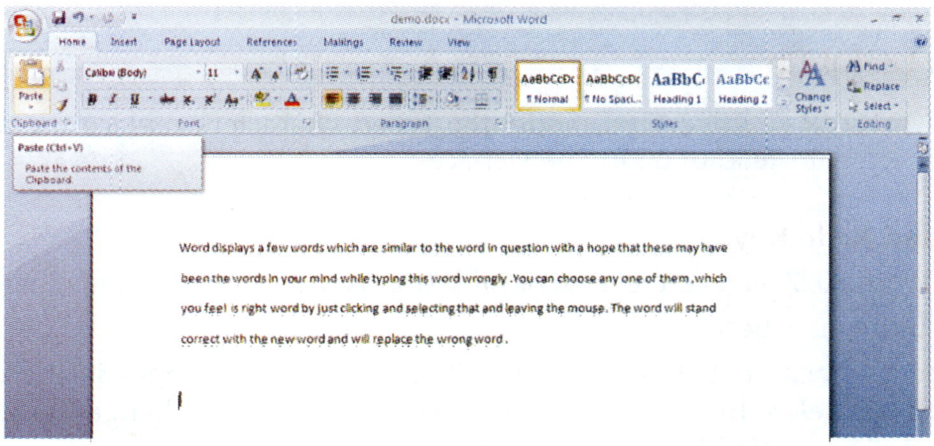

Figure 2.10 The Paste option

6. The selected text will be pasted at the place you want. (See figure 2.11)

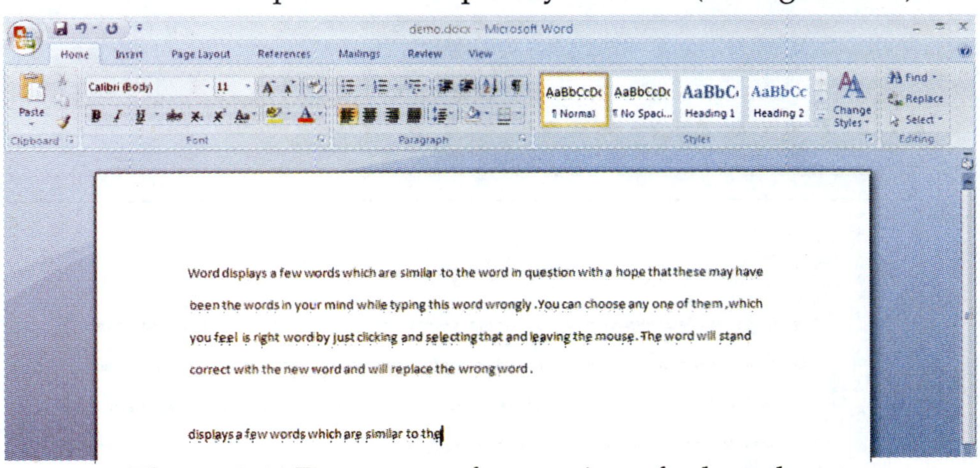

Figure 2.11 Document after pasting of selected text

7. Save and close the document.

Useful Tip

1. You can use the <Ctrl> + C keys on the keyboard to *Copy* the text.
2. You can use the <Ctrl> + V keys on the keyboard to *Paste* text.

OVR (Overtype Mode)

Overtype mode is another utility, related to the editing of text in MS Word. If you are working in overtype mode, typing of a character in the mid of two characters will replace the character to the right of the cursor. For example, if you want to add a word My before the line "Name is Sammy", place the cursor before N and type "My". The two characters typed by you, will replace the first two characters of the line and the output will be "Myme is Sammy". It is clear from the name and example, that in the overtype mode, characters are written over the presently typed characters.

You can activate the **OVR** mode by pressing the **Insert** key for once.

Useful Tip

In OVR *i.e.*, overtype mode, the typed characters replace the already typed characters instead of taking new space.

Undo and Redo Keys

In Word 2007, you can reverse or *undo* the last performed action(s) on the document. To undo an action,

1. Open a document (Refer to figure 2.11) and make changes in it (See figure 2.12). First we delete the last line of the document and then change the word "hope" to "hopr" in the first line.
2. Click the Undo icon in the title bar (See figure 2.12).

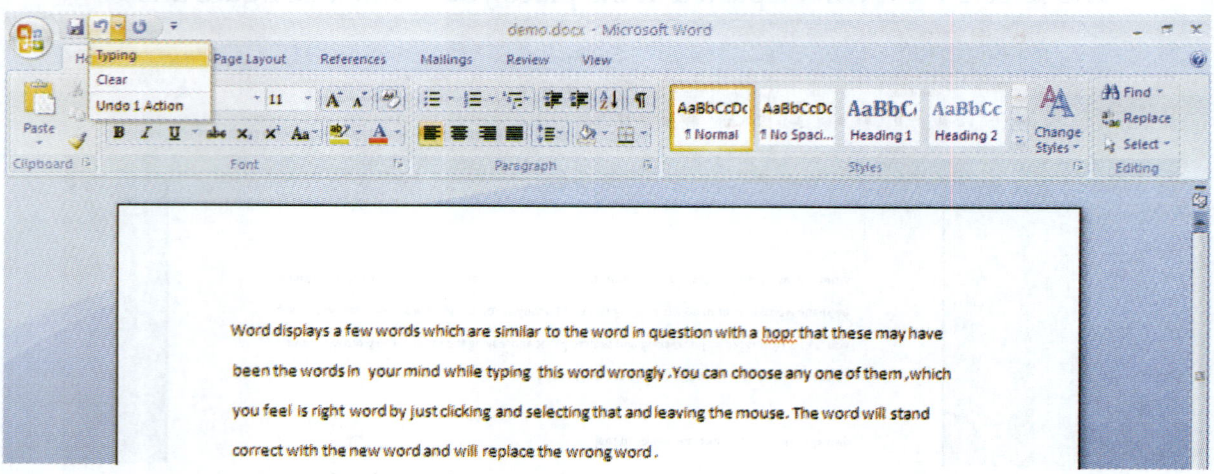

Figure 2.12 The Undo option

3. After applying Undo, the document is shown in figure 2.13.

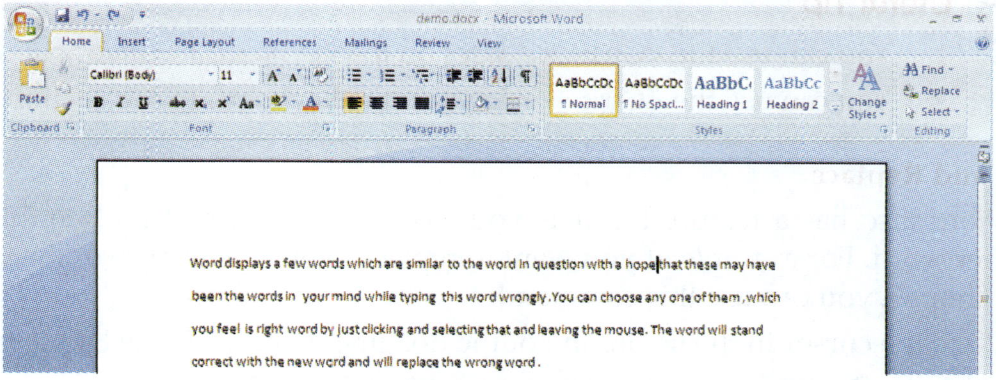

Figure 2.13 After Applying the Undo option

You can undo the other action also if you wish to do so.

Similar to an *undo* action, you can perform a *redo* action. The Redo option is used to reverse the last Undo action on the document. Let us apply Redo option on the document demo.docx shown in figure 2.13 after step 3 given above.

To redo an action,

1. Click the Redo icon in the Quick Access Toolbar. (See figure 2.14)

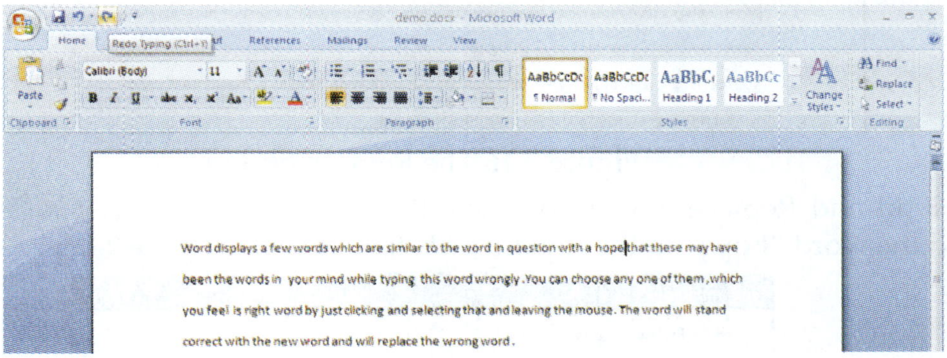

Figure 2.14 The Redo option

2. After applying Redo, the document is shown in figure 2.15. We again get back "hopr" in place of "hope".

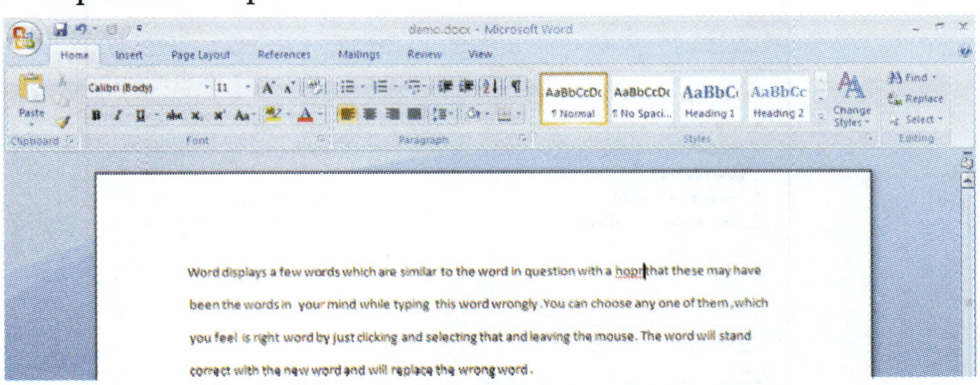

Figure 2.15 After applying the Redo option

Useful Tip

1. You can use the <Ctrl> + Z keys on the keyboard to *Undo* action.
2. You can use the <Ctrl> + Y keys on the keyboard to *Redo* action.

Find and Replace

Word also has a feature that lets you look for a word and replace the word with another word. For example, if you want to replace every occurrence of the word "hopr" with "hope", you can use this command.

1. Place the cursor in the beginning of the document and click the Home tab.
2. Click the Replace option in Editing panel (See figure 2.16).

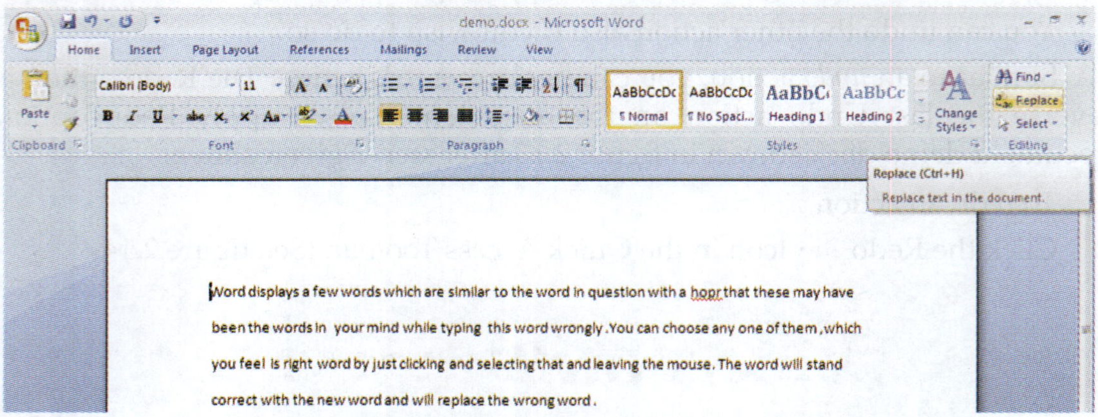

Figure 2.16 The Replace option

3. In Find and Replace dialog box, type the word *"hopr"* in the *Find what*: text box, and the word "hope" in the *Replace with*: text box. (See figure 2.17)

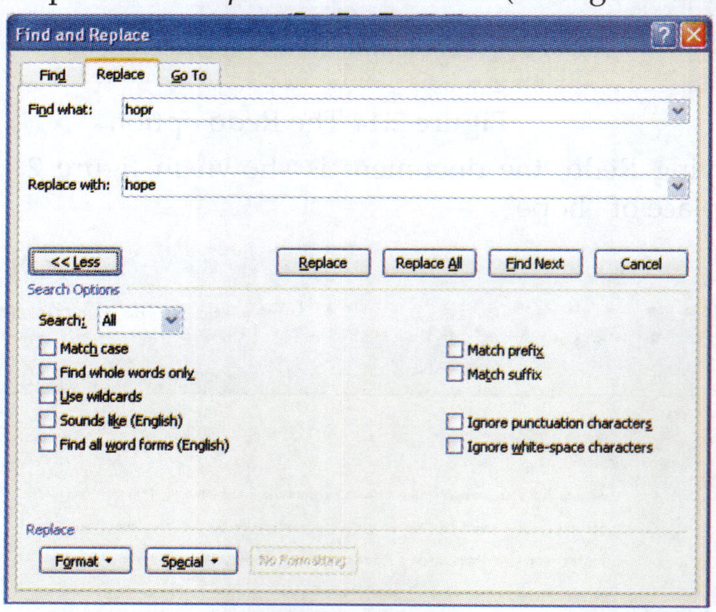

Figure 2.17 The Find and Replace dialog box

4. Click the *Replace* button. The first word to be replaced (if present) is highlighted. Again press the *Replace* button to replace it. In the same way Word replaces all the occurrence one by one and finally the following dialog box is displayed. (See figure 2.18)

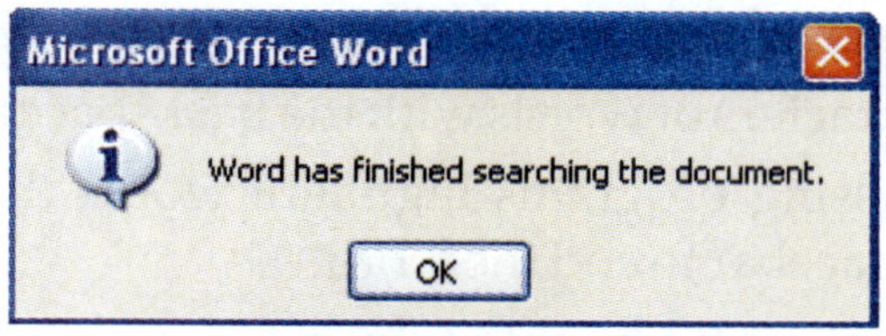

Figure 2.18

5. Click OK, close the Find and Replace dialog box and save the document.

The *Replace All* button in the Find and Replace dialog box can also be used to make all the replacements in one go.

So the Find and Replace feature is quite useful in editing text.

SUMMARY

- Editing is the act of altering documents.
- When you edit text, you change text by either inserting text, deleting text or replacing text by using mouse or keyboard.
- To edit text, place the cursor at the desired position and either insert, delete or replace text.
- You can delete words, sentences or paragraphs by selecting them and pressing the delete or the backspace key.
- You can spell check your document for wrong spellings and even wrong grammar too.
- While typing, the red lines show that the word is wrongly spelled whereas the grammatical mistakes are pointed out by the green lines.
- You can copy text from one place in a document to another place.
- When you copy text, you duplicate text.
- In OVR i.e., overtype mode the typed characters replace the already typed characters instead of taking new space.
- In Word, you can reverse the last performed action on the document using Undo option.
- The Redo action is used to reverse the last Undo action on the document.
- Word also has a feature that lets you look for a word and replace the word with another word.
- To locate words or phrases in a document, you use the Find command. To replace them, you use the Replace command.
- You must keep on saving document when working to avoid losing document when power goes off.

REVIEW QUESTIONS

STATE WHETHER TRUE OR FALSE

1. To start a new paragraph in a document you have to press the Enter key.
2. You can delete characters or words with the Backspace and Delete keys.
3. Some word processing programs highlight words that are not in their dictionary when you press Spacebar to end the word.
4. All of the words that are highlighted during a spell check are spelled incorrectly and must be changed.
5. You cannot copy text from one place in a document to another place.
6. You must keep on saving document when working to avoid losing document when power goes off.
7. The find command is used to automatically replace all occurrences of a specified word in a document with a substitute word.
8. In OVR mode the typed characters do not replace the already typed characters.
9. The Redo option is used to reverse the last Undo action on the document.
10. Find and replace is not an editing feature.

FILL IN THE BLANKS

1. The .... option is used to duplicate text.
2. The .... option is used to move text.
3. The .... option is used to place the cut or the copied text.
4. The .... option is used to reverse or undo the previous action.
5. The .... option will repeat the previous Undo action.
6. Word enables you to search and replace text in your document by using the .... option.
7. In .... mode the typed characters replace the already typed characters.
8. You can .... your document for wrong spellings and even wrong grammar too.
9. When editing a document to correct mistakes, you can move the .... point where you want to enter new text and then just type in.
10. .... is the act of altering your document.

MULTIPLE CHOICE QUESTIONS

1. Which of the following is not a feature of word processing software?
   (a) Spelling checker (b) Cell address
   (c) Cut and Paste (d) Find and replace

2. Inserting characters, words and lines in already typed text is called as
   (a) Printing (b) Formatting
   (c) Typing (d) Editing
3. When you type a character, the adjoining character is replaced by the typed character. Which of the following options is on?
   (a) Overtype Mode (b) Formatting Mode
   (c) Safe Mode (d) Editing Mode
4. Which of the following is a shortcut to copy command?
   (a) Ctrl + V (b) Ctrl + C
   (c) Ctrl + X (d) Ctrl + E
5. Which of the following is a shortcut for cutting text?
   (a) Ctrl + C (b) Ctrl + V
   (c) Ctrl + F (d) Ctrl + X

ANSWER THE FOLLOWING

1. Discuss the editing and saving of a Word document using the editing tools.
2. Explain spelling and grammar check in MS Word.
3. What are the different methods of copying text?
4. What do you mean by overtype mode? How is it activated?
5. Explain *Undo* and *Redo* Commands.

ASSIGNMENT

1. Implement the following tasks in MS Word:
   (a) Open Word and type the following document in the file "Firstfile. docx". Keep on saving document after each paragraph to avoid losing document if the power goes off.

Insert and delete. Inserting is the act of adding to the document. Simply place the cursor wherever you want to add text and start typing; the existing characters will be pushed along. If you want to write over (replace) text as you write, press the Insert key before typing. Press Insert key again to exit Insert mode when you have finished typing.

Deleting is the act of removing text, it is performed by using the *Delete* or *Backspace* keys.

The *Undo command* allows you to change your mind and restore text that you have deleted.

Find and replace. The *Find* or *Search, Command* allows you to find any word, phrase or number that exists in the document you are working. The Replace command allows you to automatically replace it with something else you wish.

Cut/copy and paste. First of all select (highlight) the portion of text you want to copy or move. Then you use the copy or cut command to move it to the clipboard, a special holding area in the computer's memory. From there, you can "paste", or transfer, the material to any point (indicated with the cursor) in the existing or a new document of your choice.

Spelling checker. Most word processors have a spelling checker, which tests for incorrectly spelled words. The spelling checker indicates words that are not in its dictionary and thus may be misspelled. Special add-on dictionaries are available. The Microsoft Word have an Auto Correct function that automatically fixes such common mistakes. For example , replaces "teh" with "the".

Grammar checker. A grammar checker, highlights poor grammar, wordiness, incomplete sentences and awkward phrases. It does not fix things automatically, but it flags possible incorrect word usage and sentence structure.

Thesaurus. While writing if you find yourself struck for the right word, you can call up an on-screen thesaurus, which will present you with the appropriate word or alternative words.

Now,

(b) Check and correct the spellings of the entire document. Close the file.

(c) Open the file "Firstfile. docx" created above and add the following text at the end:

"I am editing my first document in MS Word. Learning Word is very easy if learnt and practised carefully. That is why I am editing and saving it."

(d) Save the changes made to the file.

(e) Generate a copy of first paragraph and place it before the last paragraph, using mouse only.

(f) Overtype the first two sentences with the text of your choice.

(g) Undo the last two actions.

(h) Redo the last action.

(i) Search the word "you" and replace it by "We".

(j) Undo the last action.

(k) Save the file and Exit MS Word.

UNIT 3 FORMATTING WORD PROCESSING DOCUMENT

Specific Objective

After reading this unit, the student will be able to:

1.3.1 format and save Word document using formatting tools.

1.3.0 Introduction

When you wish to make a document both more attractive and easier to read, you use formats. All word processing programs have built-in format setting called defaults, which are designed such that you can easily override them. (See figure 3.1)

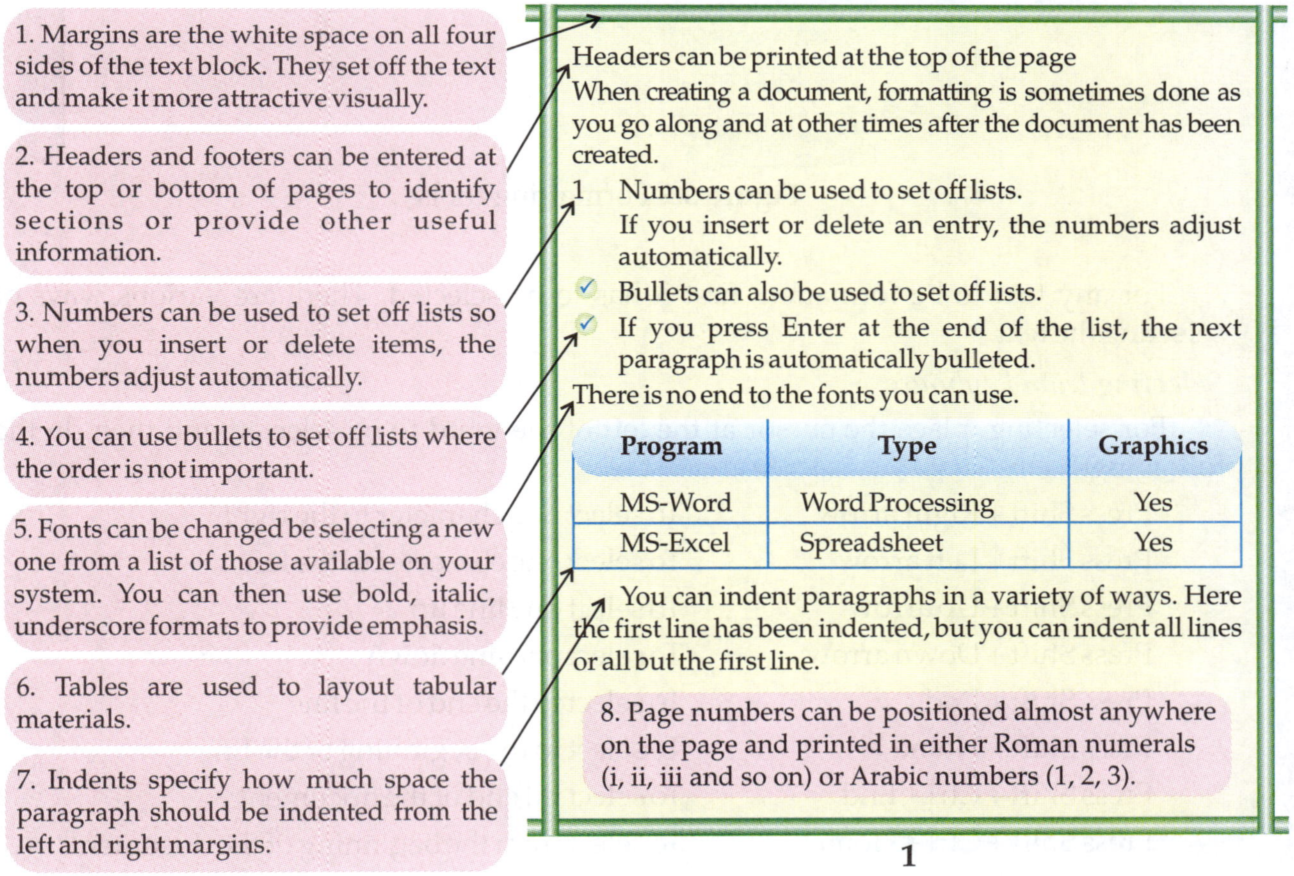

Figure 3.1 Formats for a Document

When creating a document, formatting is usually a separate stage—often completed after the document has been entered. The ease of applying and changing formats lets you play with a document's design. In this unit we will discuss the formatting and saving of a word document using the formatting tools.

1.3.1 Formatting and Saving a Word Document Using the Formatting Tools

MS Word works on the principle of "**FIRST SELECTION THAN ACTION**".

Formatting text means changing the text appearance by changing the alignment, style, font and font colour. To format text, you need to use the Home tab.

In Home tab you have all the formatting tools readily available. (See figure 3.2)

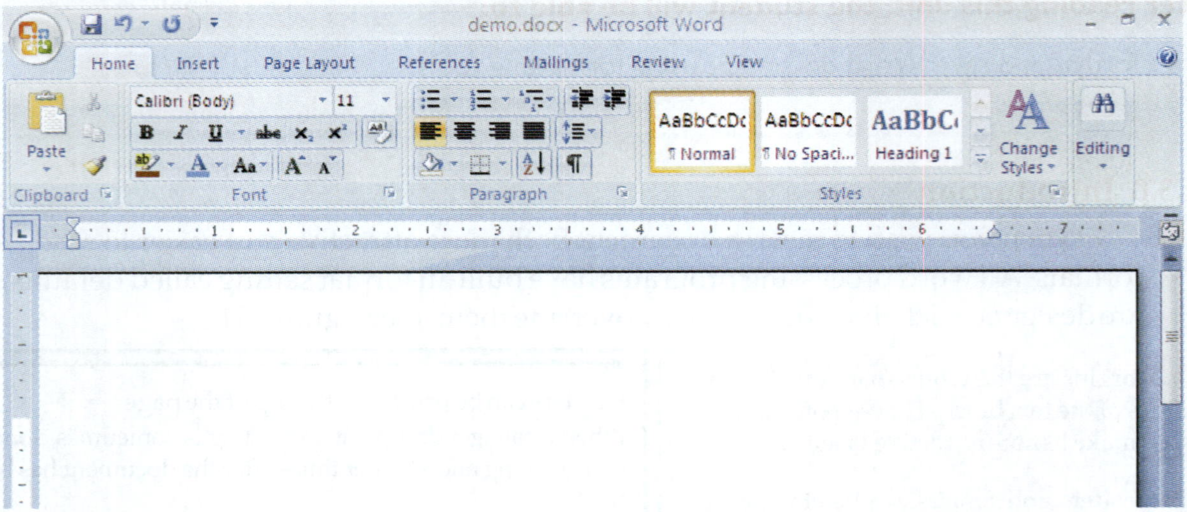

Figure 3.2 Formatting tools

- **Selecting the Text**

For any text to be formatted, first it has to be selected. There are various ways of selecting the text.

Selecting from keyboard

For selecting, place the cursor at the left of the word to be selected and then do the following:

Press Shift + Right arrow	To select one character to the right
Press Shift + Left arrow	To select one character to the left
Press Shift + Up arrow	To select one line up
Press Shift + Down arrow	To select one line down
Press Shift + End	To select to the end of the line
Press Shift + Home	To select to the beginning of the line
Press Shift + Ctrl + End	To select till end of the document
Press Shift + Ctrl + Home	To select from the beginning of the document
Press Ctrl + A	To select the complete text

Selecting the text with the mouse

For this do the following :

1. Position the cursor to the left of the first character to select.
2. Hold down the left mouse button and drag it to the position where you want to stop.
3. Release the mouse.

Selecting with mouse clicks

1. Double click to select a word.
2. Triple click to select the full paragraph.
3. Ctrl + click in a sentence to select the full sentence.

- **Change Font (style, size, colour etc.)**

You can change the font styles (type, styles) using options available in Font panel. The font size and the colour of the text can also be changed as discussed below:

Changing the Font (type style)

To change the font of your text,

1. Open the document and select the text to be formatted. (See figure 3.3)

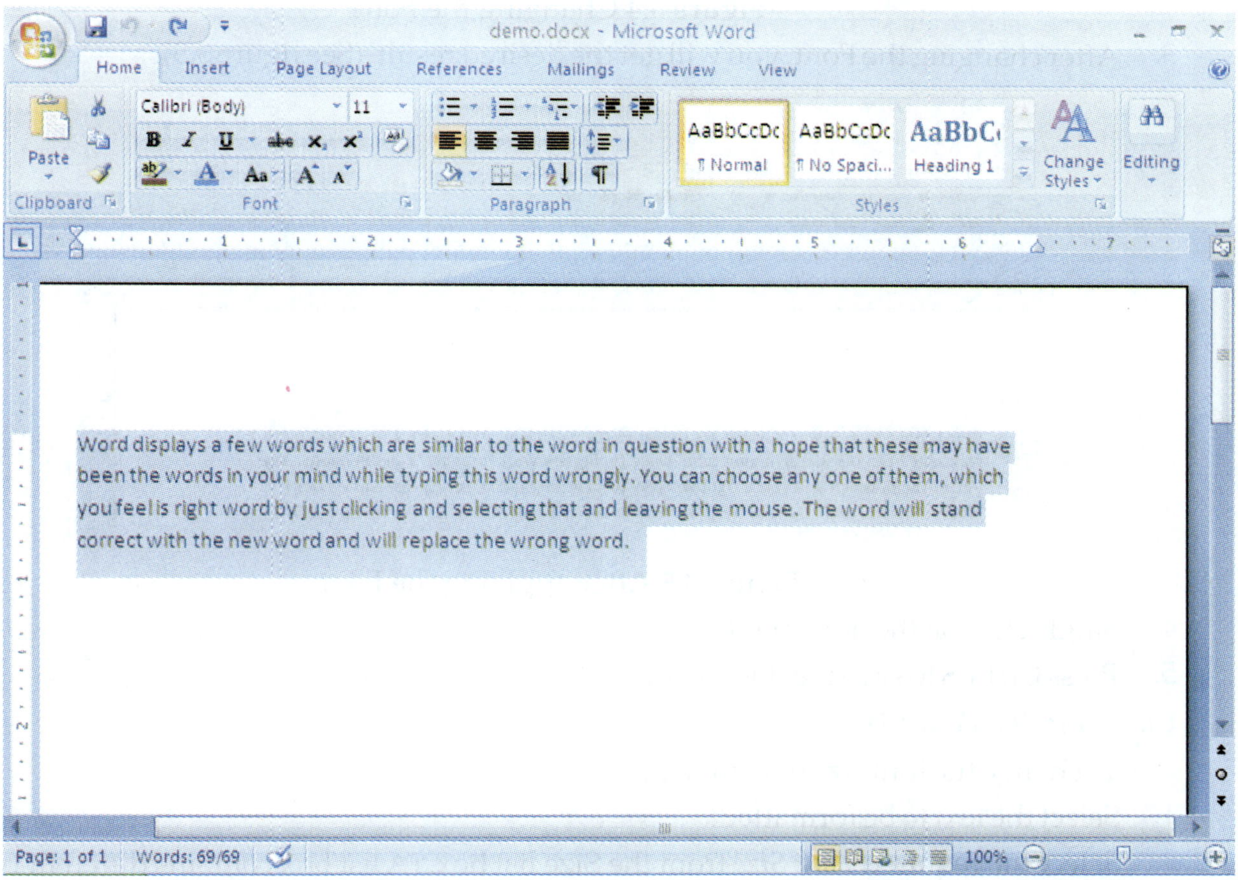

Figure 3.3 Selecting text

2. Select the required font from the *Font list* box (See figure 3.4). Here we select Albertus font.

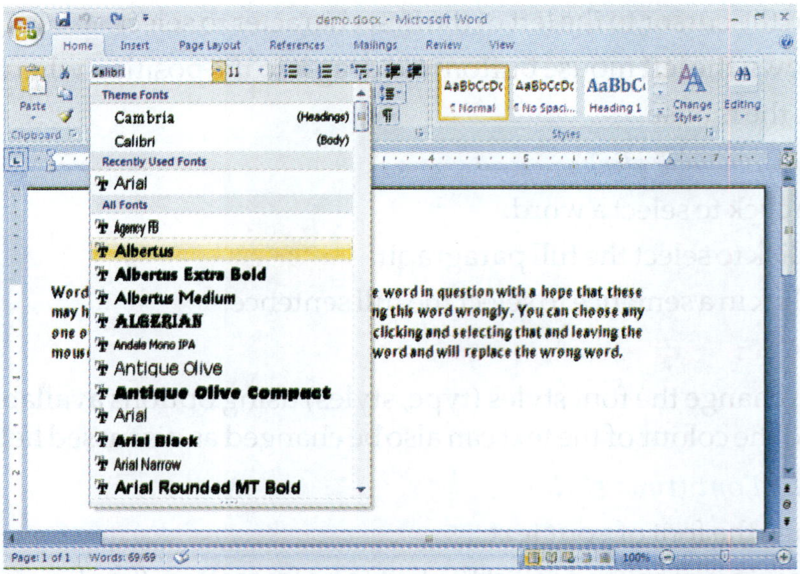

Figure 3.4 Changing the Font

3. After changing the Font, you will get the desired result. (See figure 3.5)

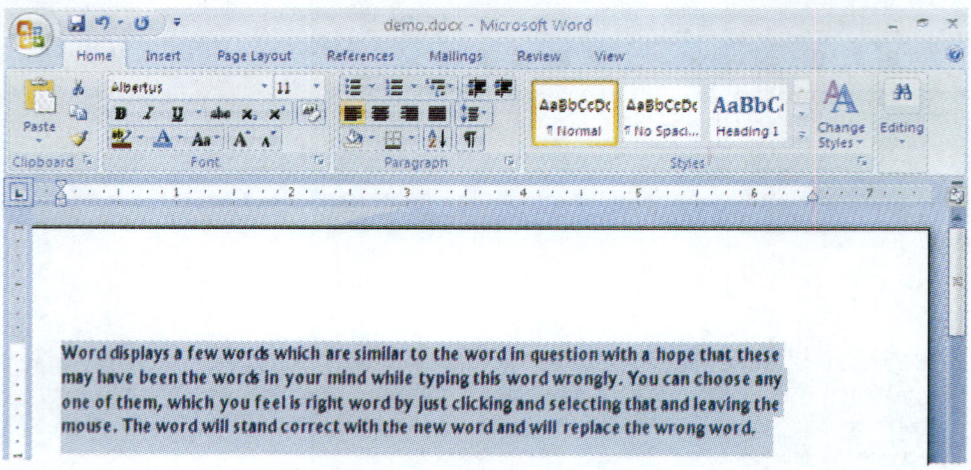

Figure 3.5 After applying the Font

4. Single click on the document.
5. Press Ctrl + S to save the document.

Changing the Font Size

To change the font size of your text,

1. Select the text to be formatted.
2. Select the required *Font Size* from the Size list box. (A list box contains different types of text from which you can select the one of your choice (See figure 3.6). Here we select font size of 16.

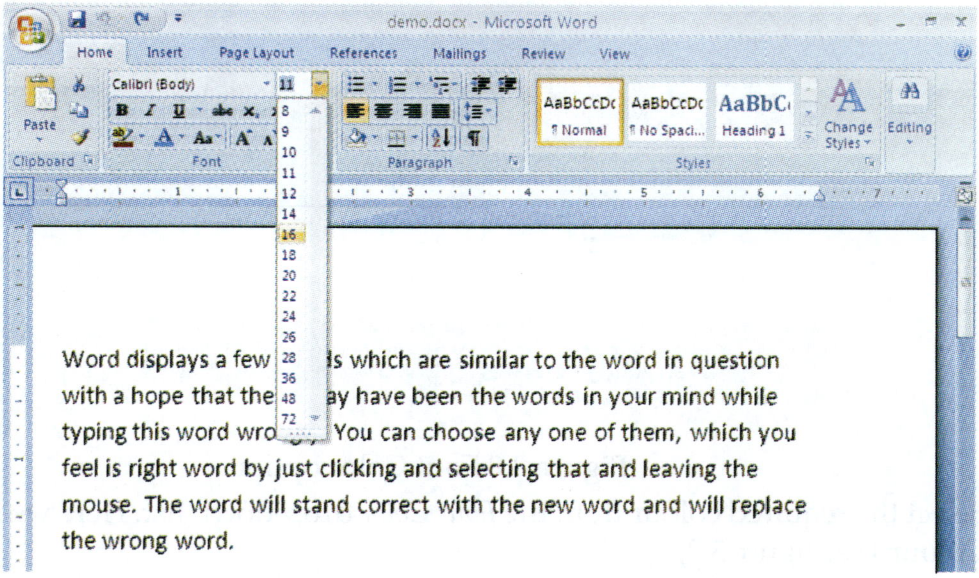

Figure 3.6 Changing the Font Size

3. After changing the font size, you will get the desired result. (See figure 3.7)

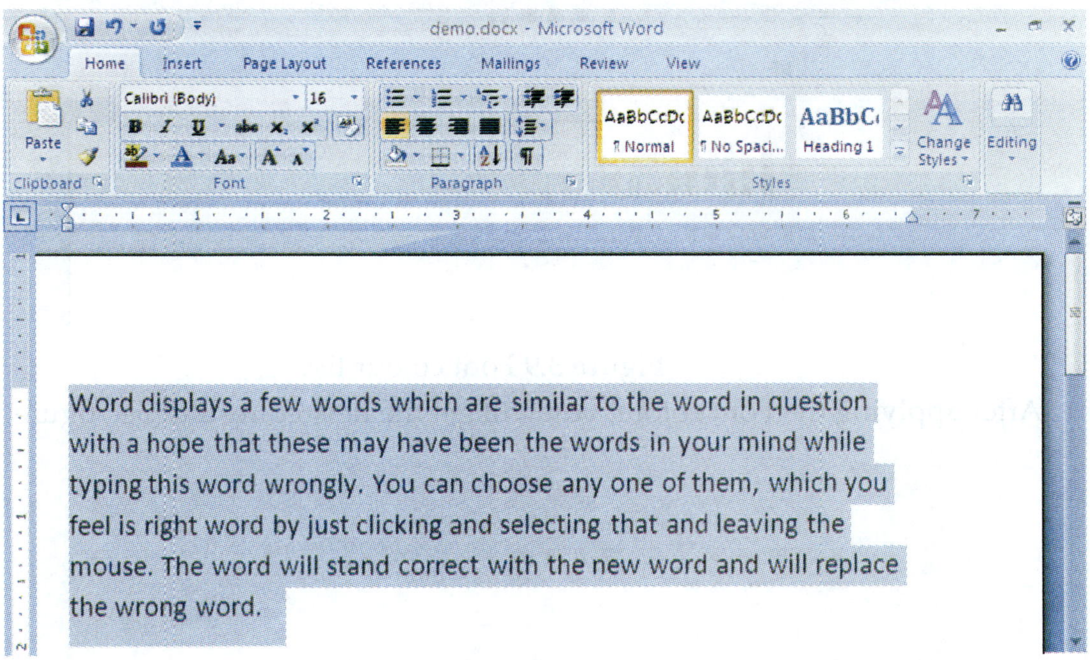

Figure 3.7 After changing the Font Size

4. Single click on the document.
5. Press Ctrl + S to save the document.

Changing the Font Colour

To change the colour of your text,

1. Select the text to be formatted
2. Select the Font Color option from the Font panel. (See figure 3.8)

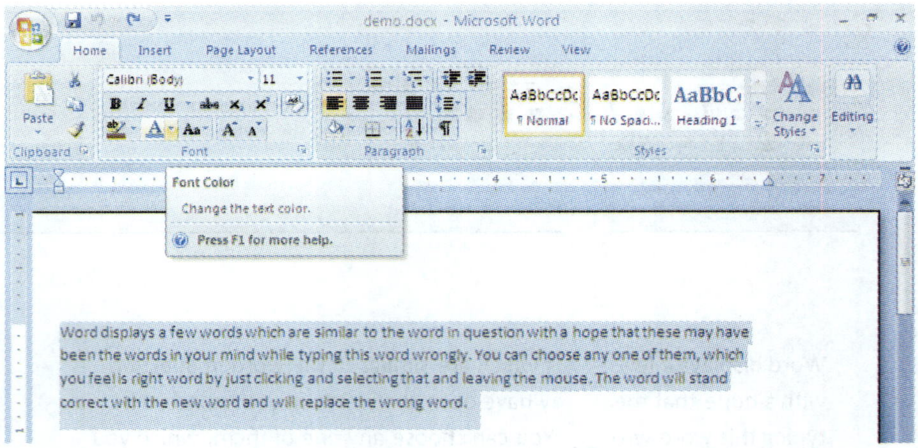

Figure 3.8 Font Color option

3. Select the required colour from the *Font Color* drop-down list. Here we select Orange Colour. (See figure 3.9)

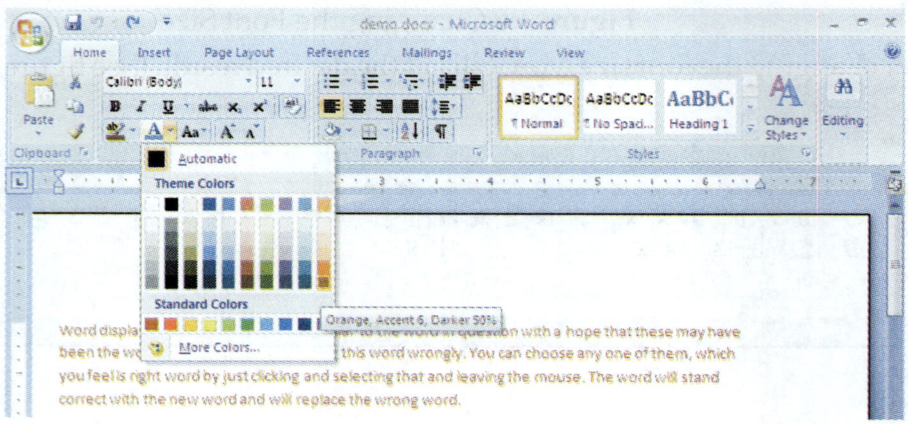

Figure 3.9 Font colour list

4. After applying the Font colour, you will get the desired result. (See figure 3.10)

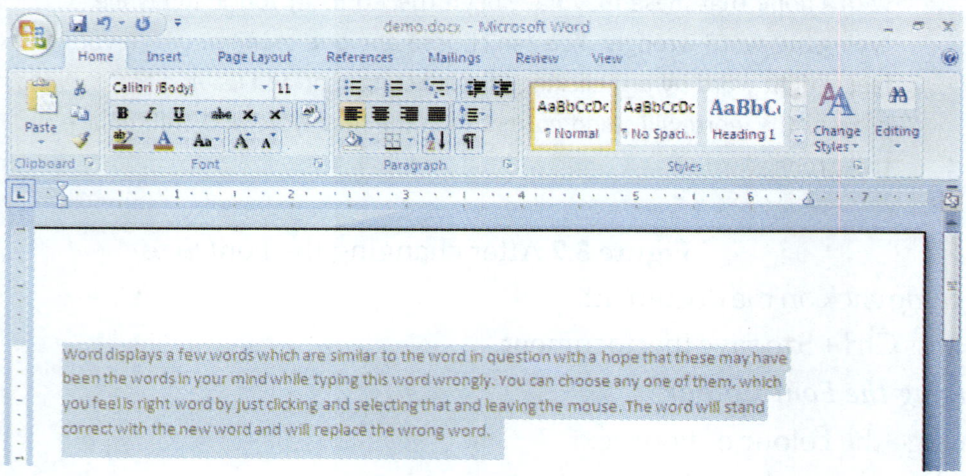

Figure 3.10 After applying Font Colour

5. Single click on the document.
6. Press Ctrl + S to save document.

Alternatively, you can also change the font, its size and colour in the following way:

1. Click the button on Font panel. (See figure 3.11)

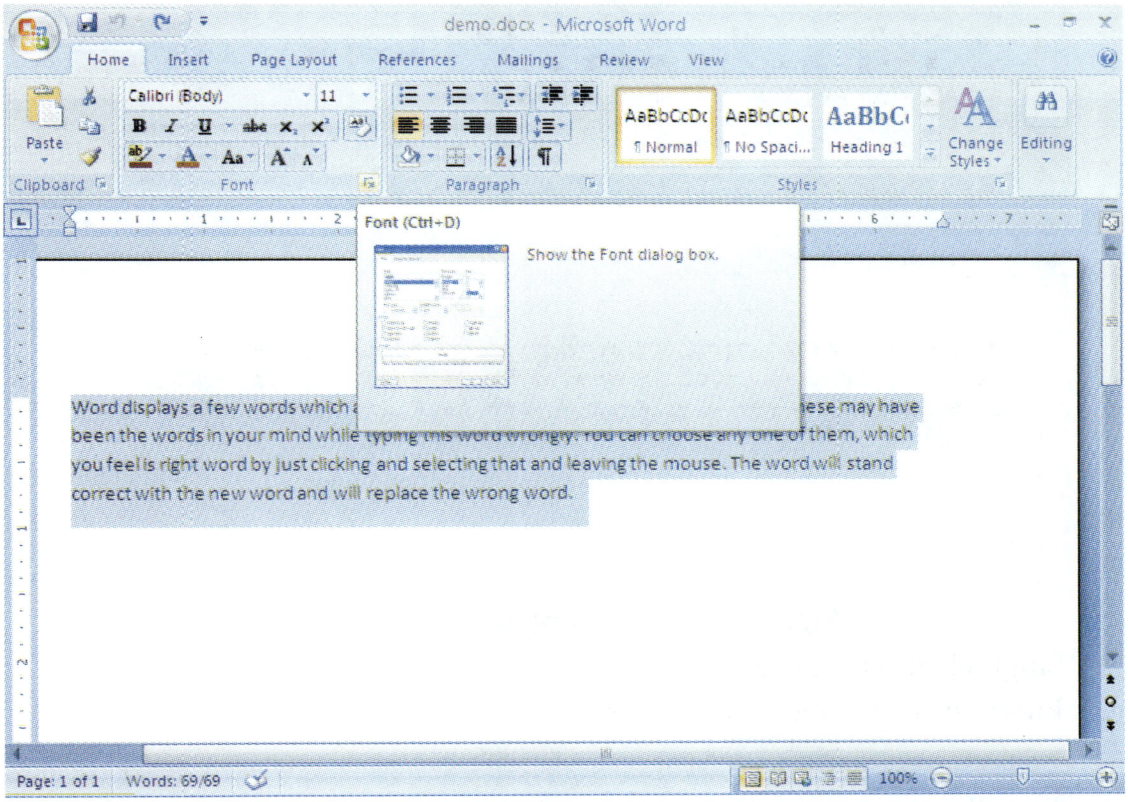

Figure 3.11 Selecting Font

2. Font dialog box is displayed. (See figure 3.12)

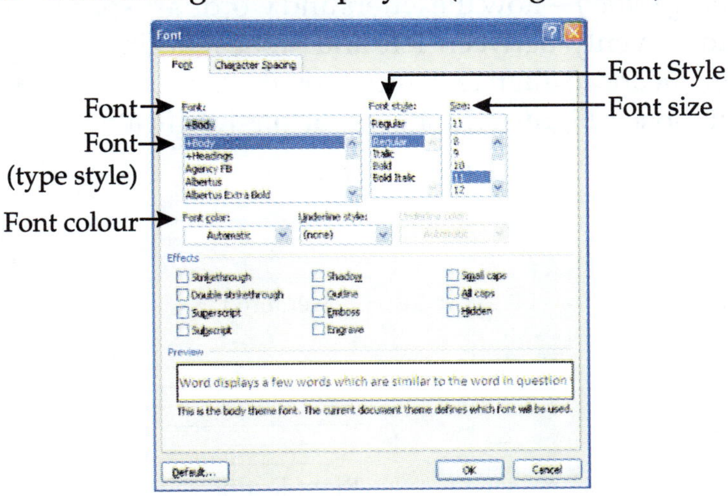

Figure 3.12 Font dialog box

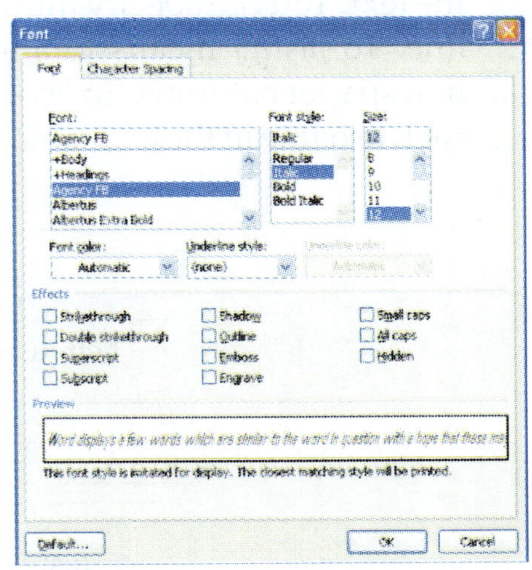

Figure 3.13 Selecting desirable options from Font dialog box

3. In the Font dialog box, select the required font, size and colour from the *Font*, *Size* and *Font color* list box (See figure 3.13). Here we select *Agency FB*, *12* and *Automatic*.
4. After applying the changes we get the desired result. (See figure 3.14)

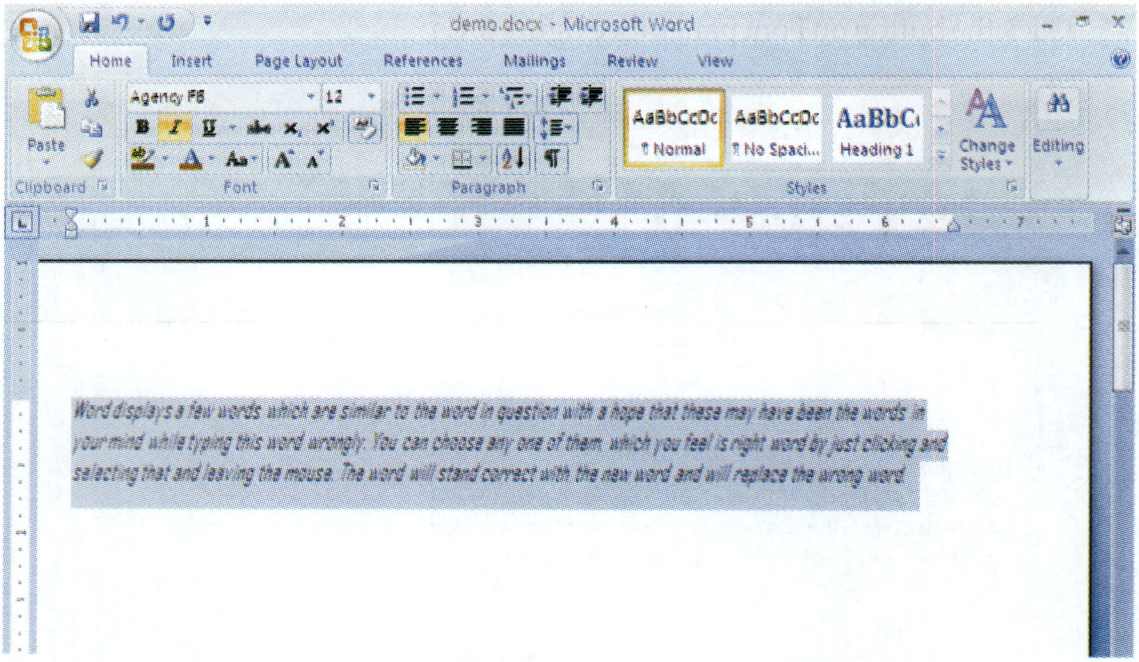

Figure 3.14 After applying various Font options

5. Single click in the document.
6. Press Ctrl + S to save the document.

- **Text Alignment**

  Text alignment means the position of the text according to the margins.

You can indicate the dimensions of the margins—left, right, top and bottom—around the text. You can specify the text *justification*—how the letters and words are spaced in each line. To *justify* means to align text evenly between left and right margins, as in most newspaper columns. To *left-justify* means to align text evenly on the left. *Centering* centres each text line in the available white space. Figure 3.15 shows various justifications:

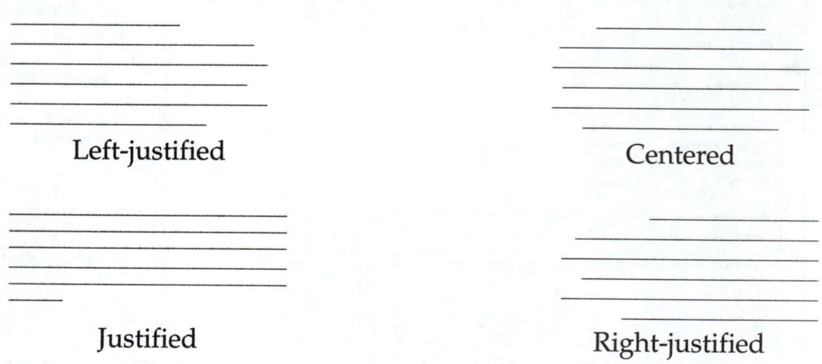

Figure 3.15 Illustration of text justification

Useful Tip

Alignment means whether the text is on the left, middle or right hand side of the page.

The text typed within a document can be aligned (centre/left/right). To understand this, let us type another document as shown in figure 3.16.

(i) **Using the buttons on Paragraph Panel**

1. Select the text to be aligned (In case, there is only one paragraph that is to be aligned, click anywhere within it.)
2. Click on the alignment buttons on the Paragraph panel.

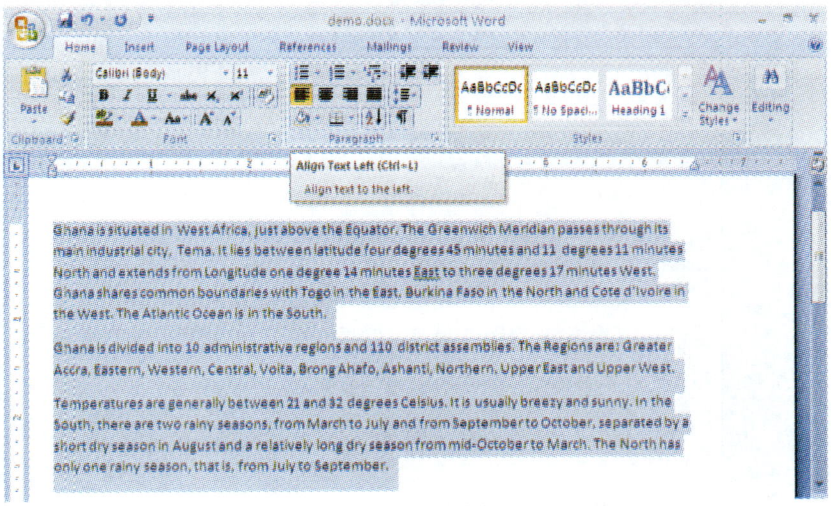

Figure 3.16 The Alignment buttons

3. The selected text alignment changes to the one that is clicked. (See figure 3.17) Here we select Justify alignment.

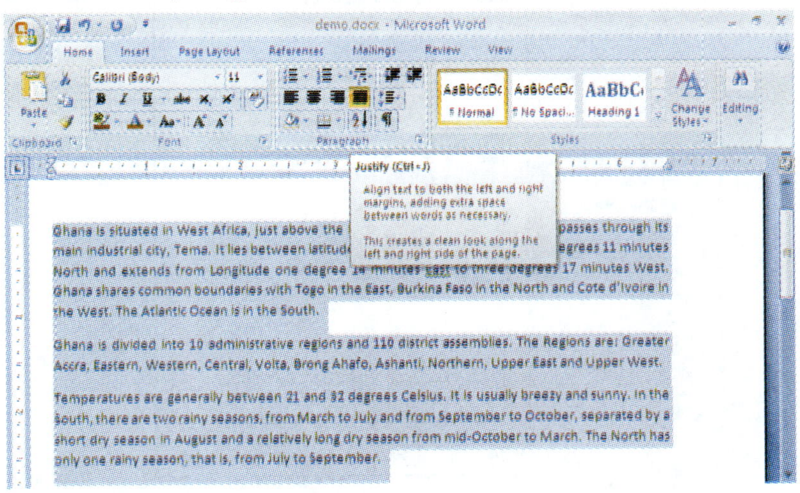

Figure 3.17 Justified text

4. Single click in the document.
5. Press Ctrl + S to save the document.

Note

Word's default alignment is Left alignment.

(ii) **Using Paragraph dialog box**

1. Select the text to be aligned.
2. Click on the button as shown in figure 3.18.

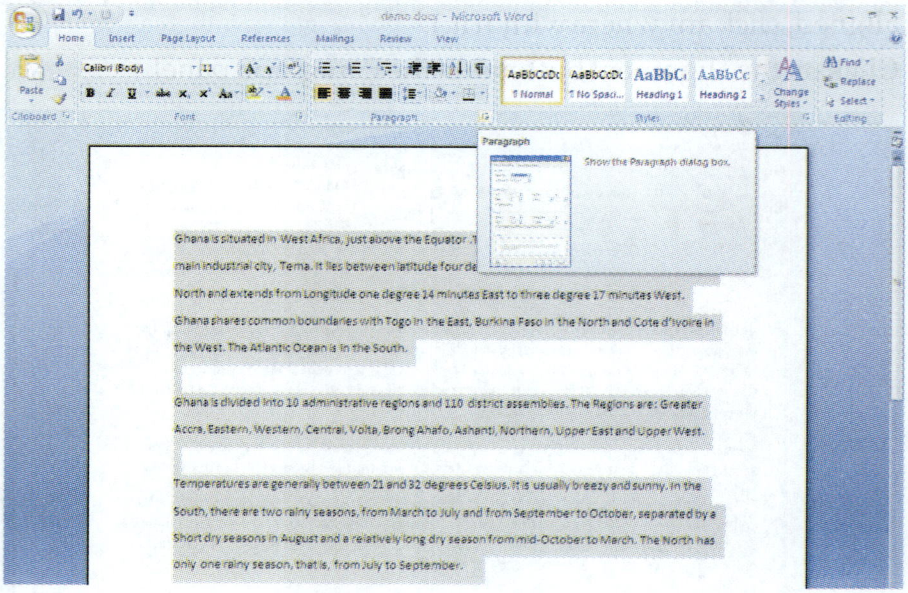

Figure 3.18 Format paragraph option

3. It will display a *Paragraph* dialog box as shown in figure 3.19.

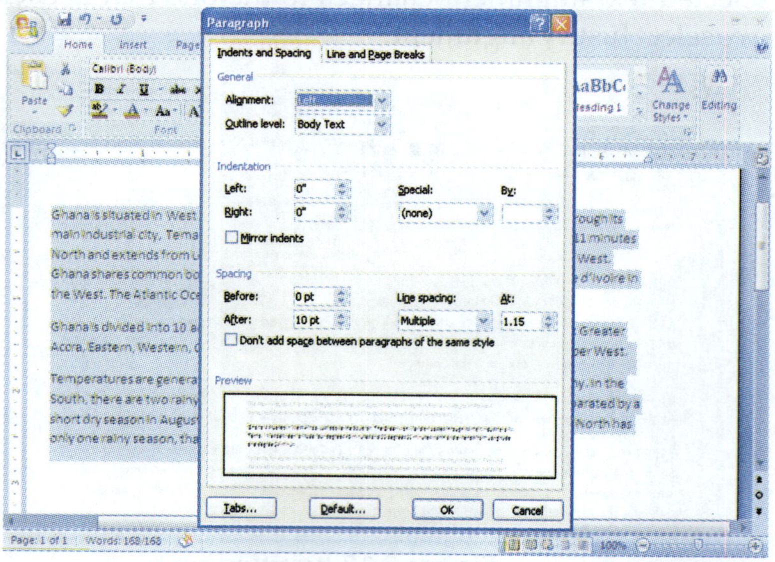

Figure 3.19 Paragraph dialog box

4. From the **'Alignment'** drop-down list, select an option. We have selected Right. (See figure 3.20)

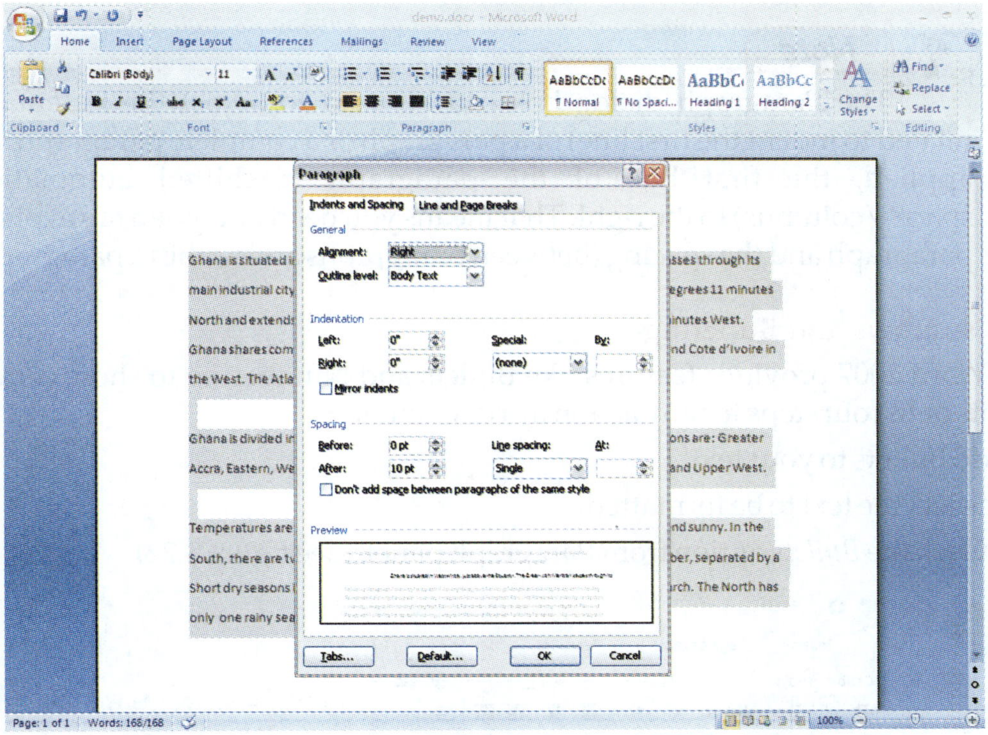

Figure 3.20 Selecting Right Alignment

5. Click on OK button to apply it. The text is aligned accordingly. (See figure 3.21)

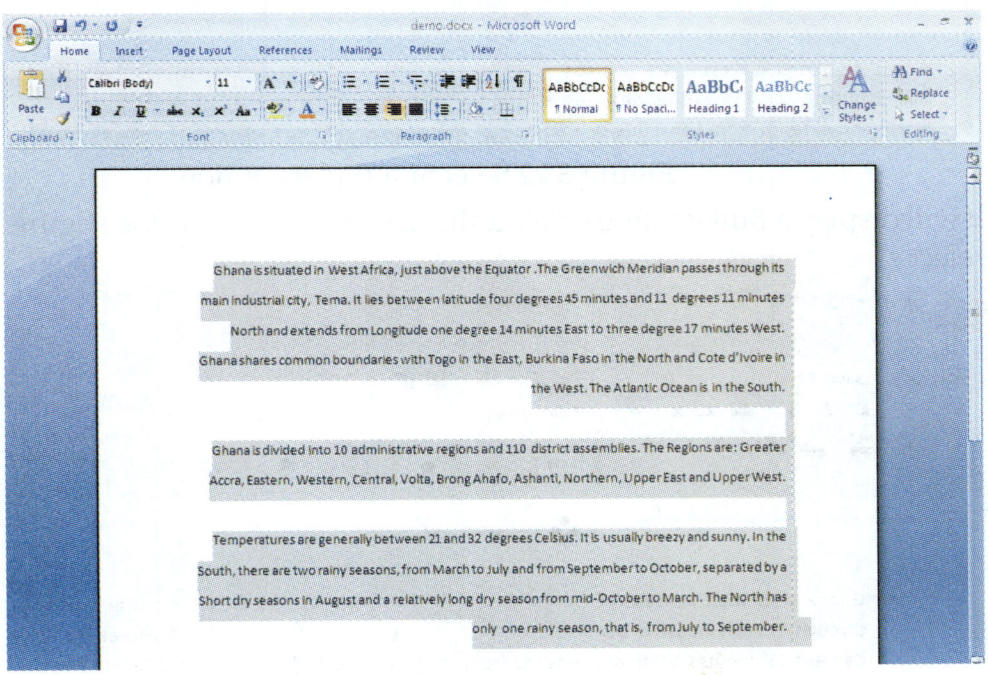

Figure 3.21 Text is Right aligned

6. Single click in the document.
7. Press Ctrl + S to save the document.

Note

The Paragraph dialog box can be used to adjust the indentation (feature related to indent the first line) of a paragraph or a complete paragraph. If indents are applied, the first line of the paragraph is shifted automatically (some spaces/columns) to the right. That means you need not type a tab explicitly to start a paragraph and the spacing (between paragraphs and within a paragraph).

- **Numbers and Bulleting**

Word 2007 provides features like Bullets and Numbering to show certain important points or list out steps for any action in a document.

To add bullets to your text,

1. Select the text to be formatted.
2. Click the *Bullets* option from Paragraph panel. (See figure 3.22)

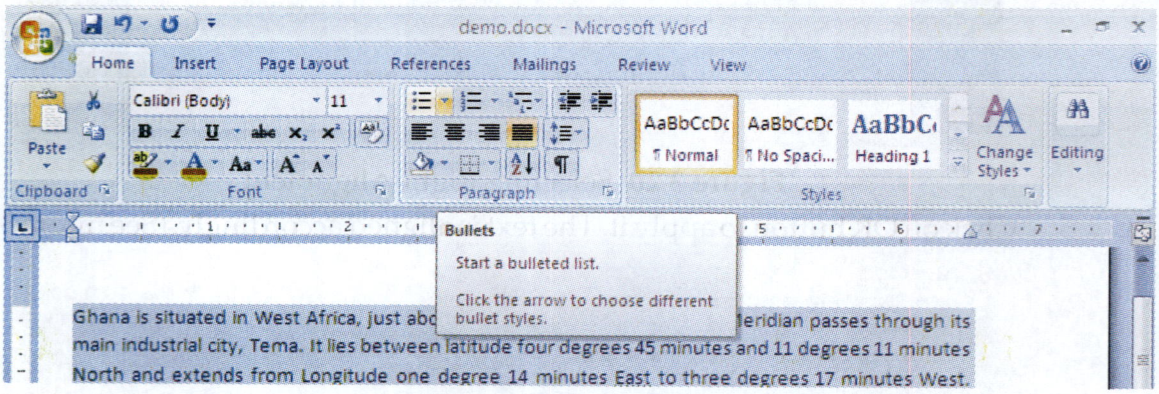

Figure 3.22 Selecting Bullets option

3. It will display a Bullet Library. Select the desired Bullet style (See figure 3.23). Here we select •.

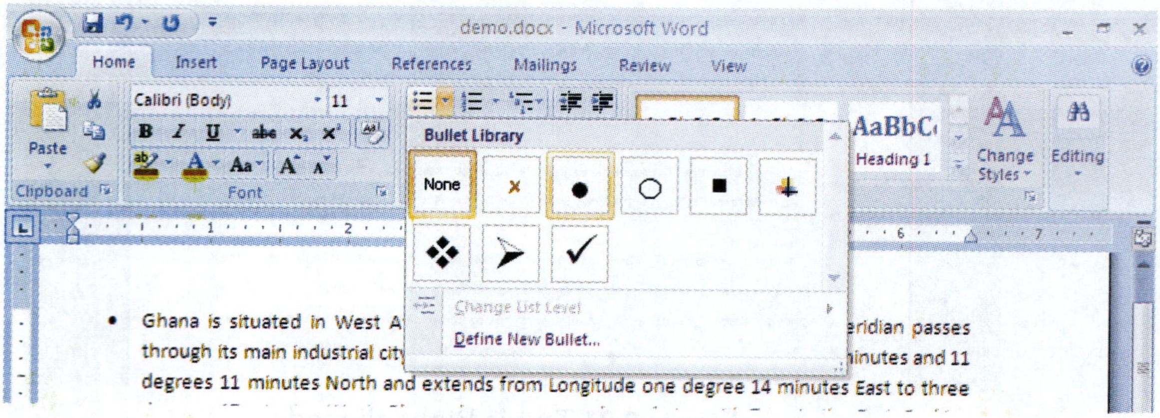

Figure 3.23 Bullet Library

4. After applying the desired bullet style, you get the bulleted text. (See figure 3.24)

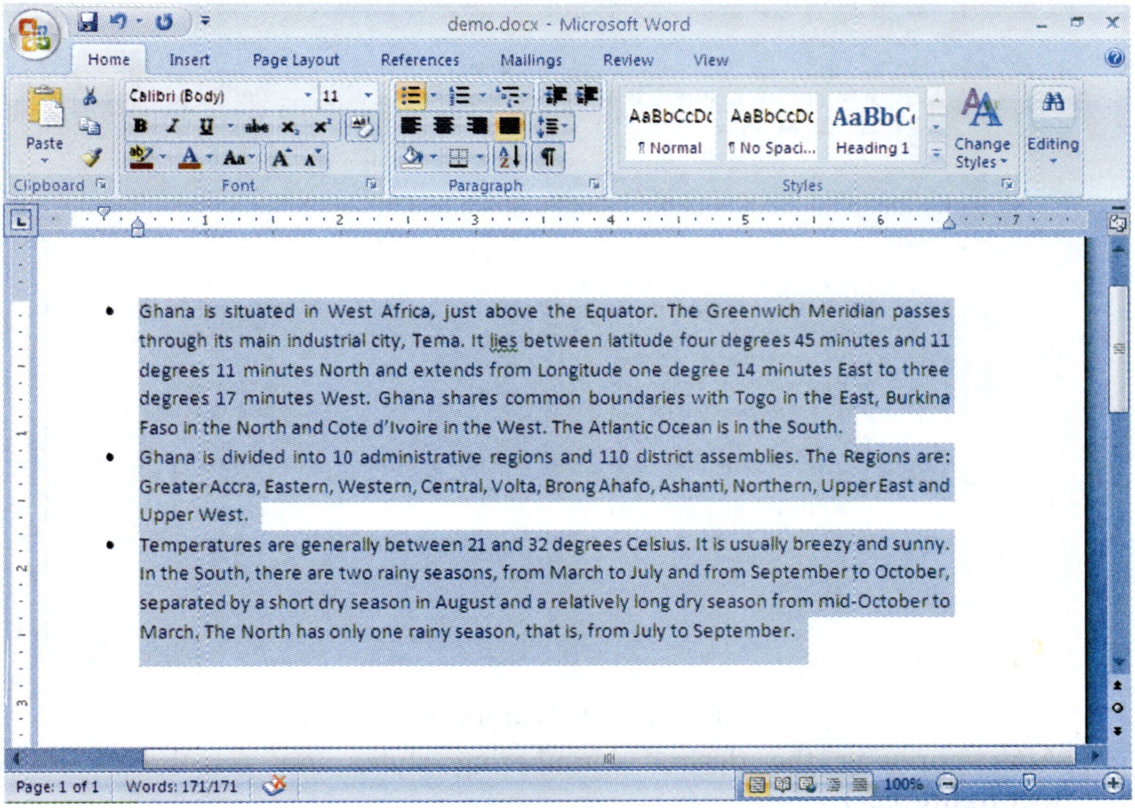

Figure 3.24 After applying Bullets

5. Single click in the document.
6. Press Ctrl + S to save the document.

To add numbers to your text,

1. Select the text to be formatted.
2. Click the Numbering option from Paragraph panel. (See figure 3.25)

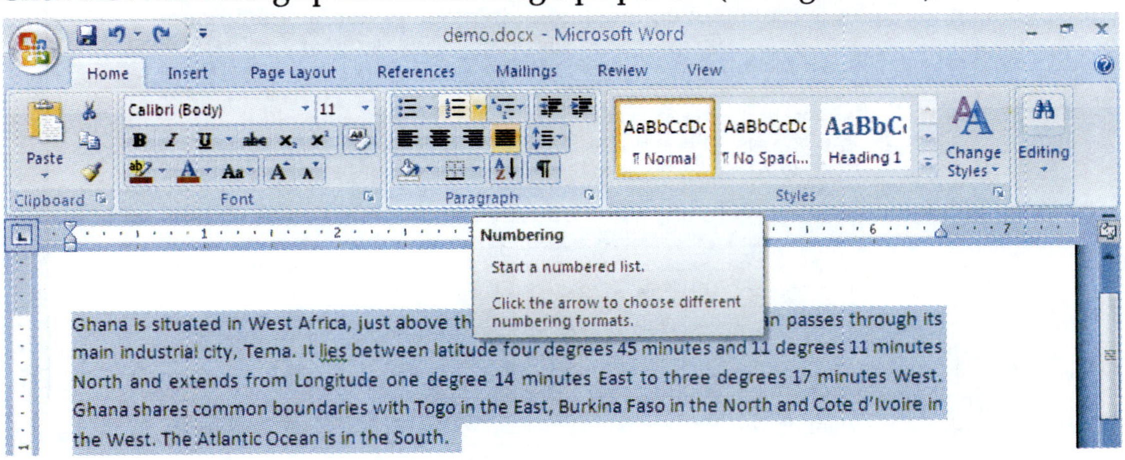

Figure 3.25 Selecting Numbering option

3. It will display a Number Library. Select the desired Numbering style. (See figure 3.26)

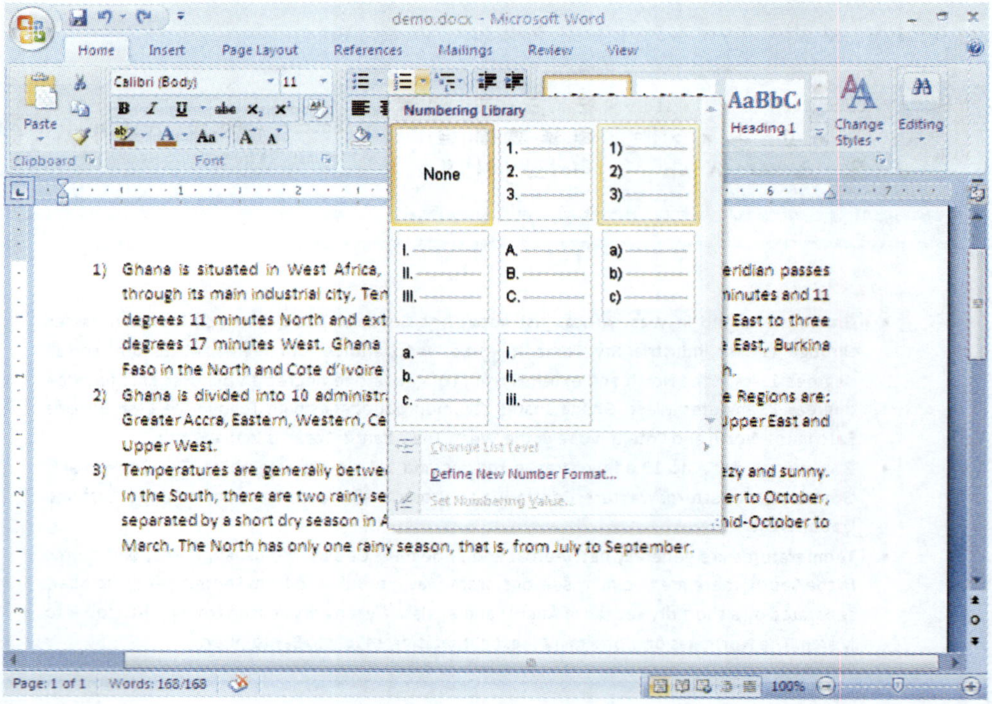

Figure 3.26 Numbering Library

4. After applying the desired Numbering style, you get the Numbered text. (See figure 3.27)

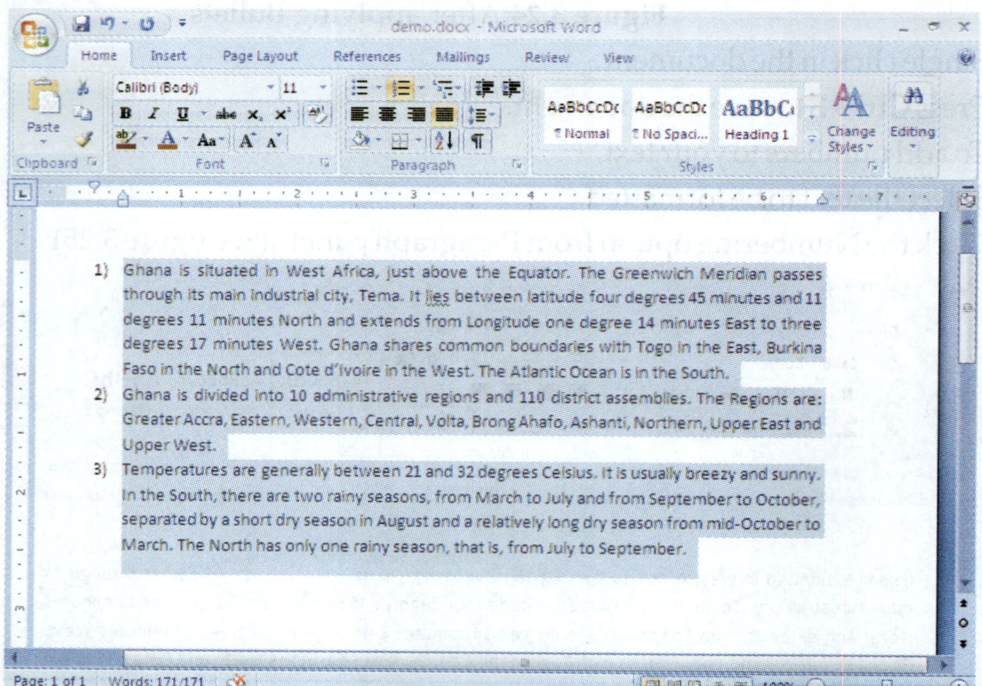

Figure 3.27 After applying Numbering

5. Single click in the document.
6. Press Ctrl + S to save the document.

- **Bold, Underline and Italics**

You can change the font styles to bold, italics and underline from the formatting toolbar by clicking on the respective options.

Table 3.1 gives a description of the options used to change font style.

Table 3.1 The Font Styles

Button Name	Button Face	Sample Output	Shortcut Keys
Bold	**B**	**Font Style**	<Ctrl> + B
Italic	I	*Font Style*	<Ctrl> + I
Underline	U	Font Style	<Ctrl> + U

To change the font style,

1. Select the text to be formatted.
2. Click the required button to change the *Font Style.*

Bold

Click at Bold button **B** from Font panel. (See figure 3.28)

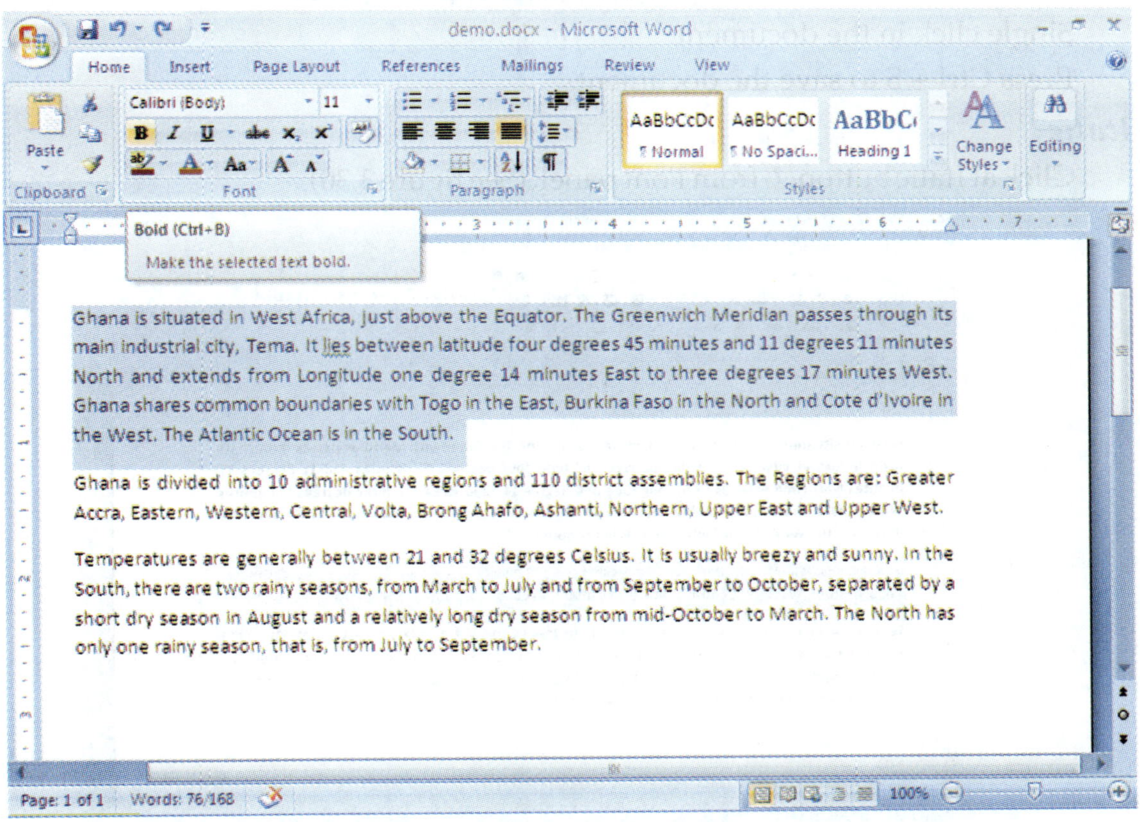

Figure 3.28 Selecting Bold option

After applying the **Bold** option, the selected text changes to bold face. (See figure 3.29)

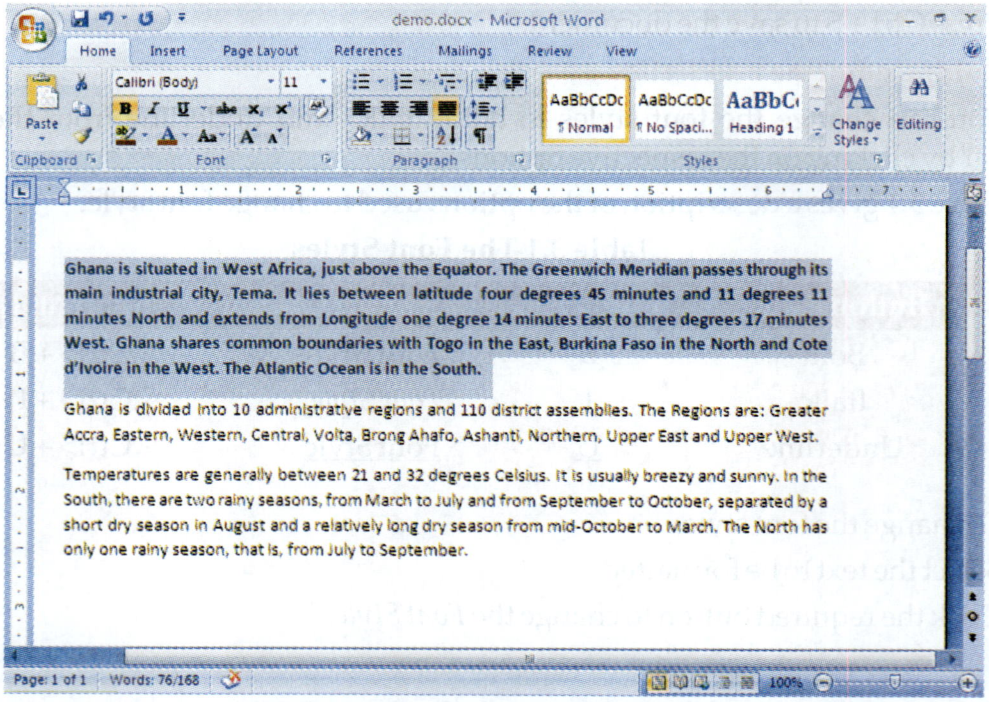

Figure 3.29 After applying Bold

Single click in the document.

Press Ctrl + S to save the document.

Italic

Click at Italic button *I* from Font panel. (See figure 3.30)

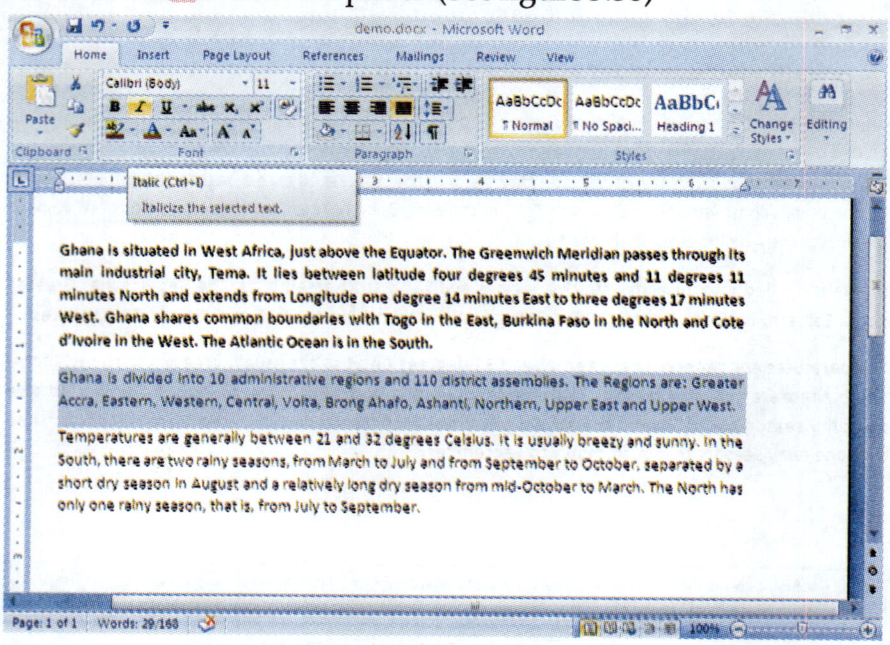

Figure 3.30 Selecting Italic option

After applying the Italic option, the selected text changes to italic. (See figure 3.31)

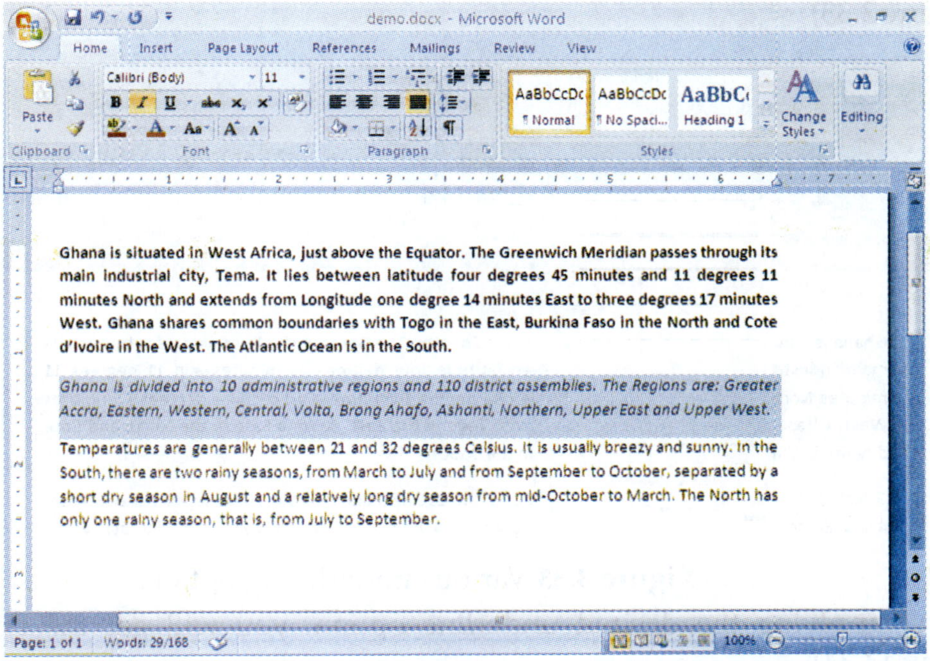

Figure 3.31 After applying Italic

Single click in the document.

Press Ctrl + S to save the document.

Underline

Click at Underline button U from Font panel. (See figure 3.32)

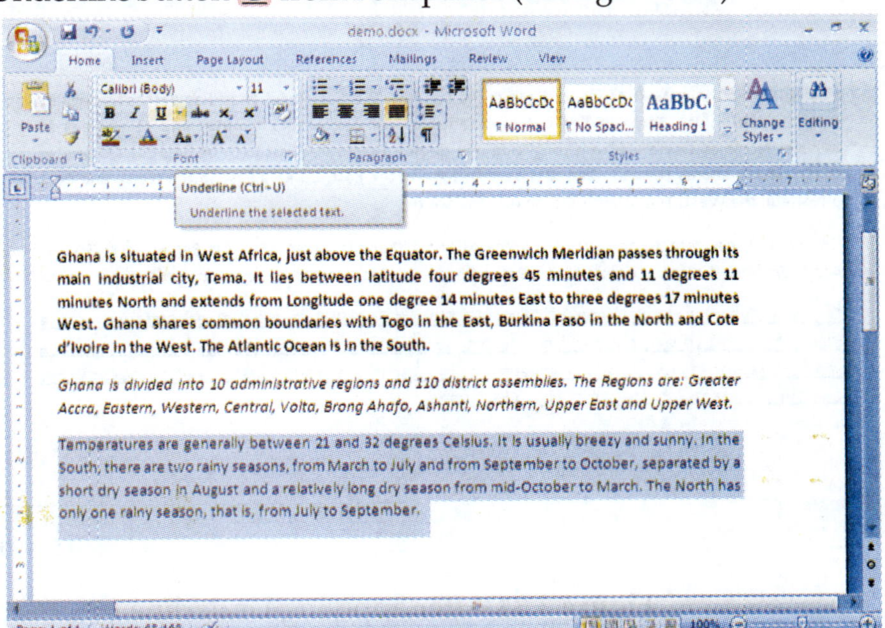

Figure 3.32 Selecting Underline option

A list of various underlining options will be displayed. Select the desired option. (See figure 3.33)

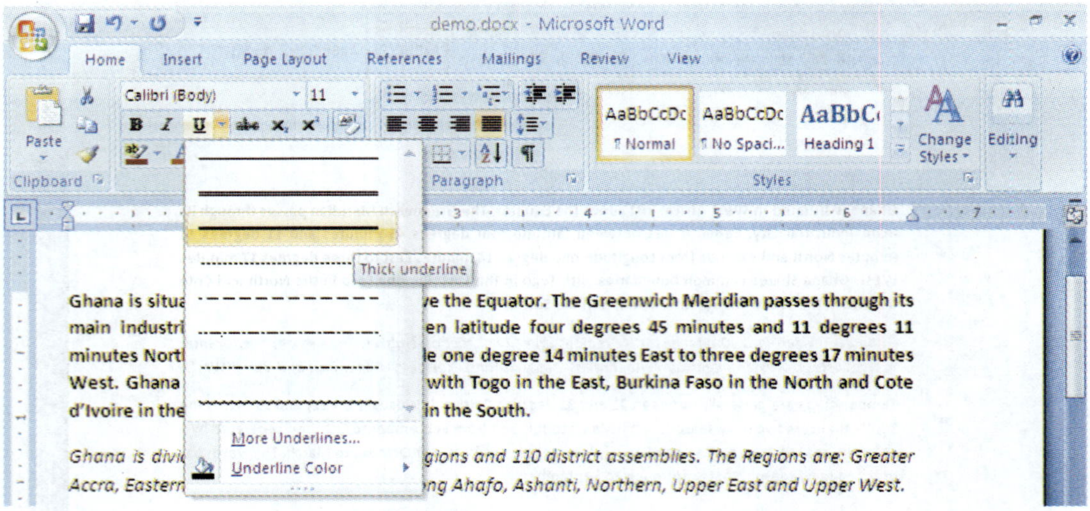

Figure 3.33 Various underlining options

After applying the desired underline option, you will get the underlined text. (See figure 3.34)

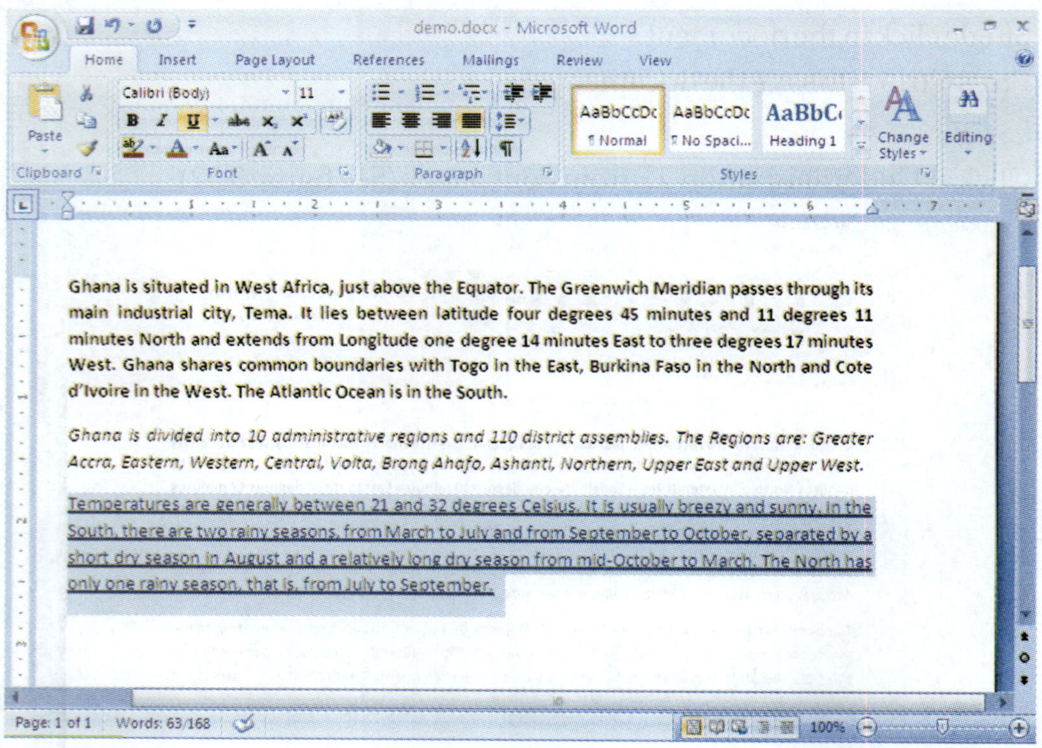

Figure 3.34 After applying Underline

Single click in the document.

Press Ctrl + S to save the document.

Alternatively, you can also change the font style, using the Font dialog box:

1. Select the text to be formatted.
2. Click the button on Font panel as shown in figure 3.35.

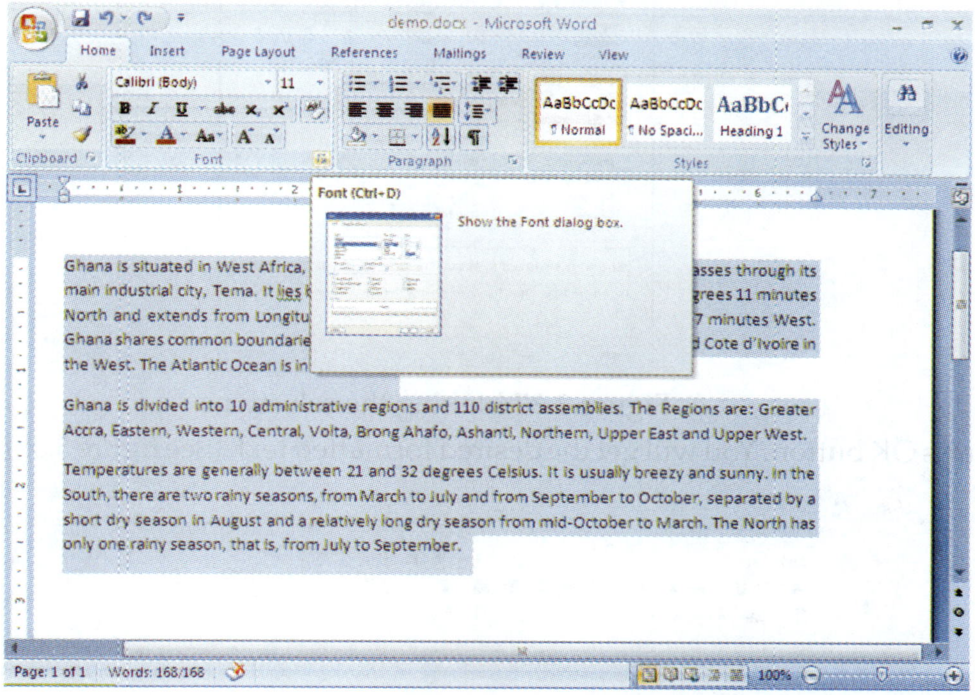

Figure 3.35 Selecting Font

3. A Font dialog box appears. (See figure 3.36)

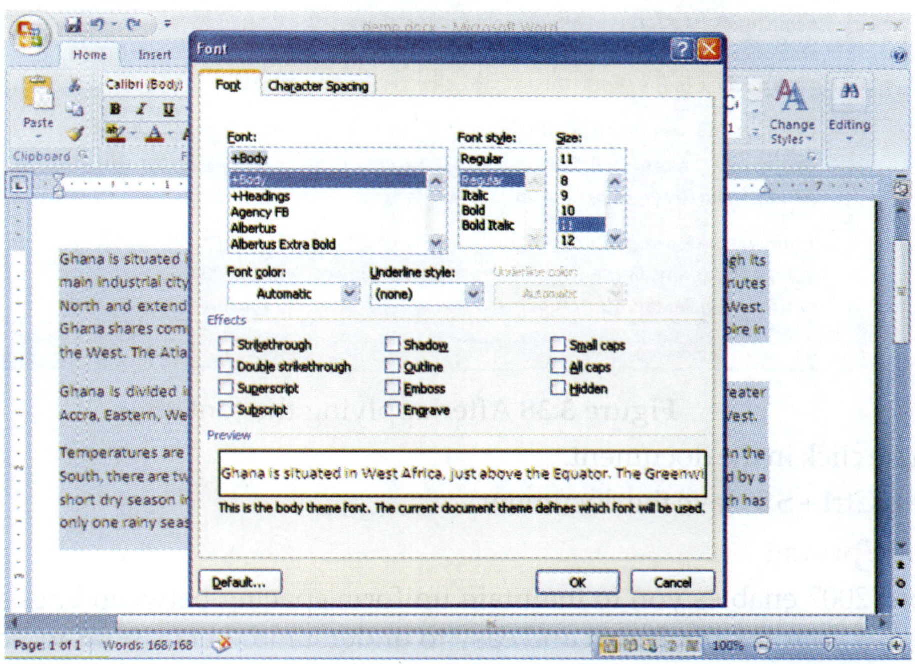

Figure 3.36 Font dialog box

4. Make the desired selections. (See figure 3.37)

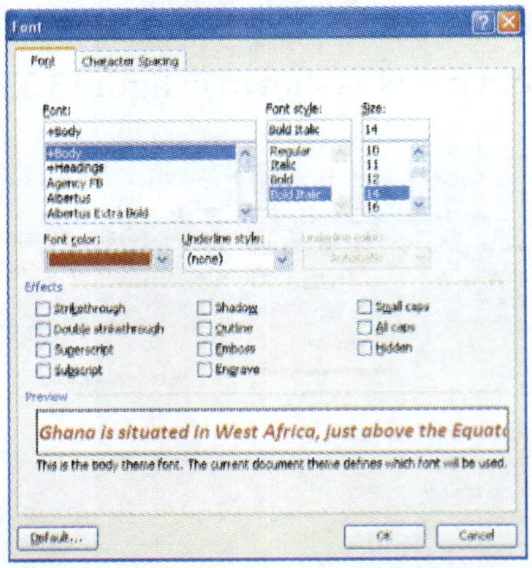

Figure 3.37 Making the selections

5. Press OK button. You will get the desired formatted text. (See figure 3.38)

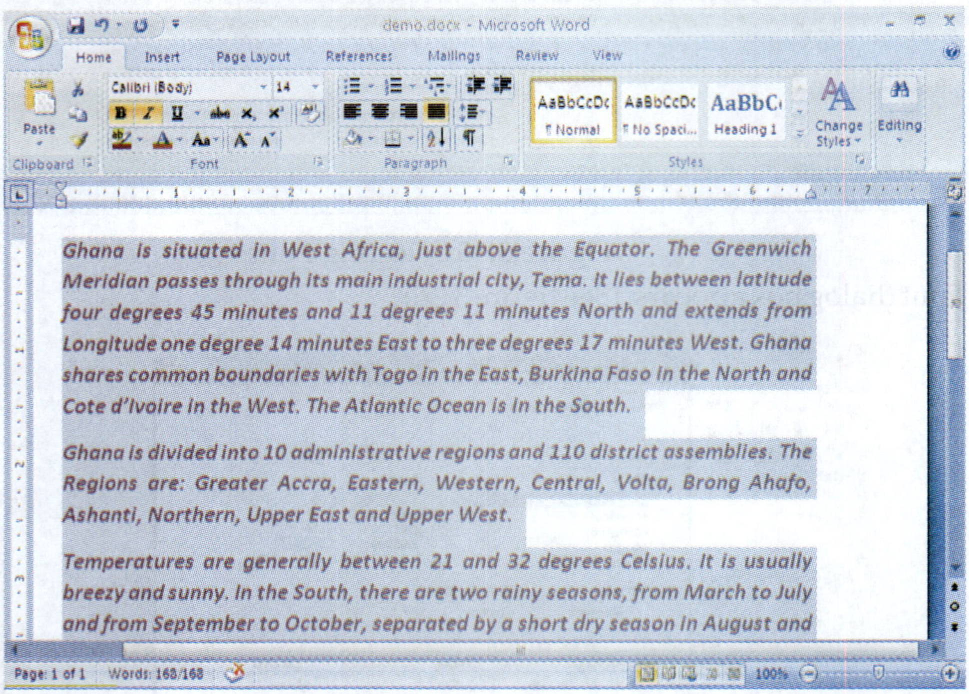

Figure 3.38 After applying the font style

6. Single click in the document.
7. Press Ctrl + S to save the document.

- **Line Spacing**

Word 2007 enables you to maintain uniform spacing between lines and paragraphs. This makes your textbook neat and easy to understand. Let us type another document as shown in figure 3.39.

To specify line spacing,

1. Select the text for line spacing.
2. Click the *Line spacing* button from Paragraph panel. (See figure 3.39)

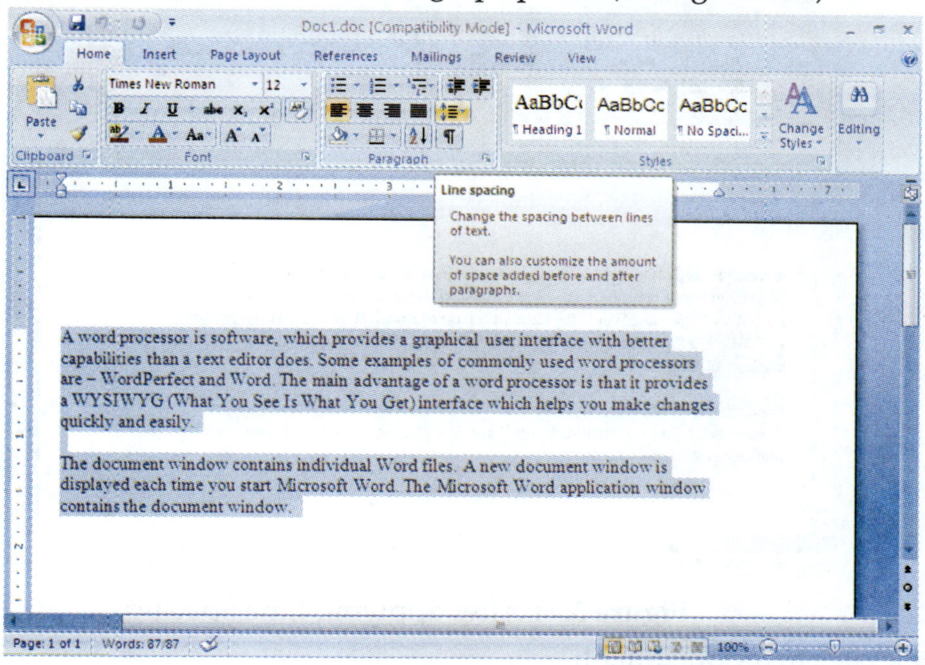

Figure 3.39 Selecting Line Spacing option

3. A list of Line Spacing Options is displayed. Select the desired option (See figure 3.40). Here we select 1.15.

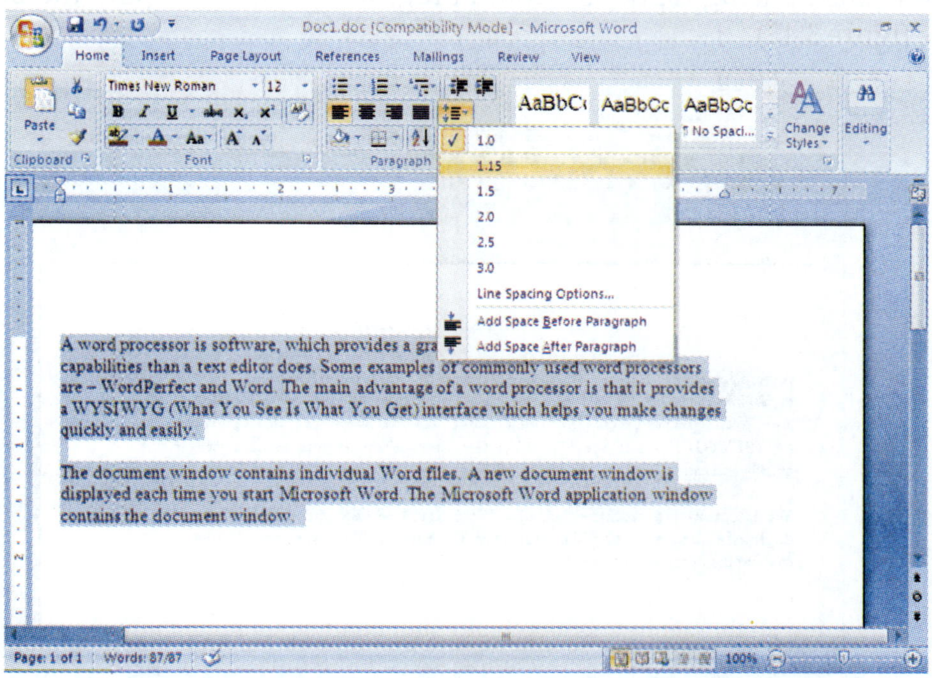

Figure 3.40 Selecting Line Spacing 1.15

4. On applying the desired Line Spacing Option, the line spaced text will be displayed. (See figure 3.41)

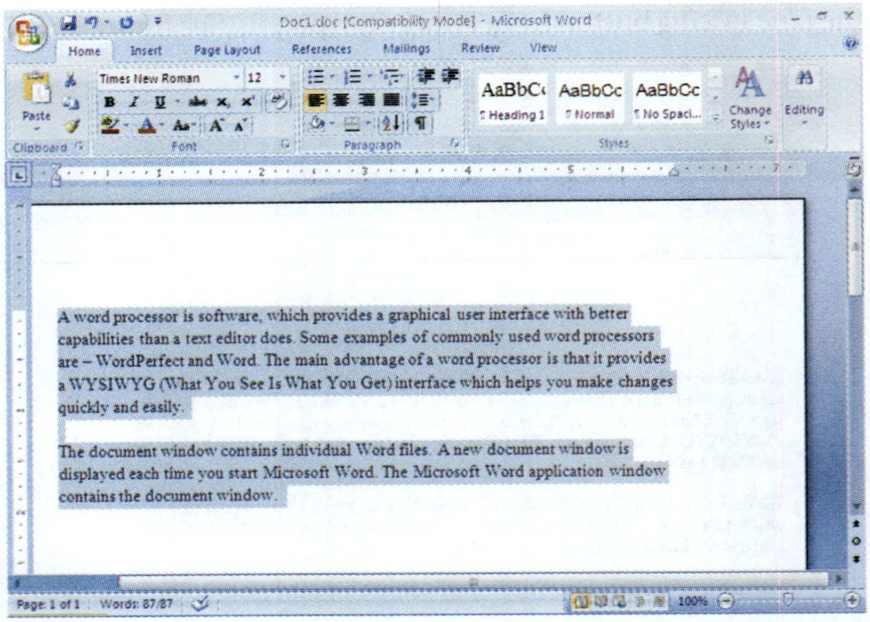

Figure 3.41 After applying Line Spacing

5. Single click in the document.
6. Press Ctrl + S to save the document.

Alternatively, you can also provide line spacing as given below:

1. Open Line Spacing Options from Paragraph panel to display the line spacing list. (See figure 3.42)

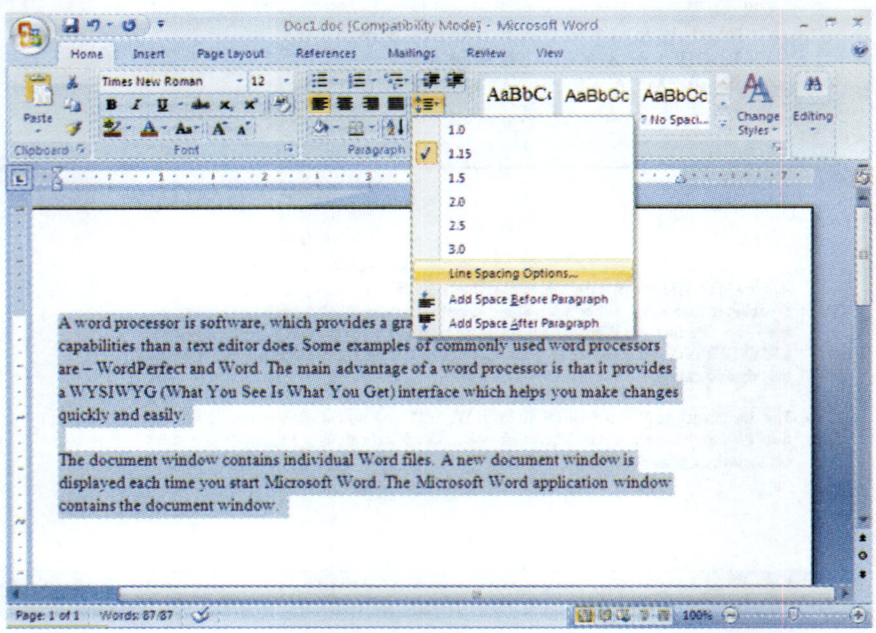

Figure 3.42 Selecting Line Spacing

2. On clicking the Line Spacing Options, you will get the Paragraph dialog Box. (See figure 3.43)

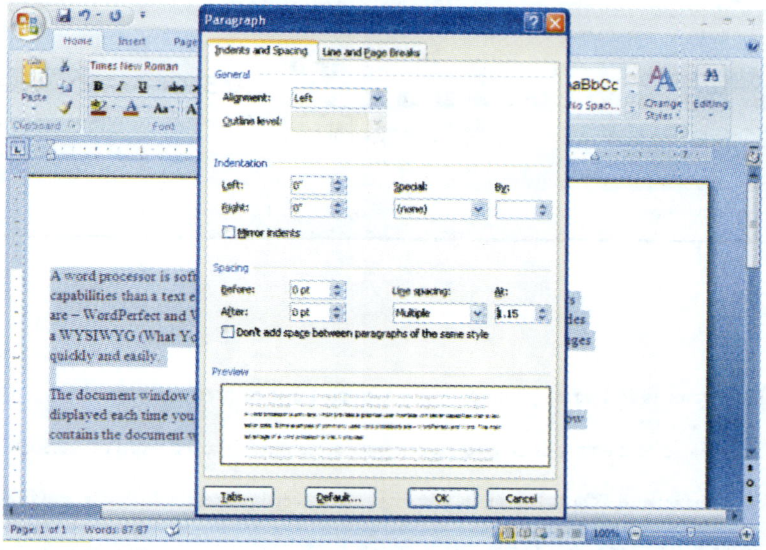

Figure 3.43 Paragraph dialog box

3. Choose the desired line spacing option from the Line spacing list (See figure 3.44). Here we select Double.

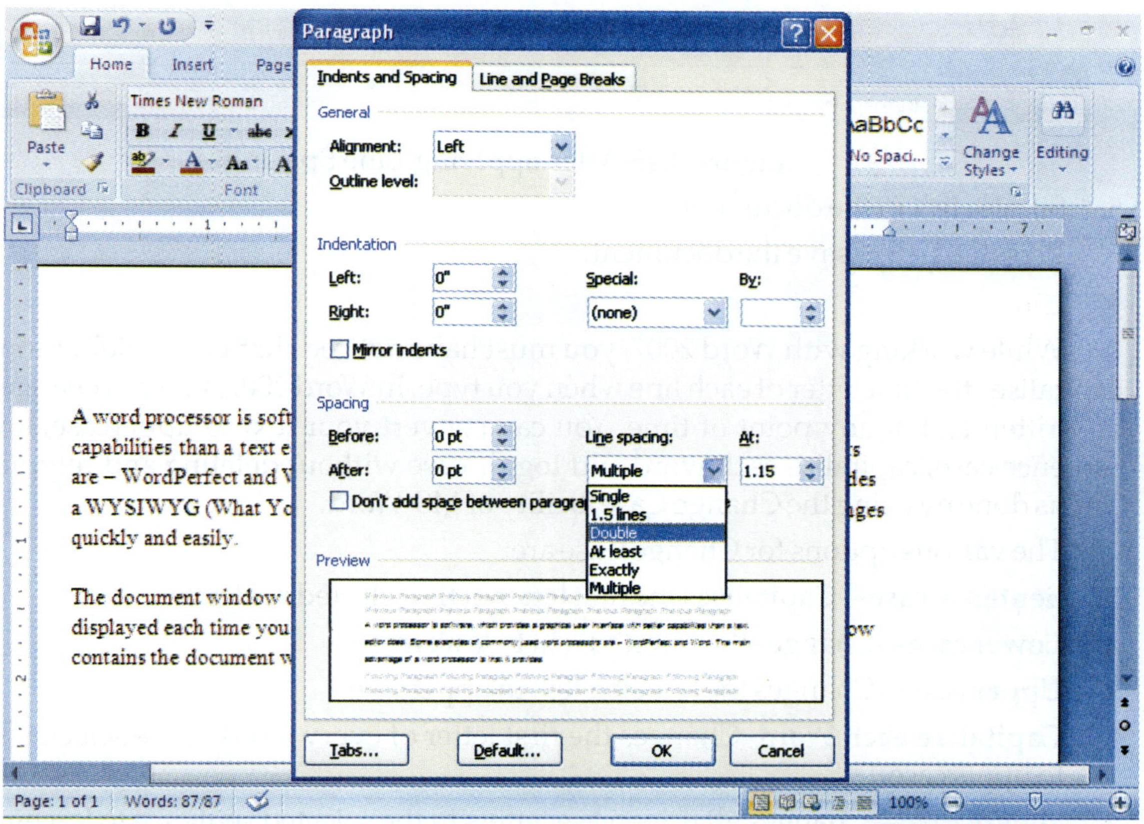

Figure 3.44 Choosing the line spacing from Line Spacing list

4. On applying it, the line spaced text will be displayed. (See figure 3.45)

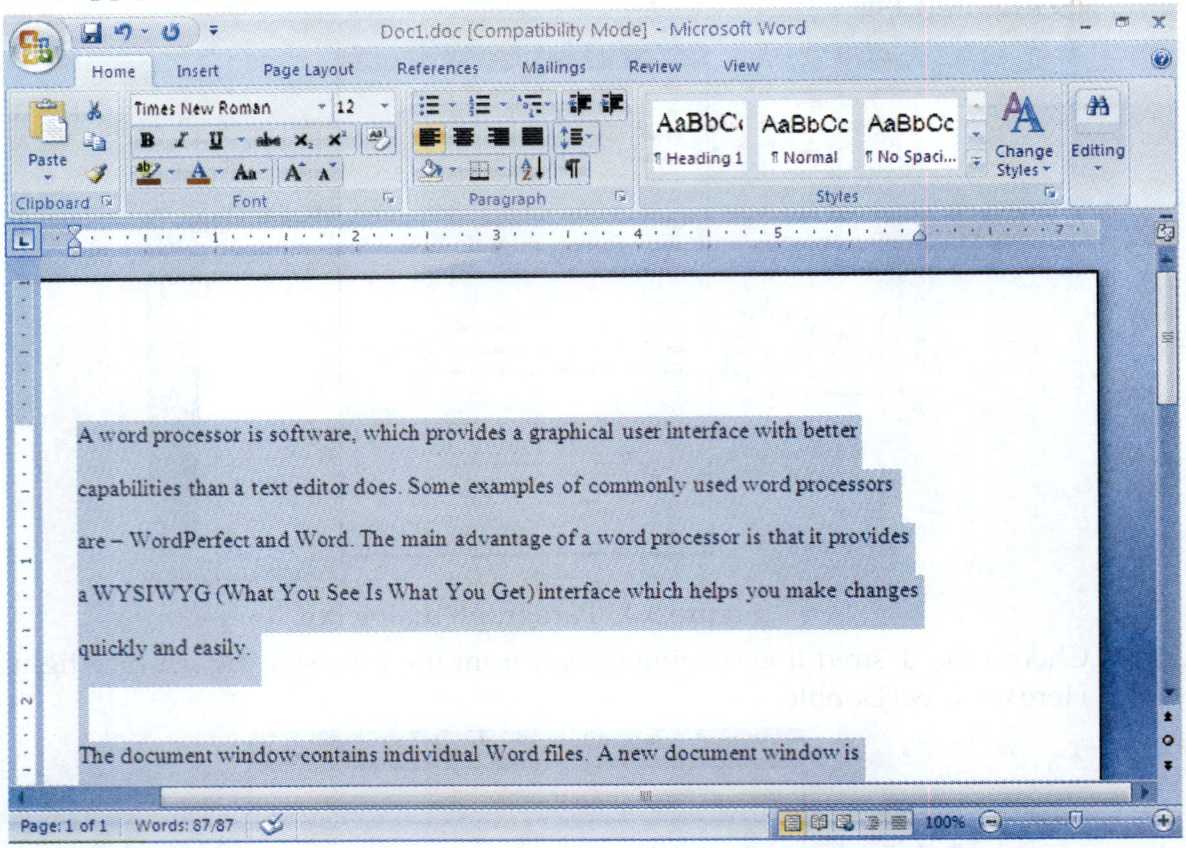

Figure 3.45 After applying Line Spacing

5. Single click in the document.
6. Press Ctrl + S to save the document.

- **Change Case**

While working with Word 2007, you must have noticed that Word 2007 automatically capitalises the first letter of each line when you type. In Word 2007, you can change the case of written text at any point of time. You can convert your text to uppercase, lowercase, sentence case, capitalise each word and toggle case without deleting and retyping them. This is done by using the Change Case facility of MS-Word.

The various options for Change Case are:

1. **Sentence case**—Capitalises the first letter of the selected sentence.
2. **Lower case**—Changes the selected text to lowercase.
3. **Upper case**—Changes the selected text to uppercase
4. **Capitalize each Word**–Changes the first letter of every word in the selected sentence to uppercase.
5. **Toggle case**—Changes all uppercase letters in the selected sentence to lowercase, and all lowercase letters to uppercase.

Useful Tip

You can change the case of typed text without retyping it. This is done by using Change Case utility.

To change the case of text,

1. Select the text to be formatted.
2. Click on the *Change Case* option from Font panel. (See figure 3.46)

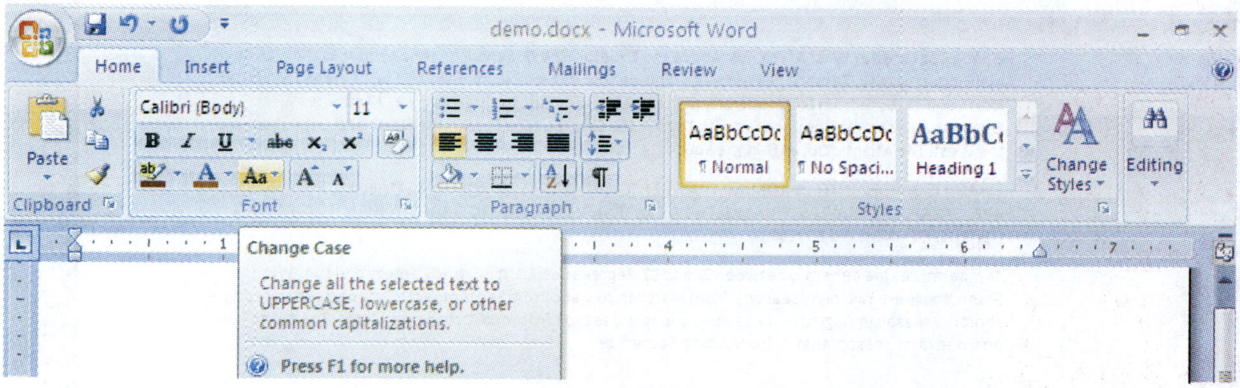

Figure 3.46 Change case option

3. On clicking, a list of various options will be displayed. Select the desired option (See figure 3.47). Here we Select UPPERCASE.

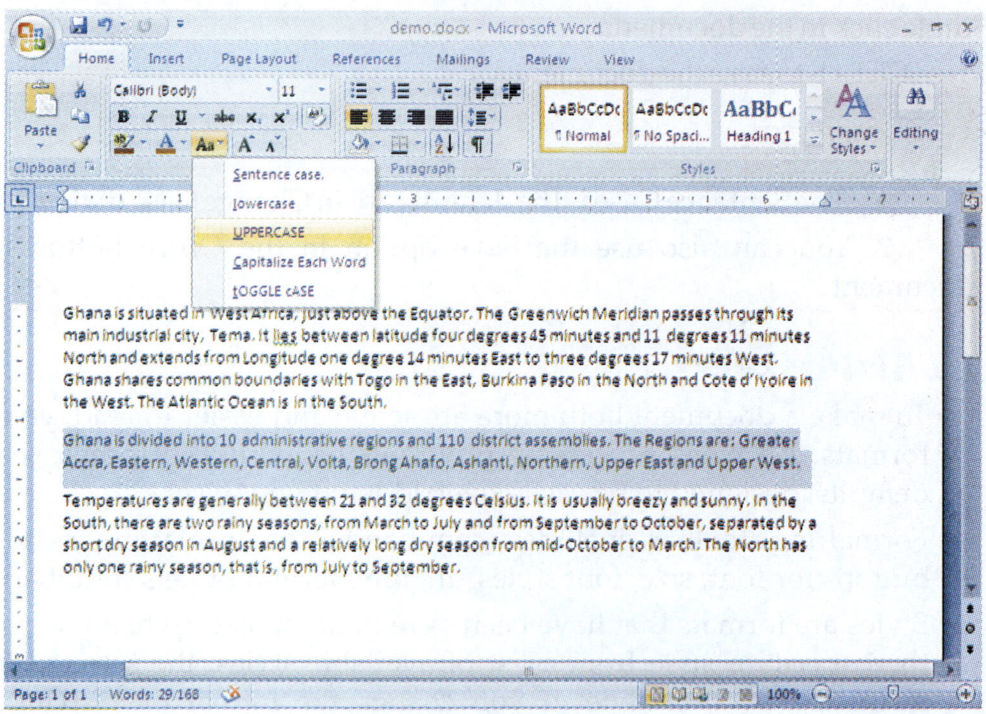

Figure 3.47 Selecting UPPERCASE

4. On applying the selected Change Case option, the selected text changes accordingly. (See figure 3.48)

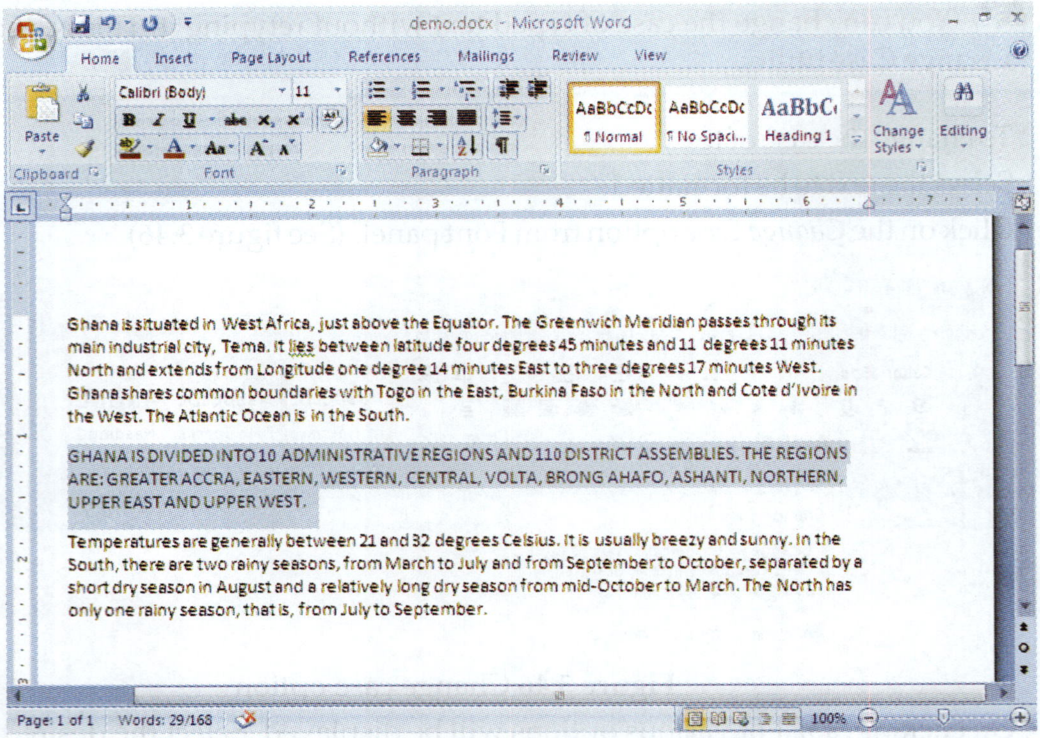

Figure 3.48 After applying UPPERCASE

5. Single click in the document.
6. Press Ctrl + S to save the document.

Note

1. The Sentence Case is the default case in Change Case dialog box.

2. You can also use the Save option in the Office button to save your document.

SUMMARY

- To make a document both more attractive and easier to read, you use various formats. All word processing programs have built-in format settings, called defaults, designed to be easily overridden if you wish.
- Formatting toolbar includes commands for formatting text. It includes buttons for font, size, font styles, alignments and bullets/numbering etc.
- Styles are formats that have been saved and named. When you select text and then specify a style from a list of available styles, the selected text becomes formatted by that style. If you change the format of a style, all elements formatted with that style will automatically reflect the change.

- MS Word works on the principle of "FIRST SELECTION THAN ACTION."
- We can select the text either from keyboard or mouse.
- Alignment means whether the text is on the left, middle or right hand side of the page.
- MS Word provides features like Bullets and Numbering to show certain important points or list out steps for any action in a document.
- You can change the font styles to bold, italics and underline from the formatting toolbar by clicking on the respective options.
- MS Word enables you to maintain uniform spacing between lines and paragraphs. This makes your text look neat and easy to understand.
- Change Case utility can change the case of typed text.
- After formatting you can save a Word document using formatting tools.

REVIEW QUESTIONS

STATE WHETHER TRUE OR FALSE

1. Formatting means changing the appearance of text.
2. You cannot change the font styles using the options available in Font panel.
3. Alignment means positioning of the text according to the margins.
4. The *Ctrl* + *R* aligns text to the left.
5. Bullets and numbering option is used to change the font size.
6. The Font options in Font dialog box can also be used to change the font characteristics of text in a document.
7. The Lines and Spacing option enables you to maintain uniform spacing between lines.
8. Different types of line spacing are not available in MS Word.
9. Word's default alignment is right alignment.
10. You can change the font styles to bold, italics and underline from the Font panel by clicking on the respective options.

FILL IN THE BLANKS

1. .... means changing the text appearance by modifying the alignment, style, font and font colour.
2. .... and .... shortcut keys are used to make the font style Italic.
3. The .... button aligns the text to the left and right margins.
4. MS Word enables you to present the information in the form of a list or points by using ....

5. The .... option enables you to maintain uniform spacing between lines.
6. The..................... option in Change Case changes the selected text to lowercase.
7. The .... option is used to change font size.
8. Text in a document can be left aligned, right aligned, ... aligned or justified.
9. Words default alignment is ....
10. You can also change the font styles to bold, italics and .... from the formatting toolbar by clicking on the respective options.

MULTIPLE CHOICE QUESTIONS

1. When you format a document, you ....
   (*a*) edit its content (*b*) add new material
   (*c*) change its appearance (*d*) None of these
2. The alignment buttons are present on the ....
   (*a*) paragraph panel (*b*) font panel
   (*c*) style panel (*d*) bear bar
3. Which of the following options changes the first letter of every word in the selected sentence to uppercase?
   (*a*) Capitalize each word (*b*) Lowercase
   (*c*) Uppercase (*d*) Autocorrect
4. A .... refers to the appearance and patterns applied to the characters in a document.
   (*a*) font (*b*) folder
   (*c*) language (*d*) editing
5. Which of the following is / are font styles?
   (*a*) Bold (*b*) Italics
   (*c*) Underline (*d*) All of these

ANSWER THE FOLLOWING

1. What do you mean by formatting? Explain.
2. What are the steps to format a document?
3. What assistance is available to help you format documents, and what aspects of formatting should be of concern to you?
4. Explain the steps and commands for the following words:
   (*i*) Change font (style, size, colour etc.)
   (*ii*) Text alignment
   (*iii*) Numbers and bulleting
   (*iv*) Bold

(v) Underline
(vi) Italics
(vii) Line spacing
(viii) Change Case.

ASSIGNMENT

1. Format the following word document and save it in file "Format.docx".

For word processing, **formatting means determining the appearance of a document.** Word processing programs provide two helpful devices—templates and wizards. **A template** is a preformatted document that provides basic tools for shaping a final document—the text, layout and style for a letter, for example. **A wizard answers your questions and uses the answers to layout and format a document.**

The useful aspects of formatting are given below:

(i) **Font:** You can decide what **font—typeface and typesize—**you wish to use.

(ii) **Spacing and columns:** You can choose whether you want the lines to be *single-spaced or double-spaced* (or something else).

(iii) **Margins and justification:** You can indicate the dimensions of the margins—left, right, top and bottom–around the text.

(iv) **Pages, headers, footers:** You can indicate page numbers and headers or footers. A *header* is common text (for example, a date or document name) printed at the top of every page. A *footer* is the same thing printed at the bottom of every page of the document.

(v) **Other formatting:** You can specify *borders* or other decorative lines, *shading*, *tables* and *footnotes*. You can even import *graphics* or drawings from files in other software programs, including *clipart*—collection of readymade pictures all illustration available online or on CD-ROM disks you have.

The word processing programs come from the manufacturer with **default setting** *i.e.*, **the setting automatically used** by a program unless the user specifies otherwise, thereby overriding them.

UNIT 4 INSERTING TABLES AND SYMBOLS IN WORD PROCESSING DOCUMENT

Specific Objectives

After reading this unit, the student will be able to:

1.4.1 insert tables in Word Processing document.

1.4.2 insert symbols and pictures in Word Processing document.

1.4.0 Introduction

Tables are used in a document to layout tabular materials. Symbols and pictures can also be inserted in a word processing document.

Tables

The table feature now included in most programs allows you to create a blank table by specifying the number of rows and columns it should contain. The intersections of the rows and columns create cells. As you type data into a cell, the text wraps within the cell and the cell's depth adjusts automatically. You can easily adjust column widths, format entire rows or columns, and insert and delete rows and columns. You can even enter numbers in some cells and formulas in others to make calculations, for example, to total a column of numbers.

Symbols and Pictures

You can insert special symbols and pictures into your text by selecting Illustrations from the Illustrations panel.

1.4.1 Inserting Tables in Word Document

Tables provide an easier and effective method of arranging the data in rows and columns. MS word offers a set of commands for creation, modification and formatting of tables. To insert a table in your document follow these steps:

1. Open a document and enter some text in it.
2. Select the *Insert* tab.
3. Select the *Table* option from Tables panel. (See figure 4.1)

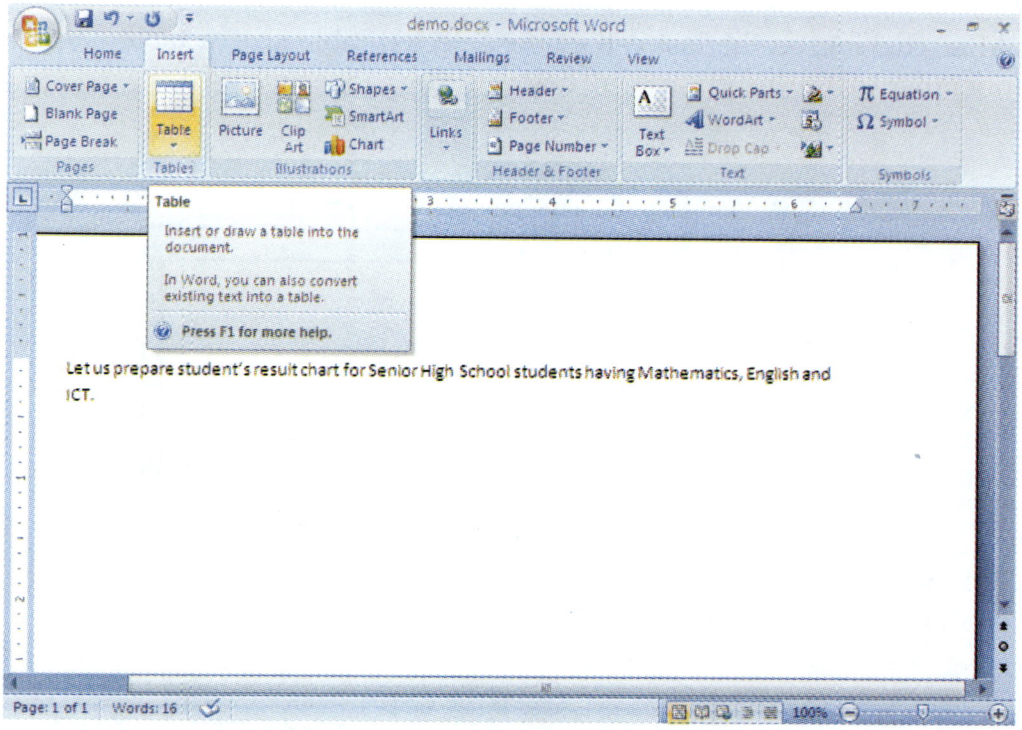

Figure 4.1 Selecting Table option

4. On clicking the *Table* option, a list will be displayed. Select the desired table size by moving the cursor on the table cells (See figure 4.2). Here we select 5 x 4 table.

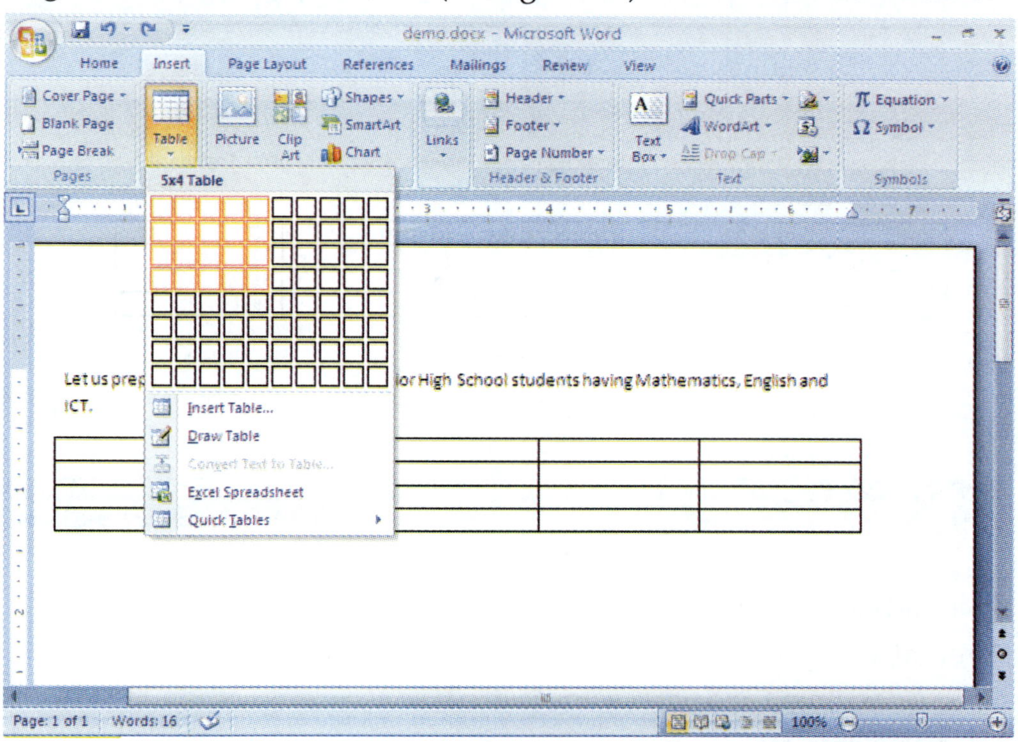

Figure 4.2 Selecting the Table size

5. After clicking on the last cell of the selected table size, a table is inserted into the document at the insertion point below the text. (See figure 4.3)

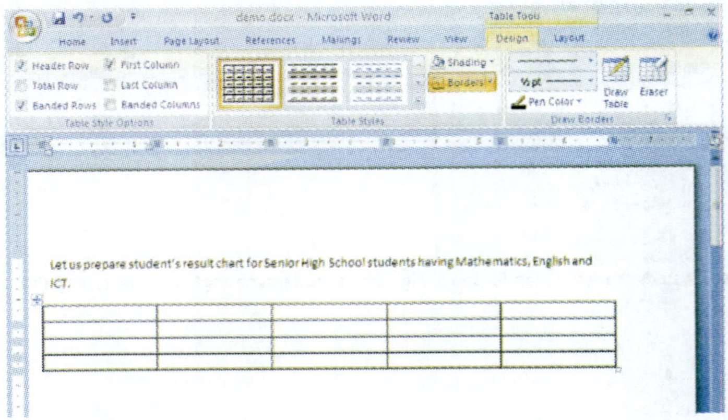

Figure 4.3 After inserting the Table

6. Fill the table as per your requirement. (See figure 4.4) Here we enter the marks of students.

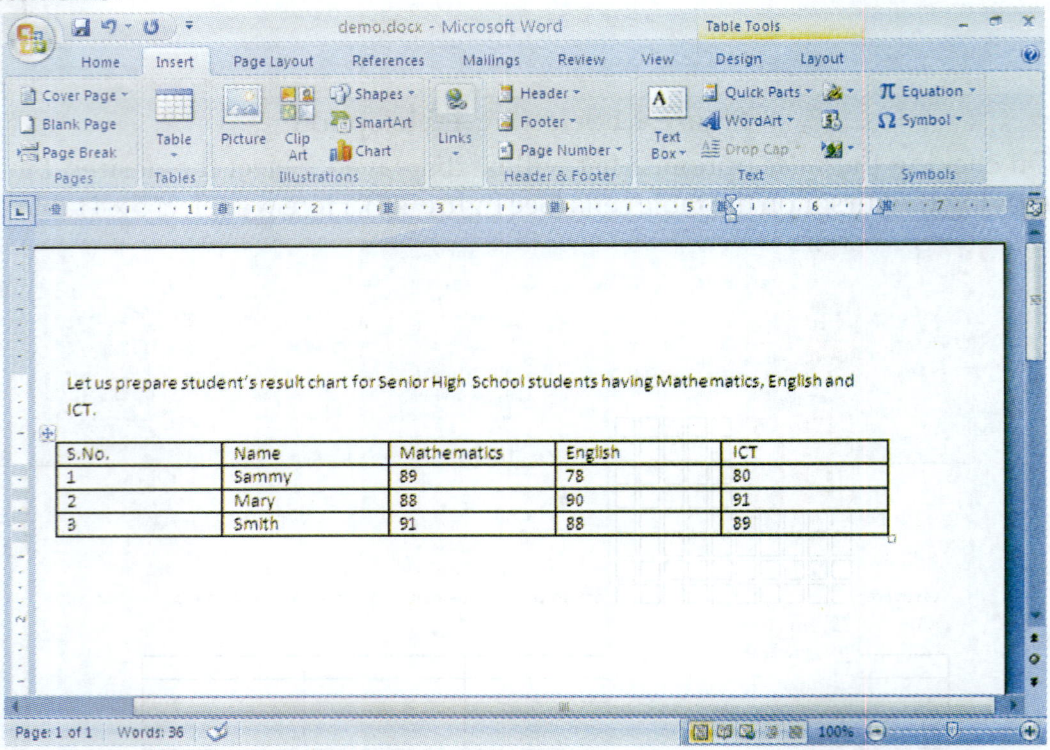

Figure 4.4 After filling the Table

7. Save and close the document.

Alternatively, you can insert a table as given below:

1. Open a document and enter some text in it.
2. Select the *Insert* tab.
3. Select the *Table* option from Table panel. (See figure 4.1)

4. On clicking the *Table* option, a list will be displayed.
5. Select the *Insert Table* option from the list. (See figure 4.5)

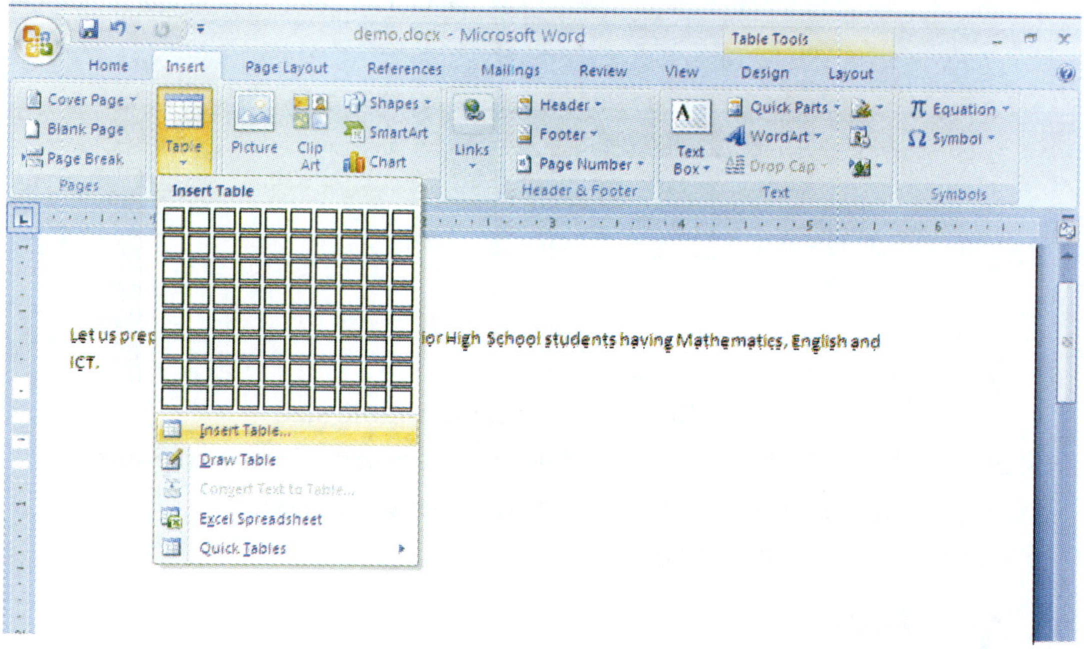

Figure 4.5 Selecting the Insert Table option

6. An *Insert Table* dialog box will appear. (See figure 4.6)

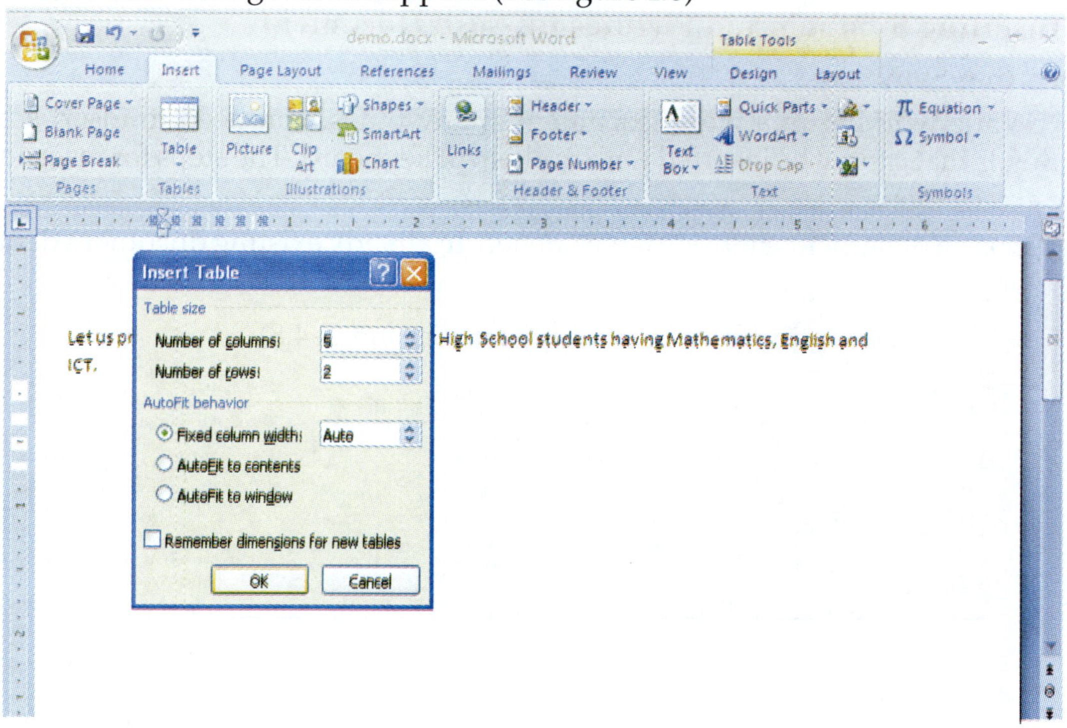

Figure 4.6 Insert Table dialog box

7. Enter the number of columns and rows as per your requirement. (See figure 4.7)

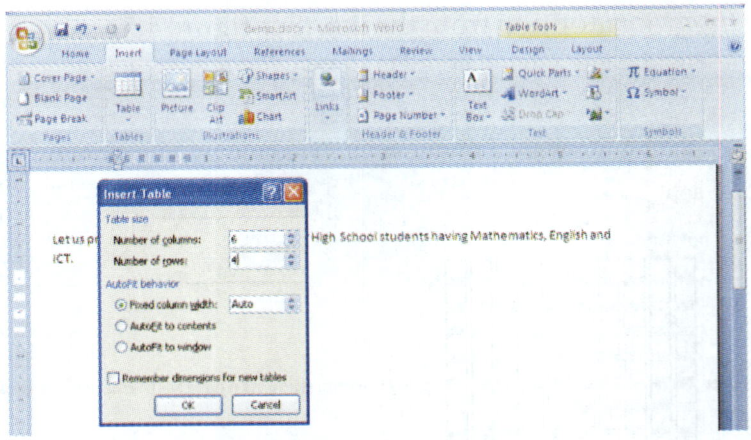

Figure 4.7 Entering the Table size

8. A blank table will be inserted into the document at the insertion point.
9. Now you can make entries into the table as per your need.
10. Save and close the document.

Note

You can also insert table using *Draw Table* option from Insert Table list, available in *Table* option of the Tables panel under Insert tab.

1.4.2 Inserting Symbols and Pictures in Word Document

Inserting Symbols

While working in a word document, many times, you need to insert some special symbols that cannot be inserted with the help of keyboard. The steps for inserting symbols are given below:

1. Open a document. Here we have opened an already existing document demo.docx.
2. Click the *Insert* tab.
3. Select *Symbol* option from Symbols panel. (See figure 4.8)

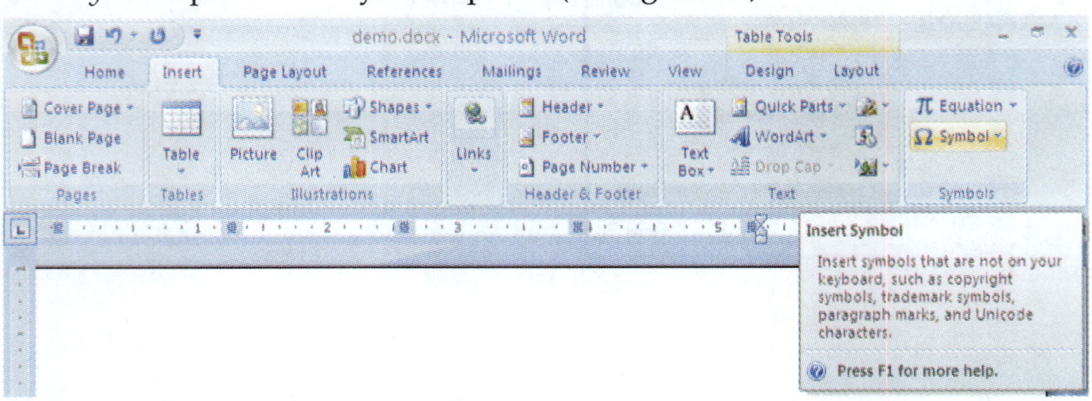

Figure 4.8 Selecting Symbol option

4. A list of symbols will be displayed. Select the desired symbol. (See figure 4.9)

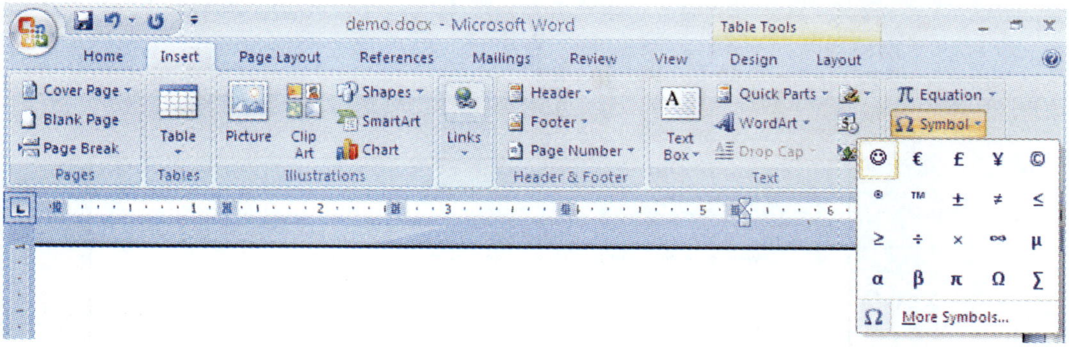

Figure 4.9 Symbol dialog box

5. On clicking the selected symbol will be inserted at the insertion point. (You can insert the symbol at as many points as you wish by changing the insertion point, see figure 4.10). Here we insert a 'Smiley' symbol where students have scored 90 or more.

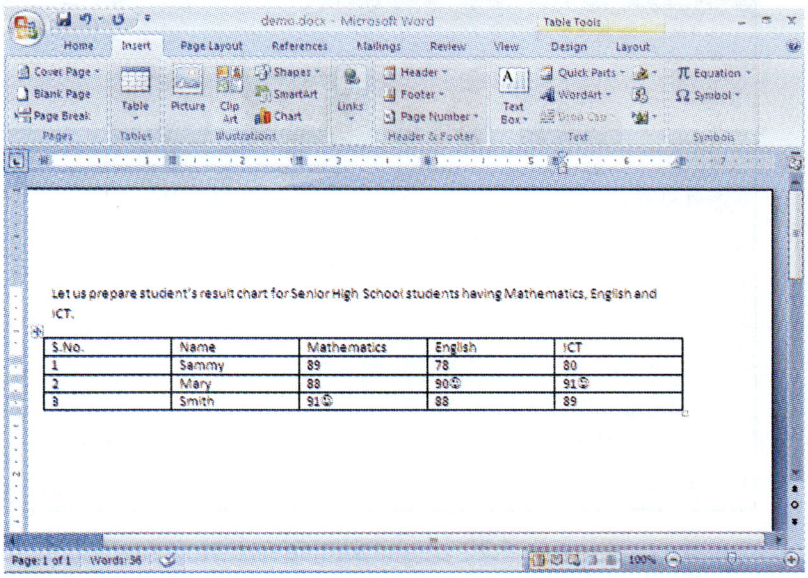

Figure 4.10 A document after inserting symbols

6. Save and close the document.

Note

Before you insert a symbol, make sure that the insertion pointer is at the proper position where the symbol is to be placed.

Inserting Pictures

While working in a word document, many times, you need to insert pictures to create effective documents. The steps for inserting pictures are given below:

1. Open a document.
2. Click the *Insert* tab.

3. Select the *Picture* option from Illustrations panel. (See figure 4.11)

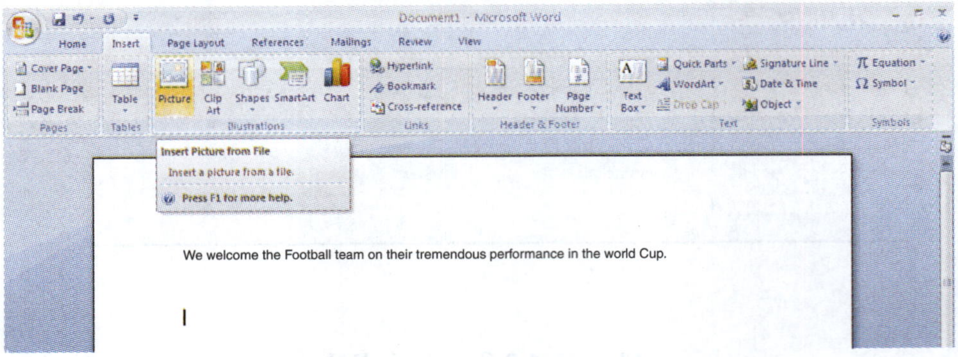

Figure 4.11 Inserting Picture

4. On clicking this button the *Insert Picture* dialog box will appear. Select the desired picture and click *Insert* button (See figure 4.12). Here we have selected Water lilies.jpg.

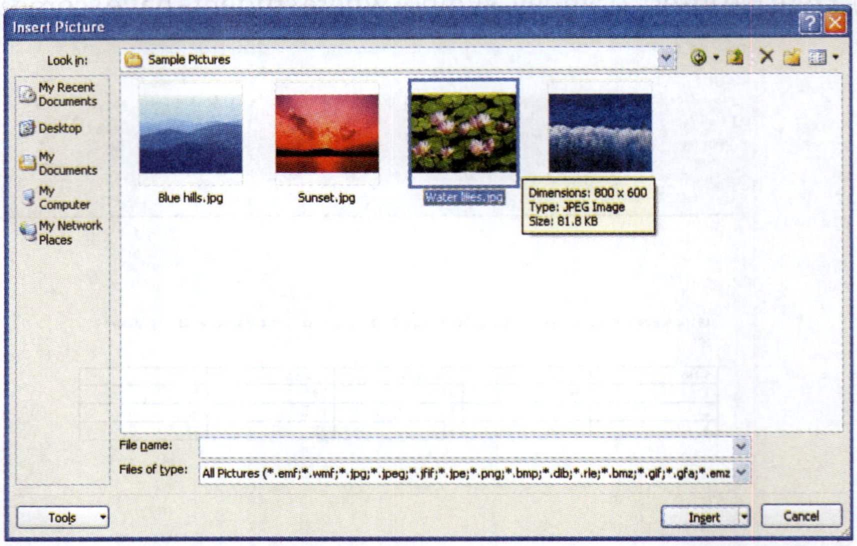

Figure 4.12 Insert Picture dialog box

5. The selected picture will be inserted in the document at the insertion point. (See figure 4.13)

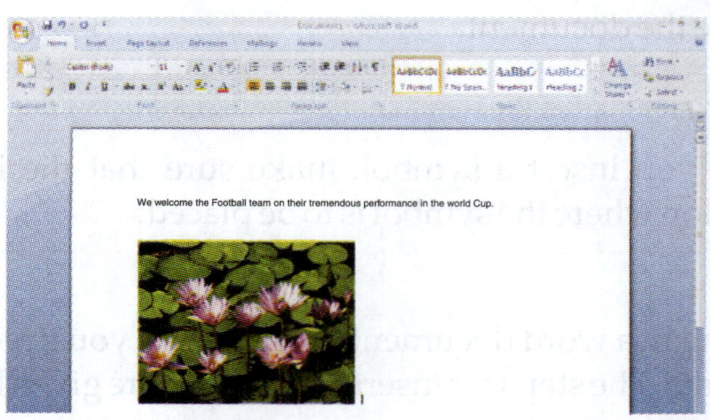

Figure 4.13 A document after inserting a picture

6. Save and close the document.

SUMMARY

- Tables provide you an easier and effective method of arranging the data in rows and columns.
- MS Word offers a set of commands for creation, modification and formatting of tables.
- Symbols, Clipart or pictures are inserted to create effective documents.

REVIEW QUESTIONS

STATE WHETHER TRUE OR FALSE

1. A table cannot be drawn in a document using MS Word.
2. Symbols cannot be drawn in a document using MS Word.
3. Picture can be inserted into the text of a document using MS Word.

FILL IN THE BLANKS

1. Insert Panel has Tables option in Word 2007 which allows you to create a .... using the intersection of rows and columns that form cells.
2. Insert Panel has Illustrations option in Word 2007 which allows you to insert .... into the text.

ANSWER THE FOLLOWING

1. How will you insert a table in Word Processing document?
2. How will you insert symbols and pictures in Word Processing document?

ASSIGNMENT

1. Write a letter to your friend inviting him/her on your birthday party. Insert proper picture also, and save it.
2. Create a document inserting tables, symbols, and pictures and save it.

UNIT 5 PRINTING

Specific Objective

After reading this unit, the student will be able to:

1.5.1 print documents using various print options.

1.5.0 Introduction

In practical environments, hard copy (printed format) is considered more relevant than the soft copy (saved format) output. All the documents are designed in such a way that they can be easily printed, whenever needed in a hard copy form.

Most word processing software gives you several options for printing. For example, you can print *several copies* of a document. You can print *individual pages* or a *range of pages.* You can even preview a document before printing it out.

1.5.1 Printing Word Documents with Various Print Options

Print Preview

As you keep working with a document, making changes to it and saving it from time to time, you get a **soft copy** of it. That is a copy of document saved in your PC, that can be referred to at any time by opening.

Previewing (print previewing) means viewing a document on screen to see what it will look like in printed form before it is printed. Whole pages are displayed in reduced size *i.e.,* print preview is actually a miniature form of a document.

When you wish to preview a document, as it will be printed, you can take the advantage of WORD's highly flexible Print Preview Feature.

Useful Tip

Print preview displays the document as it will look after printing.

For getting the Print Preview of a document the steps are:

1. Open a document and type some text in it.
2. Click the *Office Button.* (See figure 5.1)

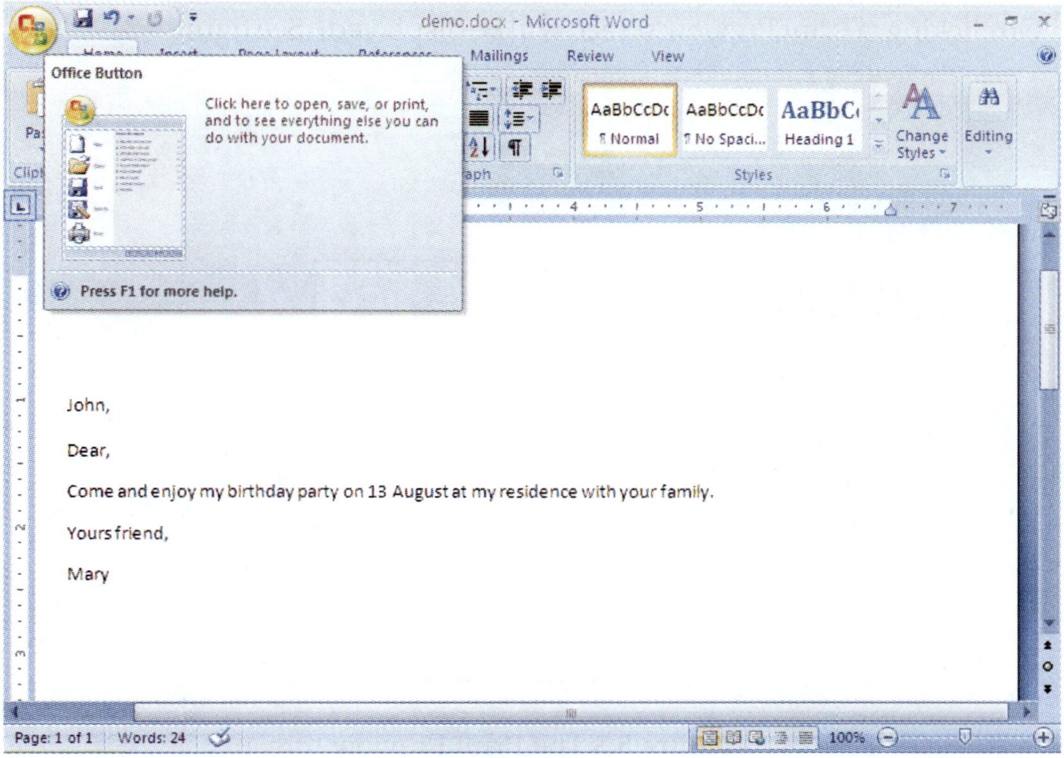

Figure 5.1

3. A list of various options will be displayed. Select the *Print* option from it. Now select *Print Preview* option from it. (See figure 5.2)

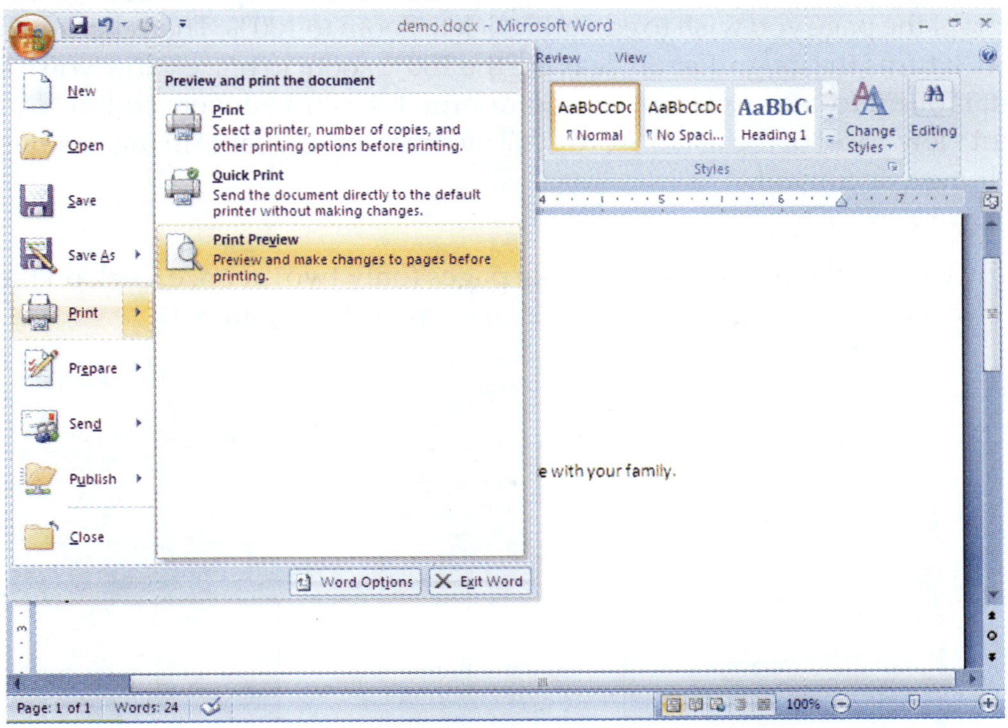

Figure 5.2

4. On clicking, a Print Preview screen will be displayed. (See figure 5.3)

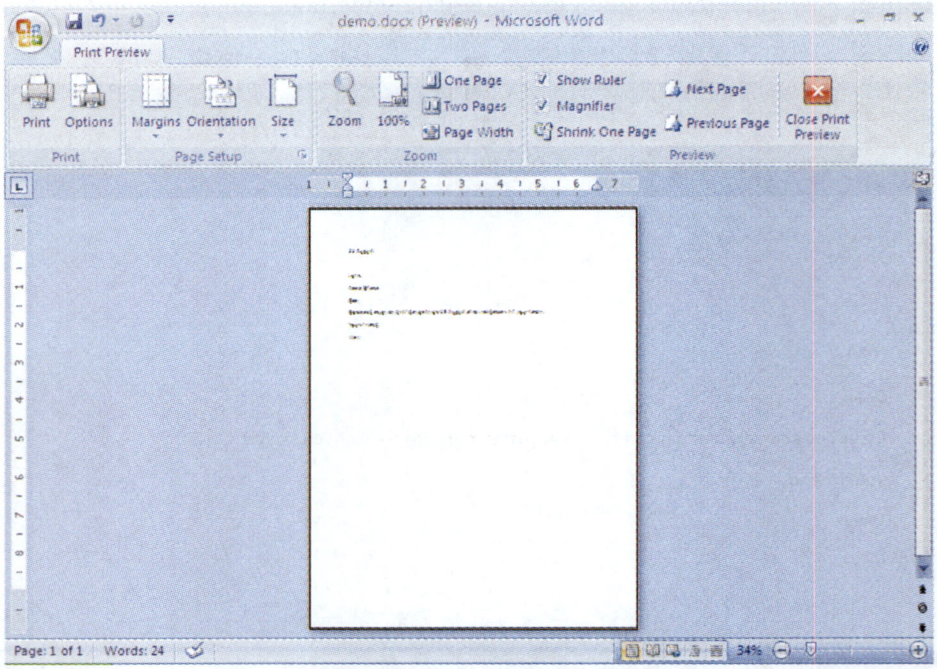

Figure 5.3 The Print Preview screen

Print Preview can save a lot of time and paper because you can quickly look at a document on screen than wait for the printout, and it does not require any sheet of paper.

The document can be edited in Print Preview. First of all place the magnifying glass on the part of the page you wish to edit and click to zoom to 100%. Then click on the Magnifier button. It turns the magnifier off, leaving the 100% zoom in place. Now you can select text, edit it, move it to some other place and reformat it as if you were still in Normal or Print Layout view. Most of the usual Word 2007 facilities are available in this case also while you are editing a document.

Viewing Multiple Pages

You can see the preview of multiple pages (only two) at once, click on the Two Pages button in the Print Preview window in Zoom panel. (See figure 5.4)

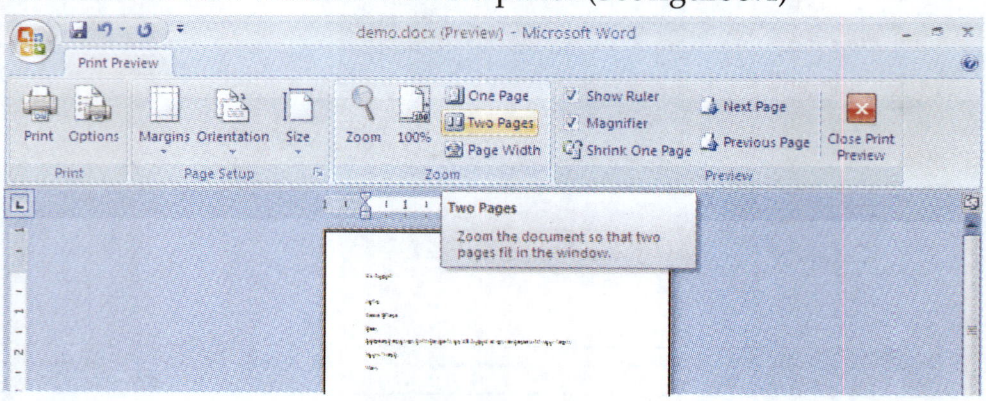

Figure 5.4 Preview of Multiple Pages

After clicking you will get preview of two pages shown side by side. (See figure 5.5)

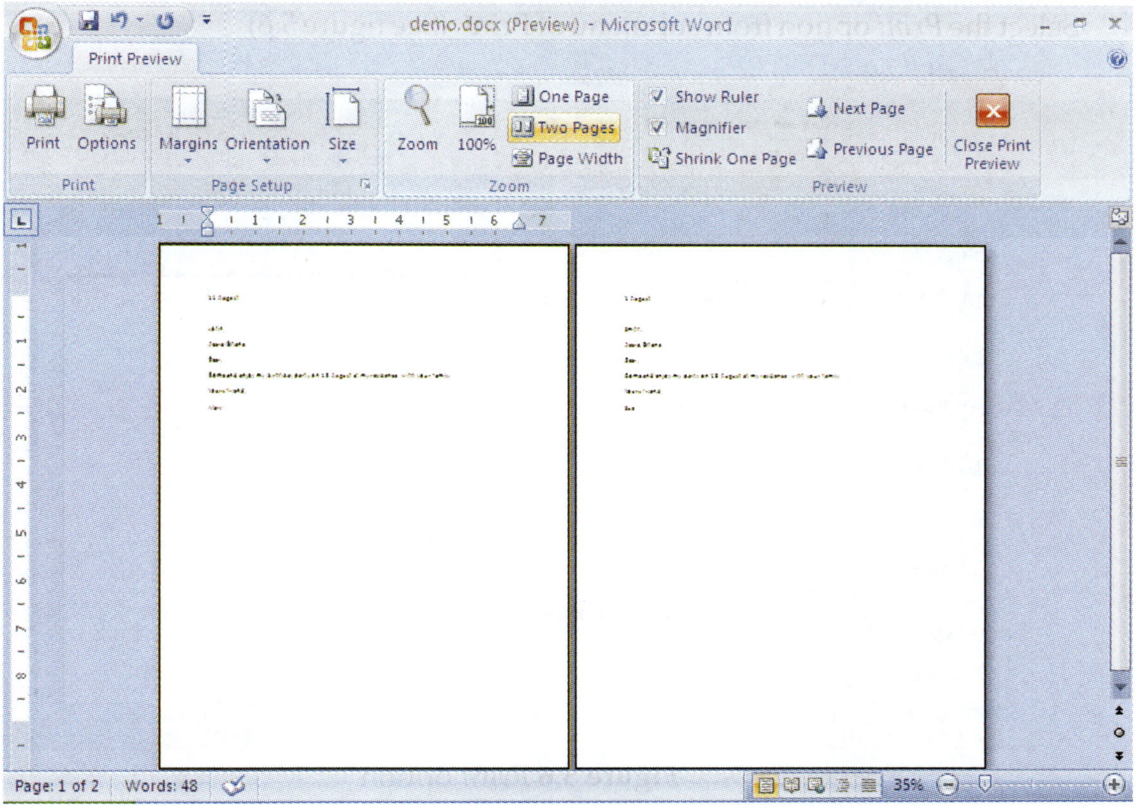

Figure 5.5 Preview of Two Pages

Click the *Close Print* Preview button to close the preview and return to normal view.

Useful Tip

Analyse the preview of the document, before giving a print command.

Printing a Document

After typing in a document, you might need to hand over your work (say for assignment or managerial purposes) further to a teacher or an executive; or otherwise need it for your own records and use. This demands a handy copy of the document at your disposal. This 'handy copy' of the document, which contains everything your document has, in printed form is called a **hard copy** of the same. To get a hard copy, you need to take a printout of the document. Word 2007 gives you several options for printing. For example, you can print *several copies* of a document. You can print *individual pages* or a *range of pages.* As discussed earlier, you can even preview a document before printing it out. To print a document :

1. Open the document which you wish to print.
2. Switch on the printer attached to your PC.

3. Click on *Office Button*. A list of various options is displayed.
4. Select the *Print* option from submenu of Print. (See figure 5.6)

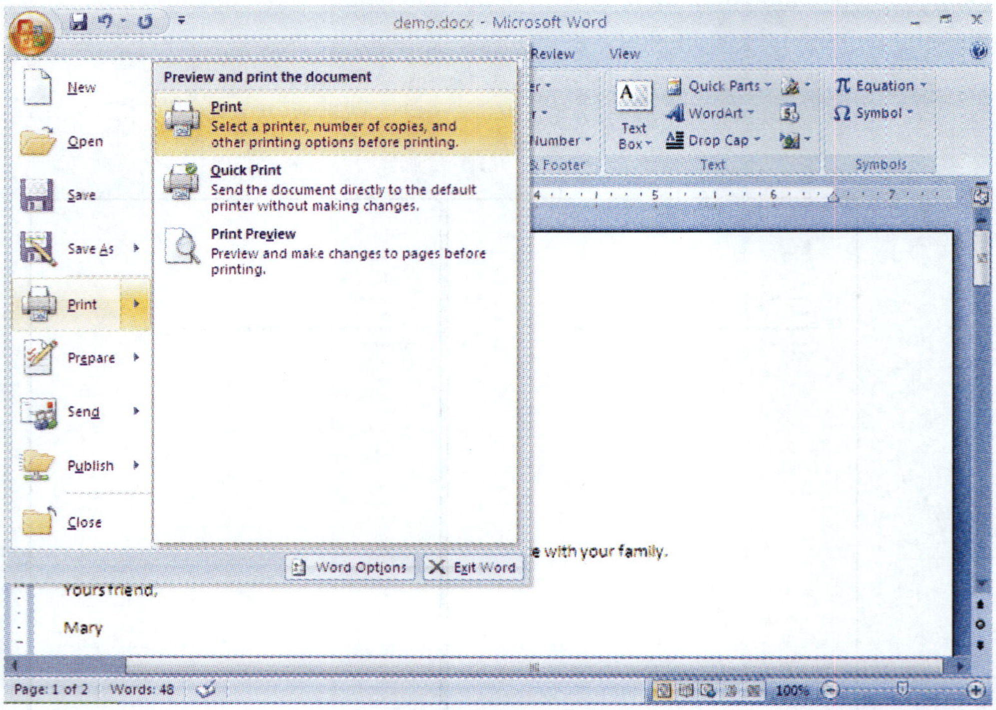

Figure 5.6 Print option

5. On clicking, a *Print* dialog box appears. (See figure 5.7)

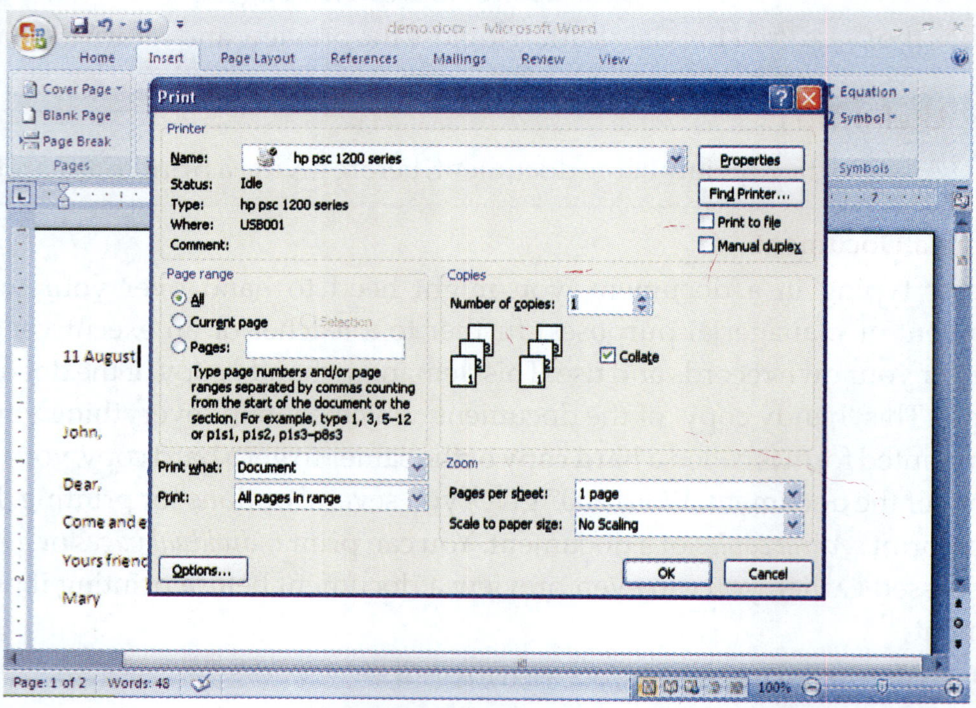

Figure 5.7 Print dialog box

It displays some general information about the printer attached to your PC, which will be used to take a print out and certain options for printing as *Page range* to be printed, *Number of copies* etc. You can enter the criteria for these options according to the need. (See figure 5.8)

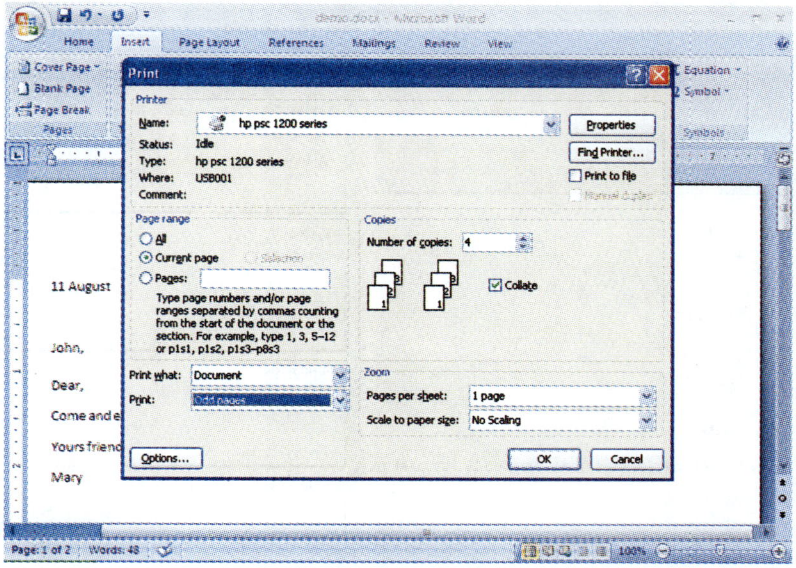

Figure 5.8

6. Click on OK button to start printing.

Page Numbering

Printed documents having more than one page should have page numbers. You can set up page numbering in two ways. Either insert a page number code while editing headers and footers, or insert page numbers from the Insert panel.

For page numbering,

1. Click the *Insert* tab and select *Page Number* from the Header & Footer panel. (See figure 5.9)

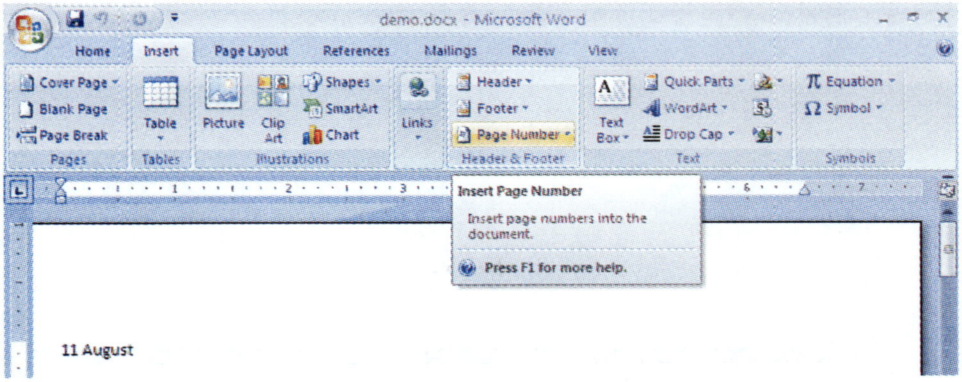

Figure 5.9 Selecting Page Number option

2. From the *Page Number* drop-down list, select the position on the page where you want your page numbers to appear. The options are:

Top of Page (Header)

Bottom of Page (Footer)

3. Select the desired option. (See figure 5.10)

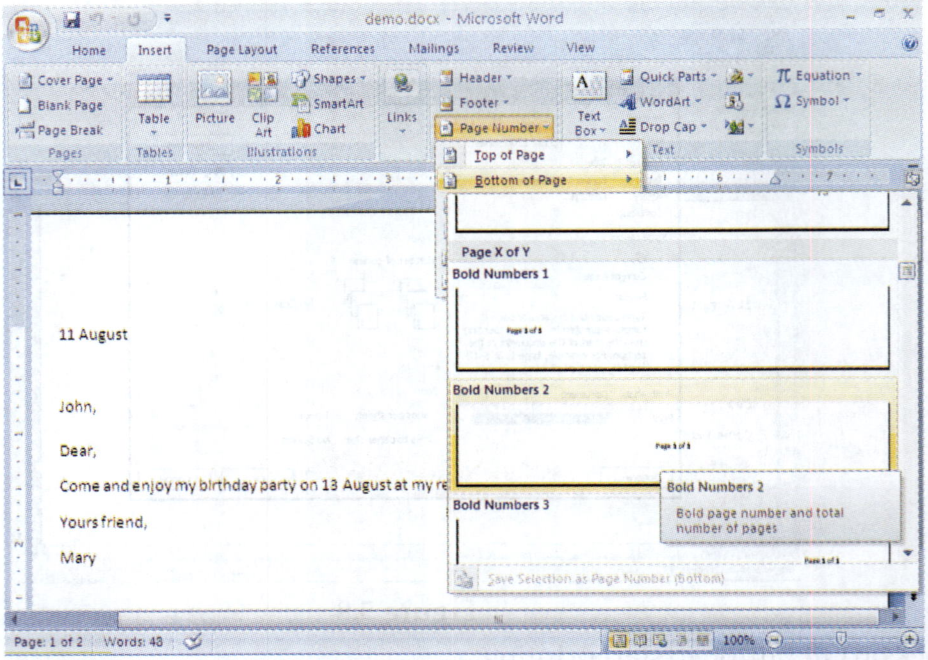

Figure 5.10 Inserting Page Number

4. After applying the selected option, you will get the page numbered document. (See figure 5.11)

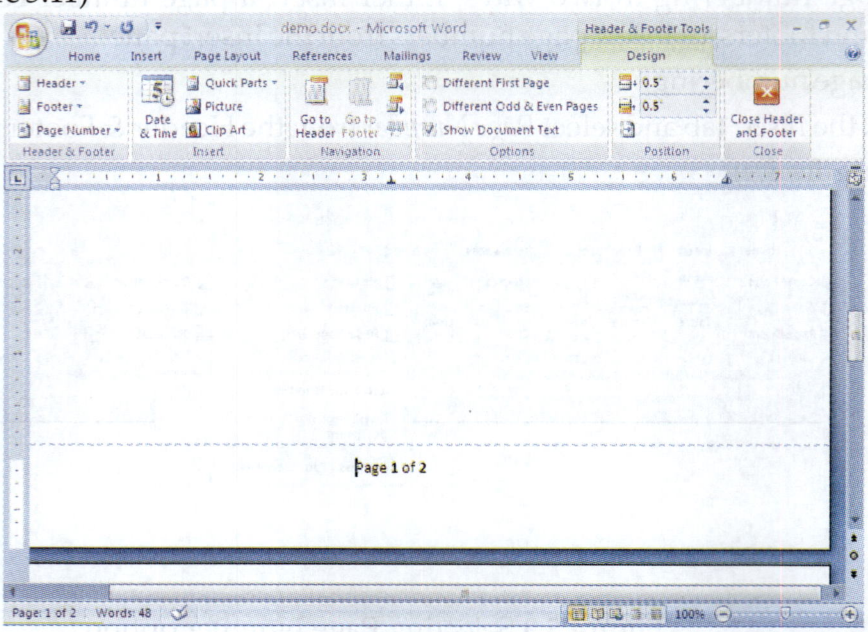

Figure 5.11 After inserting Page Number

5. Save and close the document.

SUMMARY

- Most word processing software give you several options for printing.
- You can print several copies, individual pages or a range of pages of a document.
- You can even preview a document before printing it out.
- Previewing (print previewing) means viewing a document on screen to see what it will look like in printed form before it is printed. Whole pages are displayed in reduced size.
- When you wish to preview a document, as it will be printed, you can take the advantage of word's highly flexible Print Preview feature.
- The 'handy copy' of the document, which contains everything your document has, in printed form is called a hard copy of the same.
- Printed documents having more than one page should have page numbers.

REVIEW QUESTIONS

STATE WHETHER TRUE OR FALSE

1. Word provides the option of Print Preview.
2. Print preview is not a miniature form of a document.
3. In the print preview of the document, you can zoom to a particular area of the document to have a closer look.
4. You cannot see the preview of multiple pages at once.
5. Printing the document is very easy in MS Word.

FILL IN THE BLANKS

1. Most .... software give you several options for printing.
2. .... means viewing a document before printing it out.
3. In print preview, whole pages are displayed in .... size.
4. You can see the preview of multiple pages at once by clicking on the .... button in the Print Preview window in zoom panel.
5. A document in printed form is called a ....

MULTIPLE CHOICE QUESTIONS

1. .... means viewing a document before printing it out.

   (a) Review *(b)* Preview

   (c) Printout *(d)* None of these

2. In print preview, whole pages are displayed in .... size.
   (a) Enlarged (b) Same
   (c) Reduced (d) None of these
3. A document in printed form is also called a ....
   (a) Softcopy (b) Mastercopy
   (c) Preview (d) Hardcopy

ANSWER THE FOLLOWING

1. What is print preview? Discuss.
2. How will you print Word document with various print options? Explain.
3. How can you provide page numbers in a Word document? Discuss.

ASSIGNMENT

1. Create document inserting tables, symbols, pictures, save and print three copies of it.
2. Develop a simple brochure for the school using all the features you have learned.

SECTION

TWO

TERM-TWO

THE INTERNET

UNIT 1: The Internet

UNIT 2: Using the Internet to Communicate

UNIT 3: Accessing Information from the Internet

General Objective

After reading this section, the student will be able to:

1. acquire skills in, and appreciate the importance of using the Internet.

UNIT 1 THE INTERNET

Specific Objectives

After reading this unit, the student will be able to:

2.1.1 explain basic concepts, requirements and terminologies of Internet.

2.1.2 identify the features of browser window.

2.1.3 browse the Internet with the help of some features of the browser window.

2.1.4 apply the rules and regulations in the use of the Internet.

2.1.0 Introduction

Internet (the "net") is the worldwide computer network that connects hundreds of thousands of smaller networks, linking computers at academic, scientific, and commercial institutions, as well as individuals. Using it, the users around the world can share all type of information and services.

OR

Internet is the network that connects other networks of computers around the globe into one seamless network.

The first step towards the construction of Internet was taken by U.S. Department of Defence in 1969, when they approved a project named ARPANET (acronym for Advanced Research Projects Network). In 1995, a new name was given to the collection of networks and it is now called THE INTERNET. The number of computers being connected to the Internet doubles in less than a year. Today the world of the Internet permits activities hardly imaginable 10 years age. Table 1.1 provides the main activities provided on Internet.

Table 1.1 The Main Activities Provided on Internet

Activity	Purpose
Auctions	Sell old stuff, acquire more stuff, with online auctions.
Career advancement	Search job listings, post resumes, interview online.
Distance learning	Attend online lectures, have discussions, research papers.
Download files	Get software, music, and documents such as e-books.

E-mail and discussion groups	Stay in touch worldwide through electronic mail and online chat rooms.
Entertainment	Amuse yourself with Internet games, music and videos.
E-business	Connect with coworkers, buy supplies, support customers.
E-shopping	Price anything from plane tickets to cars, order anything from books to sofas.
Financial matters	Do investing, banking and bill paying online.
News	Stay current on politics, weather, entertainment, sports and financial news.
Research and information	Find information on any subject, using browers and search tools.
Telephony and conferencing	Make inexpensive phone calls; have online meetings.

Who Governs the Internet

You will be surprised to know that there is no one who owns or runs the Internet. Every subnetwork of Internet is responsible for maintenance of its own part and does not bother about the other one. The Internet is coordinated by many volunteer organisations and no single organisation is having the complete control over it.

Note

The Protocols are the rules and regulations on which the communication proceeds in a network. In order to communicate in a network, both the sender and the receiver must agree upon some common protocol.

2.1.1 Concept, Requirements and Terminologies

- **Accessing Internet**

To connect to the Internet, we have to connect our computer to the computer server of Internet Service Provider (ISP). ISPs are companies which provide Internet related services to its users. ISPs have special computers called Internet Servers which are connected to the Internet from one end and to several users from the other end. These servers work 24 hours a day, 365 days a year to provide services to their customers.

- **Types of Connections**

The connection to service provider can be temporary as well as permanent, depending upon the choice of the customer. You can either have a dial up connection to the Internet or you can have a leased line connection.

1. Dial-up Connection

In this type of connection, user creates a temporary connection with the ISP, uses the Internet services and then disconnects the connection. The user is charged a fixed amount depending upon the time period for which the connection was active. This is the cheaper method of Internet access and most of the users connect to the Internet by using dial-up connection. To establish a dial-up connection, you only need a computer equipped with a device called "Modem" and a telephone connection to connect your computer to the ISP. In this type of connection, users are billed as per their duration of connection and not on the amount of data transfer.

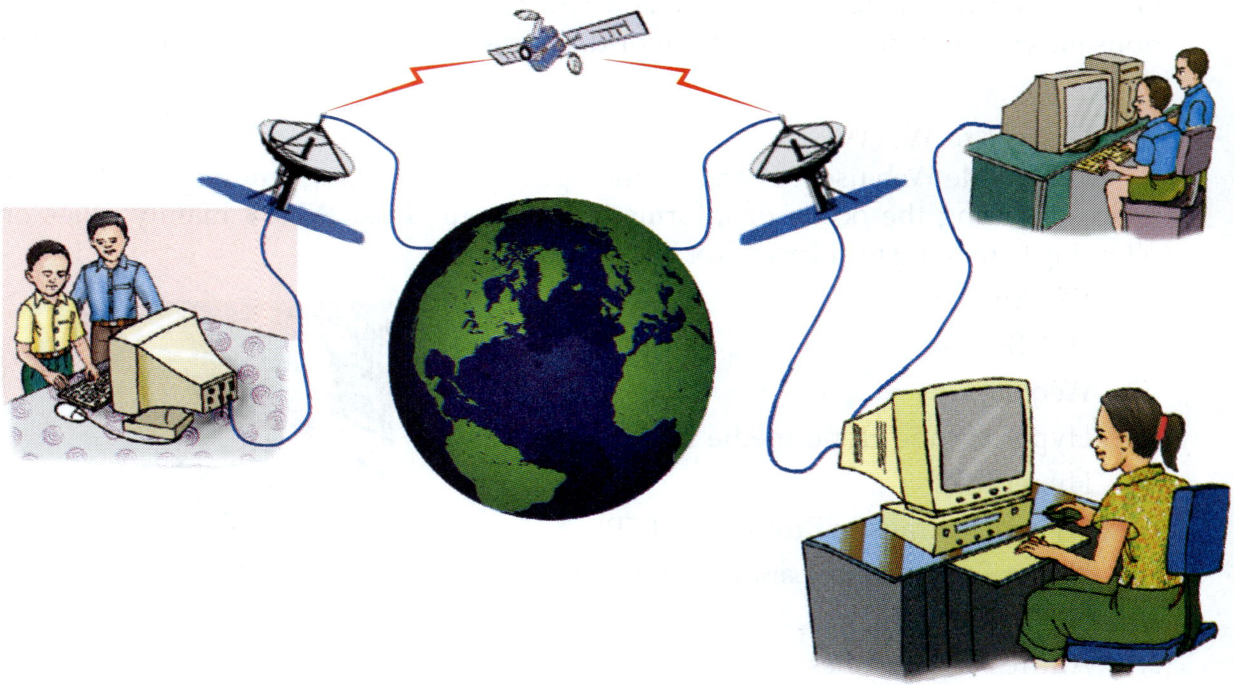

Figure 1.1 Working of Internet

2. Leased Line Connection

In leased line connection, a permanent connection is dedicated for a particular user and it is open 24 hours a day. The user is charged a fixed amount, depending upon the data transfer rate provided by the connection. The data transfer rate is measured in terms of Kbps (Kilo Bytes Per Second). More the data transfer rate of the connection, more are the charges for the connection. Leased line connections generally range from 64 Kbps to 512 Kbps. In this type of connection, the users are billed on the amount of data sent or received by them.

The amount charged for these connections is generally huge and these connections are used by large corporate houses or educational institutions like universities. These connections also require very high speed modems, having very high costs. Skilled people are also required to manage the leased line connections.

- **WWW (World Wide Web)**

World Wide Web or WWW or simply Web has changed the picture of Internet, after its creation in 1989 by Tim Berners-Lee. Earlier, Internet was used to share textual information only. There were no graphics, no animations and no links as you see in today's Internet. All credit goes to WWW, which provides an easy and effective way of storing and accessing information on the Internet.

World Wide Web is a set of programs, standards and protocols that allows the text, images, animations, sounds, videos to be stored and accessed and linked together in the form of websites. Basically, WWW is a collection of millions of web pages stored in thousands of computers all over the world. It is a safe house for storing information on the Internet.

- **Elements of WWW**

World Wide Web uses several technologies, programming languages, interfaces and devices to bring the ocean of information on your desk. WWW mainly relies on the following to making rapid access of information:

(*i*) Web Server
(*ii*) Web Browser
(*iii*) WebSite
(*iv*) Hypertext and Hypermedia
(*v*) Hyperlinks
(*vi*) Hypertext Transfer Protocol (HTTP)
(*vii*) Hyper Text Markup Language (HTML)
(*viii*) Search Engines
(*ix*) Addressing schemes

Figure 1.2 Web inventor: Tim Berners-Lee

Remember that the Internet and the World Wide Web are not the same thing. The Internet is a massive network of networks, connecting millions of computers via protocols, hardware, and communications channels. The Web is a means of accessing information available on the Internet using software called a *browser.*

Let us discuss some of the important terms associated with WWW:

Website—the domain on the computer: The top-level domains are .com, .edu, .org, and .net. A computer with a domain name is called a *website (site).* When you decide to buy books at the online site of a bookseller, you would visit its website. The website is the location of a web domain name in a computer somewhere on the Internet.

Web pages—the documents on a website: A website is composed of a web page or collection of related web pages. A *web page* is a document on the World Wide Web that can include text, pictures, sound and video. The first page you see on a website is like the title page of a book. This is the *home page,* or welcome page, which identifies the website and contains links to other pages at the site.

If you have your own personal website, it might consist of just one page—the home page. Large websites have scores or even hundreds of pages.

Note

The contents of home pages often change. Or they may disappear, and so the connecting links to them in other web pages become links to nowhere.

- **Browsers**

To use the Web, the software you use is a browser. This is an intensely competitive field right now and browsers are undergoing very rapid changes. Some are independent software programs such as those developed by Microsoft, Mozilla and Netscape. Others are integrated into application programs such as word processing programs, spreadsheets and databases. Figure 1.3 shows Mozilla Firefox browser.

Figure 1.3 Mozilla Firefox Browser

- **Chats**

Real-time chats are typed discussions among online participants. With newsgroups and mailing lists, participants may contribute to a discussion, go away, and return hours or days later to catch up on others' typed contributions. With *real-time chat (RTC)*, participants have a typed discussion ("chat") while being online at the same time, just like a telephone conversation except that messages are typed rather than spoken. Otherwise the format is much like a newsgroup, with a message board to which participants may send ("post") their contributions. To start a chat, you use a service available on your browser such as IRC (Internet Relay Chat) that will connect you to a chat server.

Unlike instant messaging, which tends to involve one-on-one conversation, real-time chat usually involves several participants. As a result, RTC is often like being at a party, with many people and many threads of conversation occurring at once.

- **Discussion Boards**

Also known as bulletin boards or discussion groups, newsgroups are used by people to share common interests. Newsgroups are used for online typed discussions on specific topics. A *newsgroup* (or *forum*) is a giant electronic bulletin board on which users conduct written discussions about a specific subject. There are thousands of Internet newsgroups—which charge no fee—and they cover an amazing array of topics. Newsgroups take place on a special network of computers called *Usenet,* a worldwide public network of servers that can be accessed through the Internet *(www.usenet.com).* To participate, you need a *newsreader,* a program included with most browsers that allows you to access a newsgroup and read or type messages. (Messages, incidentally, are known as *articles.*)

- **Synchronous and Asynchronous Transmission Modes**

Transmission modes are of two types: Asynchronous and synchronous.

Asynchronous transmission: This method, used with most microcomputers, is also called *start-stop transmission.* In asynchronous transmission, data is sent 1 byte (or character) at a time. Each string of bits making up the byte is bracketed, or marked off, with special control bits. That is a "start" bit represents the beginning of a character, and a "stop" bit represents its end.

Its advantage is that data can be transmitted whenever convenient for the sender. Its drawback is that transmitting only 1 byte at a time makes it a relatively slow method that cannot be used when great amounts of data must be sent rapidly.

Synchronous transmission: Instead of using start and stop bits, synchronous transmission sends data in blocks. Start and stop bit patterns, called synch bytes, are transmitted at the beginning and end of the blocks. These start and end bit patterns synchronise internal clocks in the sending and receiving devices so that they are in time with each other.

Synchronous transmission is rarely used with microcomputers because it is more complicated and more expensive than asynchronous transmission. It is appropriate for computer systems that need to transmit great quantities of data quickly.

- **HTML**

The format used on the web is called *hypertext markup language.* (It is not, however, a programming language.) *Hypertext Markup Language (HTML)* is the set of special instructions (called "tags" or "markups") that are used to specify document structure, formatting, and links to other multimedia documents.

In HTML, every command is surrounded by < and >. And in most commands, you need to tell the web browser when to end this command. You do this by putting a back slash (/) in front of the ending command. Since, HTML is not case sensitive, <title> is the same as <TITLE>, which is the same as <TiTLe>. Next, you need to decide what you want to put on your page. Text, links, graphics, and text fields are just a few ideas.

- **Hyper Text Transfer Protocol (HTTP)**

Hyper Text Transfer Protocol is a standard communication protocol of the Internet which governs the transfer of information between a web browser and a web server. Whenever you type the address of any web site in the address bar of the browser, it is automatically padded with "http://". For example, if you type "www.google.com", it will be changed to "http: // www.google.com". This means http is being used by your browser to display the required information.

- **FTP**

FTP is used for copying all the free files you want. Many net users enjoy "FTPing"—cruising the system and checking into some of the tens of thousands of FTP sites, which predate the web and offer interesting free or inexpensive files to download. *FTP (File Transfer Protocol)* is a method whereby you can connect to a remote computer called an *FTP site* and transfer files to your own microcomputer's hard disk via TCP/IP over the Internet. Free files offered cover nearly anything that can be stored on a computer: software, games, photos, maps, art, music, books, statistics.

Some FTP files are open to the public (at *anonymous FTP sites*); some are not. For instance, a university might maintain an FTP site with private files (such as lecture transcripts) available only to professors and students with assigned user names and passwords. It might also have public FTP files open to anyone with an e-mail address. You can download FTP files using either your web browser or special software (called an *FTP client program*), such as Fetch, Cute, and FTP pro.

- **Telnet**

Telnet allows you to connect to remote computers. *Telnet* is a protocol that runs on top of TCP/IP and allows you to connect to remote computers on the Internet by using a user name and a password and to run programs on those computers. This feature, which allows microcomputers to communicate successfully with mainframes, enables you to tap into Internet computers and access public files as though you were connected directly instead of, for example, through your ISP site.

The Telnet feature is especially useful for perusing large databases at universities, government agencies, or libraries. As an electronic version of a library card catalog, Telnet can be used to search most major public and university library catalogs. To use Telnet, you may have to open Telnet accounts for the computers you want to connect with. (Telnet software is included in recent browser versions.)

- **URL (Uniform Resource Locator)**

Each computer in a network has its own address which is unique in the network. For any type of communication, this address is required and used. As we have studied that Internet is also a network; so each computer in the Internet must have a unique address through which the information stored in that computer can be accessed. Internet uses IP addresses to uniquely identify a computer on the network. As there are millions of computers in the Internet, 32 bit addresses are used. This unique address of a web server is called as Uniform Resource Locator or URL in short.

Useful Tip

Each web server on the Internet has a unique address, called URL. A website address can be of user understandable type or machine understandable type.

- **IP**

Every computer on the Internet has an *Internet Protocol (IP) address* that consists of four sets of numbers between 0 and 255 separated by decimals—for example, 1.190.10.230. This address is similar to a street address. However, street addresses rarely change, but IP addresses often do. Each time you connect to your ISP, the ISP will assign your computer a new IP address, called a *dynamic IP address*, for your online session. When you request data from the Internet, it is transmitted to your computer's IP address. When you disconnect, your ISP frees up the IP address you were using and reassigns it to another user.

After your ISP connection has been made, your ISP functions as an interface between you and the rest of the Internet. If you are exchanging data with someone who uses the same ISP, the data may stay within the ISP's network. Large national ISPs operate their own backbones that connect their POPs (Point of Presences) throughout the country. Usually, however, data travel over many different networks before they reach your computer.

ISPs that do not run their own backbones connect to an Internet backbone through a *Network Access Point (NAP)*, a routing computer, usually a supercomputer. NAPs are owned by a *Network Service Provider (NSP)*, a large communications company.

Useful Tip

Some popular online service providers like Hotmail and Yahoo offer compatibility with Outlook Express.

- **E-MAIL**

Electronic mail is one of the most widely used services of the Internet. E-mail is used to transfer text messages from one computer to others which may be thousands of kilometres away. It is generally used to communicate with friends and family, to send business information and to stay in touch with the people near and far. With the advancement of mobile technologies, e-mail can be accessed from laptop, palmtops and even from your mobile phone.

E-mail was the first main benefit provided by the Internet. Through e-mail, we can rapidly transfer text messages electronically (by using computers). No matter how far are sending and receiving computers from each other, the message is delivered in seconds. You can also attach documents, images or presentations etc., with your e-mail message. In the modern world, it is a cheap and the best way of communication.

Some of the popular e-mail service providers are
www.yahoo.com
www.gmail.com
www.hotmail.com

Useful Tip

E-mail offers cheap, reliable, speedy communication with patience and user friendliness. It is helpful in reducing the volume of papers in offices. It has completely changed the modern communication system.

- **TCP/IP**

The key to sharing data across the Internet is the data transmission format. For everyone to be able to use the Internet, all computers must be able to "understand" the data being transmitted. For computers to do this, the data must be formatted according to the same *protocol,* or set of conventions (standards or rules), that govern the format of data transmitted electronically. Protocols can be implemented with either hardware or software. The protocol that enables all computers to use data transmitted on the Internet is called *Transmission Control Protocol/Internet Protocol,* or *TCP/IP.* This protocol determines

1. the type of built-in error checking to be used;
2. the data compression method, if any;
3. how the sending device will indicate that it has finished sending a message; and
4. how the receiving device will indicate that it has received a message.

TCP/IP was developed in 1978 by the U.S. Department of Defence's Advanced Research Projects Agency for Space and Computer Research.

TCP/IP breaks data into *packets,* which are the largest blocks of data that can be sent across the Internet (less than 1,500 characters, or 128 kilobytes). IP is used to send the packets across the Internet to their final destination, and TCP is used to reassemble the packets in the correct order. (Note that the packets do not have to follow the same network routes to reach their destination; but because all the packets have the same IP address, they all arrive—usually—at the same destination.) Internet computers use TCP/IP for all Internet transactions, from sending e-mail to downloading stock quotes or pictures off a friend's website.

- **Search Engines**

It is time-consuming to hop around the world clicking on whatever happens to catch your eye, especially when doing research or looking for specific information. A better way to locate specific information is to use search engines, Web tools that help you find specific sites on the Internet.

When you use a keyword to search for a topic, you are using a piece of software known as a *search engine*. Whereas, directories are lists of websites classified by topic (as offered by portals), search engines allow you to find specific documents through keyword searches and menu choices.

When you enter a word or phrase to look up, the search engine locates any documents containing those key words and lists their titles, brief descriptions, and addresses. The listed documents are called "hits" because the computer "hit" on them using your key word. Clicking on the title or address of one of the listed documents jumps you to that page, wherever it is? There are a number of popular search engines on the Web, and each works a little differently. The type of search engine you use depends on what you are looking for.

There are four types of such search tools:

1. **Human-organized search sites:** Yahoo! and Open Directory.
2. **Computer-created search sites:** Google, Excite, and Web Crawler.
3. **Hybrid search sites:** AOL Search, Alta Vista, MSN Search, Ask Jeeves, Teoma, Alltheweb, HotBot, and Snap.
4. **Metasearch sites:** Copernic, Meta Crawler, and Dogpile.

- **Blogs**

Many users of the Internet have fun keeping journals or web logs—called blogs for short—accessible to other users. Blogs are often updated daily and reflect the personality and views of the blogger. Blog sites—for example, blogging network (www.bloggingnetwork.com) and Pyra Labs (www.blogger.com)—provide information about how you can create and maintain your own web log for a small fee.

- **Listserv**

Listserv is an automatic mailing list server that sends e-mail to subscribers who regularly participate in discussion topics. To subscribe, the user sends an e-mail to the listserve moderator and asks to become a member, after which he or she automatically receives e-mail messages from anyone who responds to the server.

Anyone connected to the Internet can subscribe to listserv services. Subscribers receive information on particular subjects and can post e-mail to other subscribers.

- **How the Internet Functions**

To send information from one computer to another on the Internet, the following procedure is followed:

(*i*) At the sender computer, the information is divided into packets of equal length. These packets contain the data and control information. The length of data and control information depends on the type of the protocols used.

(*ii*) Each packet is given a unique identification number by TCP and IP puts the destination address on each packet.

(*iii*) These packets are routed by using either circuit switching or packet switching technology.

(*iv*) On receiving the packets, the protocols at the receiving end check for arrival of packets. The correctness of the information contained in packets is also checked. If there is some packet loss or packet damage during the way, it is demanded again by the receiving computer.

(*v*) The packets are assembled in the predefined order and the original message is generated again.

2.1.2 Features and Use of Browser Window

Browsers are software for connecting with websites. A *web browser*, or simply *browser*, is software that enables users to locate and view web pages and to jump from one page to another. It is what you use to get around the web. The three best-known browsers are Microsoft Internet Explorer, most commonly used, Netscape Navigator, once the leader but now used by fewer people and Mozila Firefox, coming up very fast. When you connect to a particular website with your browser, the first thing you will see is the home page. Then, using your mouse, you can move from one page to another by clicking on hypertext links. A web page may contain text, graphics, animations, sounds, movies and a variety of interactive elements. A web browser makes it easy to navigate (or "surf") the web and to download items.

Internet Explorer (IE) is one of the most popular web browsers. Before you can use IE to browse the web, you must be connected to the Internet. When you are connected to the Internet, you are said to be online.

There are three ways to start Internet Explorer:

1. Choose Start, All Programs, Internet Explorer.
2. Click the Internet Explorer icon on the Quick Launch bar (on the taskbar).
3. Double-click the Internet Explorer icon on the desktop.

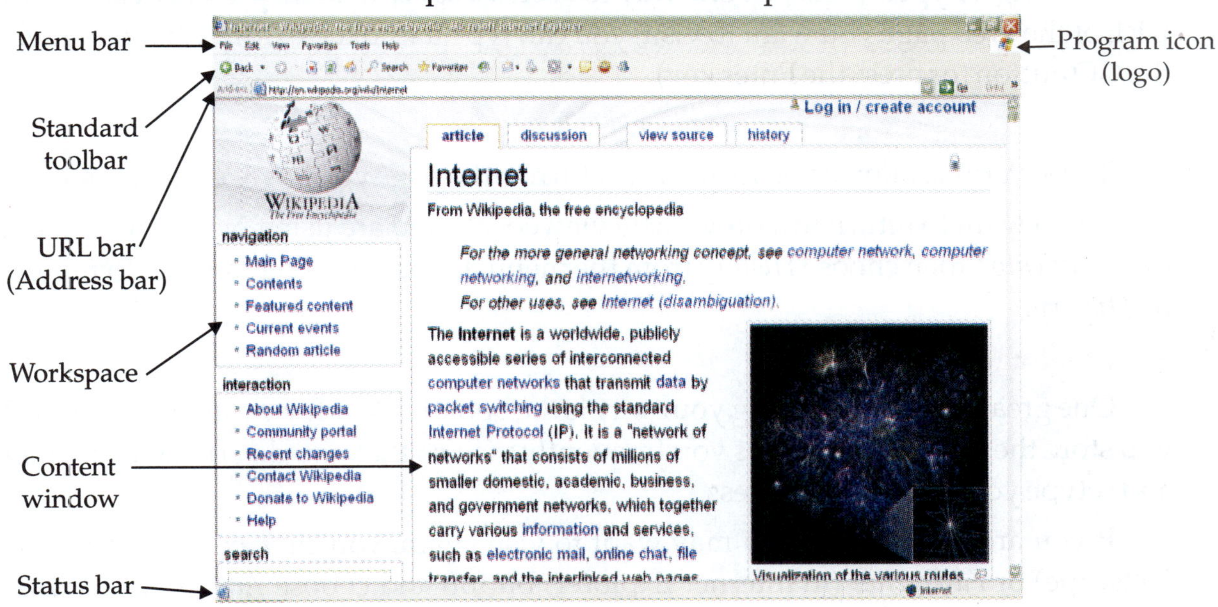

Figure 1.4 Internet Explorer browser window

When IE opens, you will see the browser interface that contains the standard Windows components: a title bar, a menu bar, a content window and a status bar. It also includes a *Standard toolbar* and *Address bar* similar to those in the Windows Explorer and My Computer windows.

In addition to the Standard toolbar and the Address bar, IE also includes a Links bar and a Radio toolbar. Like the toolbars in other Windows programs, you can show, hide, size and arrange the IE toolbars to suit your work style.

- **Address Bar**

The *Address bar* indicates the location of the Web page currently displayed in the content window. This location is also known as *Uniform Resourse Locator* (URL). You can think of a URL as the Internet address of a web page. The Address bar also provides a drop-down list of the recently visited sites. To access a web page, you can type its URL in the Address bar and, then, click the GO button (or press the Enter key). (See figure 1.5)

Figure 1.5 Address bar

Hyperlinks enable you to navigate the Web by clicking words, icons, pictures or other graphics on a web page. When you point to a hyperlink, your mouse pointer changes to a pointing hand. At the same time, the IE status bar shows you the URL associated with the hyperlink to which you are pointing.

Text-based hyperlinks are often underlined or displayed in a different colour than the rest of the text on a Web page. Graphics-based hyperlinks can be icons, logos, buttons, photographs and so on.

Clicking a hyperlink is just one way to access a specific URL. If you already know the URL of the Web page you want to visit, you can type it into the Address bar and then click the GO button (or press the Enter key).

- **History**

The *history list* allows you to quickly return to the page you have recently visited.

If you want to return to a previously viewed site and are using Netscape, you click on *Communicator*, then choose *History* from the menu. If you are using Internet Explorer, click on *History*.

- **Bookmarks/Favourites**

One great helper for finding your way is the bookmark or favourite system, which lets you store the URL or web pages you frequently visit so that you do not have to remember and retype your favourite address.

If you are at a website you may want to visit again, you click on your *Bookmarks* (in Netscape) or *Favourites* (in Internet Explorer) button and choose *Add Bookmark* or *Add to*

Favourites. Later, to revisit the site, you can go to the bookmark menu, and site will reappear.

- **Standard Toolbar**

The *Standard toolbar* provides buttons to facilitate navigation, searching, printing and other common tasks. You can customise this toolbar to include other buttons—such as cut, copy and paste—and you can delete any of the default buttons that you do not commonly use. Figure 1.6 shows the Standard toolbar.

Figure 1.6 Standard toolbar

2.1.3 Browsing the Internet with the Help of Some Features of Browser Window

The World Wide Web consists of more than 1 billion web pages. Moreover, the web is constantly changing; more sites are created and old ones get retired. Without a browser and various kinds of search tools, there would be no way any of us could begin to make any kind of sense of this enormous amount of data.

If you buy a new computer, it will come with a browser already installed. Most browsers have a similar look and feel. Note that the web browser screen has five basic elements: *menu bar, toolbar, URL bar, workspace,* and *status bar.* To execute menu bar and toolbar commands, you use the mouse to move the pointer over the word, known as a *menu selection,* and click the left button of the mouse. This will result in a pull-down menu of other commands for other options.

After you have been using a mouse for a while, you may find moving the pointer around somewhat time-consuming. As a shortcut, if you click on the right mouse button, you can reach many of the commands on the toolbar *(Back, Forward,* and so on) via a pop-up menu.

- **Starting out from home:** The first page you see when you start up your browser is the *home page* or *start page.* (You can also start up from just a blank page, if you do not want to wait for the time it takes to connect with a home page.) You can choose any page on the web as your start page, but a good start page offers links to sites you want to visit frequently.

- **Personalising your home page:** You can probably personalise your home page following the directions provided with the first start page you encounter. Or if you have an older Microsoft or Netscape browser, you can get a customising system from either company. A customised start page is also provided by Yahoo!, Google, AltaVista, and similar services.

- **Getting around—Back, Forward, Home, and Search features:** *Back* takes you back to the previous page. *Forward* lets you look again at a page you returned from. If you really get lost, you can start over by clicking on *Home,* which returns you to your home page. *Search* lists various other search tools. Other navigational aides are history lists and bookmarks. (See figure 1.7)

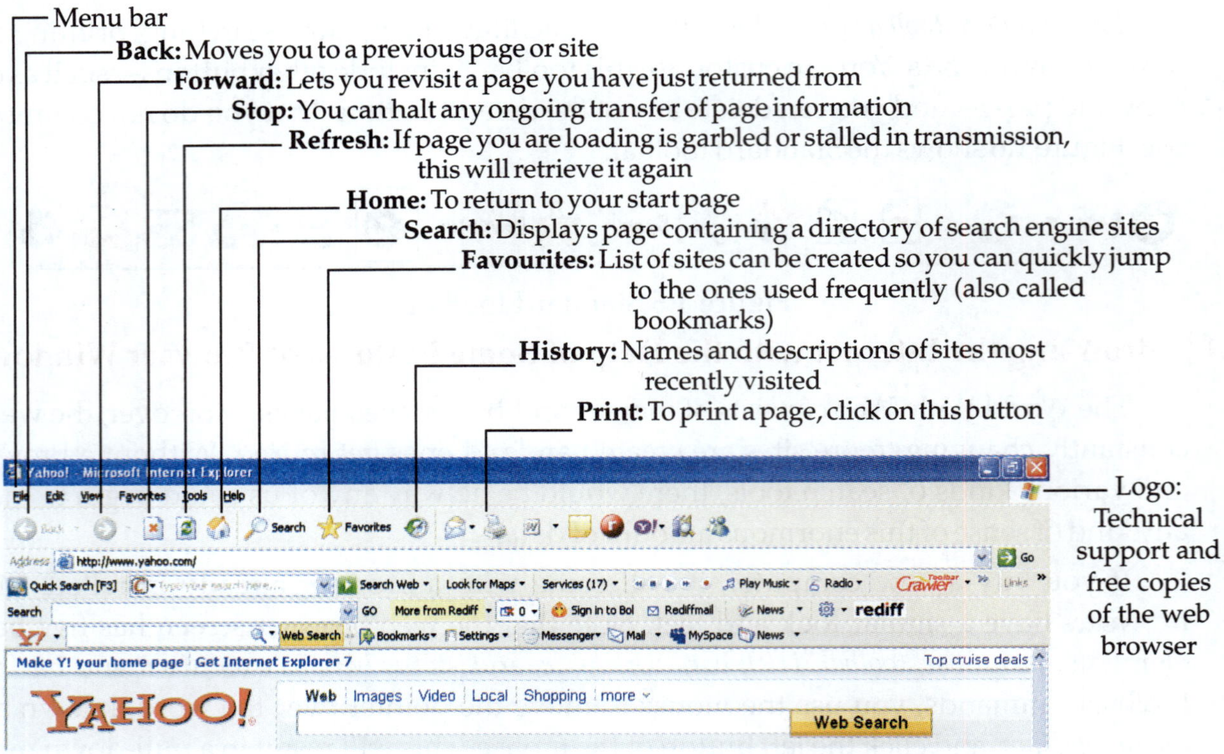

Figure 1.7 Getting around the Web

- **History lists:** If you are browsing through many web pages, it can be difficult to keep track of the locations of the pages you have already visited. The *history list* allows you to quickly return to the pages you have recently visited. (See figure 1.8)

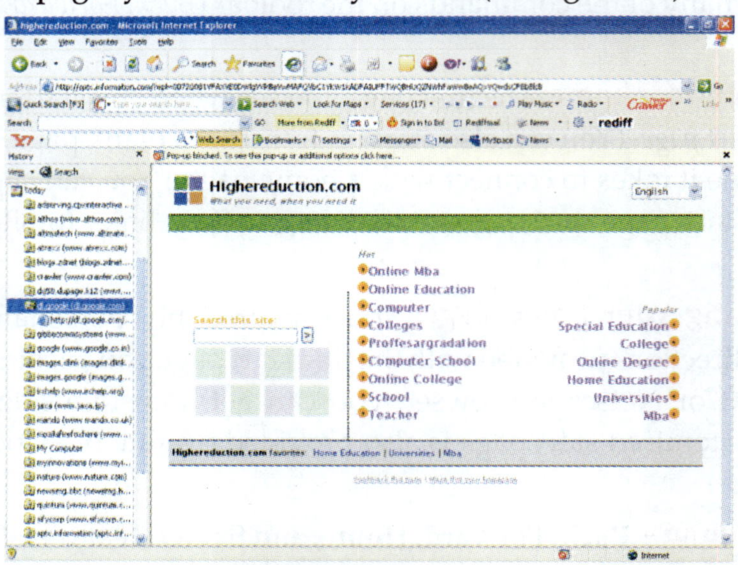

Figure 1.8 History List

If you want to return to a previously viewed site and are using Netscape, you click on *Communicator,* then choose *History* from the menu. If you are using Internet Explorer, click on *History.*

- **Bookmarks or favorites:** One great helper for finding your way is the bookmark or favorites system, which lets you store the URLs of web pages you frequently visit so that you do not have to remember and retype your favourite addresses (See figure 1.9). Say you are visiting a site that you really like and that you know you would like to come back to. You click on your *Bookmark* or *Favorites* feature, which displays the URL on your screen, and then click on *Add,* which automatically stores the address. Later you can locate the site name on your bookmark menu, click on it, and the site will reappear. (When you want to delete it, you can use the right mouse button and select the Delete command.)

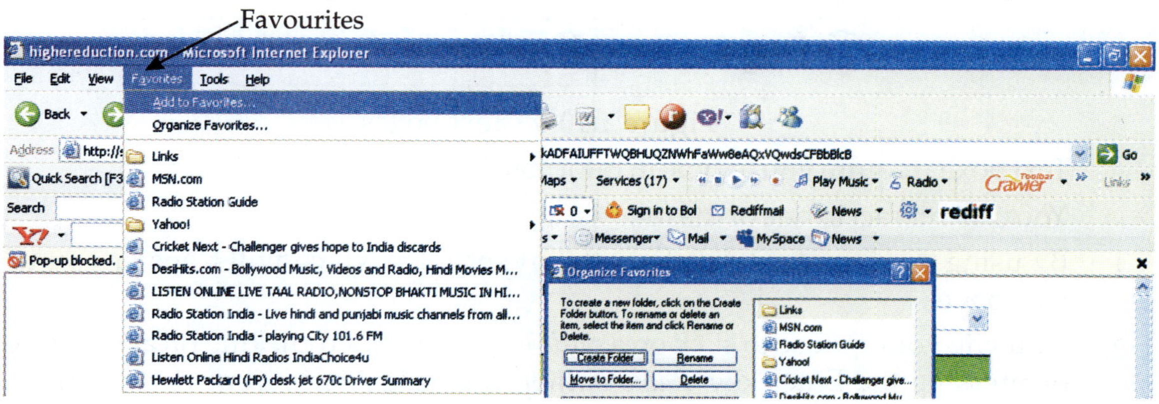

Figure 1.9 Adding Favourites

If you are at a website you may want to visit again, you click on your *Bookmarks* (in Netscape) or *Favorites* (in Internet Explorer) button and choose *Add Bookmark* or *Add to Favorites.* Later, to revisit the site, you can go to the bookmark menu, and the site will reappear.

- **Interactivity—hyperlinks, radio buttons, and fill-in text boxes:** For any given web page that you happen to find yourself on, there may be one of three possible ways to interact with it—or sometimes even all three on the same page. (See figure 1.10)

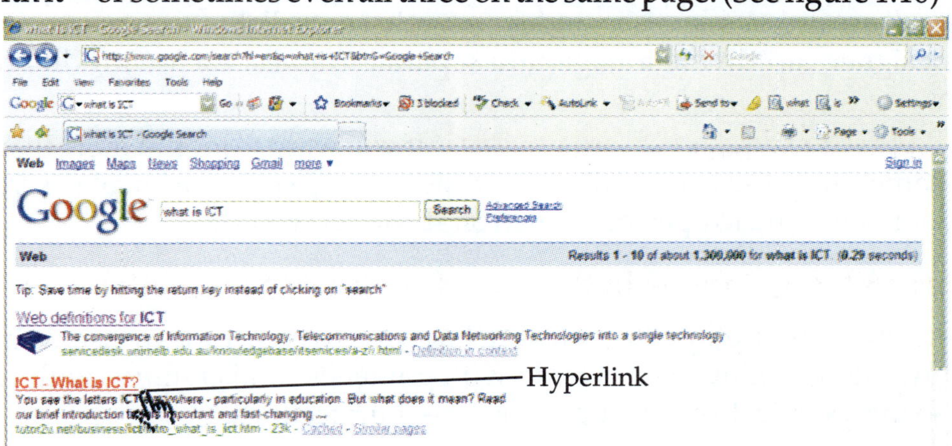

Figure 1.10(*a*) Hyperlinks

Clicking on underlined or colour term transfers you to another web page.

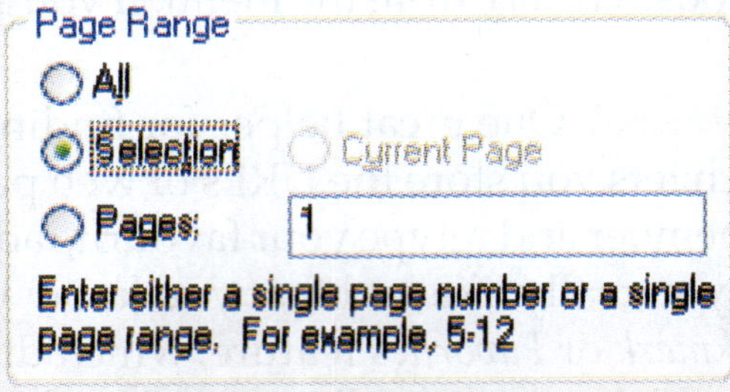

Figure 1.10(*b*) Radio button

Radio buttons act like station selector buttons on a car radio.

Figure 1.10 (*c*) Text boxes

Text boxes require you to type in information.

You can interact in one of the following ways:

1. By using your mouse to click on the hyperlinks, which will transfer you to another web page.
2. By using your mouse to click on a *radio button* and then clicking on a *Submit* command or pressing the Enter key. *Radio buttons* are little circles located, in front of various options; selecting an option with the mouse places a dot in the corresponding circle.
3. By typing text in a fill-in text box, and then hitting the Enter key or clicking on a Go or *Continue* command, which will transfer you to another web page.

- **Scrolling and frames:** To the bottom and side of your screen display, you will note *scroll arrows,* small up/down and left/right arrows. Clicking on scroll arrows with your mouse pointer moves the screen so that you can see the rest of the web page, a movement known as *scrolling.* You can also use the arrow keys on your keyboard for scrolling.

Some web pages are divided into different rectangles known as *frames,* each with its own scroll arrows. A *frame* is an independently controllable section of a web page. A web page designer can divide a page into separate frames, each with different features or options.

- **Looking at two pages simultaneously:** If you want to look at more than one web page at the same time, you can position them side by side on your display screen. Select *New* from your File menu to open more than one browser window.

2.1.4 Rules and Regulations in the Use of Internet (Netiquette)

You may think etiquette is about knowing which fork to use at a formal lunch. Basically, though, etiquette has to do with politeness and civility—with rules for getting along so that people do not get upset or suffer hurt feelings.

New Internet users, known as "newbies", may accidentally offend other people in a discussion group or in an e-mail simply because they are unaware of *netiquette* or "network etiquette"—appropriate online behaviour. In general, netiquette has two basic rules:

(*a*) do not waste people's time, and

(*b*) do not say anything to a person online that you would not say to his or her face.

Some more specific rules of netiquette are given below:

- **Consult FAQs:** Most online groups post *FAQs (frequently asked questions)* that explain expected norms of online behaviour for a particular group. Always read these first—before someone in the group tells you, you have made a mistake.
- **Avoid flaming:** A form of speech unique to online communication, *flaming* is writing an online message that uses derogatory, obscene, or inappropriate language. Flaming is a form of public humiliation inflicted on people who have failed to read FAQs or have otherwise not observed netiquette (although it can happen just because the sender has poor impulse control and needs a course in anger management). Something that smoothes communication online is the use of *emoticons,* keyboard-produced pictorial representations of expressions. (See figure 1.11)

:-)	Happy face	<g>	Grin
:-(	Sorrow or frown	BTW	By the way
:-o	Shock	IMHO	In my humble opinion
:-/	Sarcasm	FYI	For your information
;-)	Wink		

Figure 1.11 Some emoticons

- **Do not SHOUT:** Use of all-capital letters is considered the equivalent of SHOUTING. Avoid, except when they are required for emphasis of a word or two (as when you cannot use italics in your e-messages).
- **Be careful with jokes:** In e-mail, subtleties are often lost, so jokes may be taken as insults or criticism.
- **Avoid sloppiness, but avoid criticising others' sloppiness:** Avoid spelling and grammatical errors. But do not criticise those same errors in others' messages. (After all, they may not speak English as a native language.) Most e-mail software comes with spell-checking capability, which is easy to use.
- **Do not send huge file attachments, unless requested:** Your friend living in the country may find it takes many minutes rather than seconds for his or her computer to download a massive file (as of a video that you want to share). This may tie up the system at a time when your friend badly needs to use it. Also, most e-mail programs can be set to refuse e-mails larger than a designated size—say, 1 megabyte. Better to query in advance before sending large files as attachments. Also, whenever you send an attachment, be sure the recipient has the appropriate software to open your attachment (you both are using Microsoft Word 2007, for example).
- **When replying, quote only the relevant portion:** If you are replying to just a couple of

matters in a long e-mail posting, do not send back the entire message. This forces your recipient to wade through lots of text to find the reference. Instead, edit his or her original text down to the relevant paragraph and then put in your response immediately following.

- **Do not "overforward":** Do not automatically forward e-mails to your friends without checking if the contents are true and appropriate.

Spam-unsolicited mails

Spam refers to unsolicited e-mail, or junk mail, in the form of advertising or chain letters. Usually you would not recognise the sender on your list of incoming mail, and often the subject line will give no hint, stating something such as "The status of your application" or "It's up to you now." The solicitations can range from money-making schemes to online pornography. So, annoying is spam that the members of the European Union have voted to outlaw bulk e-mail, which includes spam.

Useful Tip

Handling the Annoyance of Spam

To better manage spam, some users get two e-mail boxes. One is used for online shopping, business, research, etc.,—which will continue to attract spam. The other is used (like an unlisted phone number) only for personal friends and family—and will probably not receive much spam.

Some ways to deal with this nuisance are given below:

- Delete without opening the message
- Never reply to a spam message
- Enlist the help of your ISP or use spam filters
- Fight back

Useful Tip

Getting Antispam Software

Make sure that the antispam program you want to buy or download supports your e-mail format. Some spam programs are sold, and others are free. You can find out what is available by doing a keyword search for antispam software or something similar.

A few tips for spam-fighting are given below:

1. Guard your in-box.
2. Use free web mail accounts.
3. Use a disposable e-mail address.
4. Use fake addresses.
5. Do not post your address.

6. Do not answer spam. Ever.
7. Opt out.
8. Read the privacy policy.
9. Use a spam filter.

People's Privacy

It primarily consists of privacy over the media of the Internet. It is the ability to control what information one reveals about oneself over the Internet. To control who can access that information has become a growing concern. These concerns include whether *email* can be stored or read by third parties without consent, or whether third parties can track the websites someone has visited. Another concern is whether websites which are visited collect, store and possibly share *personally identifiable information* about users. The advent of various *search engines* and the use of *data mining* has created a capability for data about individuals to be collected and combined from a wide variety of sources very easily.

Risks to Internet Privacy

Those concerned about Internet privacy often cite a number of privacy risks—events that can compromise privacy—which one may encounter through Internet use. These risks are due to the following:

1. Cookies
2. ISPs
3. Data logging
4. Other potential Internet privacy risks (Spyware, Web bug, Social engineering, etc.)

Pornography

Due to the international nature of the Internet, *Internet pornography* carries with it special issues with regards to the law. There is no one set of laws that applies to the distribution, purchase, or possession of Internet pornography. Only the laws of one's home nation apply with regard to distributing or possessing Internet pornography. This means that, for example, even if a pornographer is legally distributing pornography, the person receiving it may not be legally doing so due to legal laws.

Pornography is a computer crime, so the students must avoid visiting pornographic sites.

Intellectual Property Rights

Intellectual Property Rights (IPR), very broadly, are rights granted to creators and owners of works that are results of human intellectual creativity. These works can be in the industrial, scientific, literacy and artistic form. They can be in the form of an invention, a manuscript, a suite of software, or a business name.

In general, the objective of IPR is to protect the copyright of authors in their work and at the same time allow the general public to access their creativity.

Types of Intellectual Property Rights

The Principal Intellectual Property Rights are given below:

1. Copyright
2. Patents
3. Trade Marks
4. Design Rights
5. Passing Off
6. The Law of Confidential Information

You must always follow the rules and regulations for the responsible use of the Internet and in turn obey the Intellectual Property Rights.

SUMMARY

- Internet (the "net") is the worldwide computer network that connects hundreds of thousands of smaller networks linking computers at academic, scientific, and commercial institutions, as well as individuals.
- The first step towards the construction of Internet was the project named ARPANET.
- Broadband is a very high speed connection. Access to information is much faster than with traditional phone lines.
- Protocol is set of communication rules for exchanging information.
- Telnet is a program or command that allows you to connect to remote computers on the Internet and to run programs on those computers.
- Transmission Control Protocol/Internet Protocol (TCP/IP) is a protocol that enables all computers to use data transmitted on the Internet. IP is used to send the packets across the Internet to their final destination, and TCP is used to reassemble the packets in the correct order.
- Internet computers use TCP/IP for all Internet transactions, from sending e-mail to downloading stock quotes or pictures off a friend's website.
- URL (Universal Resource Locator) is a string of characters that points to specific piece of information anywhere on the web.
- Usenet is worldwide network of servers that can be accessed through the Internet. Newsgroups take place on Usenet.
- Web browser (browser) is software that enables users to locate and view web pages and to jump from one page to another.
- Users cannot surf the web without a browser. The three most well-known browsers are Microsoft Internet Explorer, Mozilla Firefox and Netscape Communicator.
- Internet Protocol (IP) address is an address that every computer on the Internet has; consists of four sets of numbers between 0 and 255 separated by decimals—for example, 1.190.10.230.

- Internet service provider (ISP) is a company that connects you through your communications line to its servers, or central computer, which connects you to the Internet via another company's network access points.
- Web page is a document on the World Wide Web that can include text, pictures, sound, and video.
- Hyper Text Transfer Protocol (HTTP) are communications rules that allow browsers to connect with web servers. Without HTTP, files could not be transferred over the web.
- FTP (File Transfer Protocol) is a method whereby you can connect to a remote computer called an FTP site and transfer publicly available files to your own microcomputer's hard disk via TCP/IP over the Internet.
- Home page is also called welcome page; web page that, somewhat like the title page of a book, identifies the website and contains links to other pages at the site. The first page you see at a website is the home page.
- Hypertext Markup Language (HTML) is a set of special instructions (called "tags" or "markups") used to specify web document structure, formatting, and links to other documents. HTML enables the creation of web pages.
- Log on means to make a connection to a remote computer. Users must be familiar with log on procedures to go online.
- Modem is a device that sends and receives data over telephone lines to and from computers.
- Discussion board or Newsgroup, also called forum, is a giant electronic bulletin board on which users conduct written discussions about a specific subject.
- Real-time chart (RTC) is a typed discussion ("chat") among participants who are online at the same time; it is just like a telephone conversation, except that messages are typed rather than spoken.
- Search engine is a search tool that allows you to find specific documents through keyword searches and menu choices, in contrast to directories, which are lists of websites classified by topic.
- Site is a computer with a domain name. Sites provide Internet and web content.
- Spam is unsolicited e-mail in the form of advertising or chain letters.
- Domain is a location on the Internet.
- Download means to transmit data from a remote computer to a local computer.
- Emoticons are keyboard-produced pictorial representations of expressions.
- Website is a location of a web domain name in a computer somewhere on the Internet. Websites provide multimedia content to users.
- Blog is Web log, an Internet journal.

- Listserv is an automatic mailing list server that sends e-mail to subscribers who regularly participate in discussion topics.
- Netiquette means "Network etiquette," or appropriate online behavior.

REVIEW QUESTIONS

STATE WHETHER TRUE OR FALSE

1. The largest network in the world is not called Internet.
2. To make a connection to the Internet over the phone lines, you use what is called dial-up access.
3. The term surfing refers to the way you click the links to move from site to site.
4. Unsolicited e-mail in the form of advertising or chain letters is known as URL.
5. People's privacy must be ignored while using the Internet.

FILL IN THE BLANKS

1. A company that connects you through your communications line to its server, which connects you to the Internet, is a(n) ....
2. To navigate the web and display the contents of its pages, you use a software program called a ....
3. Students must desist from visiting .... site and intruding on people's privacy.
4. TCP Stands for ....
5. .... is the language used to format web pages.

MULTIPLE CHOICE QUESTIONS

1. Who owns the Internet?
   (a) Microsoft
   (b) IBM
   (c) U.S. government
   (d) No one owns the Internet
2. A location on the Internet is called a(n) ....
   (a) User ID (b) domain
   (c) browser (d) web
3. Which of the following is *not* a netiquette rule?
   (a) Consult FAQs (b) Flame only when necessary
   (c) Always SHOUT (d) Avoid huge file attachments

4. A .... is set of communication rules for exchanging information on the Internet.
   (a) Protocol
   (b) Email
   (c) URL
   (d) Pornography
5. Which of the following is/are search engines?
   (a) Yahoo!
   (b) Google
   (c) Meta Crawler
   (d) All of these

ANSWER THE FOLLOWING

1. What is Internet? Who owns it?
2. How has the Internet affected your life? Discuss.
3. What are the means of connecting to the Internet, and how fast are they?
4. What is an Internet Service Provider, and what do ISPs provide?
5. What are websites, web pages, browsers, URLs, and search engines?
6. Write a short note on the following:
   (i) Chat
   (ii) Discussion boards
   (iii) Synchronous and Asynchronous transmission modes
   (iv) WWW (World Wide Web)
   (v) HTML (Hypertext Markup Language)
   (vi) HTTP (Hypertext Transfer Protocol)
   (vii) FTP (File Transfer Protocol)
   (viii) URL (Uniform Resource Locator)
   (ix) IP (Internet Protocol)
   (x) E-mail
   (xi) TCP (Transmission Control Protocol)
   (xii) Search engines
   (xiii) Blogs
   (xiv) Listservs
7. What is a browser? Discuss the features of browser window.
8. How will you browse the Internet with the help of the features of browser window?
9. What are the rules and regulations in the use of Internet (Netiquette), and why are these important?
10. What is spam? Give some spam fighting tips.

11. Write a short note on the following:
    (i) People's privacy
    (ii) Pornography
    (iii) Intellectual Property Rights.
12. How does the Internet function?

ASSIGNMENT

Locate the name and telephone number of a local Internet access provider. Also, get the name, telephone number, and e-mail address of their help desk so they can help if you have any questions getting connected. Ask the following questions.

(i) What is the one-time connect charge, if any?

(ii) What is the monthly charge?

(iii) How many free hours are there?

(iv) What is the cost per hour after you exceed the maximum free hours?

(v) Do they provide an e-mail address?

(vi) What browser is required? Do you have a choice?

UNIT 2 USING THE INTERNET TO COMMUNICATE

Specific Objectives

After reading this unit, the student will be able to:

2.2.1 send and access e-mail message with attachments.

2.2.2 use Internet to chat.

2.2.0 Introduction

You have already studied in your junior classes how to create an e-mail account. We will review the same and learn about attachments and Internet chatting.

You need to send/access e-mail messages to/from your friends, relatives and classmates. Using Internet to chat is also very important in today's world. As mentioned earlier netiquette refers to politeness and consideration for others in your use of Internet services like e-mail and chat. So it is essential for you to get a grip on your netiquettes before you send an e-mail or start chatting.

2.2.1 Sending, Accessing E-mail Messages with Attachments

E-mail or electronic mail is the exchange of messages stored on computers, through a communication channel. E-mail was one of the first uses of the Internet and is still the most popular. To send and receive e-mail, you need to create an account with an e-mail service provider. The Internet does not limit you to one e-mail address. You can create multiple e-mail addresses. There are many Internet based e-mail service providers.

Here is a list of sites that provide you with the e-mail facility.

http://www.yahoo.com/

http://www.mailandnews.com/

http://www.everyone.net/

http://www.mail.com/

http://www.excite.com/

http://www.hotmail.com/

Let us use the site http://www.yahoo.com/ to create an E-mail account, *i.e.*, a mail ID (See figure 2.1). Go ahead and create your e-mail ID by accessing the site, http://www.yahoo.com/.

Figure 2.1 Using the site yahoo.com

OR

You can directly open the site by typing http://www.yahoomail.com.

Click the 'Mail' link on Yahoo!.

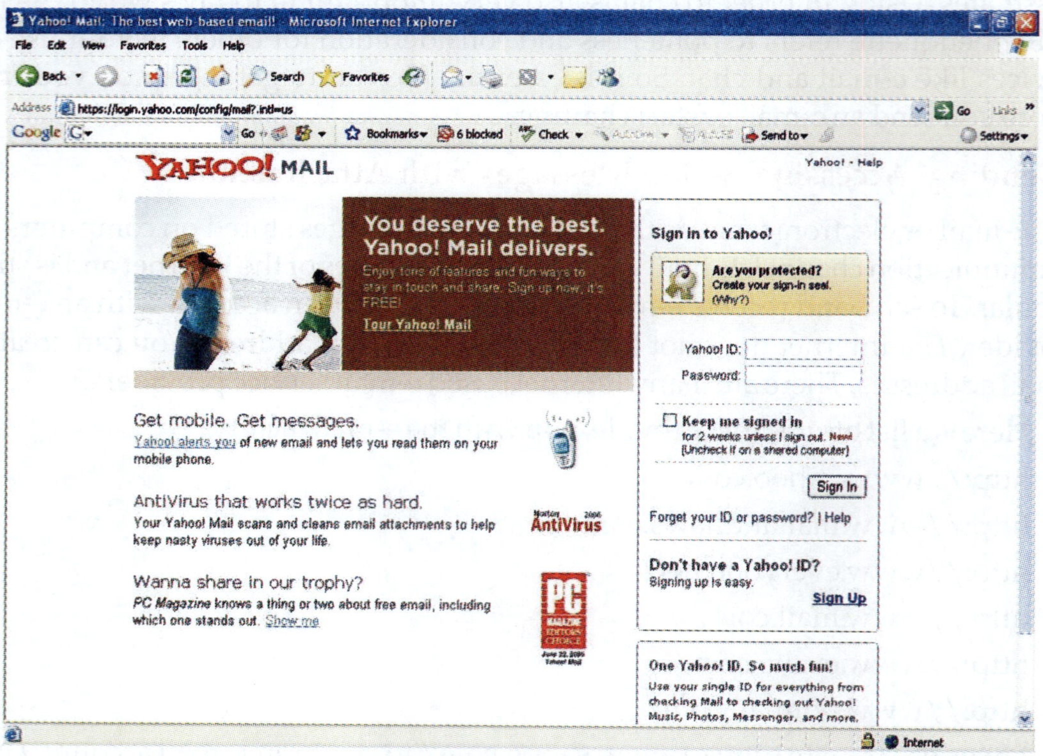

Figure 2.2 Selecting the Mail link on Yahoo!

Since you are a new user, click the 'Sign Up' link.

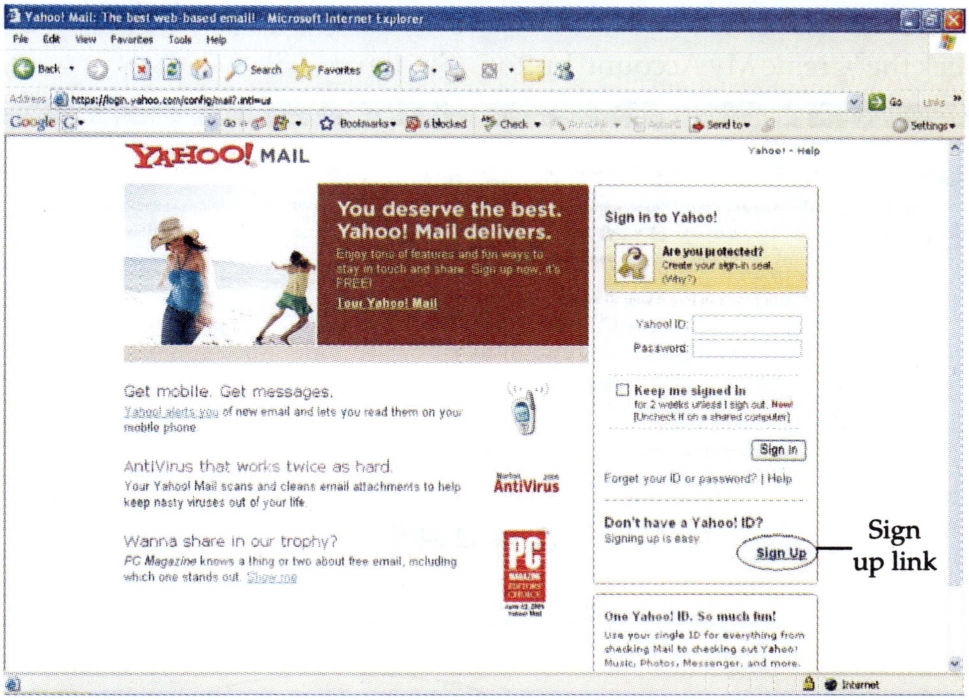

Figure 2.3 Selecting the Sign Up link

Type in your details in the spaces provided.

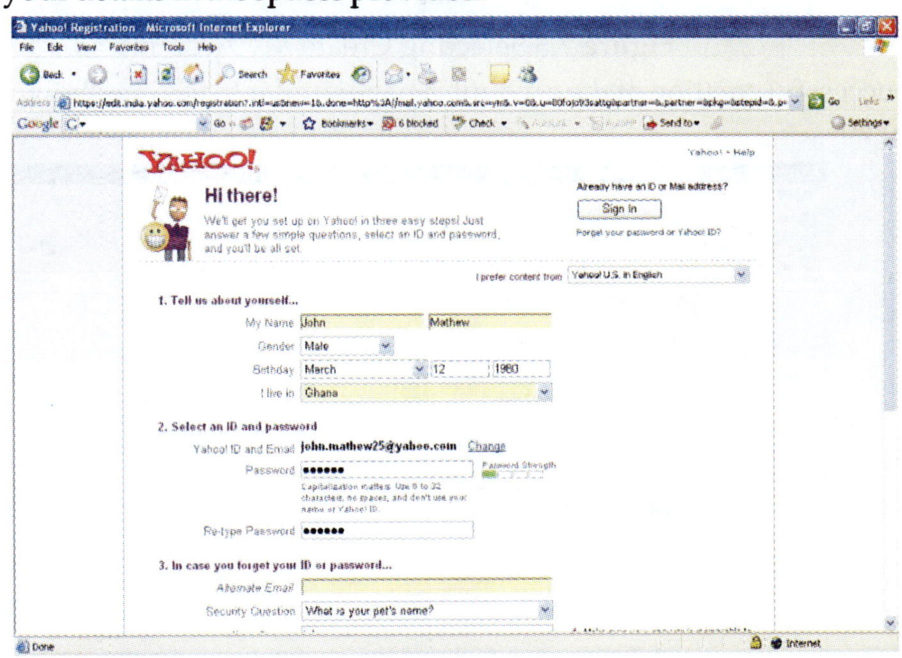

Figure 2.4 Typing the details

The name that you enter in the Yahoo ID text box is your yahoo mail ID. You can choose any name for the ID, but it should be one that you can identify easily. It has to be unique, since two people cannot have the same ID. For example, let us assume your name is John Mathew and you choose your name as your ID. If there is already another user with the same ID, you will be asked to choose a different ID.

Click the 'Create My Account' button. (See figure 2.5)

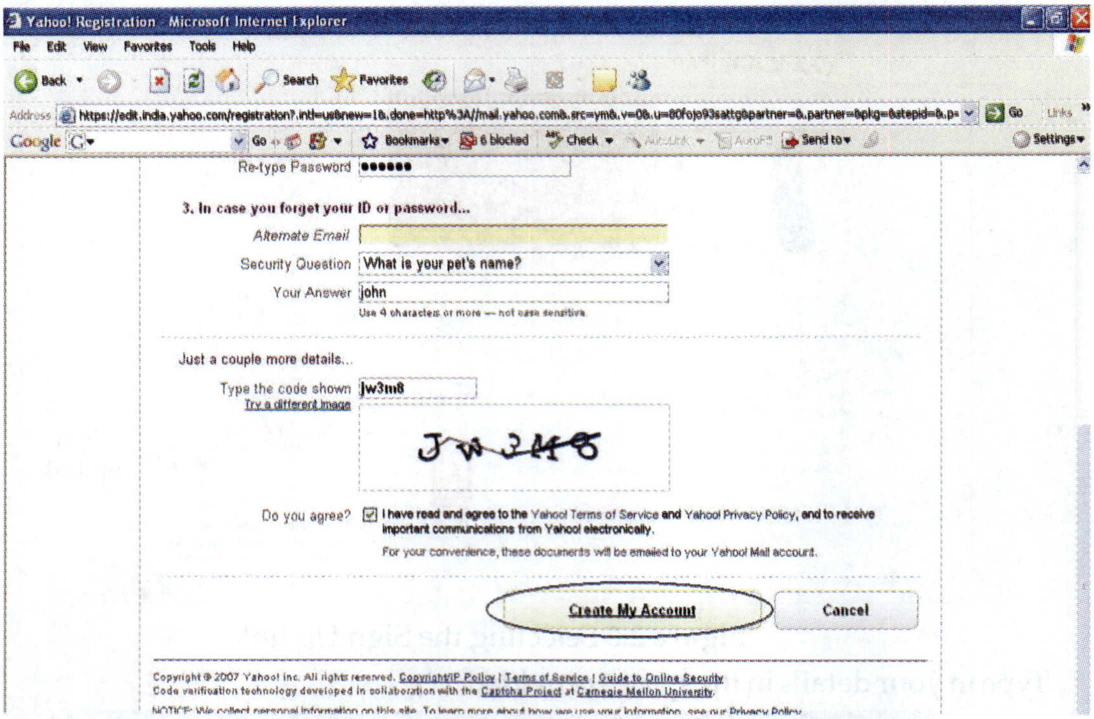

Figure 2.5 Selecting Create My Account

On successful creation of the account, a page similar to the one shown in figure 2.6 will be displayed.

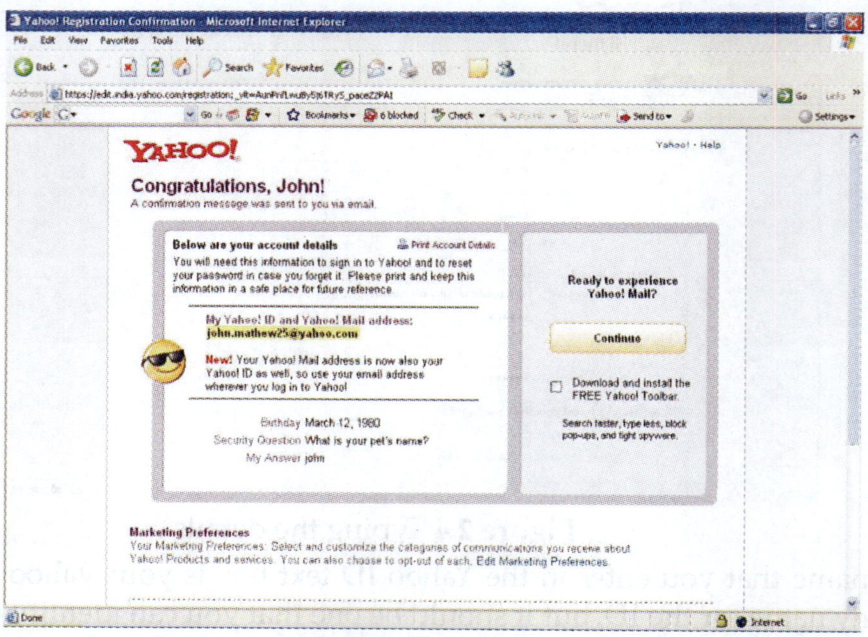

Figure 2.6 Ready to explore the created account

Your account is created. You are asked to enter your password to verify your account. Enter your password, and click the 'Sign In' button. (See figure 2.7)

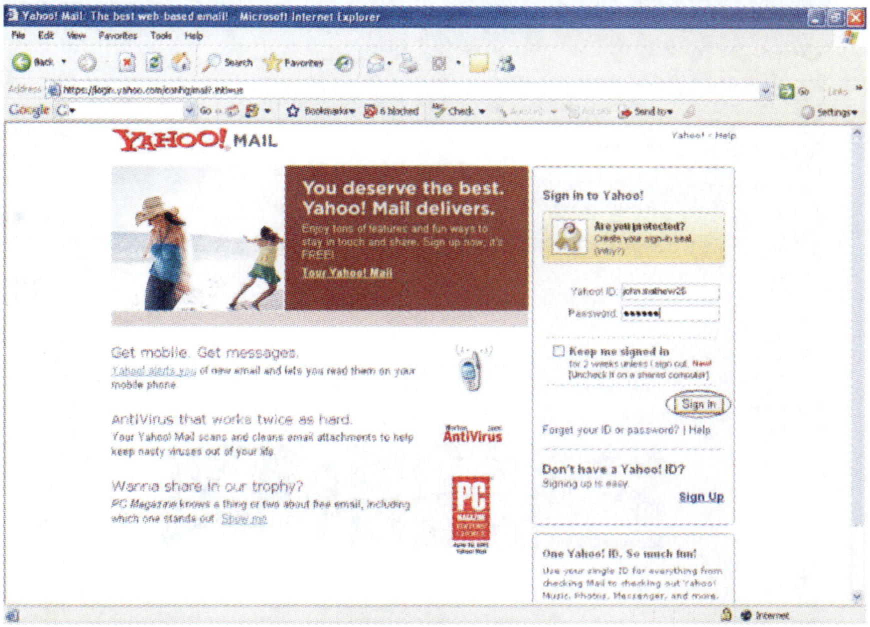

Figure 2.7 Selecting Sign In

After correct Sign In, you will see the open mail box as shown in figure 2.8.

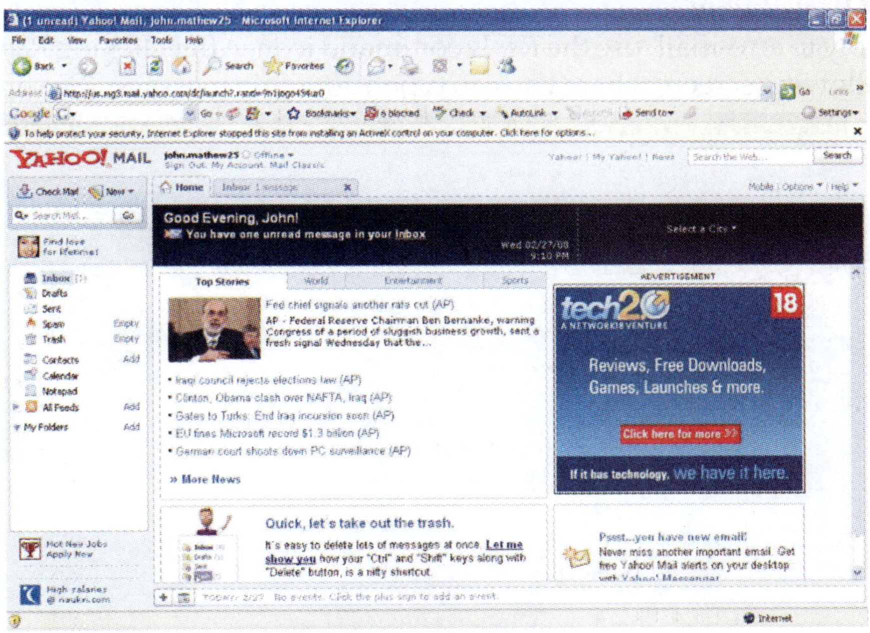

Figure 2.8 Open mail box

Receiving an e-mail

To send and receive mails, log on to the site using the Yahoo ID and the password.

To read the received mails, click on the *Inbox* shown on the left side of the screen. (See figure 2.8)

On clicking the Inbox you will see the list of received mails. Select anyone of these and click to read it. (See figure 2.9)

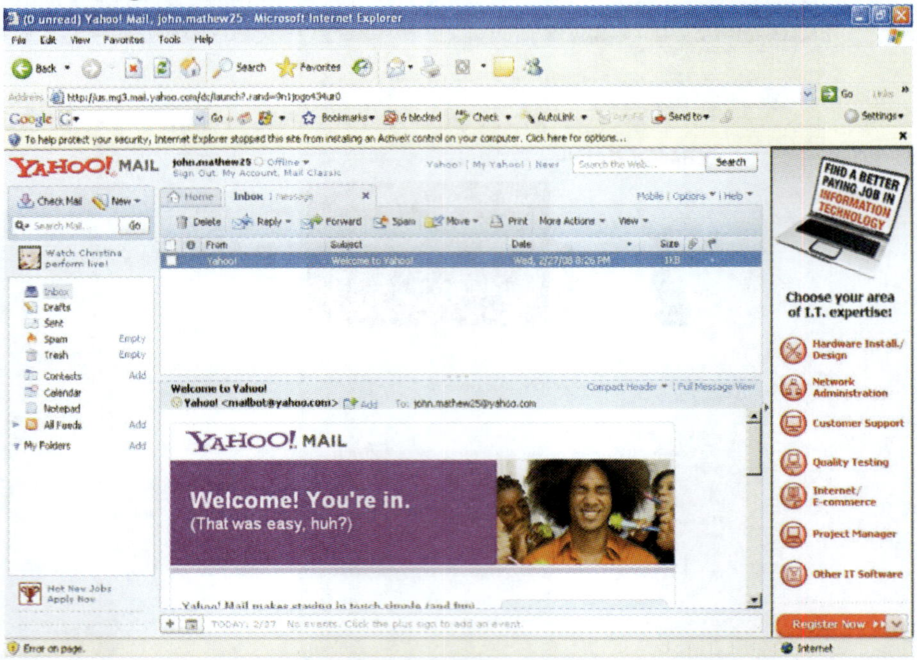

Figure 2.9 Receiving an e-mail

Replying to an e-mail

To reply to an e-mail, use the *Reply* command icon. After clicking *Reply* button you will see the following screen, where you can type your reply message. (See figure 2.10)

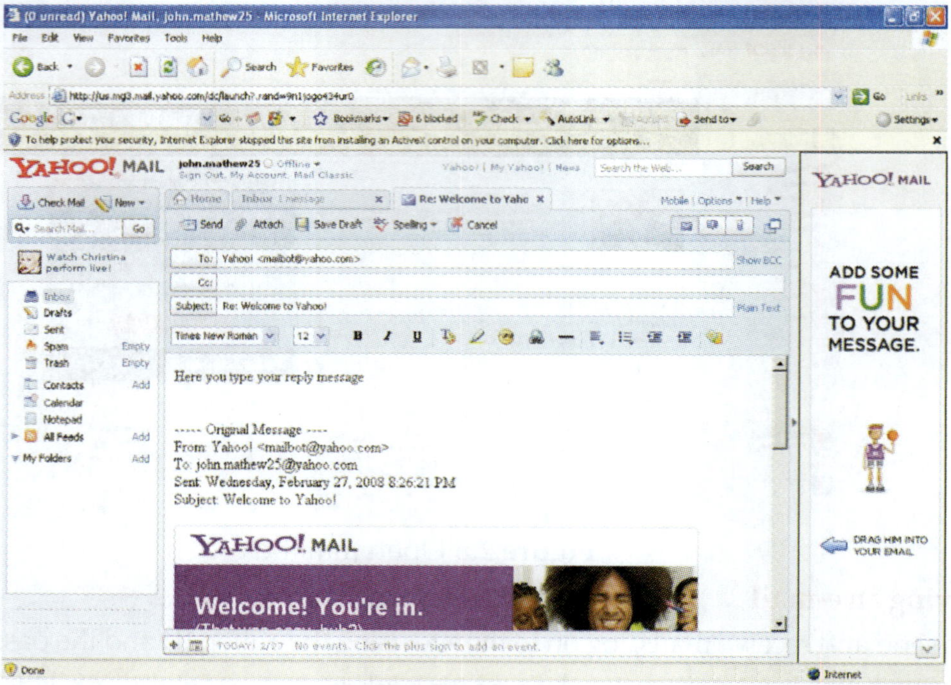

Figure 2.10 Replying to an e-mail

Composing and editing a new e-mail

Click the 'New' link on the left side of the screen to write a new mail.

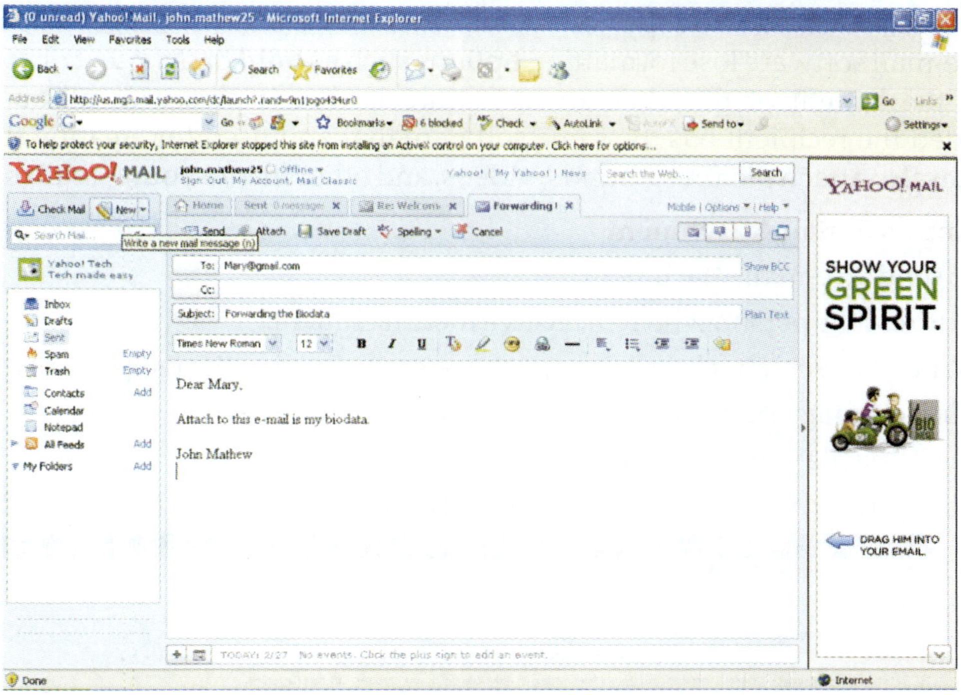

Figure 2.11 Sending an e-mail

Enter the recipient's e-mail address in the 'To' option. You can send copies of the mail to other users by using the 'Cc' option. You can enter the contents and addresses in the appropriate places provided.

Composing of an e-mail message is done very much like a paper letter. It consists of three parts, the header, the body and the signature. The header, at the top of the message, is the envelope, the body is the actual message, the signature comes at the end.

You do not have to be online while composing your e-mail messages. E-mail lets you write messages offline, so you can save them, then go online, and send them all at once.

Editing of an e-mail message can be done like editing of text in MS Word. Various editing features like font, font size, bold, italic, underline, text colour, emoticons, text alignment, bullets, numbering etc. are available in the mail box.

Spell checking must be done before sending e-mail messages by the user. You can spell check by clicking the *Spelling* button in the mail box.

Sending an e-mail

Click the 'Send' button when you have typed in the message and addresses and you are ready to send the e-mail. **Make sure that you have spell checked the message before sending it.**

Attachments

If a file of your matter exists in the computer from which you are sending e-mail, you can write your e-mail message, (your cover note) and then use the Attach link to attach the document. Such attached documents may be in MS Word or Excel and are called attachments.

While you could also copy your document into the main message and send it that way, some e-mail software lose formatting options such as **bold** or *italic* text or special symbols. Thus, the benefit of the attachment feature is that it preserves all such formatting, provided the recipient has the same software that you used for creating the attachment. You can also attach pictures, sounds, videos, and other files to your e-mail message.

Sending an e-mail Attachment

To send an e-mail attachment,

1. Address the person who will receive the attachment.
2. Write a "cover letter" e-mail or your message advising the recipient of the attachment.
3. Click on *Attach* button on your e-mail software's toolbar.
4. Select the file you want to attach.
5. Click on *Send* to send the e-mail message and the attachment. (See figure 2.12)

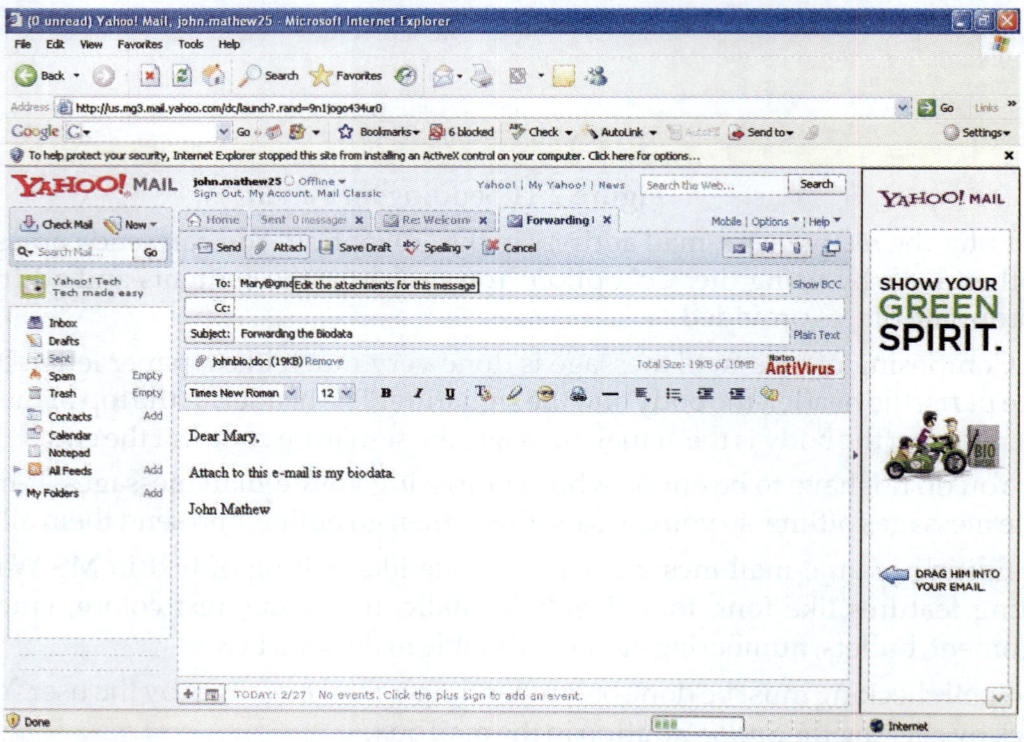

Figure 2.12 Sending an e-mail attachment

Receiving an e-mail Attachment

When you receive a file containing an attachment, you will see an icon indicating that the message contains more than just text. You can click on the icon to see the attachment. If you have the software the attached file was created in, you can open the attachment immediately to read or print, or you can save the attachment in a location of your choice (on your computer). You can also forward the attachment to another person.

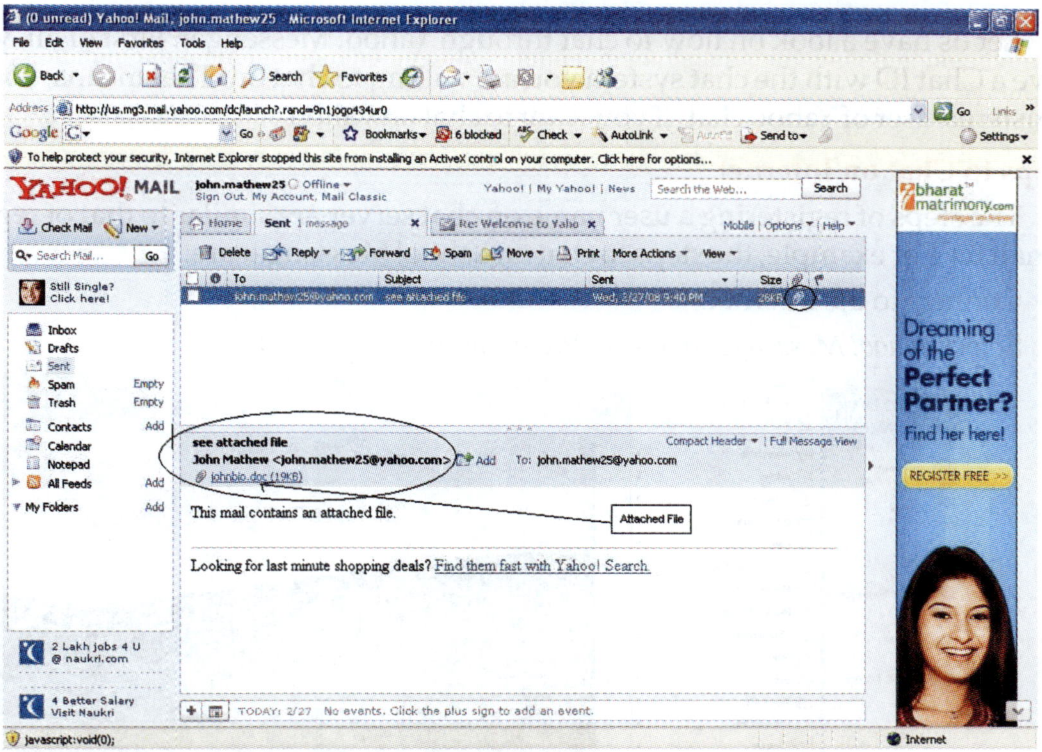

Figure 2.13 Receiving an e-mail attachment

To exit your mailbox, click the 'Sign Out' link.

Note

1. It is important that the persons receiving the e-mail attachment have the exact same software that created the attached file, such as Microsoft Word 2007, or have software that can read and convert the attached file.

2. Many viruses—those rogue programs that can seriously damage your PC or programs—ride along with e-mail as attached files. Thus, you should *never open an attached file from an unknown source*.

2.2.2 Using Internet to Chat

Once connected with an ISP (Internet Service Provider), you immediately join the millions of users who are online. Your friends, relatives and classmates might also be amongst these users.

Chat provides a means of immediate electronic communication. *Chatting* is online text and voice conversation on the Internet.

Chatting is a fast and instant way of communicating with your friends, relatives and classmates. It is also called Instant Messaging System. Examples of present instant-message systems are AOL Instant Messenger, MSN Messenger, ICQ, AT&T IM anywhere, and Yahoo! Messenger. Some of these, such as Yahoo's, allow voice chats among users if their PCs have microphones and speakers.

Let us have a look on how to chat through Yahoo! Messenger. First of all, you need to have a Chat ID with the chat system you are willing to chat on. That means, you must be a registered user of Yahoo chat, if you want to chat on yahoo.

Steps to Chat on Internet

The steps of registering a user name on chat server are similar to that of registering an e-mail ID. For example, the steps to chat on Yahoo! Messenger are:

1. Connect to the Internet.
2. Select *Yahoo! Messenger* from *All Programs*. (See figure 2.14)

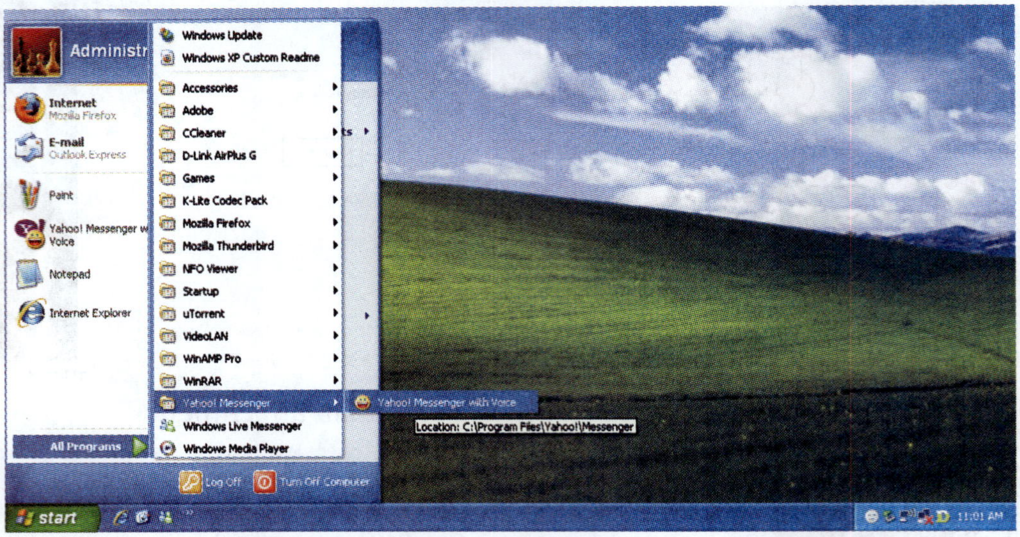

Figure 2.14 Selecting Yahoo! Messenger

3. The Yahoo! Messenger page will open. Fill-in your e-mail ID and password and click on 'Sign In' (See figure 2.15)

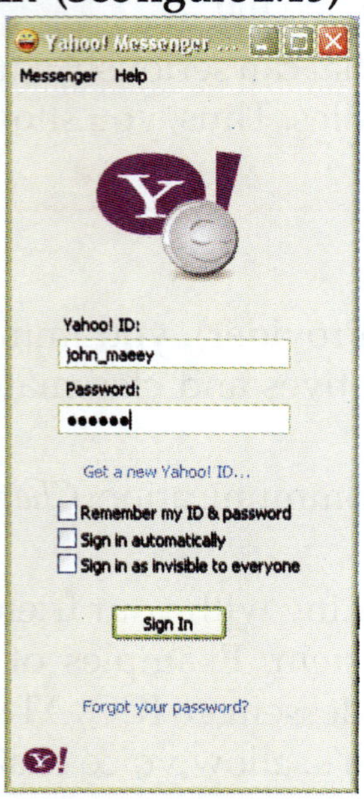

Figure 2.15 Selecting 'Sign In' option

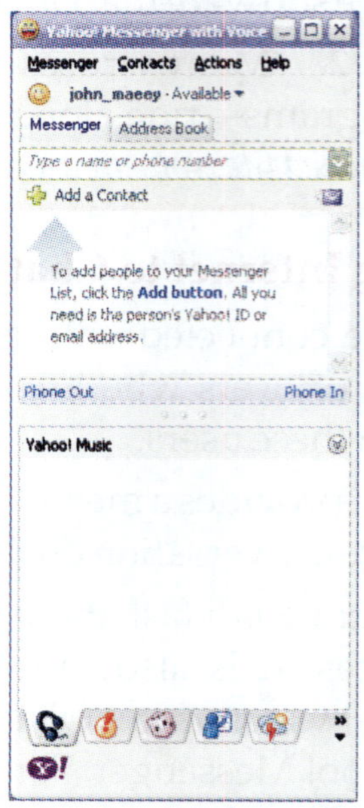

Figure 2.16 Entering the chat room

4. After Sign In you will get the options for entering the chat room. (See figure 2.16).
5. Click on *Messenger* tab.
6. Select *Yahoo! Chat* and click on *Join a Room...* (See figure 2.17)

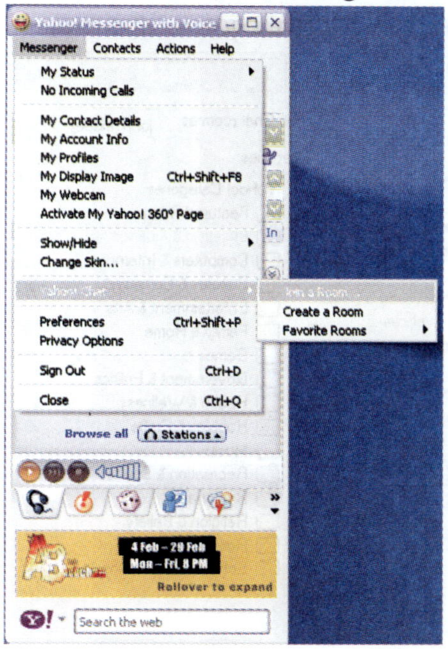

Figure 2.17 Selecting *Join a Room...*

7. Select any category from *Yahoo! Categories.* (See figure 2.18)

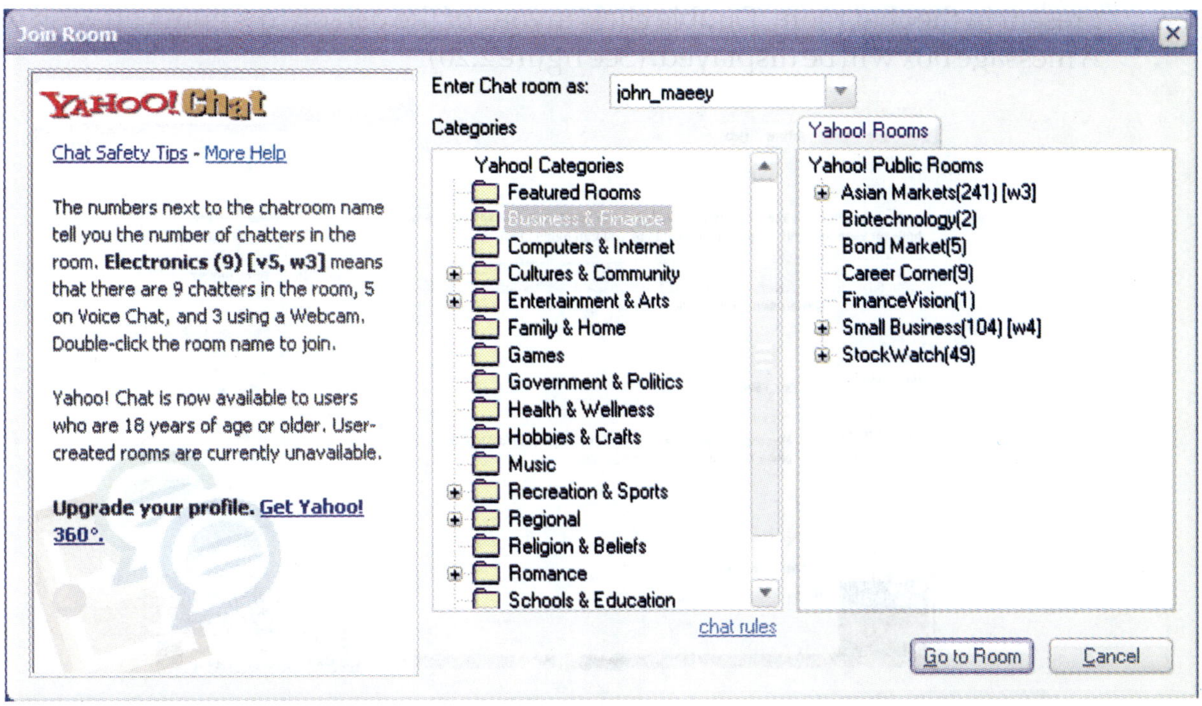

Figure 2.18 Selecting from Yahoo! categories

8. On selecting the category, the Yahoo! Rooms are made available.
9. Select any Yahoo! Room and click on *Go to Room.* (See figure 2.19)

OR

Double click on the Yahoo! Room to join a Room.

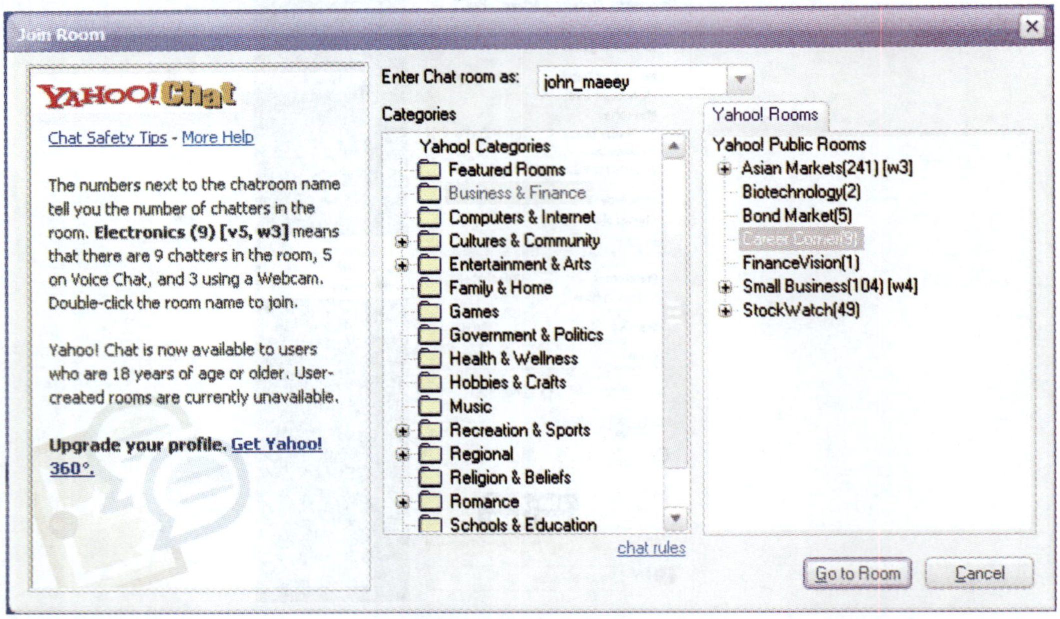

Figure 2.19 Joining Room

10. The chat room is displayed for chatting. The chatter list box contains the list of people present in the chat room. Double click anyone of the person to whom you wish to chat. A message box will be displayed. (See figure 2.20)

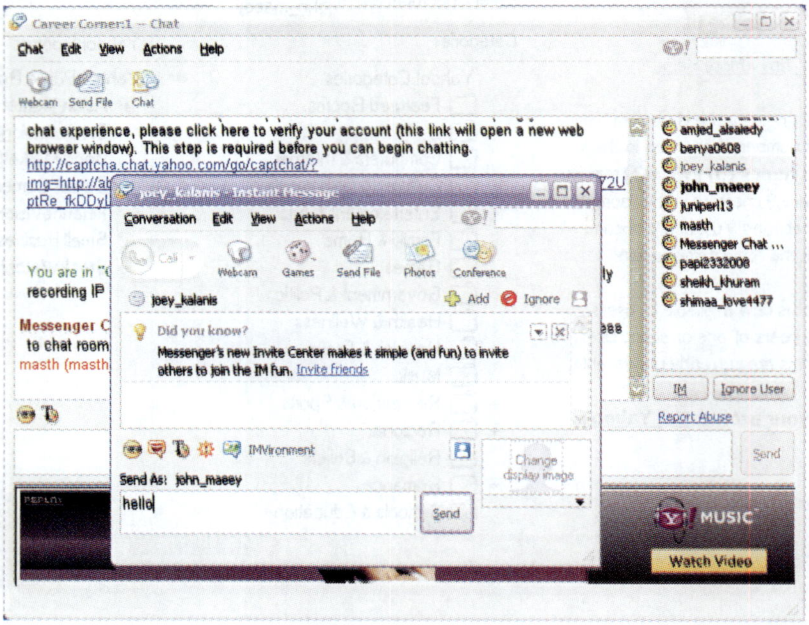

Figure 2.20 Chatting

11. You can type your message in the 'Chat' text box and click the 'Send' button or press Enter Key.
12. When you have finished the chat, close the Yahoo! Chat Room.
13. Click on the Messenger tab.
14. Select 'Sign Out' option.

SUMMARY

- E-mail or electronic mail is the exchange of messages stored on computers, through a communication channel.
- E-mail was one of the first uses of the Internet and is still the most popular.
- To send and receive e-mail, you need to create an e-mail account with an e-mail service provider.
- There are many sites that provide you with the e-mail facility, for example,
  http://www.yahoo.com/
  http://www.hotmail.com/
- The name that you enter in the Yahoo ID text box is your yahoo mail ID.
- Your mail ID must be unique.
- To send and receive mail, log on to the site using the yahoo ID and the password.
- Netiquette refers to politeness and consideration for others in your use of Internet services like e-mail and chat.
- The Internet does not limit you to one e-mail address. You can create multiple e-mail addresses.
- Using a chat facility, you can reach out and befriend people all over the world.
- Chat provides a means of immediate electronic communication.

REVIEW QUESTIONS

STATE WHETHER TRUE OR FALSE

1. Electronic mail is a utility, used to transfer text messages from one computer to the other on the Internet.
2. There is no need of an e-mail account to send and receive mail.
3. Chat does not provide a means of immediate electronic communication.

FILL IN THE BLANKS

1. .... was one of the first uses of the Internet and is still the most popular.
2. The Internet does not limit you to one e-mail address. You can create .... e-mail addresses.

3. You must properly compose, edit and .... an e-mail message.
4. .... is online text and voice conversation on the Internet.

MULTIPLE CHOICE QUESTIONS

1. The service used to transfer text messages across the Internet is called ....
   (*a*) Newgroup (*b*) E-mail
   (*c*) Telnet (*d*) FTP
2. .... is appropriate online behaviour.
   (*a*) Netiquette (*b*) HTML
   (*c*) Modem (*d*) URLs

ANSWER THE FOLLOWING

1. How will you create an e-mail account? Discuss.
2. What are the components of an e-mail address? Give an example.
3. How will you send and access e-mail messages with attachments? Explain.
4. What is chat? How will you use Internet to chat?

ASSIGNMENT

1. How will you access and print an e-mail attachment? Discuss.
2. Make groups in your class, log on and chat using the Internet.

UNIT 3 ACCESSING INFORMATION FROM THE INTERNET

Specific Objectives

After reading this unit, the student will be able to:

2.3.1 use Uniform Resource Locators (URLs) and Search Engines to access Information.

2.3.2 download Information from the Internet.

2.3.3 access, copy and paste information from Internet to a different Application e.g., Word Processing.

2.3.0 Introduction

As you already know, the Internet is a giant network of computers all over the world. It has facilitated the speedy transfer of information across the globe. Any entity that wants to display information on the Internet must acquire a unique address known as a Website address. This address will be used to uniquely identify this information on the Internet.

2.3.1 Using Uniform Resource Locators (URLs) and Search Engines to Access Information

URLs are the addresses for web pages. Before your browser can connect to a website, it needs to know the site's address, the URL. The *Uniform Resource Locator* or the URL is a string of characters that points to a specific piece of information anywhere on the Web. In other words, URL is a website's unique address. A URL consists of

1. the web *protocol,*
2. the name of the web *server,*
3. the *directory* (or folder) on that server, and
4. the *file* within that directory (perhaps with an extension such as html or htm).

Consider the following example of a URL for a website offered for African studies. (See figure 3.1).

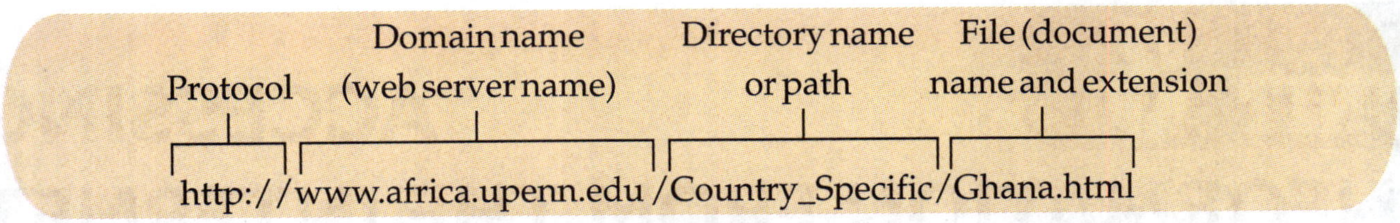

Figure 3.1 URL

URLs are necessary to distinguish between websites.

Search engines are search tools that allow you to find specific documents through keyword searches and menu choices. Search engines enable users to find information and websites of specific interest or use to them.

Following are some famous search engines which you can use to search the required information:

http://www.google.com/

http://www.excite.com/

http://www.yahoo.com/

http://www.infoseek.com/

How to Search the Internet

Computers cannot yet read your body language to find out what it is you are searching for. The search engine cannot read your mind and will not make the first move. So you need to learn how to "talk" with your search engine.

There are two basic ways to search:

1. Start at the top with broad concepts and work down to specific ones.
2. Work up from specific topics to broad ones.

If you are searching for something that on a broad level could return millions of results, be as specific as possible. For something that is obscure, be as broad as possible.

Unfortunately, many search results are useless, even though your keywords appear somewhere in the Web pages, their content does not pertain to what you are looking for. Learning to distinguish quickly between commercials and real information is a big time saver.

Once you learn to filter out the garbage, your searches will speed up. Searching the Internet effectively is a skill that comes with experience.

2.3.2 Downloading Information from the Internet

Downloading means transmitting data from a remote computer to a local computer.

Downloading enables users to save files on their own computers for later use, which reduces the time spent online and the corresponding charges.

You can download information (*e.g.*, pictures, video clips, sounds and software) from the Internet. The Internet has lot of information you can download. Some are copyrighted but many are free. Let us find *TypingMaster* software on the Internet.

1. Open Internet Explorer and connect to the Internet.
2. In the Address box enter *http://www.download.com/TypingMaster* and click *Go*. (See figure 3.2)

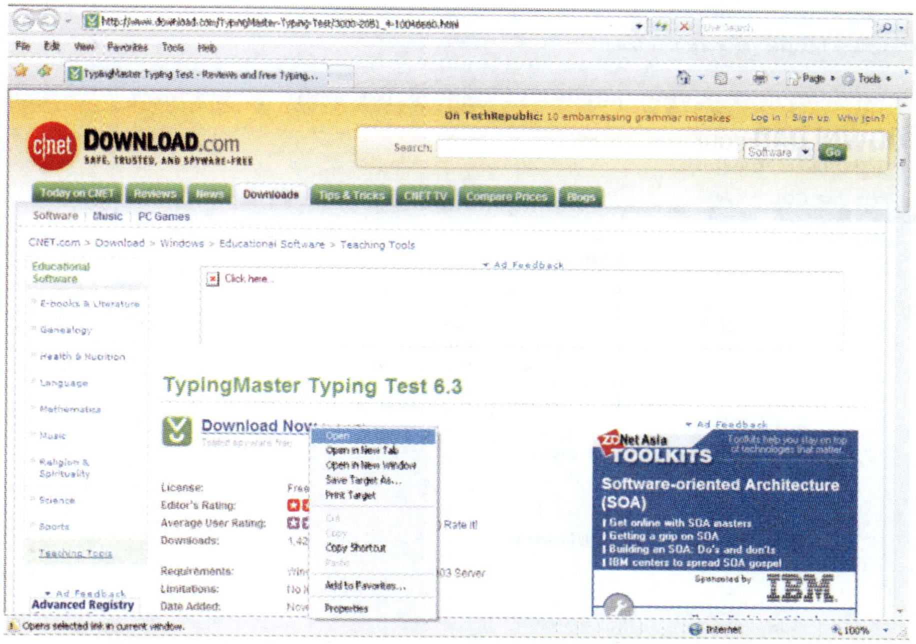

Figure 3.2 Preparing to Download from Internet

3. Select *Download* option. The File Download message box appears. When you click on 'Save', downloading starts. (See figure 3.3)

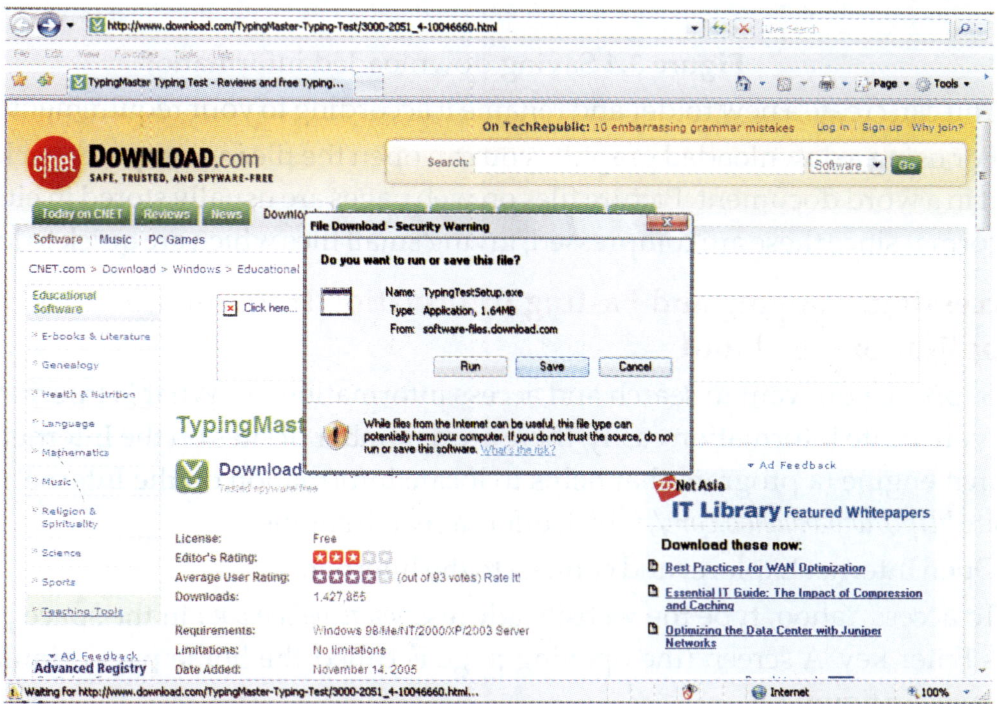

Figure 3.3 File Download message box

4. A dialog box may ask where you want to save the file. (See figure 3.4)

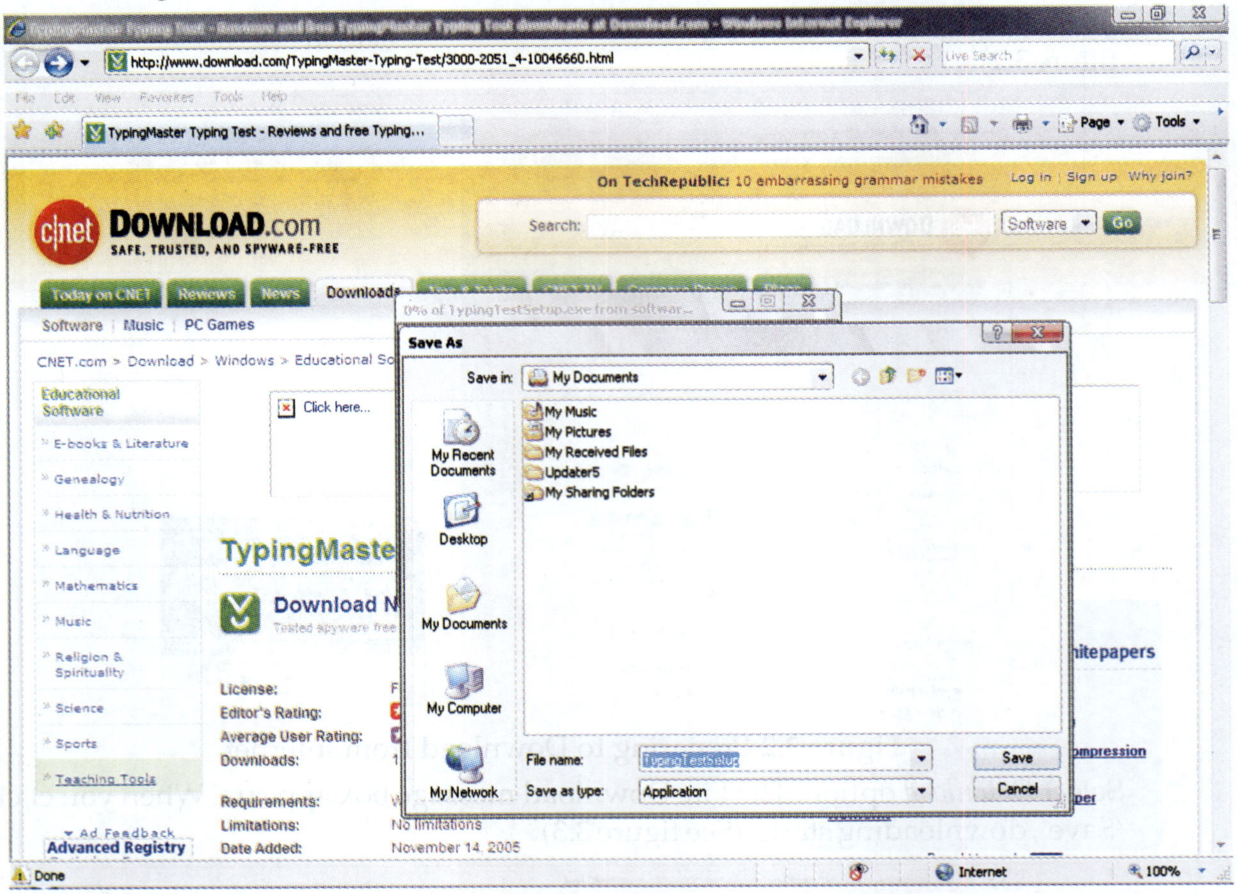

Figure 3.4 Saving downloaded information

5. You can create a new folder and rename it according to your requirement.
6. For using a downloaded graphic, you can open the file in a graphics package, or paste it in a word document. Picture files on web pages are usually stored in either *.jpg* or *.gif* format since these are compressed, giving small files which are quick to load.

2.3.3 Accessing, Copying and Pasting Information from Internet to a Different Application *e.g.*, Word

Suppose you want to search and access information on 'What is Internet'. In order to help you locate information easily, there are a number of sites on the Internet that provide a search engine (a program that helps to locate information on the Internet). Let us go to the site *http://www.yahoo.com/*, which offers a search engine.

Open Internet Explorer and connect to the Internet.

To access Yahoo, type the website address *www.yahoo.com* in the space provided and press Enter key. A screen (the opening page is called the home page) similar to the one displayed in figure 3.5.

Figure 3.5 The Yahoo home page

Note

The screen you see on your monitor may look slightly different from the one displayed in figure 3.5 because websites are frequently updated and modified. Some sites are modified daily. Therefore, when you access a site, you may notice differences in the contents displayed everyday.

In the space provided for the search, you need to enter the word or words that describe the information you wish to search. For example, we enter 'What is Internet' and click the 'Web Search' button. (See figure 3.6)

Figure 3.6 Searching on Internet

The result of search will be displayed as a list of websites that contain the required information with a short description of each site. (See figure 3.7)

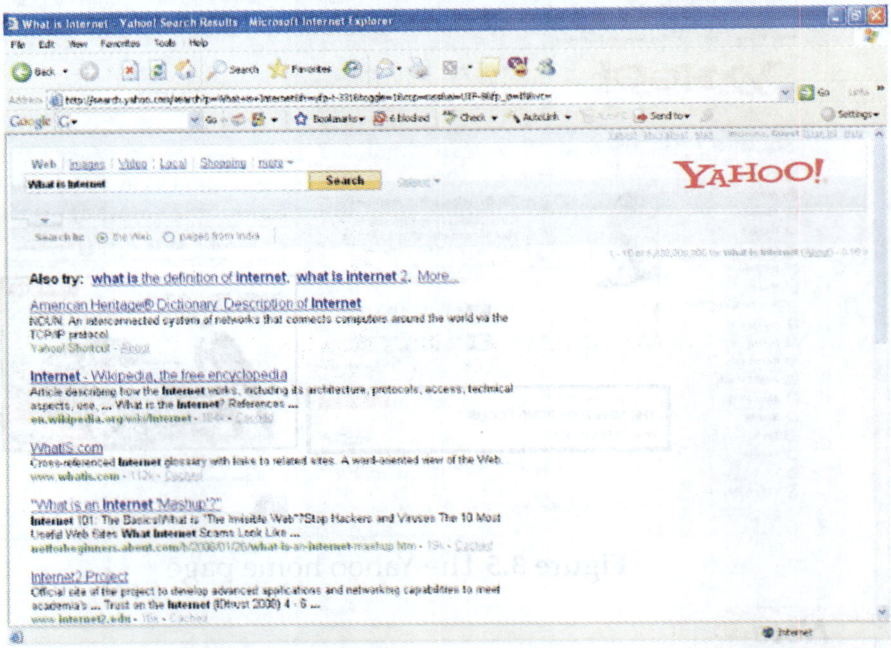

Figure 3.7 Search result on the Internet

You can click any of these sites to access the required information. (See figure 3.8)

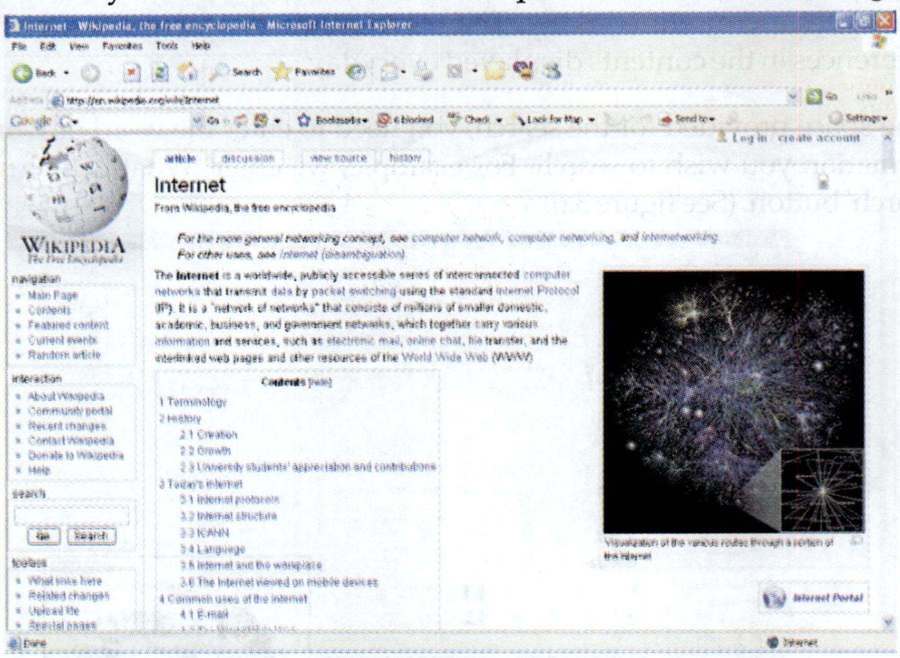

Figure 3.8 Accessing the required page

Here we click on the Wikipedia site link and find a whole lot of information on 'What is Internet'. We select the text to be copied. This highlights the text. Click the right mouse button on the highlighted text.

A shortcut menu is displayed near the highlighted text. (See figure 3.9)

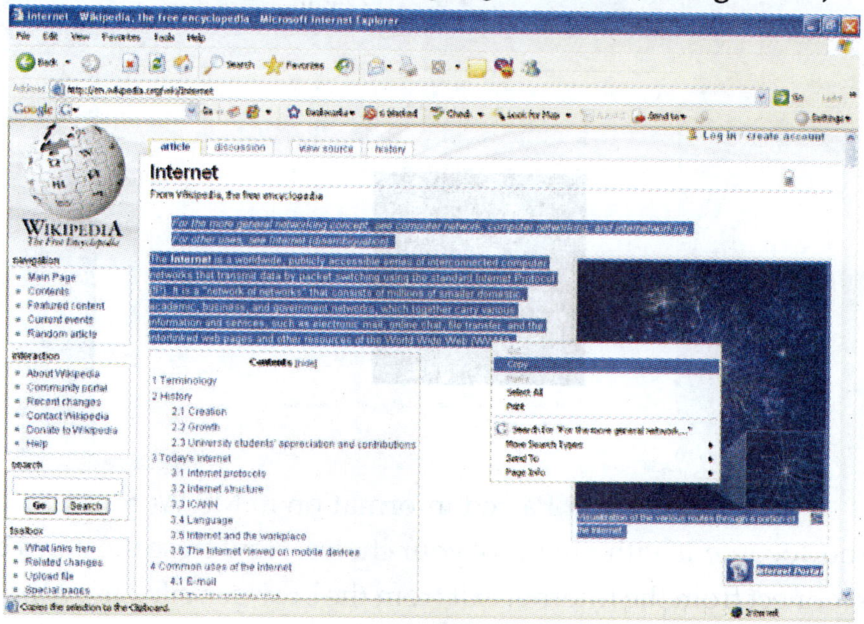

Figure 3.9 Copying the information

Select the 'Copy' option from the shortcut menu to copy the selected text to the clipboard.

Open the Microsoft Word 2007 document.

Select the Paste option. (See figure 3.10)

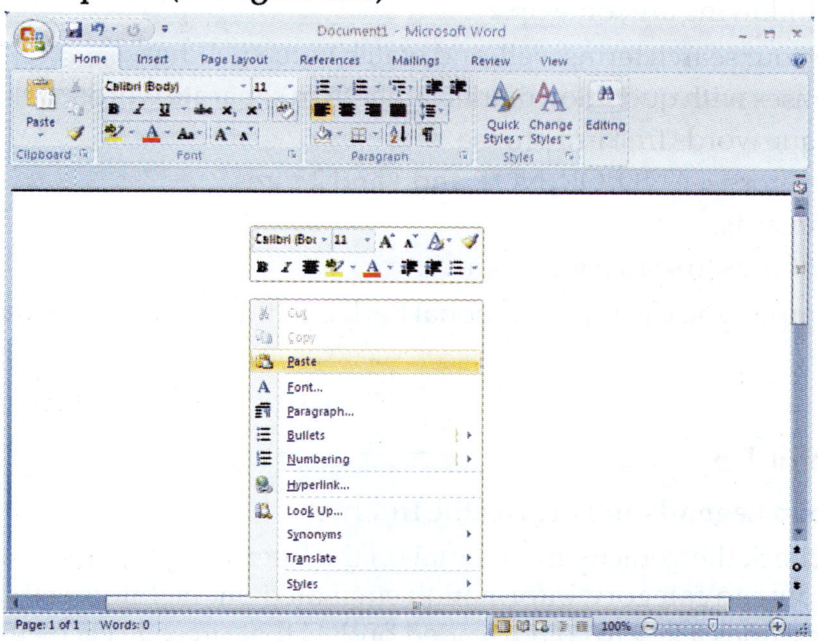

Figure 3.10 Pasting the information in MS Word 2007

On applying Paste, the selected information is pasted in the word document. (See figure 3.11)

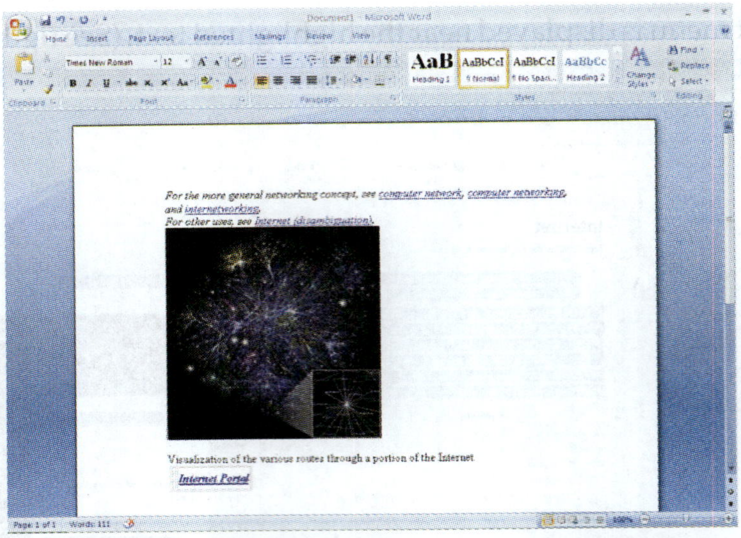

Figure 3.11 Pasted information in MS Word 2007

Save the document with a name of your choice. Now close the Word document.

To disconnect from the Internet exit from the browser, click the × button on the upper right corner of the browser screen.

Tips for Smart Searching

The phrase "trying to find a needle in a haystack" will come vividly to your mind the first time you type a word into a search engine and back comes a response on millions of results. Clearly, it becomes mandatory that you have a strategy for narrowing down your search. The following are some tips:

1. Choose your search terms well, and watch your spellings.
2. Use phrases with quotation marks rather than separate words.
3. Put unique words first in a phrase.
4. Use operators—AND, OR, NOT, and 1 and 2 signs.
5. Use wildcards.
6. Use keywords to search for a topic.

   For example, you can type "National Parks" in the space provided for the search.

Useful Tip

Urban Legends and Lies on the Internet

To check the veracity of material on the Internet, go to www.snopes.com, which lists, according to category, information circulated on the Internet that is not true. Each category includes a key to colour-coded bullets that precede each entry; the colour lets you know how much truth there is to each item. Green=true; red=false; yellow=based on fact but has become fictionalised, white=of indeterminate origin but really old and has been repeatedly "updated."

SUMMARY

- The Internet is a giant network of computers all over the world.
- Any entity that wants to display information on the Internet must acquire a unique address known as a website address.
- The URL (Uniform Resource Locator) is a string of characters that points to a specific piece of information anywhere on the Web.
- Search engines are search tools that allow you to find specific documents through keyword searches and menu choices.
- Searching the Internet effectively is a skill that comes with experience.
- Downloading means transmitting data from a remote computer to local computer.
- Downloading enables users to save files on their own computers for later use, which reduces the time spent online and the corresponding charges.
- In order to help you locate information easily, there are a number of sites on the Internet that provide a search engine (a program that helps to locate information on the Internet).
- You can access, copy and paste information from Internet to a different Application *e.g.*, Word Processing.

REVIEW QUESTIONS

STATE WHETHER TRUE OR FALSE

1. The largest network in the world is the one called Internet.
2. URLs (Uniform Resource Locators) are addresses of pages on the Web.
3. Search engines on the Web do not let you look up information using keywords that might be in the document you want to find.
4. Searching the Internet effectively is not a skill that comes with experience.

FILL IN THE BLANKS

1. Unfortunately, many search results are .... , even though your keywords appear somewhere in the web pages.
2. When you visit a site on the web, the first page you often see is called a ....
3. Web addresses are called ....
4. .... means transmitting data from a remote computer to local computer.

MULTIPLE CHOICE QUESTIONS

1. A browser ....
   (a) Displays Web documents
   (b) Allows you to navigate
   (c) Allows you to copy, print, and transfer documents
   (d) All of these
2. Which of the following is not one of the four components of a URL?
   (a) Web protocol
   (b) Name of the web server
   (c) Word processing
   (d) Name of the directory on the web server

ANSWER THE FOLLOWING

1. How will you access information using URLs and Search Engines? Discuss.
2. How will you download information from the Internet? Discuss.
3. How will you access, copy and paste information from the Internet to a different Application *e.g.*, Word? Discuss.

ASSIGNMENT

1. Student to access information on "What is ICT" using URLs and Search Engines.
2. Student to prepare Word document using the information accessed from the Internet.

SECTION ONE

TERM-THREE

SPREADSHEET APPLICATION

UNIT 1: Spreadsheet

UNIT 2: Application of Selected Formula and Functions

UNIT 3: Formatting Worksheet

UNIT 4: Editing Worksheet

UNIT 5: Printing Worksheet

General Objectives

After reading this section, the student will be able to:

1. acquire basic skills in using Spreadsheet Packages.
2. appreciate the importance of spreadsheet in data management.

UNIT 1 SPREADSHEET

Specific Objectives

After reading this unit, the student will be able to:

1.1.1 identify Spreadsheet Packages.

1.1.2 explain related concepts and terminologies.

1.1.3 identify features in Spreadsheet window.

1.1.4 identify types of data and state their uses.

1.1.5 launch and exit Spreadsheet Application.

1.1.6 create and save Workbook.

1.1.7 construct and insert simple formula.

1.1.0 Introduction

The electronic spreadsheet is the brain child of *Dan Bricklin* and *Bob Franktor.* Behind the invention of first electronic worksheet *VisiCalc* (Visible Calculator) was this duo. *Bricklin,* a Harvard Business school student, got the idea of VisiCalc while spending hours manually to solve financial-planning problems.

The spreadsheets are one of the most widely used software in the world. These are used everywhere from a small store to a large manufacturing house. These can be used for calculating accounts, managing inventory, managing payroll, managing and analysing the sales and marketing. These software are also used to manage household data like recording expenditures. As spreadsheets are much easier to learn than programming languages, these can be operated by any user having a moderate knowledge of programming.

1.1.1 Spreadsheet Packages

A *spreadsheet package* is a numeric data analysis tool, which not only allows us to quickly calculate and analyse numbers, but also lets us quickly explore a variety of possible outcomes. *The spreadsheet allows users to create tables and financial schedules by entering data and formulae into rows and columns arranged as a grid on a display screen.* Today the principal spreadsheets are Microsoft Excel, Corel Quattro Pro, Lotus 123 and Linux.

The Spreadsheet

All spreadsheets (sometimes called worksheets) have a similar look. Basically a spreadsheet is the arrangement of rows and columns that appears on the screen when we first load the program in the computer's memory.

The spreadsheet on the computer screen is a window to the larger spreadsheet. *For example,* MS-Excel and Lotus 123 have over 4 million cells in each spreadsheet. If printed, the spreadsheet would cover an area 21 feet wide by 341 feet long.

Let us discuss some of the popular spreadsheet packages:

Excel

MS-Excel 2007 is a GUI based spreadsheet package that is part of Microsoft Office 2007 suite of software. It is a powerful spreadsheet package that supports data of various formats, pictures, graphs and drawing objects. There are 1,048,576 rows and 16,384 columns in an Excel worksheet. It has got many user friendly features that makes it the first choice of its users.

Microsoft Excel 2007 is equipped with a support of very large files, called workbooks. A single file of Excel can hold monthly data of a small organisation. Excel supports the following features:

(*i*) Automatic recalculation
(*ii*) What if analysis
(*iii*) Fill handle
(*iv*) Sharing of workbooks
(*v*) Grouping and outlining data
(*vi*) Graphical data representation through charts
(*vii*) Conditional formatting
(*viii*) Wide variety of dates
(*ix*) Several types of data
(*x*) Specialised printing to print the data from worksheets.

Quattro Pro

Quattro Pro is a *spreadsheet* program developed by *Borland* and now sold by *Corel,* most often as part of Corel's *WordPerfect Office.*

It currently runs under the Windows operating system. Quattro Pro avoids Excel's long-standing worksheet size limitation of 65,536 rows by 256 columns (excluding Excel 2007), with a maximum worksheet size of one million rows by 18,276 columns. However, since about 1996, it has run a distant second to Excel's market domination.

As of 2008, Microsoft still dominates the market for Windows business application software, though Quattro Pro and WordPerfect are still both updated and sold. The latest version 9 of Quattro Pro is in use these days.

Quattro Pro supports the following features:

(*i*) Display multiple, linked worksheets and live graphics on the screen at the same time

(*ii*) Superior graphics and spreadsheet publishing

(*iii*) High speed and small memory needs

(*iv*) Charting capabilities

(*v*) Provides a robust query function that can pull relevant information from any file stored in Lotus 123 or database format without loading the entire database into memory first.

Lotus 123

Lotus 123 is a GUI based spreadsheet package from *Lotus Development Corporation, USA*. Although not the first spreadsheet program designed, Lotus 123 was one of the best-selling micro-computer business software few years back. By learning spreadsheet operations with Lotus 123, you can gain most of the necessary skills. Further, the knowledge you acquire is directly applicable in the business world. When you learn to use Lotus 123, you pick up enough competence to work in any of the other spreadsheet packages used today. Basically the working principles as applied to all spreadsheet packages remain the same.

It is believed to be named because of the following reasons:

1. It is as simple to learn as 1, 2, 3,... .
2. It can be used in applications belonging to the following three areas:

Calculations. It is one of the fastest calculating program ever developed for the microcomputers. These calculations are done in what are called electronic spreadsheets or worksheets.

Data Management. You can use 123's tabular format to create databases and perform various database functions.

You can create graphs of your tabular data to give a visual display to your presentations.

In addition to the above three, you can use Lotus 123 for limited word processing tasks also.

You can use Lotus 123 for producing photo-ready documents which can be sent directly for publishing.

Undoubtedly the newer versions offer a number of improvements over the earlier versions, such as the ability to display three-dimensional spreadsheets with 3-D graphs, charts and even graphical pictorials.

Linux

Linux is a popular open source, multi-user operating system. Linux has a graphical user interface called the X Window System. Linux consists of three main software components. The components are: Kernel, Shell, and Utilities and Application Programs.

Spreadsheet software is available under Linux. Spreadsheet and Word Processor software are of particular interest to those who wish to see Linux more widely adopted for use in office applications. Some Linux based spreadsheets are given below:

1. The Gnumeric spreadsheet
2. Table Editor and Planner, or : Teapot!
3. SIAG Office
4. MOODSS (Modular Object Oriented Dynamic Spreadsheet)
5. OpenOffice.org
6. IBM Lotus Symphony
7. SOT Office

In the next section, you will understand some basic concepts of the most popular spreadsheet program—Microsoft Excel 2007.

1.1.2 Related Concepts and Terminologies

Spreadsheets are much more structured than word processing packages. *For example,* a word processing package allows to enter data anywhere on the page while in a spreadsheet program we can enter data only into the cells. The data are not always typed in, but rather are copied from the organisation's mainframe computer or network server to a user's PC (known as downloading). It saves time and eliminates the possibility of introducing errors. Some of the key features of spreadsheet package are shown in figure 1.1.

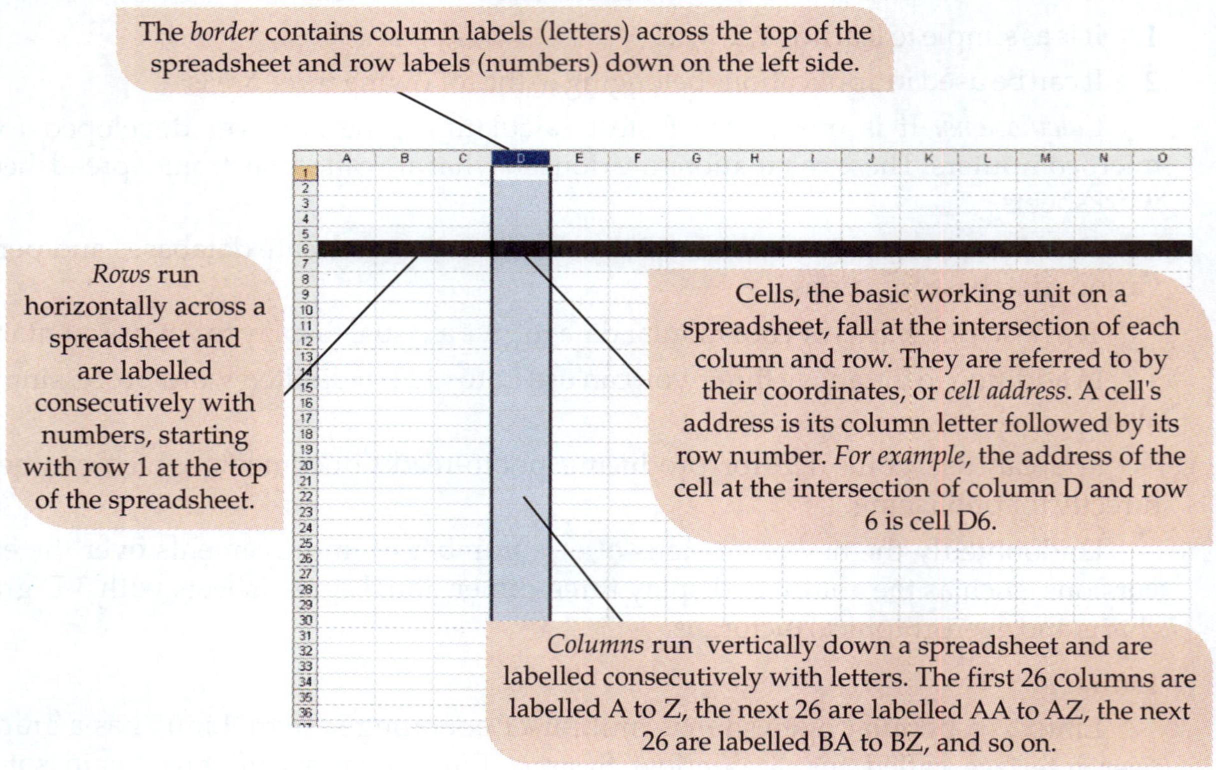

Figure 1.1 The spreadsheet

- **Rows and Columns**

A spreadsheet is an arrangement of rows and columns. Rows run horizontally across the spreadsheet and are labelled consecutively with numbers, starting with row 1 at the top of the worksheet. Columns run vertically down a worksheet and are labelled consecutively with letters. The first 26 columns are labelled A to Z, the next 26 are labelled AA to AZ, the next 26 are labelled BA to BZ, and so on.

- **Cells**

Cells, the basic working unit on a spreadsheet, fall at the intersection of each column and row. They are referred to by their coordinates, or cell address. A cell's address is its column letter followed by its row number. *For example,* the address of the cell at the intersection of column D and row 6 is cell D6. (See figure 1.1)

A cell pointer, or spreadsheet cursor, indicates where data is to be entered. The cell pointer can be moved around like a cursor in a word processing program. Each worksheet has more than 16 million cells.

- **Cell Range**

The cell range specifies the spreadsheet where to look for the values or data we want to use in a formula. We can have following types of cell ranges:

(i) **Row Range**—includes a set of adjacent cells in the same row. *For example,* the range A6..H6 refers to the cells A6, B6, C6, D6, E6, F6, G6 and H6.

(ii) **Column Range**—includes a set of adjacent cells in the same column. *For example, the range* A1.. A4 refers to the cells A1, A2, A3 and A4.

(iii) **Block Range**—includes a set of adjacent cells in a rectangular group of cells. *For example,* the range A1..C3 refers to the cells A1, A2, A3, B1, B2, B3, C1, C2 and C3.

Note that a specific range is denoted by the address of the endpoint cells separated by two periods (A1.. C3) or a colon (A1 : C3).

- **Label**

A label is a name for the information in a spreadsheet. For example, 'Name' is a label.

- **Values**

A number or date entered in a cell is called a *value.* The values are the actual numbers used in the spreadsheet—Cedi/Pesewa (100 Pesewas = one Cedi), percentages, grade points, temperatures or whatever. Headings, labels and formulas also go into cells.

- **Worksheet**

A spreadsheet is a collection of rows and columns. It is also known as a worksheet. A worksheet is a primary document used to store data.

- **Workbook**

A collection of worksheets is a workbook.

1.1.3 Features in the Spreadsheet window Toolbars

The features in the spreadsheet window toolbars are shown in figure 1.2.

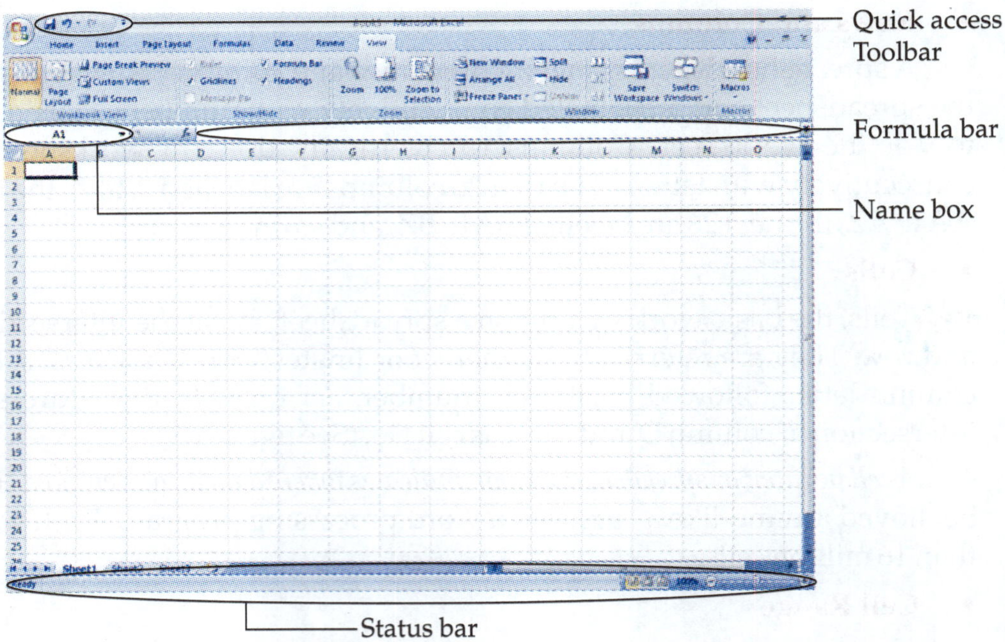

Figure 1.2 Features in spreadsheet window

- **Formatting bar**

  It is a horizontal toolbar situated below the standard toolbar. It mainly contains the command buttons for formatting of text in spreadsheet, such as commands for setting font name and size, setting font styles, alignment, currency style, percentage, increase or decrease decimal precision, font colours and file colours etc.

- **Standard bar**

  It is a horizontal bar that appears below the menu bar. It contains shortcut command buttons. These buttons are the shortcuts to access standard menu commands like creating new workbook, opening existing workbook, saving the current workbook etc.

- **Formula bar**

  It is the horizontal bar that is located below the formatting toolbar. It displays the formula applied in the active cell of the worksheet.

- **Help facilities**

  The online Help feature in Excel 2007 has been completely redesigned, and the new design does not include the Microsoft Office Assistant.

  You can find Help for Excel 2007 in more than one place. Help is installed on your computer when you install MS Office 2007, and you can get additional Help content from Microsoft Office Online. You can specify where you want to search for Help, and you can restrict the scope of your search to online or offline or to a specific category within a program.

  If *Connected to Office Online* appears in the lower-right corner of the Help window, you are searching and getting Help from Office Online. If *Offline* appears in the lower-right corner, you are searching and getting Help from the files stored on your computer.

- **Title Bar**

  It shows the name of the workbook.
- **Status Bar**

  It shows the status of the active workbook.

  You will become more familiar with these features after studying this unit.

Useful Tip

Formula bar is only present in Excel. MS Excel 2007 has panels in place of menus available in earlier versions of Excel.

1.1.4 Types of Data and their Uses

The types of data and their uses in spreadsheets are given below:

- **Number**

  As the name suggests, this type of data includes numbers. You can specify the number of decimal places you want to see after a number, put commas in a number and select format for representing negative numbers. You can specify up to 30 decimal places. For example, 154, 23.6.
- **Date**

  As the name suggests, this type of data includes dates. Spreadsheets store dates as numbers by automatically converting them to numbers but display it as per the date format. Spreadsheets offer different kinds of date formats. For example, 25-Mar-2008 or 3/25/2008.
- **Text**

  It is used when you do not want the spreadsheet to treat some values as numbers. When you format some data as text, they will be displayed exactly as they are typed and will be treated as text. For example, John, 123.
- **Currency**

  It is used with financial data. Select the currency sign you want to display in front of the number. Select the desired decimal precision and format for the negative numbers. For example, £20,500.00, USD 1000.00.
- **Fraction**

  It is used to convert values to their equivalent fractions. For example, if you enter 17.52, it will be converted to 17½ automatically.

1.1.5 Launching and Exiting Spreadsheet Application

To launch MS-Excel 2007,

Double-click on the MS-Excel 2007 icon on the desktop.

OR

1. Click the *Start* button.
2. Choose *All Programs*.
3. Click the *Microsoft Office* option.
4. Click the *Microsoft Office Excel* 2007 option. (See figure 1.3)

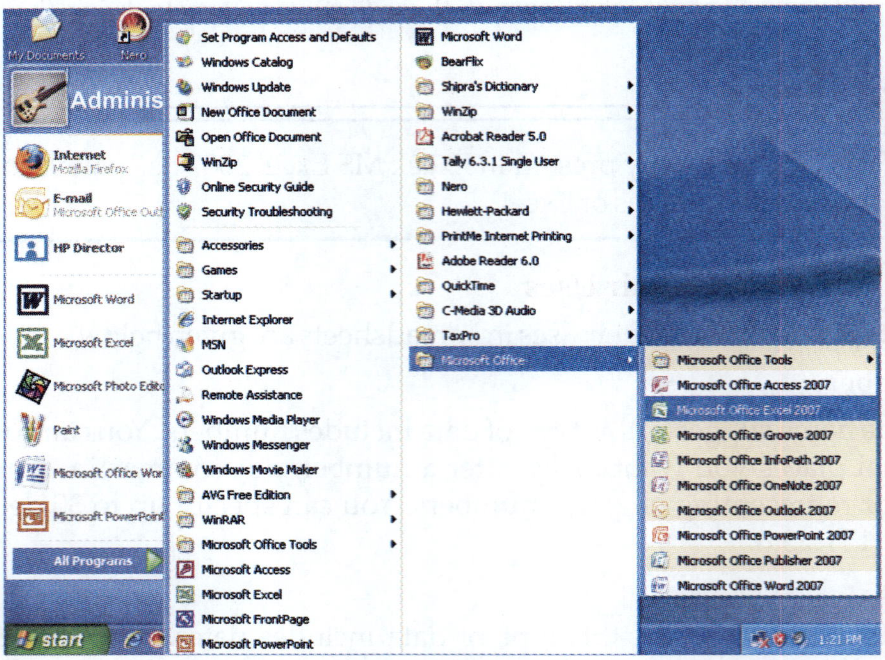

Figure 1.3 Launching MS-Excel 2007

To exit MS-Excel 2007,

Click on the close button ☒ on the far right corner of the Title bar. (See figure 1.4)

Figure 1.4 Exiting Excel 2007 using Close button

OR

Double-click the *Office Button*. (See figure 1.5)

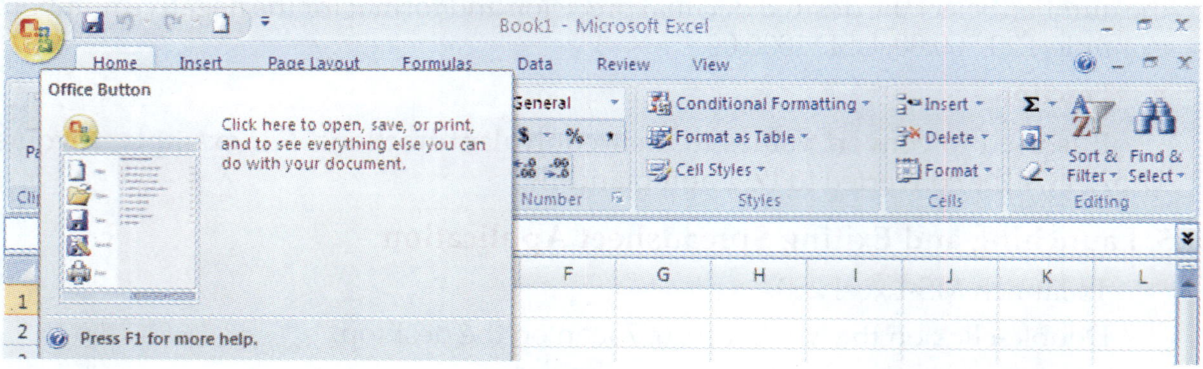

Figure 1.5 Exiting Excel 2007 using Office Button

OR

1. Click the *Office Button*.
2. Click the *Exit Excel* option. (See figure 1.6)

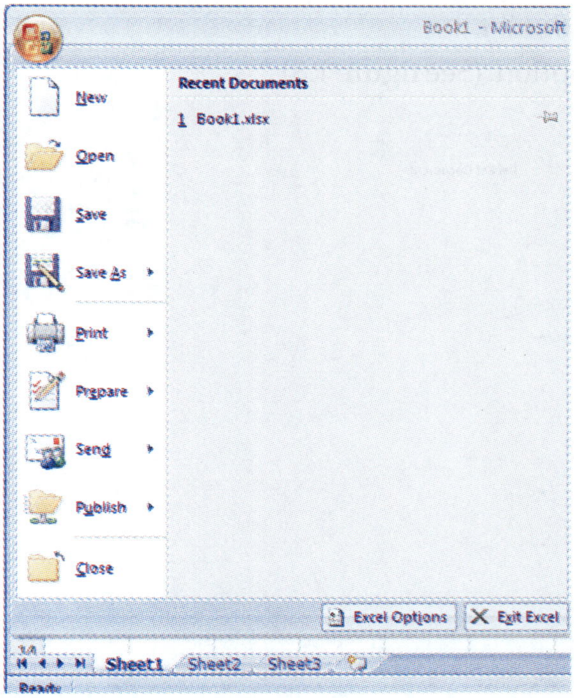

Figure 1.6 Exiting Excel 2007 using Exit Excel option

OR

1. Right click the workbook Title bar.
2. Click the Close option from the Pop-up menu or press Alt + F4. (See figure 1.7)

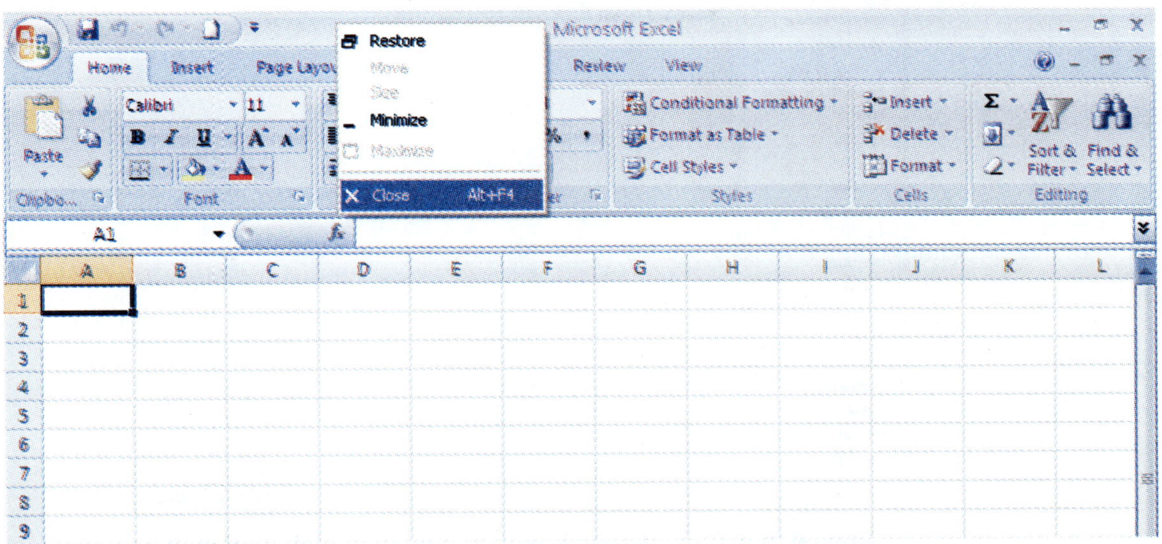

Figure 1.7 Exiting Excel 2007 using Close option

1.1.6 Creating and Saving Workbook

Creating Workbooks

To create a workbook,

1. Click the *Office Button*.
2. Click the *New* option. (See figure 1.8)

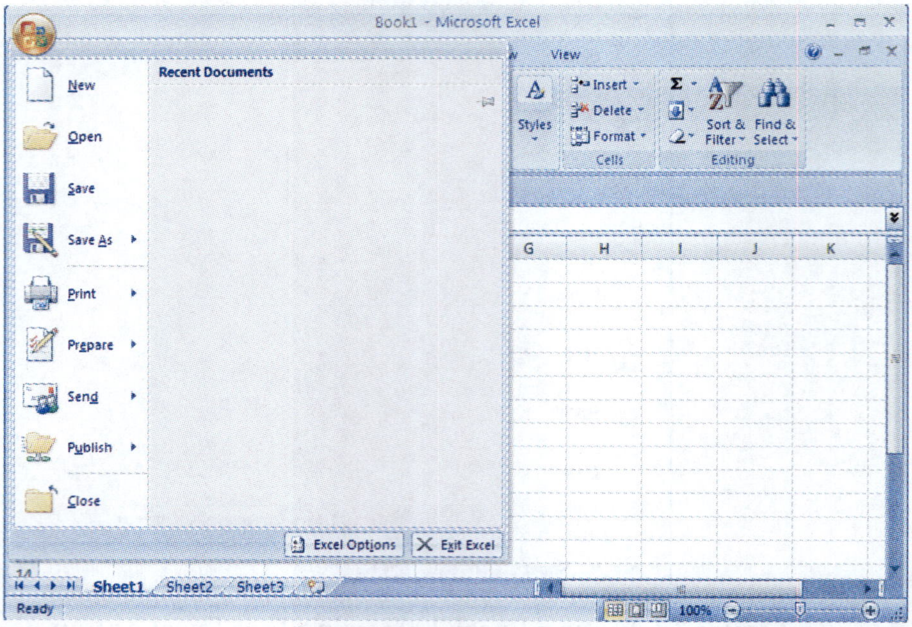

Figure 1.8 Selecting New option

3. Double click the *Blank Workbook* or click on the *Create* button. (See figure 1.9)

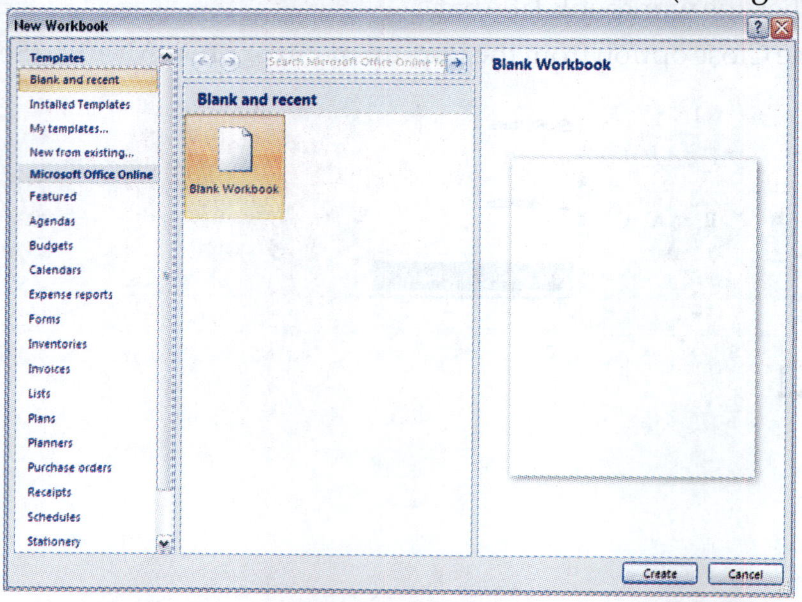

Figure 1.9 Double clicking the Blank workbook

A new workbook is created.

Navigating Workbooks

It means moving across the worksheet using the mouse and keyboard. The various navigation techniques are shown in table 1.1.

Table 1.1. Illustration of Various Navigation Techniques

Navigation Technique	Purpose
Click a cell	Make the cell active.
Arrow keys	Move the active cell left, right, up or down one row or column.
Shift + Enter	Move the active cell one row up.
Enter	Move the active cell one row down.
Shift + Tab	Move the active cell one column to the left.
Tab	Move the active cell one column to the right.
Ctrl + Home	Move the active cell to the cell A1.
Click the scroll arrow	Scroll view of the worksheet, one row or column. Does not move the active cell.
Click scroll bar	Scroll view of the worksheet one screen up, down, left or right, depending on which of the scroll box we click. Does not move the active cell.
Drag scroll bar	Scroll view of the worksheet quickly without moving the active cell.

Entering Data

To enter data,

1. Select the cell where the data has to be added.
2. Type the data.

After entering the data, the workbook may look as shown in figure 1.10.

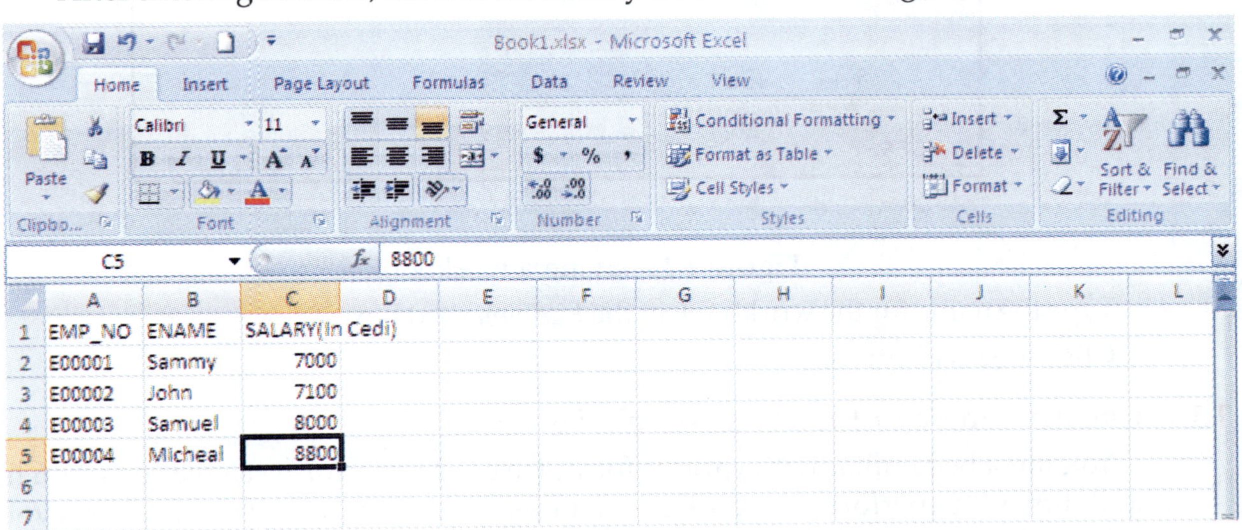

Figure 1.10 Entering data in a workbook

Editing Data

To edit data (in case we have made mistakes),

1. Double-click the cell, which has to be edited.
2. Use the Backspace or Delete key to edit the content of the cell.
3. Press the Enter key.

OR

1. Select the cell, which needs to be edited.
2. Click the Formula bar.
3. Use the Backspace or Delete key to edit the content of the cell.
4. Press the Enter key.

Saving Workbooks

For saving a workbook the first time,

1. Click the *Office Button*.
2. Click the *Save As* option.
3. Click the *Excel Workbook* option. A *Save As* dialog box appears. (See figure 1.11)

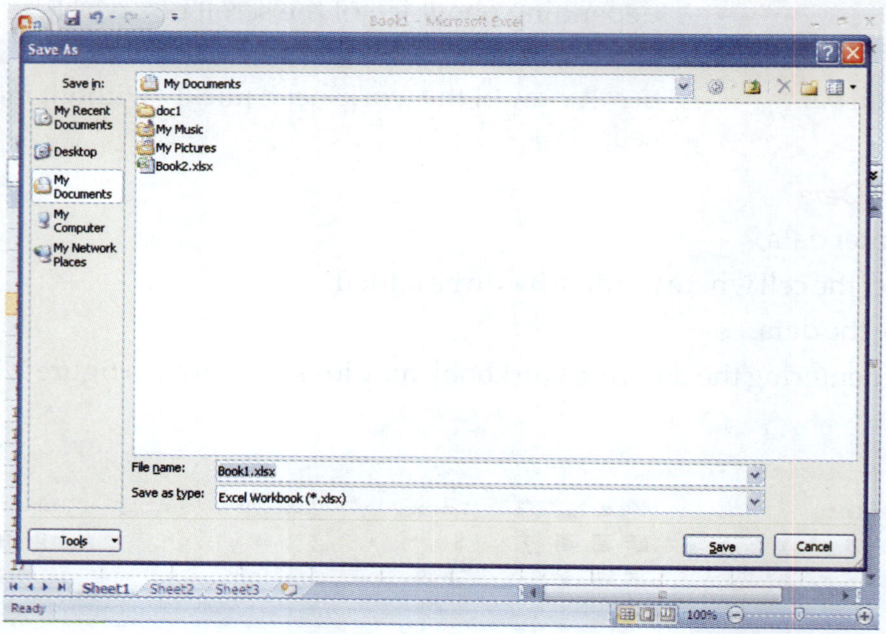

Figure 1.11 Saving a workbook

4. Type the name for the workbook in the *File name* text box.
5. Click the *Save* button.

1.1.7 Constructing and Inserting Simple Formula

You must be familiar with various formulae used to perform calculations. You might find it difficult to perform complex calculations on your own. In such situations you can use the built-in functions available in MS-Excel 2007.

Formulae

(*i*) can be used for numeric calculations such as adding, subtracting, multiplying, dividing and averaging.

(*ii*) begin with the equal sign (=).

(*iii*) use functions and operators for calculations.

Functions

Functions are predefined formulae that perform simple to complex calculations.

Operators

Operators point to the type of operation that the formula would perform. Table 1.2 illustrates the arithmetic operators.

Table 1.2 Arithmetic Operators

Operator	Purpose	Example
+	Add numbers	= A3+B3
–	Subtract numbers	= A3–B3
*	Multiply numbers	= A3*B3
/	Divide numbers	= A3/B3
%	Specify the percentage of a number	20%
^	Specify the exponent	= 2^3 (2 raised to the power of 3 or 2*2*2)

Inserting Formulae

You can enter formulae in cells the same way as you enter normal data values. The formula is seen in the Formula bar when the cell is active. An example of a formula is = A3 + B3 (See figure 1.12). Here, A3 and B3 are the cell references.

To enter a formula,

1. Enter the data and select the cell where the result has to be seen.
2. Type the formula in the selected cell.
3. Press the Enter key.

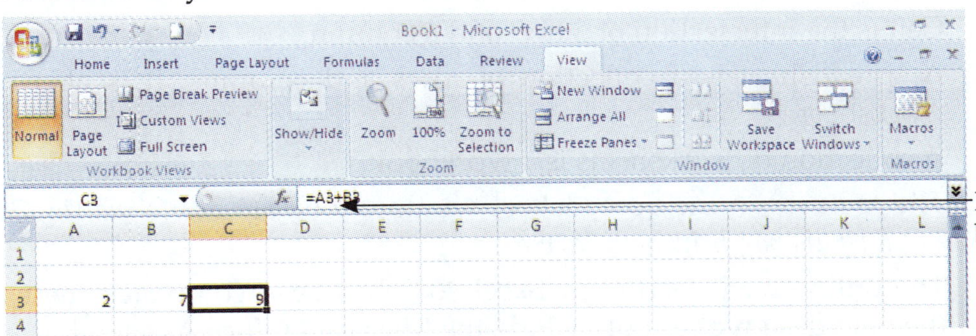

Figure 1.12 Adding Two Numbers

In figure 1.12, the cell A3 has the value 2. The cell B3 has the value 7. The cell C3 has the formula = A3 + B3. This adds the values 2 and 7. So cell C3 has the value 9. If you change the value in cell A3 or B3, the value in cell C3 also changes automatically.

Editing Formulae

To edit a formula,

1. Select the cell having the formula.
2. Edit the formula in the Formula bar.

OR

Alternatively, Double-click the cell having the formula and make corrections.

SUMMARY

- The spreadsheets are one of the most widely used software in the world.
- A spreadsheet package is a numeric data analysis tool, which not only allows us to quickly calculate and analyse numbers, but also lets us quickly explore a variety of possible outcomes.
- Today the principal spreadsheets are Microsoft Excel, Corel Quattro Pro, Lotus 123 and Linux etc.
- Spreadsheets are much more structured than word processing applications.
- *Microsoft Excel 2007* is a GUI spreadsheet package that is part of Microsoft Office 2007 suite of software.
- *Quattro Pro* is a spreadsheet program developed by *Borland* and now sold by Corel, most often as part of the *Corel's WordPerfect Office.*
- *Lotus 123* is a GUI based spreadsheet package from *Lotus Development Corporation, USA.*
- Linux is an operating system that supports many spreadsheet packages.
- Row is a group of data arranged horizontally.
- Column is a group of data arranged vertically.
- Cell is the intersection of a row and a column.
- A spreadsheet is a collection of rows and columns. It is also known as a worksheet.
- A collection of worksheets is a workbook.
- The features in the Spreadsheet window toolbars are *formatting bar, standard bar, formula bar, help facilities etc.*
- The online Help feature in Excel 2007 has been completely redesigned, and the new design does not include the Microsoft Office Assistant.
- The various types of data are *number, date, text, currency, fraction* etc.

- For working efficiently with a spreadsheet package you must know how to launch and exit Spreadsheet Application.
- To enter data in a worksheet, you first need to create a workbook.
- After entering data in a worksheet, you should save a workbook.
- A function is a built-in formula that performs calculations on a range of values. It allows you to perform mathematical, statistical and date-time functions.
- Formulae must be defined by the user.

REVIEW QUESTIONS

STATE WHETHER TRUE OR FALSE

1. Excel is a spreadsheet program that is used to organise, calculate and analyse data.
2. The row-and-column sheet-Spreadsheet is also called Hardsheet in Excel.
3. Worksheets can be grouped into a file called the workbook.
4. You can work in a spreadsheet application without launching it.
5. You cannot navigate a workbook using the mouse and keyboard.
6. Moving across the worksheet using the mouse and keyboard is called investigation.
7. Formulae begin with the equal sign (=).

FILL IN THE BLANKS

1. Commonly used spreadsheet packages are Excel, ..., Lotus 123 and Linux.
2. A .... is a group of data arranged horizontally.
3. Moving across the worksheet using the mouse and the keyboard is called ....
4. To enter data in a workbook, you first need to .... a workbook.
5. The types of data in spreadsheet packages are number, date, text, ... and ....
6. To save a workbook the first time, choose .... option in Office Button.
7. .... can be used for numeric calculations.

MULTIPLE CHOICE QUESTIONS

1. In a spreadsheet, the place where a row and a column intersect is called a ....
   (*a*) cell (*b*) worksheet
   (*c*) workbook (*d*) None of these

2. Features in the Spreadsheet window toolbars is/are
   (a) Formatting bar (b) Standard bar
   (c) Formulae bar (d) All of these
3. When working with a spreadsheet, you can only enter ....
   (a) Numbers and formulas
   (b) Numbers, formulas, and functions
   (c) Labels, numbers, formulas, functions, and formats
   (d) All of these

ANSWER THE FOLLOWING

1. What are spreadsheet packages? Give examples.
2. Discuss some useful spreadsheet packages.
3. What is a spreadsheet? A worksheet?
4. What are the components of a spreadsheet?
5. Discuss the features of Spreadsheet window.
6. What are the types of data in spreadsheets? State their uses.
7. How will you launch and exit Spreadsheet Application? Discuss.
8. How will you create and save workbook? Discuss.
9. How will you construct and apply a simple formula in spreadsheet? Discuss.

FIELD TRIP

Using the Internet or computer magazines, look up information on Microsoft Excel. List any features you find. List which of these features appeal to you and describe why they do.

ASSIGNMENT

1. Perform the following:
   (i) Start MS-Excel 2007.
   (ii) Make the cell A10 an active cell.
   (iii) Make the cell AY6 an active cell.
   (iv) Click on Sheet 2 and see what happens.
   (v) Make cell C20 active. Check the Name box to see what it shows.
   (vi) Change the address in the Name box to B20.
   (vii) Identify the Title bar.

(viii) Write down the name of the workbook.

(ix) Identify the Quick Access Toolbar.

(x) Identify the Status bar.

(xi) Identify the buttons in the Quick Access Toolbar by using the ToolTip.

(xii) Ask any question by getting Help. *For example,* "What are rows and columns?" Write down the answer you get.

(xiii) Make the Help Online and then Offline.

(xiv) Exit MS Excel 2007.

2. Label the features of the workbook given below.

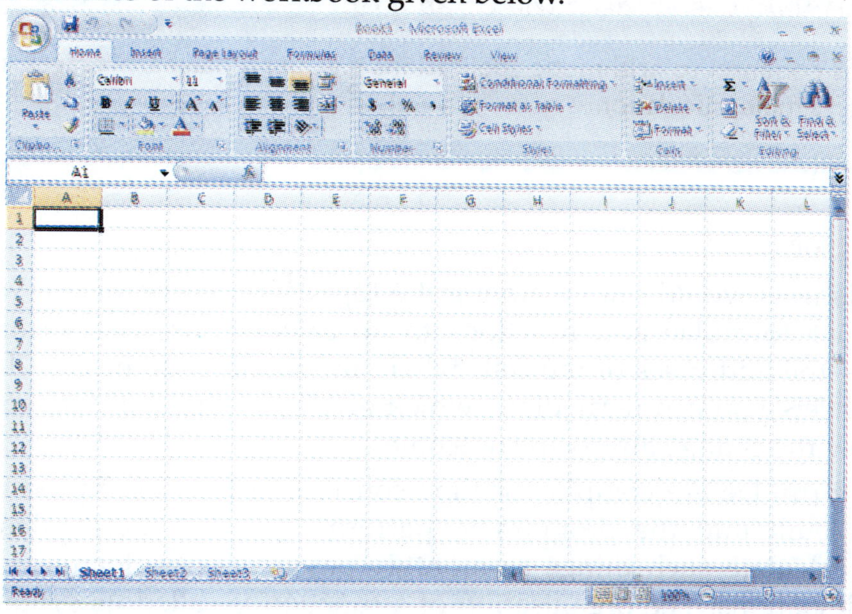

3. Create the following Students' Marks List database in a new worksheet and perform the following functions.

	A	B	C	D	E	F	G
1	**Students Marks List**						
2							
3	**Name**	**English**	**ICT**	**Maths**	**Science**	**History**	
4	Anthony	78	94	85	67	86	
5	Mary	88	88	87	98	98	
6	Nancy	86	67	86	88	65	
7	Hussen	96	84	88	56	84	
8	Michael	84	96	84	82	90	

(i) Find the total marks obtained by each student and display it in the column G with label Total Marks.

(ii) Save the workbook as *Exam Result.*

UNIT 2 APPLICATION OF SELECTED FORMULA AND FUNCTIONS

Specific Objective

After reading this unit, the student will be able to:

1.2.1 use functions common to arithmetic applications e.g., percentages, averages, count, maximum, minimum for simple calculation.

1.2.0 Introduction

Spreadsheets would not be among the top-selling program if it were not for their ability to use formulae and functions to do calculations. The formulae contain cell references—the addresses of the cells where the numbers to be calculated are entered. In spreadsheets you can recalculate, which gives you the ability to easily change data and see how the change affects the outcome.

Many formulae are complex or time consuming to enter. In these cases functions have been built into the program to perform many of these calculations for you. Functions calculate such things as monthly payments of a loan, average, totals, and standard deviations. The organisation of a function is called its syntax. The values on which a function performs operations are called its arguments and these can be numbers and cell references. Parentheses tell the program where arguments begin and end. The functions begin with an equal sign followed by name that describes their functions.

1.2.1 Using Functions Common to Arithmetic Applications

You can apply formulae and functions to arithmetic applications. In this unit we will discuss functions common to arithmetic applications.

Functions

A function is a built-in formula that performs calculations on a range of values. It allows you to perform mathematical, statistical and date-time functions. Some examples of functions are:

- Sum
- Average
- Count

- Max
- Min

Parts of a Function

Every function in Excel has two parts:

1. Function name
2. Function arguments

Function Arguments

Arguments are data received by the function. Each function receives a specific kind of arguments. It can be numbers, text, data or logical values such as True or False.

The syntax is,

=<Function name> (<List of arguments>)

The following example illustrates the usage of the *SUM* function.

=SUM(C2:E2)

Here, SUM is the name of the function, which finds the sum of the specified range.

Rules for Using Functions

Just like a formulae, functions also follow certain rules. These are:

1. All functions must begin with an = sign.
2. The arguments of a function must be enclosed within parentheses.
3. The arguments should be separated by a comma.
4. The cell range should be mentioned using a colon.

Cell Range

The cell range specifies Excel where to look for the values or data you want to use in a formula. Consider the case where you want to find total marks obtained by a student in three subjects. Assume that the marks of the students are entered in a worksheet as given in figure 2.1.

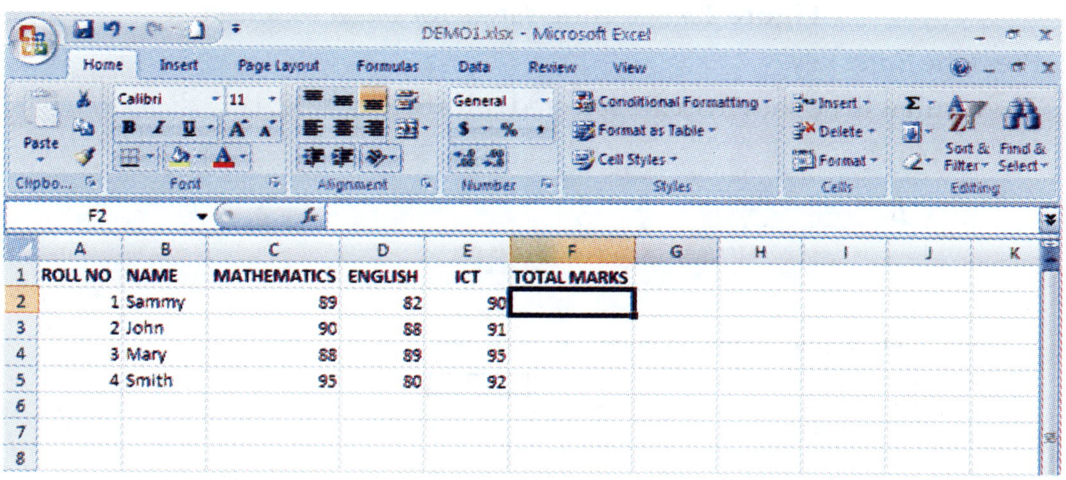

Figure 2.1 Worksheet showing student data

To calculate the total marks using the *SUM* function,

1. Select the cell where the result should be displayed. In this case, cell F2 is selected.
2. Type = SUM(<starting cell address>,<ending cell address>) or use the built in function SUM by applying the steps given below:
   (*i*) Select the *Formulas* tab.
   (*ii*) Select *AutoSum* option from *Function Library.*
   (*iii*) Select the desired option (here *Sum*). See figure 2.2.

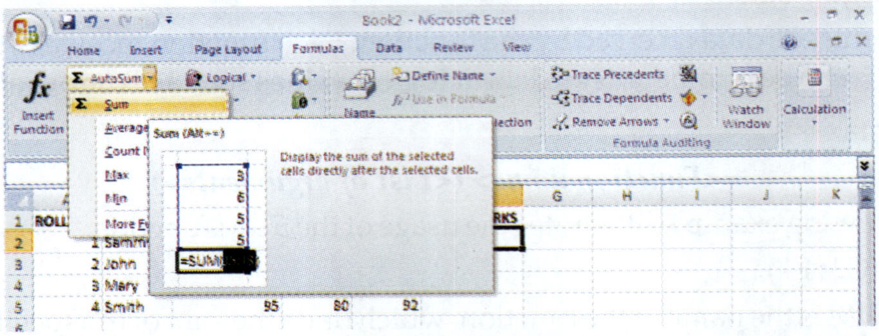

Figure 2.2 Selecting SUM function

   (*iv*) The selected function appears along with the Cell range. If you want to change Cell range then type the desired range. (See figure 2.3)

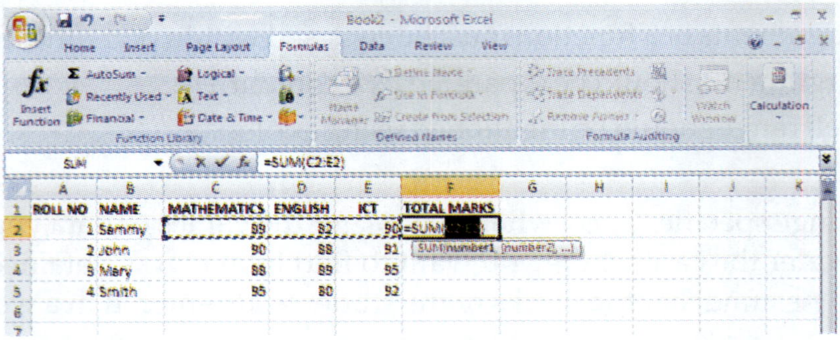

Figure 2.3 Selecting range for SUM function

3. Press the *Enter* key.
   The result will be shown in the selected cell. (See figure 2.4)

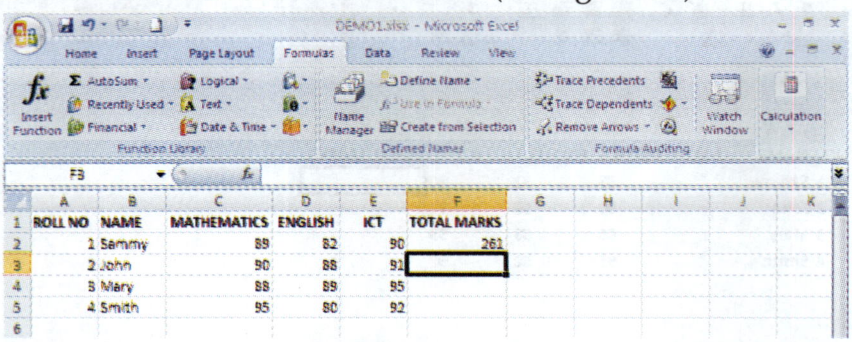

Figure 2.4 Result after applying SUM function

Alternatively, you can also select the cell range using the mouse. To do so,

1. Select the cell where the result should be displayed.
2. Type =SUM(
3. Click the first cell in the range and drag it till the last cell in the range.
4. Close the parentheses and press the *Enter* key.

You can see that the cell range is automatically displayed in the function. Excel highlights the starting and ending cell of the range with different colours.

Note

If there are any character values in the cell above or to the right of the selected cell, then the AutoSum feature will not generate any errors. It will calculate the sum only for the numeric values.

Editing Functions

Excel allows you to make any changes to the functions entered in a cell. The various editing operations that can be done on functions are:

- Changing the cell reference
- Copying functions
- Moving functions

Changing the Cell Reference

Sometimes you might add new data or delete an existing data in the worksheet. In such cases, you have to change the cell reference in the function to include the new values.

To change the cell reference,

1. Double-click the cell that contains the result of the function.
2. The formula will be displayed. Type the new range.
3. Press the *Enter* key.

The result will be recalculated.

Copying or Moving Functions

Excel allows you to copy or move a function in one cell to another rather than entering the same function again for a new range of values.

To copy a function,

1. Select the cell that contains the function.
2. Click the *Copy* option from *Clipboard* panel present in *Home* tab.
3. Click the destination cell (or range of cells) where the function has to be pasted.
4. Click the *Paste* option from *Clipboard* panel present in *Home* tab.

Note

When a function is copied to another cell, the cell range will change automatically.

When a function is copied to another cell, any changes made to the source cell will not be reflected in the destination cell. If you want the changes to be reflected, you should choose the *Paste Special* option available in *Paste* from the *Clipboard* panel present in *Home* tab instead of the *Paste* option.

To move a function,

1. Select the cell that contains the function.
2. Click the *Cut* option from *Clipboard* panel in *Home* tab.
3. Click the destination cell (or range of cells) where the function has to be pasted.
4. Click the *Paste* option from *Clipboard* panel in *Home* tab.

Fill Handle

You can copy using the fill handle. The fill handle is a small square that is seen at the right bottom corner of a selected cell or range. You cannot move data or formulae using a fill handle.

When you point to the fill handle,

1. The pointer changes to a cross + sign.
2. Drag the fill handle over the neighbouring cells to which you want to copy the formula.

AVERAGE

The average function returns the arithmetic mean of the values passed as arguments. This function takes 255 values as the maximum number of arguments.

The syntax is,

Average(number 1, number 2,...)

Consider the following examples, which illustrate the Average function.

= Average (12, 75, 15, 62) —Returns 41.

= Average (–3, –6, –9) —Returns –6.

COUNT

The count function returns the count of the cells that contain only numeric values in the specified range.

The syntax is,

Count (value 1, value 2, ...)

Here, value 1, value 2, ... are 1 to 255 arguments that can contain or refer to a variety of different types of data, but only numbers are counted.

The following examples illustrate the use of the Count function using the data given in figure 2.5.

= Count (A5 : B6) — Returns 2.

= Count (B5 : B10) — Returns 6.

	A	B	C
1		**Shop**	
2			
3	**Product**	**Availability**	
4			
5	Cricket bat	190	
6	Basket ball	82	
7	Volley ball	90	
8	Hockey stick	80	
9	Cricket bat	35	
10	Football	500	
11			
12			

Figure 2.5 Sample data

MAX

This function takes 255 values as the maximum number of arguments and returns the highest value in the specified range.

The syntax is,

Max (number 1, number 2, ...)

Here, number 1, number 2, ... are 1 to 255 numbers for which you want to find the maximum value.

Consider figure 2.5 for the example given below:

= Max (B5 : B10) — Returns 500.

MIN

This function takes 255 values as the maximum number of arguments and returns the least value in the specified range.

The syntax is,

Min (number 1, number 2, ...)

Here, number 1, number 2, ... are 1 to 255 numbers for which you want to find the minimum value. Consider figure 2.5 for the example given below:

= Min (B5 : B10) — Returns 35.

The Insert Function Feature

By now, you must be familiar with various functions available in Excel. Working with these functions is as easy as learning them. Excel provides a feature called *Insert Function*, which helps you to work with these functions more easily.

To invoke the Insert Function dialog box,

1. Click the *Formulas* tab.
2. Click the Insert Function. (See figure 2.6)

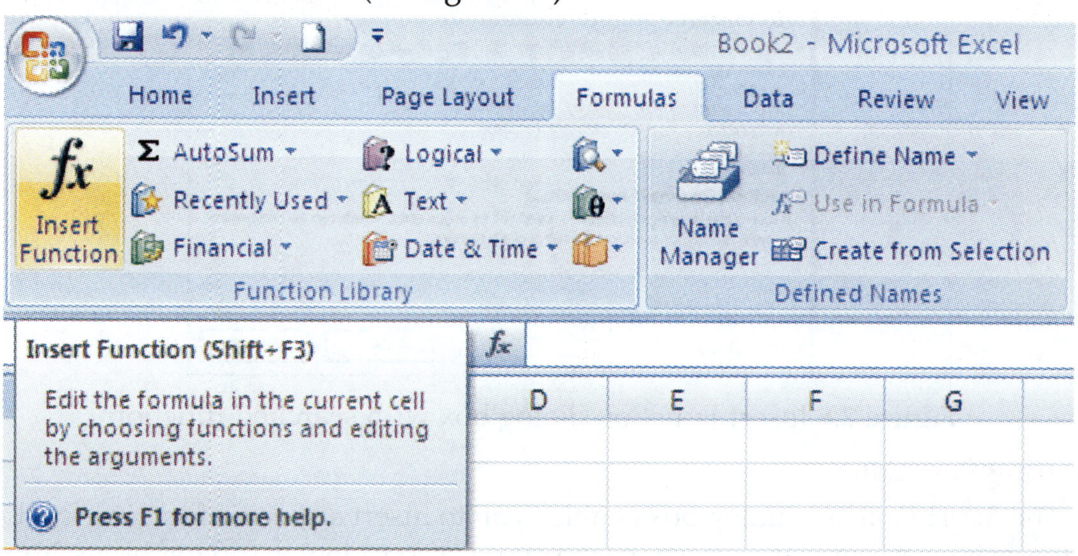

Figure 2.6 Inserting Function

3. The *Insert Function* dialog box appears. (See figure 2.7)

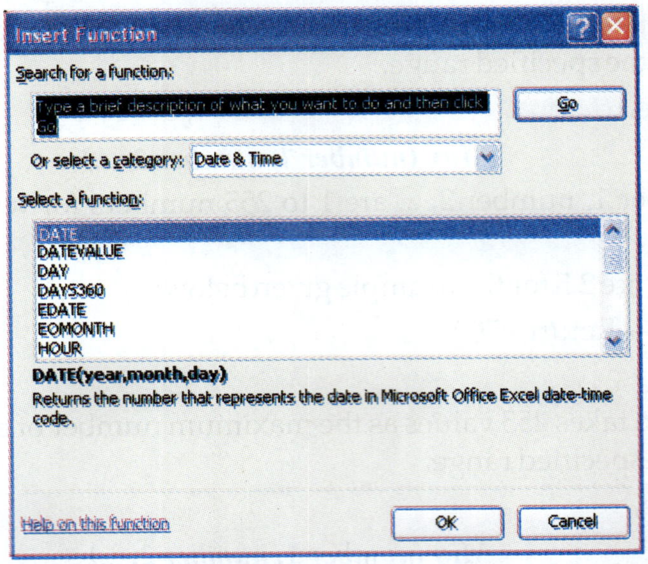

Figure 2.7 Insert Function dialog box

The *Insert Function* dialog box allows you to search for a specific function or choose a function from the available categories.

To search for a particular function,

1. Type the function in the *Search for a function* text box. (See figure 2.8)
2. Click the *Go* button.

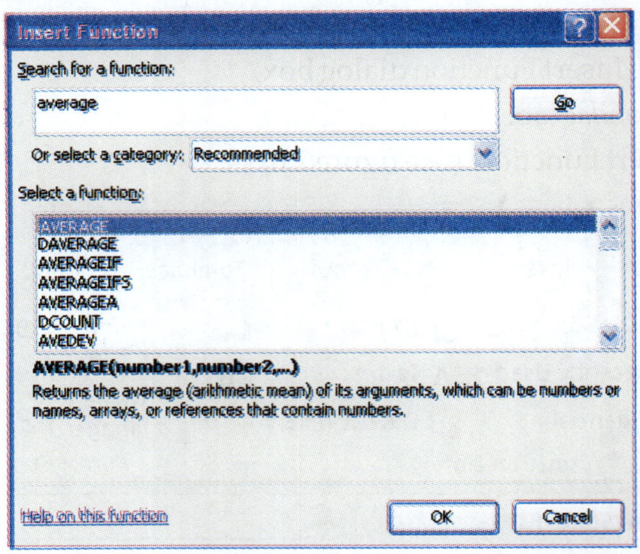

Figure 2.8 Insert Function dialog box with searched function

Inserting Functions

The *Insert Function* dialog box enables you to insert a specific function for the data in the worksheet. Assume that you have the marks of a student in three subjects. You can find the average marks of the student using the *Average* function under the *Statistical* category.

To do so,

1. Select the *Statistical* category from the *Or select a category* list box.
2. Select the *Average* function from the *Select a function* list.
3. Click the *OK* button. The *Function Arguments* dialog box will appear. (See figure 2.9)

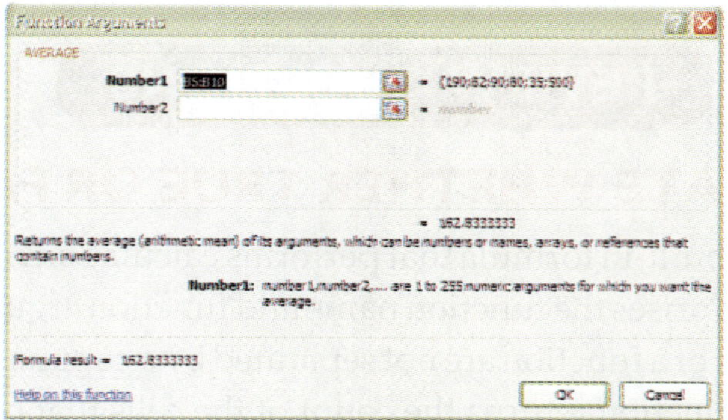

Figure 2.9 Function Arguments dialog box

4. Enter the cell range in the *Number1* text box. Here we select the range B5:B10 of sample data shown in figure 2.5.
5. Click the *OK* button.
6. You will get the desired result.

   You can click the *Help on this function* link to know more about the function.

SUMMARY

- Formulae can be used for numeric calculations such as adding, subtracting, multiplying, dividing and averaging.
- All formulae begin with the = sign.
- Functions are predefined formulae that perform simple to complex calculations.
- The organisation of a function is called its syntax.
- Formulae use functions and operators for calculations.
- Operators point to the type of operation that the formula would perform.
- Formulae are based on the values of the cells referred in the formula.
- If you change or delete the cell references in a formula, the result will change accordingly.
- The formula can be edited in the *Formula bar*.
- The SUM function returns the sum of the numbers passed as arguments to it.
- The AVERAGE function returns the average of the numbers passed as arguments to it.
- The COUNT function returns the count of the cells that contain only numeric values in the specified range.

- The MAX function returns the highest value in the specified range.
- The MIN function returns the least value in the specified range.
- Excel provides a feature called Insert Function, which helps you to work with the functions more easily.

REVIEW QUESTIONS

STATE WHETHER TRUE OR FALSE

1. A function is a built-in formula that performs calculations on a range of values.
2. A function comprises the function name and function argument.
3. The arguments of a function are not separated by a comma.
4. The COUNT function returns the count of the cells that contain data of any type in the specified range.

FILL IN THE BLANKS

1. All functions must begin with a .... sign.
2. The organisation of a function is called its ....
3. The formula can be edited in the ....
4. The .... function returns the least value in the specified range.

MULTIPLE CHOICE QUESTIONS

1. MAX function in Excel 2007 can have maximum upto .... arguments.
   (a) 200 (b) 100
   (c) 355 (d) 255
2. Which of the following function will you use to calculate the average of data range?
   (a) SUM (b) MIN
   (c) AVERAGE (d) MAX
3. Which of the following feature(s) will you use to work with the functions more easily?
   (a) Insert Function (b) ICT
   (c) PRINT (d) All of these

ANSWER THE FOLLOWING

1. Discuss the functions common to arithmetic applications.
2. Give the syntax and an example for each of the following MS-Excel functions:
   (i) COUNT (ii) AVERAGE
   (iii) MAX (iv) MIN
3. What are library functions? Explain five such functions of Excel.

ASSIGNMENT

1. Create an employee database in Excel worksheet. Create a maximum of 25 records. The sample is given with the required fields.

   Name Dept Grade Basic HRA DA PF Gross Pay Net Pay

   (i) Calculate HRA, DA, PF as follows:
   - HRA = 10% of Basic
   - DA = 35% of Basic
   - PF = 10% of Basic

   (ii) Perform the following calculations on the employee database:
   - Calculate Gross Pay for each employee using functions.
     [Gross Pay = Basic + HRA + DA]
   - Calculate the Total Salary to be disbursed every month.
   - Calculate the Net Pay for each employee using formulae [Gross Pay – PF].

   (iii) Save the workbook as *Employee Salary*.

2. Enter a given data in Worksheet and do the following:

   (i) Find averages

   (ii) Percentages

3. Create the following Students Measurement List database in a new worksheet and perform the given functions and save the workbook as *Students List*.

	A	B	C	D	E
1	**MEASUREMENTS**	**LIST**	**CLASS X**		
2					
3	**Name**	**Height**	**Weight (kg)**	**Foot length (cm)**	
4	Mathew	142.5	46.3	20.5	
5	Timothy	138	40	20.4	
6	John	146	39.5	22	
7	Maria	138.7	44.8	20.3	
8	Stephen	147.5	43	20	
9	Julie	132	44	20	
10					
11	TOTAL				
12					
13	AVERAGE				
14					
15	MAXIMUM				
16					
17	MINIMUM				
18					

UNIT 3 FORMATTING WORKSHEET

Specific Objective

After reading this unit, the student will be able to:

1.3.1 format worksheet.

1.3.0 Introduction

Formatting refers to the act of changing the appearance of data in cells. Data in MS Excel can be grouped into two broad categories: text and numbers. Different formatting options are available for these two categories of data. Excel allows many formats for numeric data, for example, general number, positive number, decimal number and its precision, currency etc.

For textual data, Excel allows you to change fonts, colours, sizes and other features. Excel has a complete dialog box for formatting cells.

1.3.1 Formatting Worksheet

Formats control the way numbers are displayed on the screen and the way labels are aligned in their cells. These are used to make screen displays and printed reports more readable and attractive. One thing to be aware of is that the same number can be displayed in a variety of ways, just by changing its format.

- **Changing Column width**

  You can change the width of a column so that the desired text fits into that cell.

  To change column width,

1. Open an existing worksheet DEMO1.xlsx.
2. Position the pointer so that it is on the line between column headers. The pointer will change to a double-headed arrow. (See figure 3.1)
3. Press the left mouse button and hold it down while you drag to the left or right. The column width will change. Make it wide enough to contain the whole text. (See figure 3.2)

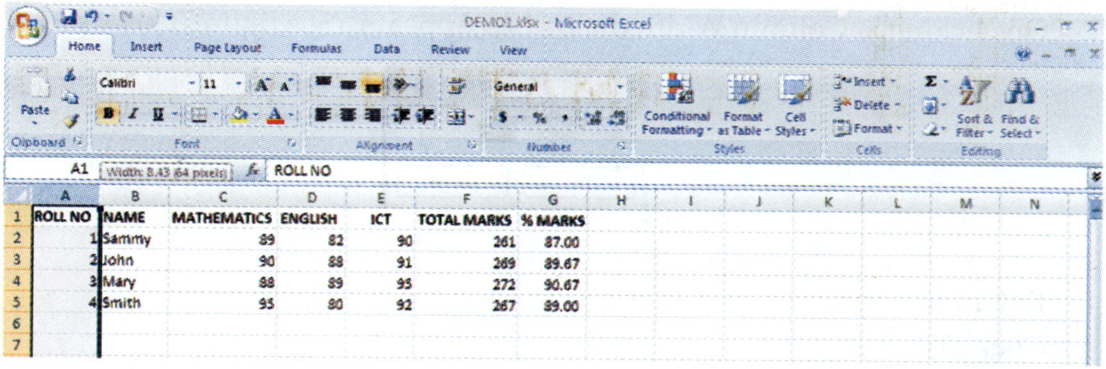

Figure 3.1 Changing column width

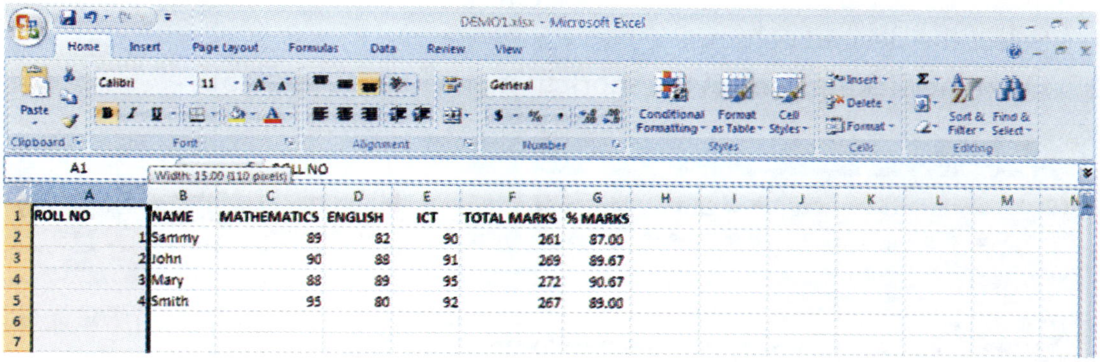

Figure 3.2 Column after changing width

4. Save your workbook.

OR

1. Position the pointer between the column headers of the desired columns.
2. Double click. The column automatically widens so that the text will fit in the cell.
3. Save your workbook.

OR

1. Select the desired column.
2. Click the *Column Width* option from *Format* available in Cells panel of Home tab. (See figure 3.3).

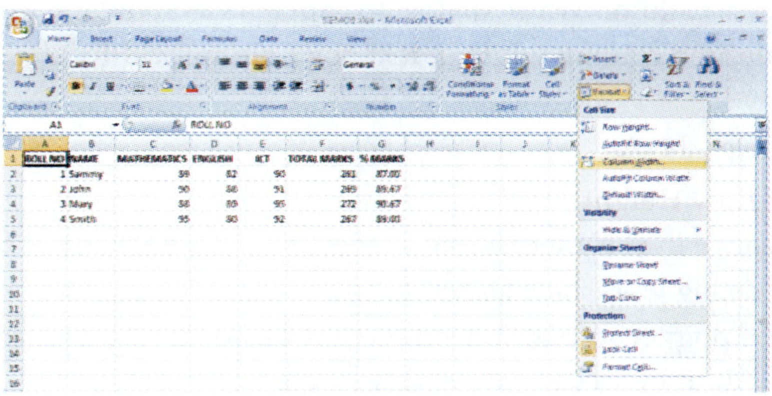

Figure 3.3 Changing column width

3. On clicking, a Column Width dialog box appears. (See figure 3.4).

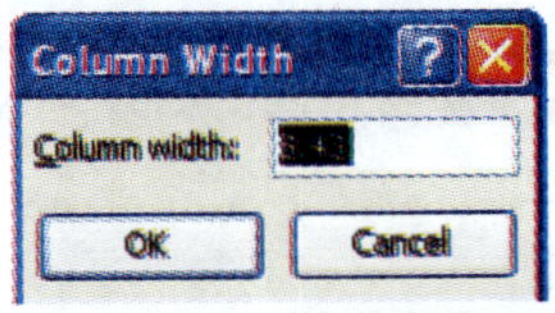

Figure 3.4 Column width dialog box

4. Enter the desired column width in the text box Column width.
5. Click OK.
6. Save your workbook.

OR

1. Select the desired column.
2. On right clicking, we get the shortcut menu. (See figure 3.5).

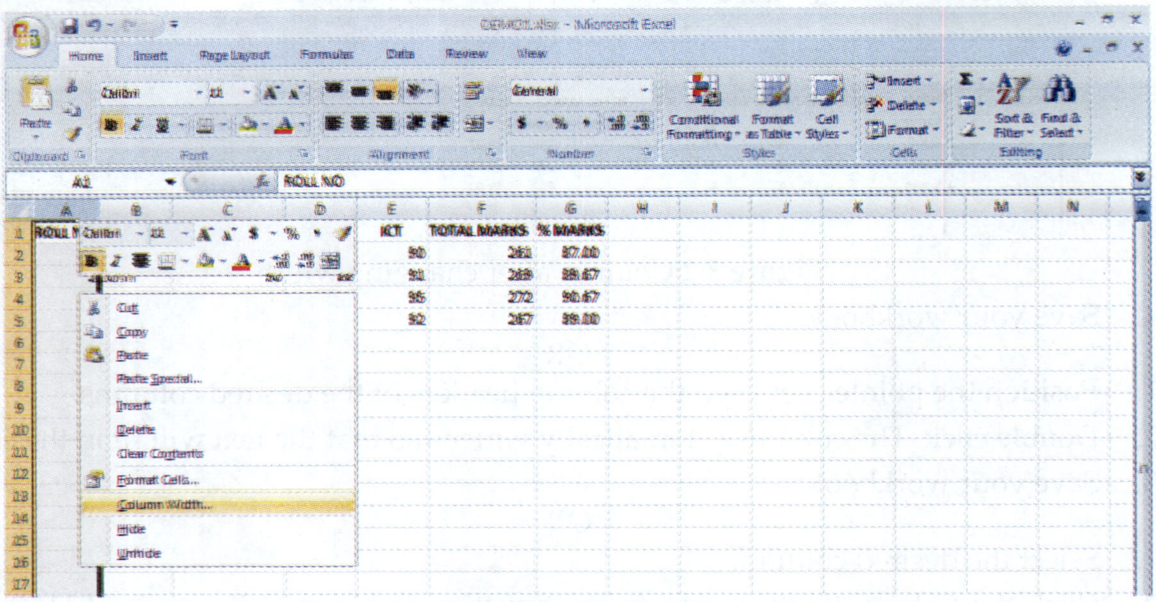

Figure 3.5 Changing Column width

3. On clicking, a Column Width dialog box appears as shown in figure 3.4.
4. Enter the desired column width in text box Column width.
5. Click OK.
6. Save your workbook.

- **Changing Row Height**

  You can change the height of a row so that the desired text fits into the cell. To do so:

1. Open an existing worksheet DEMO1.xlsx.
2. Position the pointer so that it is on the line between row headers. The pointer will change to a double-headed arrow. (See figure 3.6)

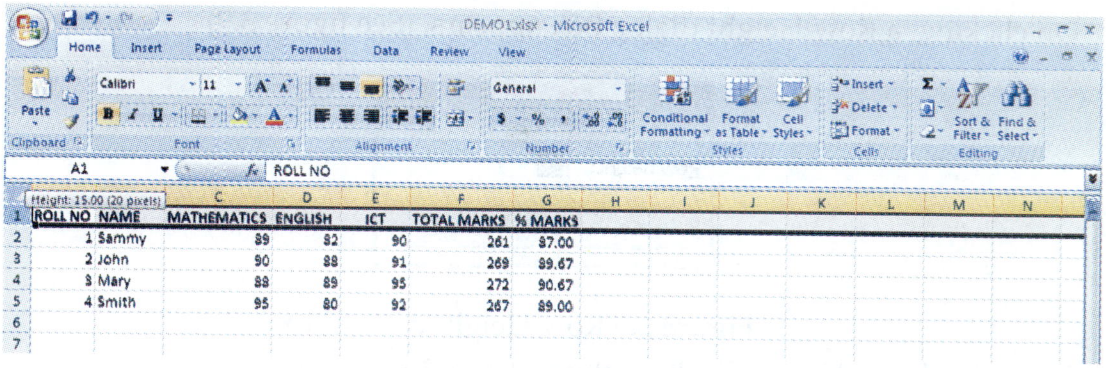

Figure 3.6 Changing row height

3. Press the left mouse button and hold it down while you drag up or down. The row height will change. Make the height appropriate to contain the whole text. (See figure 3.7)

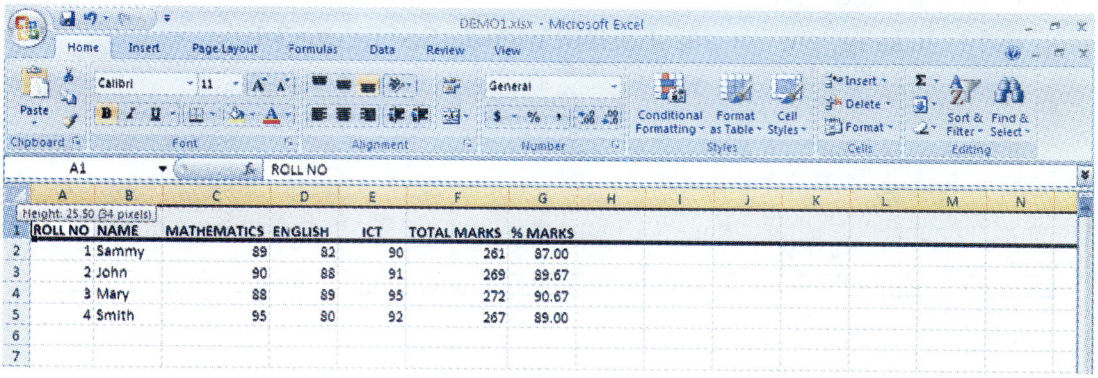

Figure 3.7 After changing row height

4. Save your workbook.

OR

1. Select the desired row.
2. Click the *Row Height* option from *Format* available in Cells panel. (See figure 3.8)

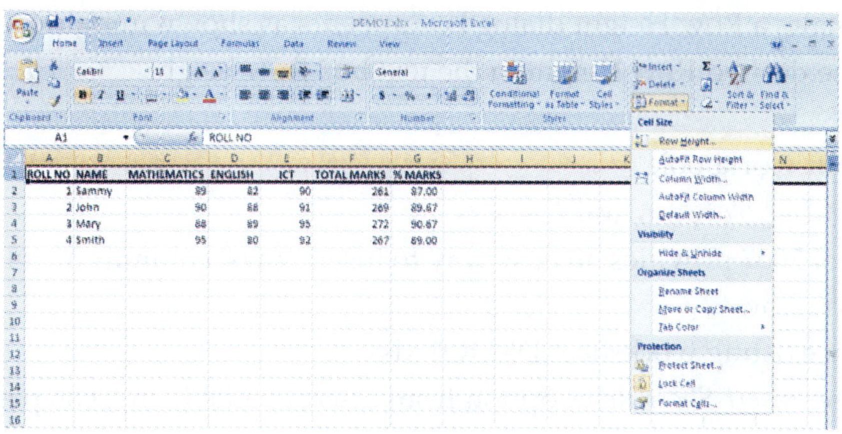

Figure 3.8 Changing row height

3. On clicking, a Row Height dialog box appears. (See figure 3.9)

Figure 3.9 Row Height dialog box

4. Enter the desired Row Height in the text box Row height.
5. Click OK.
6. Save your workbook.

OR

1. Select the desired row.
2. On right clicking, we get the shortcut menu. (See figure 3.10)

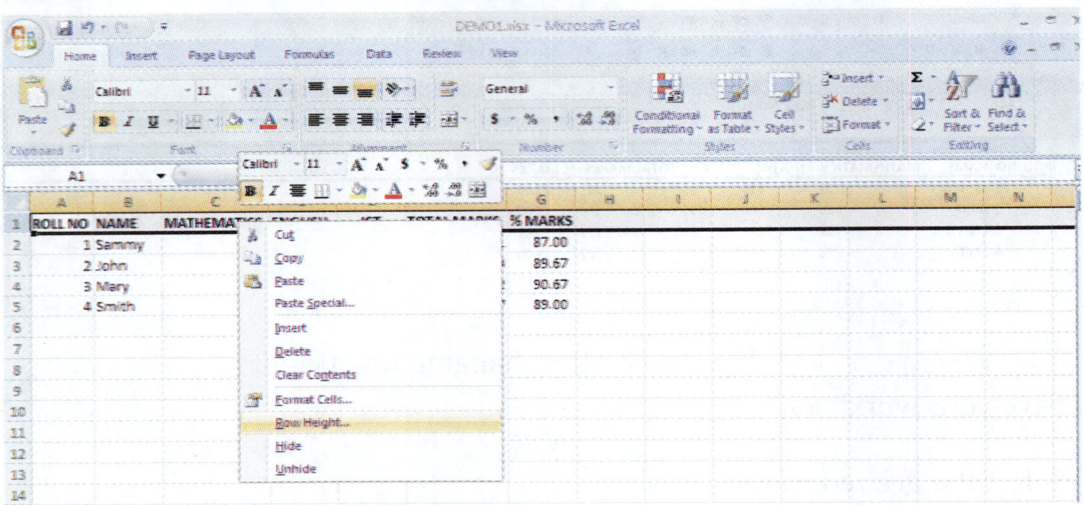

Figure 3.10

3. On clicking, a Row Height dialog box appears as shown in figure 3.9.
4. Enter the desired Row Height in the text box Row height.
5. Click OK.
6. Save your workbook.

- **Insert: Row, Column and Cells**

  MS-Excel 2007 provides an easy way to insert rows, columns or cells.

  To insert a row,

1. Open an existing worksheet DEMO1.xlsx.
2. Select the *Insert Sheet Rows* option from *Insert* available in Cells panel of Home tab. (See figure 3.11)

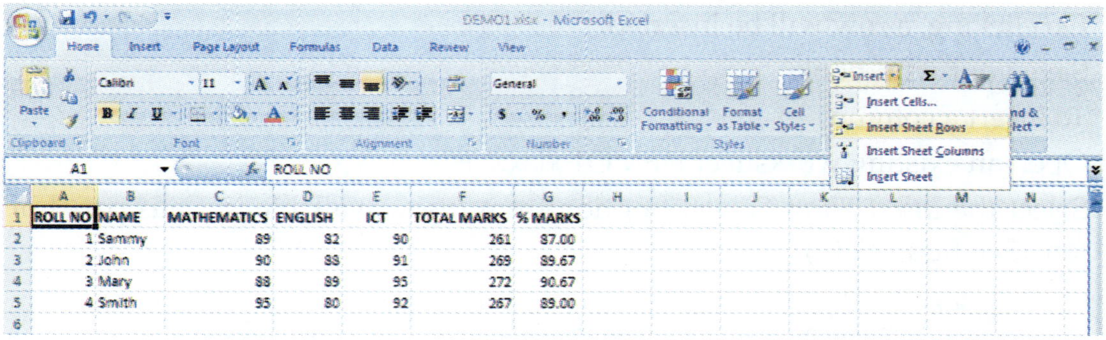

Figure 3.11 Inserting a row

3. On clicking, a row will be inserted above the insertion point (See figure 3.12)

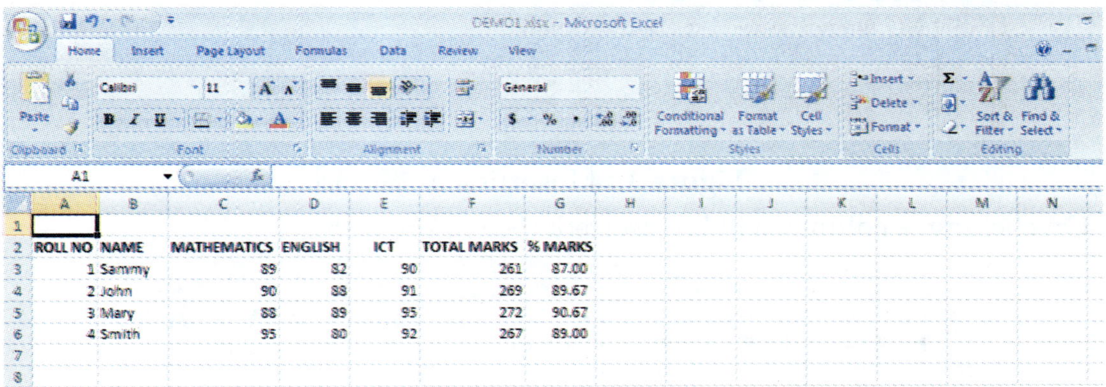

Figure 3.12 Worksheet after inserting a row

4. Save your workbook.

OR

1. Select the desired row above which a new row is to be inserted.
2. On right clicking the selected row, a shortcut menu appears.
3. Select the *Insert* option from shortcut menu. (See figure 3.13)

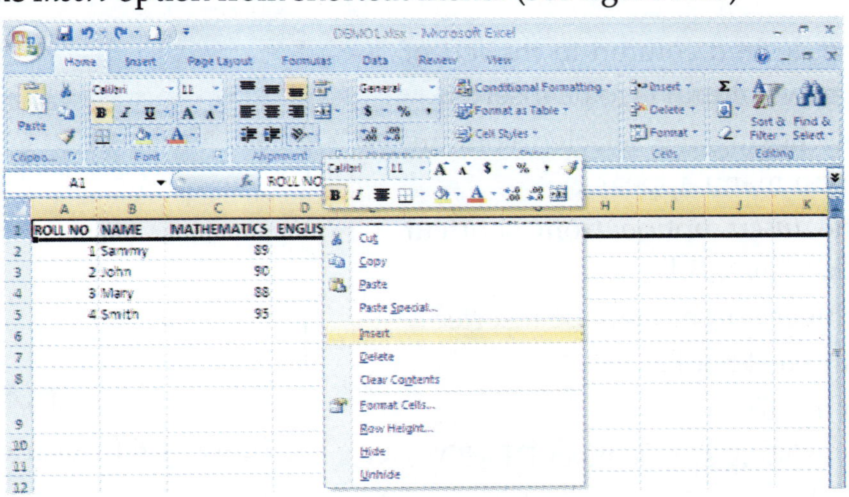

Figure 3.13 Inserting a row

4. On clicking, a row will be inserted.
5. Save your workbook.

To insert a column,

1. Open an existing worksheet DEMO1.xlsx.
2. Select the *Insert Sheet Columns* option from *Insert* available in Cells panel of Home tab. (See figure 3.14)

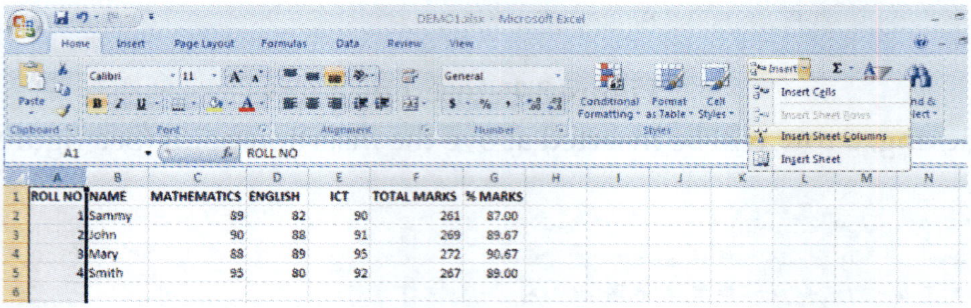

Figure 3.14 Inserting a column

3. On clicking, a column will be inserted. (See figure 3.15)

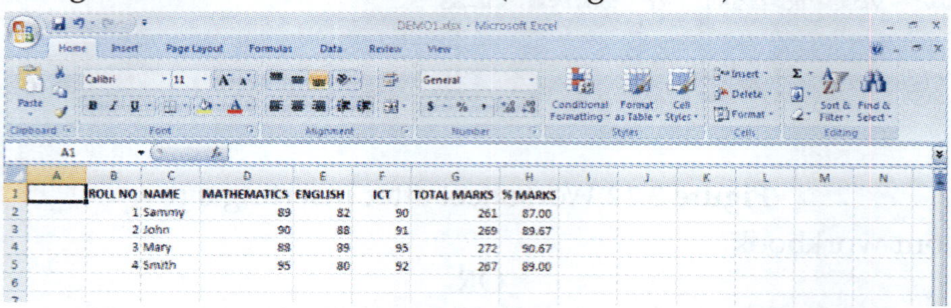

Figure 3.15 Worksheet after inserting a column

4. Save your workbook.

OR

1. Select the desired column to the left of which a new column is to be inserted.
2. On right clicking the selected column, the shortcut menu appears.
3. Select the *Insert* option from shortcut menu. (See figure 3.16)
4. On clicking, a column will be inserted.
5. Save your workbook.

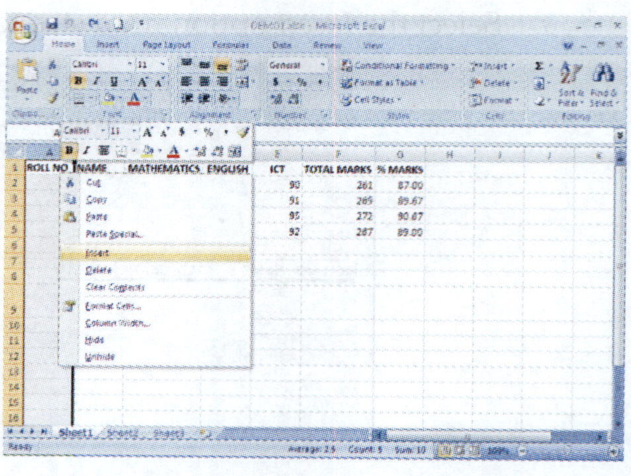

Figure 3.16 Inserting a column

To insert a cell,

1. Open an existing spreadsheet DEMO1.xlsx.
2. Select the *Insert Cells....* option from *Insert* available in Cells panel of Home tab. (See figure 3.17)

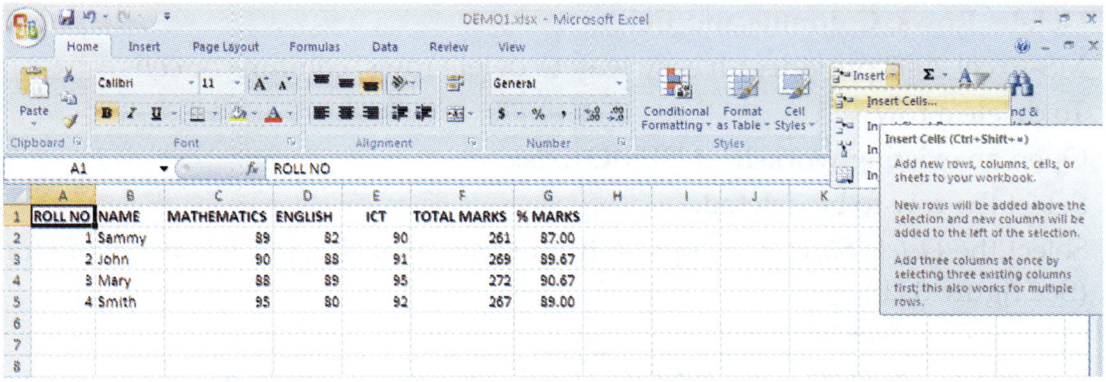

Figure 3.17 Inserting a cell

3. On clicking, an *Insert* dialog box appears. The dialog box has 4 options out of which 2 are *Shift cells right* and *Shift cells down*. The *Shift cells right* option shifts the data of the selected cell one position right. The *Shift cells down* option shifts the data of the selected cell one position down. Select the desired option (See figure 3.18). Here, we select the *Shift cells down* option.

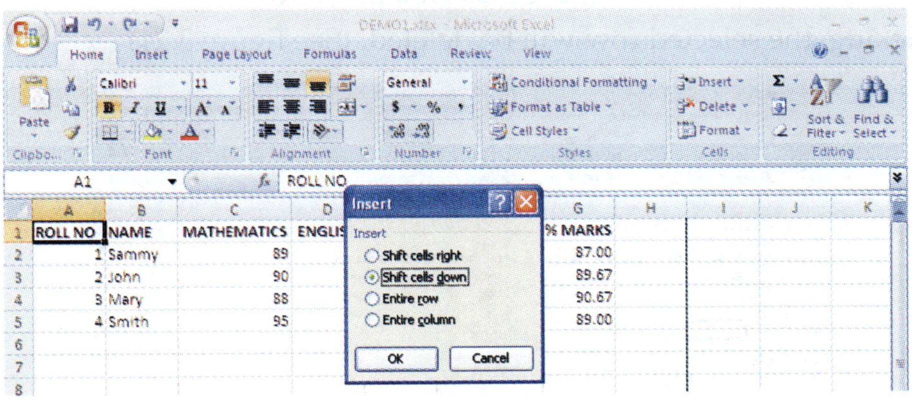

Figure 3.18 Insert dialog box

4. Click OK.
5. A cell will be inserted at the applied location. (See figure 3.19)

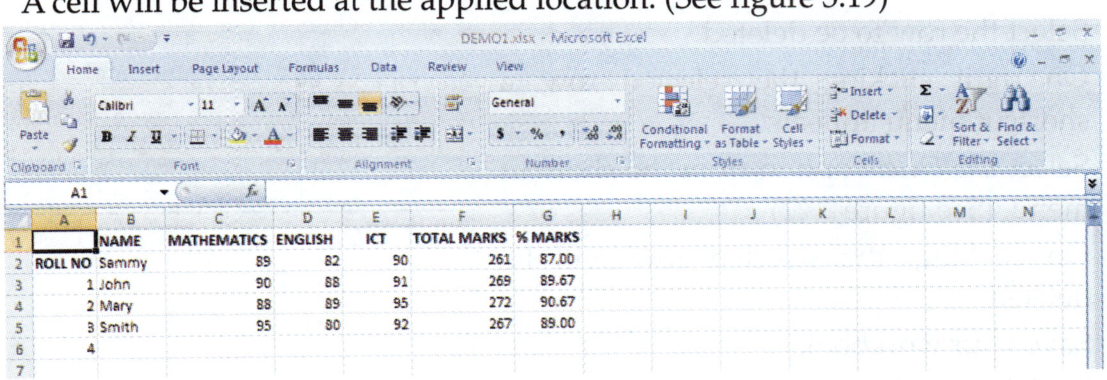

Figure 3.19 Worksheet after inserting a cell

6. Save your workbook.

- **Delete: Rows, Columns and Cells**

  MS-Excel 2007 provides an easy way to delete rows, columns or cells.

  To delete a row,

1. Open an existing worksheet DEMO1.xlsx.
2. Select the row to be deleted.
3. Select the *Delete Sheet Rows* option from *Delete* available in Cells panel of Home tab. (See figure 3.20)

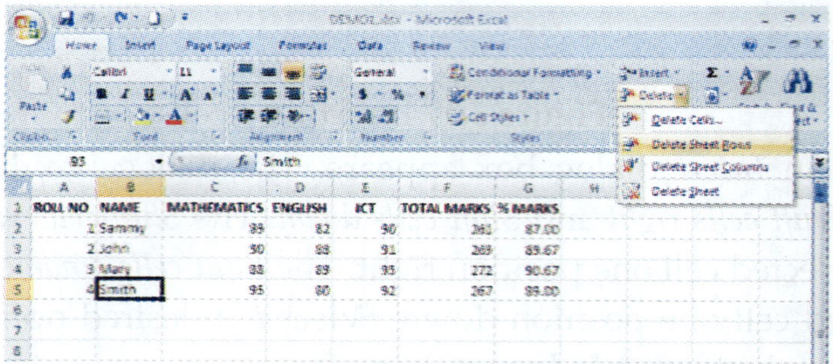

Figure 3.20 Deleting a row

4. On clicking, the selected row will be deleted. (See figure 3.21)

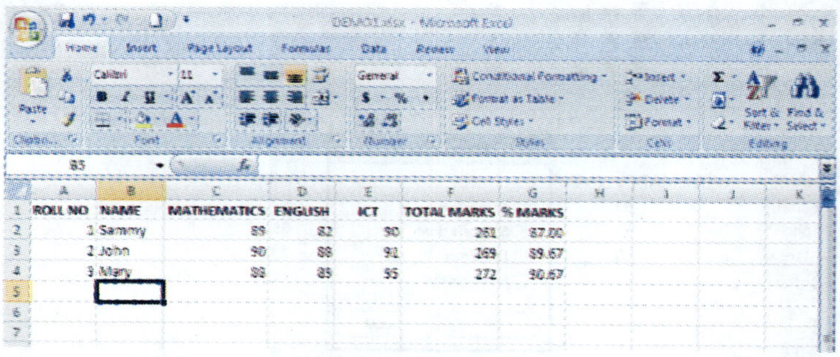

Figure 3.21 Worksheet after deleting a row

5. Save your workbook.

OR

1. Select the row to be deleted.
2. On right clicking the selected row, a shortcut menu appears.
3. Select the *Delete* option from the shortcut menu. (See figure 3.22)
4. On clicking, the selected row will be deleted.
5. Save your workbook.

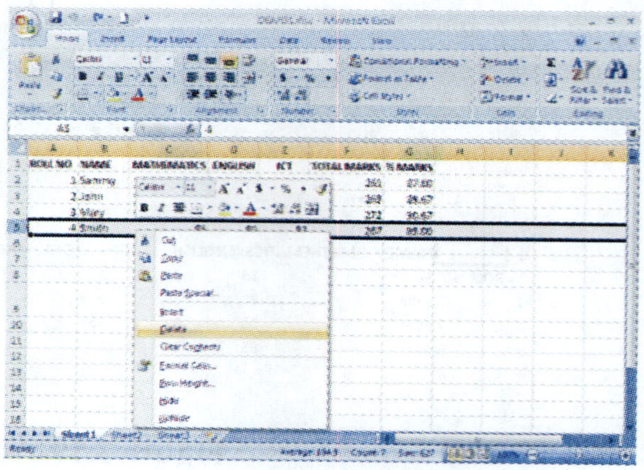

Figure 3.22 Deleting a row

To delete a column,

1. Open an existing worksheet DEMO1.xlsx.
2. Select the column to be deleted.

3. Select the *Delete Sheet Columns* option from *Delete* available in Cells panel of Home tab. (See figure 3.23)

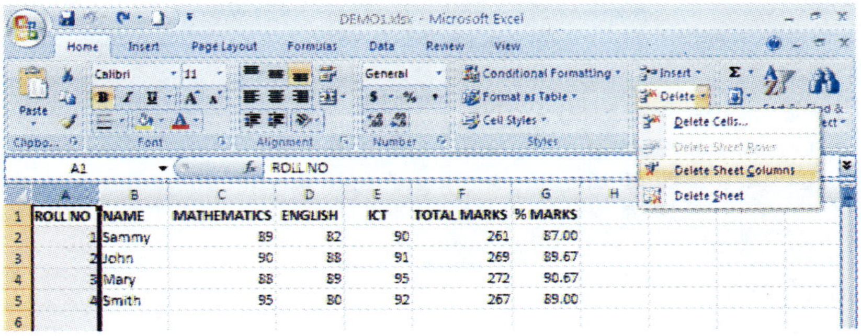

Figure 3.23 Deleting a column

4. On clicking, the selected column will be deleted. (See figure 3.24)

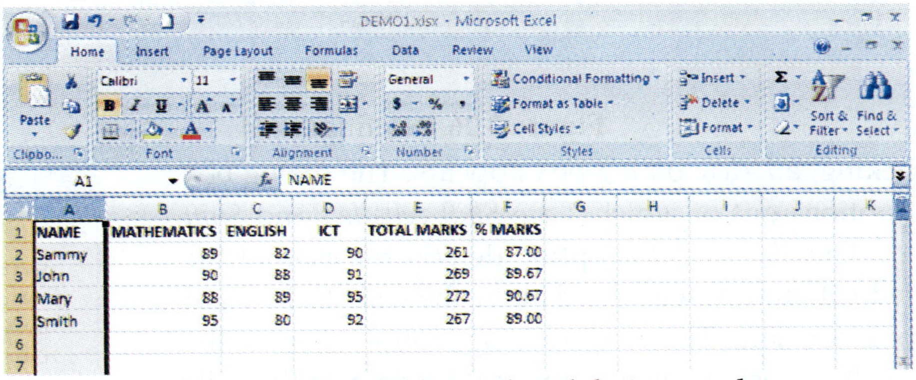

Figure 3.24 Worksheet after deleting a column

5. Save your workbook.

OR

1. Select the column to be deleted.
2. On right clicking the selected column, a shortcut menu appears.
3. Select the *Delete* option from the shortcut menu. (See figure 3.25)
4. On clicking, the selected column will be deleted.
5. Save your workbook.

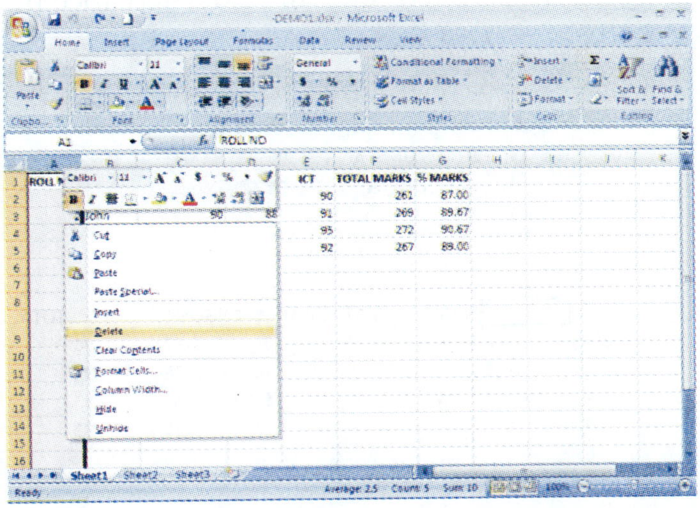

Figure 3.25 Deleting a column

To delete a cell,

1. Open an existing worksheet DEMO1.xlsx and make some changes in it, if you have already deleted some data from it. (See figure 3.26)

2. Select the cell to be deleted.
3. Select the *Delete Cells...* option from *Delete* available in Cells panel of Home tab. (See figure 3.26)

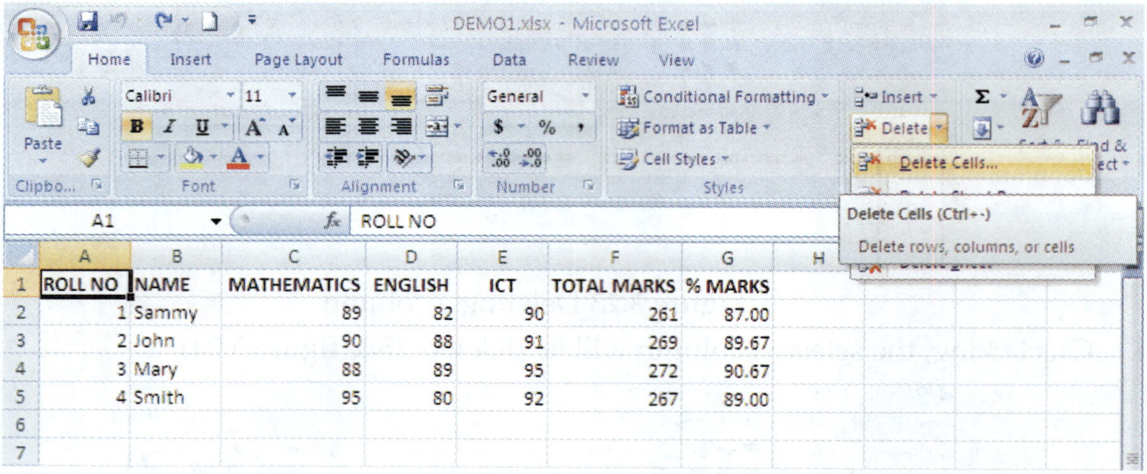

Figure 3.26 Deleting a cell

4. On clicking, a *Delete* dialog box appears. The dialog box has 4 options out of which 2 are *Shift cells left* and *Shift cells up*. The *Shift cells left* option deletes the data of the selected cell and moves the data of the cells to its right one position left. The *Shift cells up* option deletes the data of the selected cell and moves the data of the cells below it one position up. Select the desired option (See figure 3.27). Here we select the *Shift cells up* option.

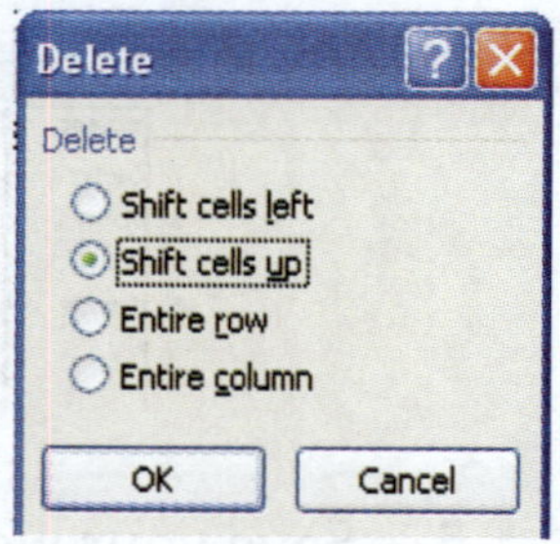

Figure 3.27 Delete dialog box

5. Click OK.
6. The selected cell will be deleted. (See figure 3.28)

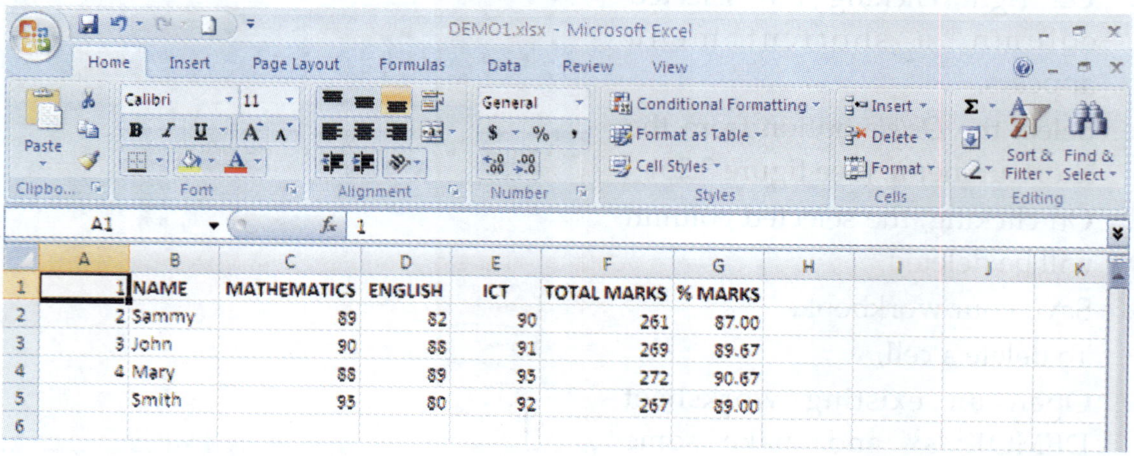

Figure 3.28 Worksheet after deleting a cell

7. Save your workbook.

OR

1. Select the cell to be deleted.
2. On right clicking the desired cell, a shortcut menu appears. (See figure 3.25)
3. On selecting the *Delete* option, a dialog box appears. (See figure 3.27)
4. Select the desired option.
5. Click OK.
6. The selected cell will be deleted. (See figure 3.28)
7. Save your workbook.

- **Merge Cells**

The *Merge cells* option is used to combine two or more cells into a single cell. This option will be useful in places where you want to display the heading for a worksheet. You can merge cells that span several columns or rows.

To merge cells,

1. Open an existing worksheet DEMO1.xlsx and add some data in it. (See figure 3.29)
2. Select the cells that contain the text.
3. From the Alignment panel of Home tab, select the *Merge Cells* option of *Merge & Center*. (See figure 3.29)

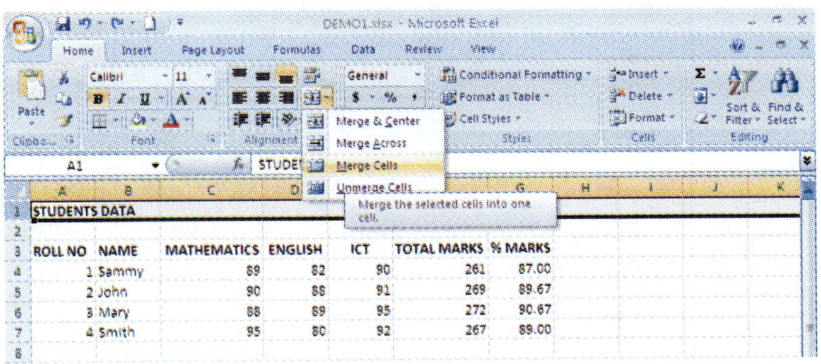

Figure 3.29 Merging cells

4. On clicking, the cells will be merged. (See figure 3.30)

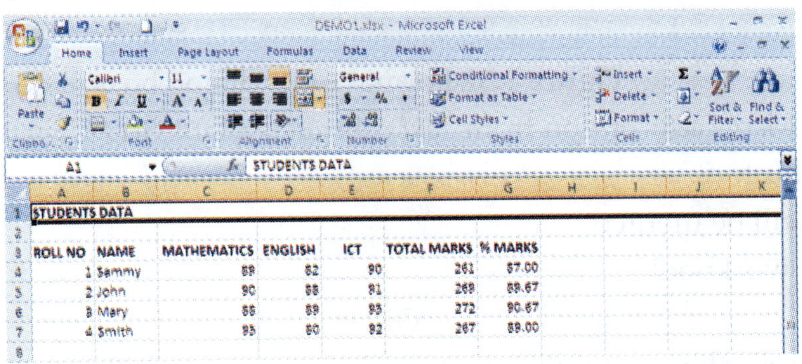

Figure 3.30 Worksheet after merging of cells

5. Save your workbook.

OR

1. Select the cells that contain the text.
2. Click the button on Alignment panel. (See figure 3.31)

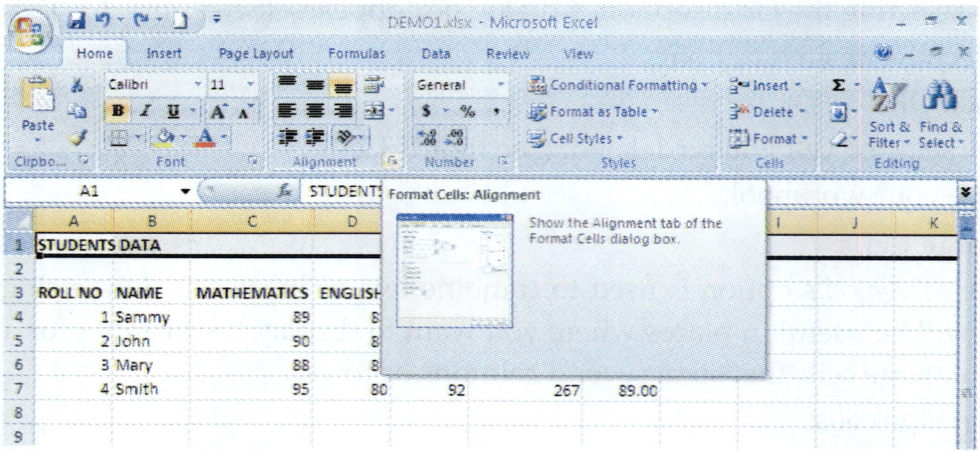

Figure 3.31 Merging cells

3. A *Format Cells* dialog box appears. (See figure 3.32)

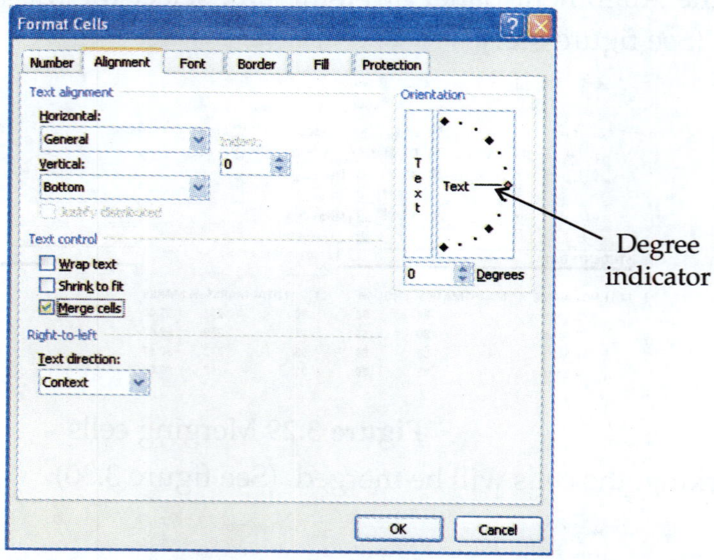

Figure 3.32 Format Cells dialog box

4. Select the *Merge cells* option from *Text control* available in *Alignment* tab.
5. Click OK button.
6. The cells will be merged.
7. Save your workbook.

OR

1. Select the cells that contain the text.
2. On right clicking the selected cells, a shortcut menu appears. (See figure 3.33)

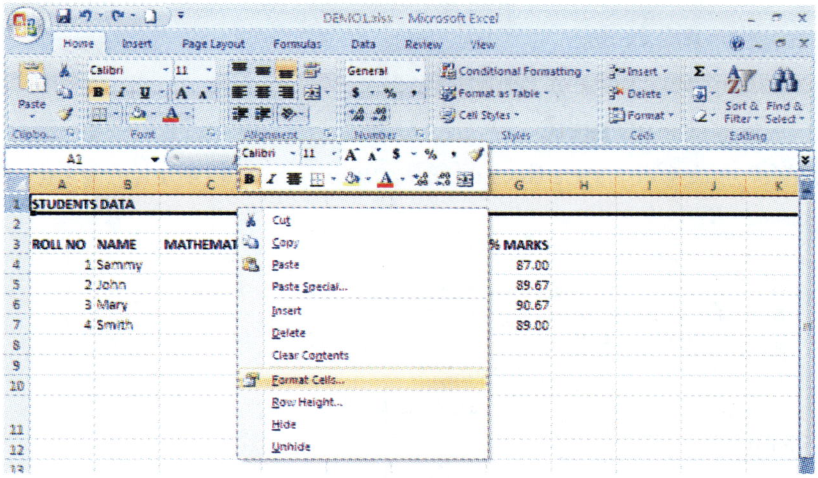

Figure 3.33 Merging cells

3. Select the *Format Cells...* option.
4. Repeat the steps 3 to 7 of the method given above.

OR

1. Select the cells that contain the text.
2. Select the *Format Cells...* option from *Format* of Cells panel. (See figure 3.34)

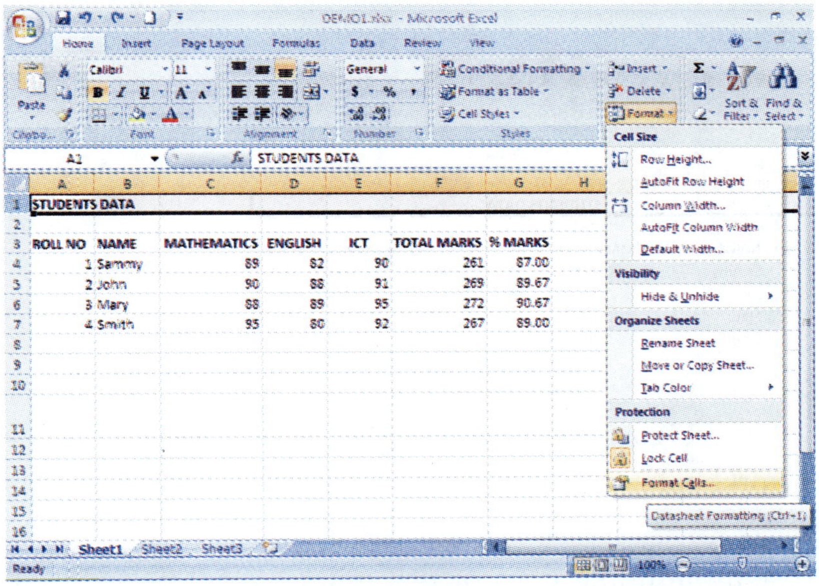

Figure 3.34 Merging cells

3. Repeat the step 4 of the method given above.

- **Merge and Center**

The *Merge & Center* option of *Alignment* panel on Home tab is used to combine and centre two or more cells into a single cell. This option will be useful in places where you want to display the heading in the centre for a worksheet. You can merge and centre cells that span several columns or rows.

To merge and centre cells,

1. Open an existing worksheet DEMO1.xlsx.
2. Select the cells to be merged.
3. Select the *Merge & Center* option of *Alignment* panel on Home tab. (See figure 3.35)

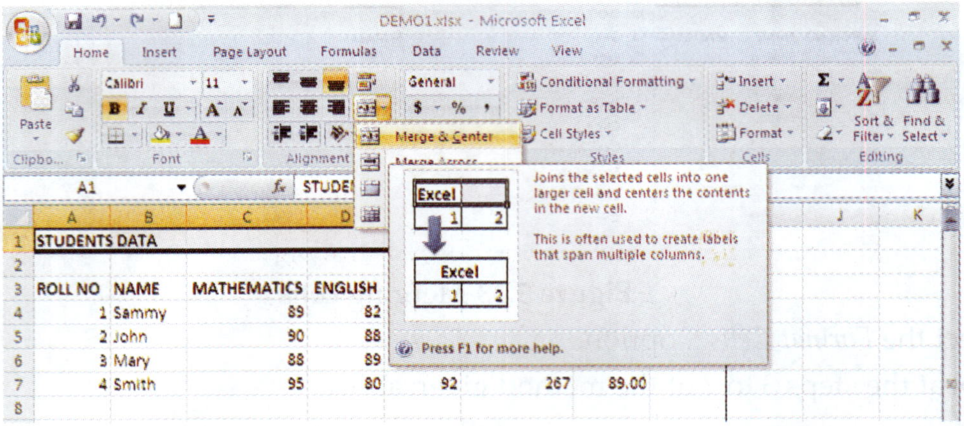

Figure 3.35 Merging and centering

4. On clicking, the selected cells are merged and centred. (See figure 3.36)

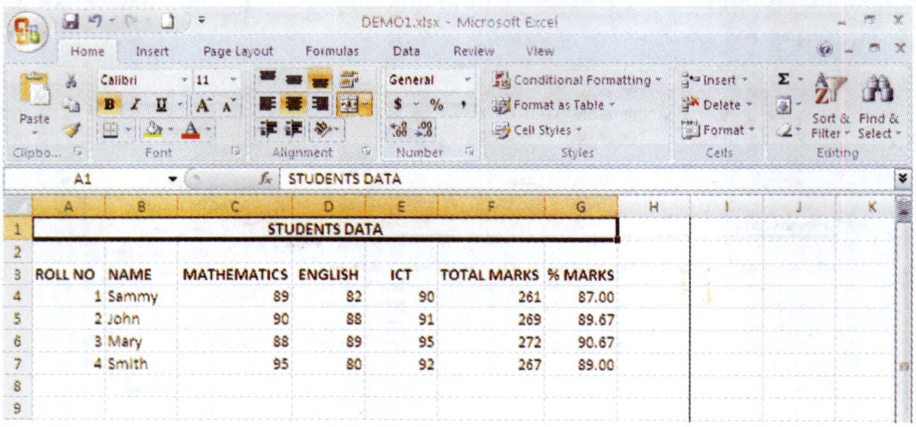

Figure 3.36 After merging and centering

5. Save your workbook.

- **Text Wrap**

You can display multiple lines of text within a cell using the *Wrap Text* option. When you wrap a lengthy text, it will be displayed in multiple lines within the cell.

To wrap text,

1. Open an existing worksheet DEMO1.xlsx and make some changes in it. (See figure 3.37) Here, we have written surnames of students and changed the text STUDENTS DATA in it.
2. Select the cells you want to format.
3. Click the *Wrap Text* button on Alignment panel. (See figure 3.37)

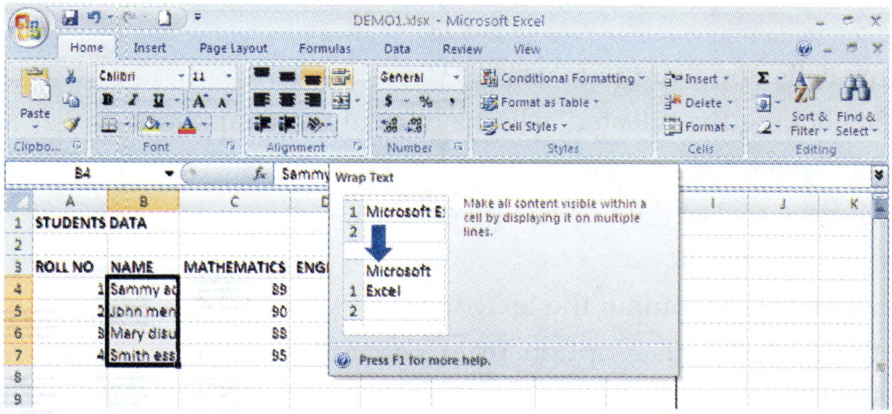

Figure 3.37 Text Wrap

4. On clicking, the text in selected cells will be wrapped. (See figure 3.38)

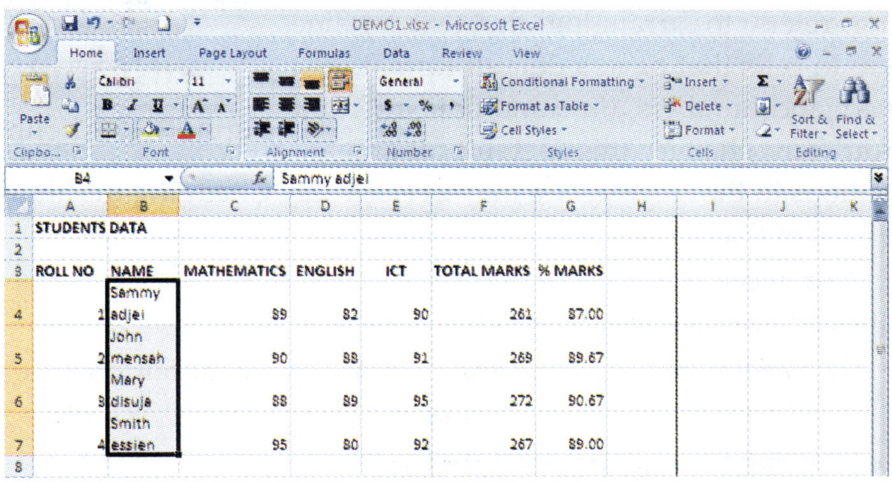

Figure 3.38 After Text Wrap

5. Single click in the worksheet.
6. Save your workbook.

OR

1. Select the cells you want to format.
2. Click the button on Alignment panel. (See figure 3.31)
3. A *Format Cells* dialog box appears. (See figure 3.39)
4. Select the *Wrap text* option from *Text control* available in Alignment tab.
5. Click OK button.
6. The text will be wrapped.
7. Save your workbook.

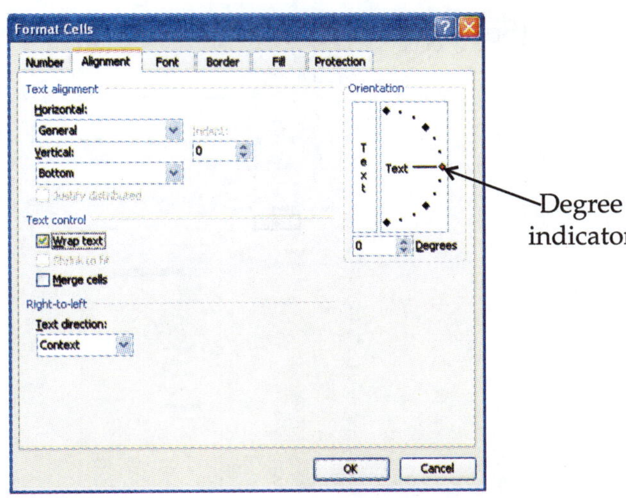

Figure 3.39 Selecting Wrap Text

OR

1. Select the cells you want to format.
2. On right clicking the selected cells, a shortcut menu appears.
3. Select the *Format Cells...* option.
4. Repeat steps 4 to 7 of the method given above.

OR

1. Select the cells that contain the text.
2. Select the *Format Cells...* option from *Format* of Cells panel.
3. Repeat the step 4 of the method given above.

- **Cell Alignment**

Aligning refers to arranging the text in line within a cell. In cells that have a default format, text is left aligned, and numbers, time and date are right aligned. You can change this default alignment using the options in the *Alignment* panel on *Home* tab. Changing the alignment does not change the type of data.

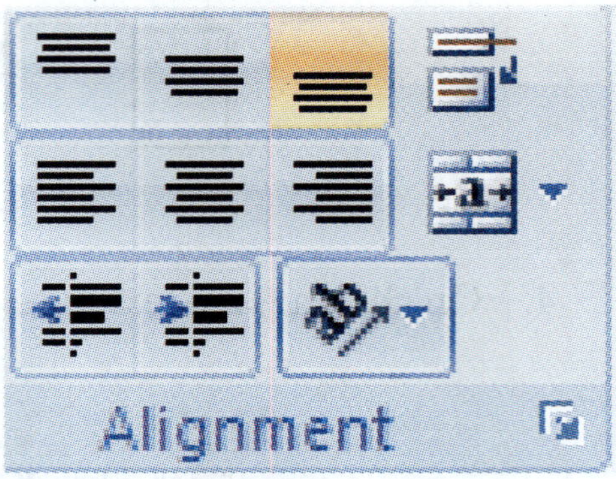

Figure 3.40 Alignment buttons

To align text in cell,

1. Select the cell or range of cells that has to be aligned.
2. On the *Alignment* panel, click the appropriate alignment button. (See figure 3.40)

OR

1. Open an existing worksheet DEMO1.xlsx.
2. Select the cell or range of cells that has to be aligned.
3. From the *Format Cells* dialog box, select the appropriate text alignment option. (See figure 3.41)

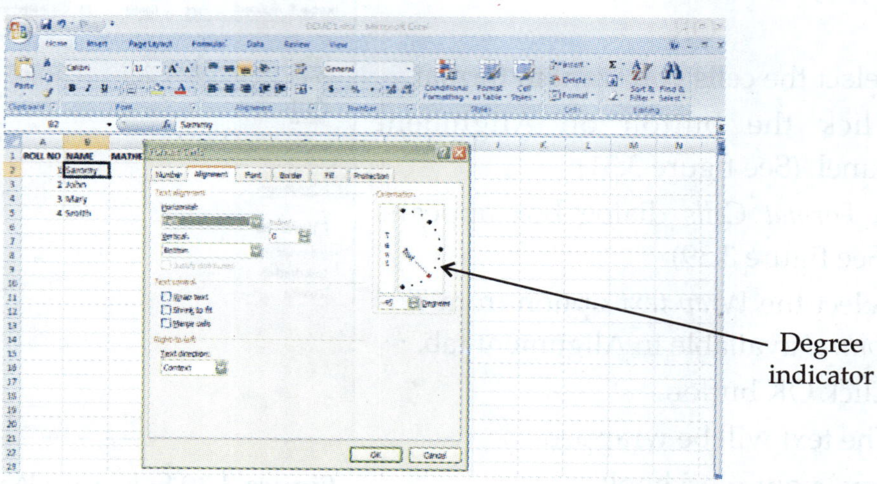

Figure 3.41 Alignment using Format Cells

4. Click OK button.
5. The selected cell or range of cells will be aligned. (See figure 3.42)

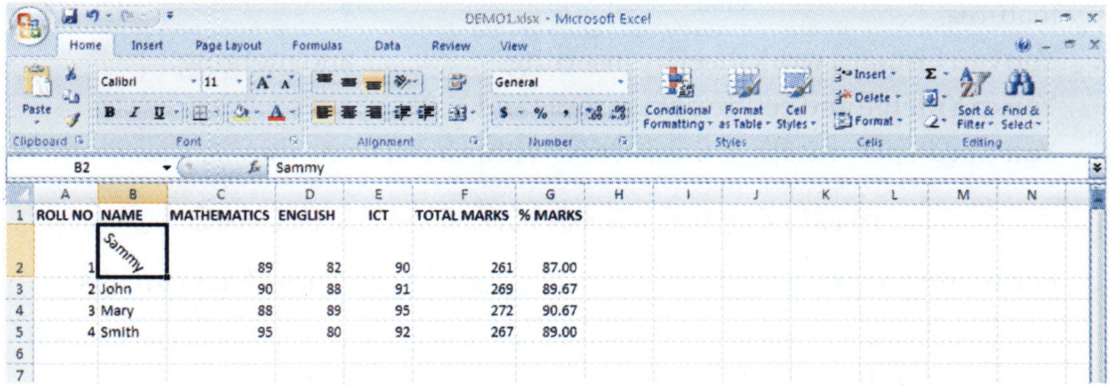

Figure 3.42 Worksheet after cell alignment

6. Save your workbook.

SUMMARY

- Formatting refers to changing the appearance of text in a cell or range of cells.
- Excel allows you to specify the attributes of rows and columns of a worksheet.
- You can change (increase or decrease) the column width or row height.
- You can insert rows, columns and cells in a worksheet.
- You can delete rows, columns and cells in a worksheet.
- The *Merge Cells* option is used to combine two or more cells into a single cell.
- You can merge and centre to combine and centre two or more cells into a single cell.
- You can display multiple lines of text within a cell using the *Wrap text* option.
- Aligning refers to arranging the text in line within a cell.
- In cells that have a default format, text is left aligned, and numbers, time and date are right aligned.
- You can change the cell alignment using the *Format Cells* dialog box.

REVIEW QUESTIONS

STATE WHETHER TRUE OR FALSE

1. Formats cannot control the way numbers are displayed on the screen and the way labels are aligned in their cells.
2. You can format a worksheet by changing column width and row height.
3. You cannot insert rows, columns and cells in a worksheet.
4. You can delete rows, columns and cells in a worksheet.

FILL IN THE BLANKS

1. For .... data, Excel allows you to change fonts, colours, sizes and other features.
2. You can format a worksheet by inserting, ... and merging.
3. You can merge and centre data in rows and ....
4. You can display multiple lines of text within a cell using the .... option.

MULTIPLE CHOICE QUESTIONS

1. Formatting refers to the act of .... the appearance of data in cells.
   (a) Changing (b) Printing
   (c) Calculating (d) None of these
2. The .... option allows you to display multiple lines of text within a cell.
   (a) Wrap text (b) Insert
   (c) Delete (d) None of these
3. You can change the cell alignment using the .... dialog box.
   (a) Column Width (b) Row Height
   (c) Format Cells (d) None of these

ANSWER THE FOLLOWING

1. What is formatting?
2. What are the various options of formatting rows and columns?
3. Discuss the formatting of a worksheet by changing column width and row height.
4. Explain the insertion and deletion of rows, columns and cells in Excel.
5. Discuss the formatting of a worksheet by inserting, deleting and merging.
6. Explain the merging and centring of data in rows and columns of a worksheet.

ASSIGNMENT

1. Create your own worksheet and format it by inserting, deleting, merging.
2. Create a Students Personal Information database with the following fields: Student Name, Enrolment Number, Date of Birth, Father's name, Occupation, Annual Income.
   - Enter at least 20 records in the worksheet.
   - Change the column width and row height for the heading row of the database.
   - Insert rows and columns of your choice.
   - Merge and Centre the heading STUDENT DETAILS so that it spans all the columns of the database.
   - Save your workbook.

3. Implement the following tasks in MS EXCEL:

- Open the file "Formatted.xlsx" and insert a new sheet.
- Design a solution for the following problem:

  A manufacturer of leather goods purchases raw leather and after dyeing, cutting, stitching and polishing, the leather apparel is manufactured. The expenses incurred at different stages can be classified into Raw material, Manufacturing expenses @ 45% of raw material cost, colouring and stitching @ 35% of raw material cost, Packing and transportation @ 18% of raw material cost. Find the value in the empty cells of the following figure. (First design the following figure on your computer)

	A	B	C	D	E	F
1	**Item**	**Raw Mat.**	**Mfg. Exp.**	**Col & St. Exp.**	**Packg & Tpt.**	**Sale Price**
2	Jacket	600				
3	Gloves	200				
4	Trouser	450				
5	Shoes	350				

- You are required to calculate the sale price of the item at which the manufacturer will earn 25% profit. Do not add any other column. Notice the formatting of rows and columns and try to make the same.
- Save your workbook.

UNIT 4 EDITING WORKSHEET

Specific Objective

After reading this unit, the student will be able to:

1.4.1 demonstrate skills in editing and printing a worksheet.

1.4.0 Introduction

Editing means modifying the content and location of the data in a worksheet. Editing consists of modifying, copying and moving data from a location to the other either in the same worksheet or different worksheets. Editing features allow you to change the contents of a cell, copy or move cells, inserting and deleting cells and inserting and deleting rows and columns in between existing cells. The MS Excel 2007 provides tools that can help you correct the spelling and grammar mistakes faster. You decide if you want to set up the MS Excel 2007 so that you can easily see the mistakes while you work or, if you find the wavy red and green lines distracting, you can just check your document when you are ready to finish it.

Print command is used to take the hard copy of the information stored in a worksheet. It is better to preview the worksheet before giving the print command.

1.4.1 Editing and Printing Worksheet

As mentioned earlier editing consists of modifying, copying and moving data from a location to the other either in the same worksheet or different worksheets. Print command is used to take the hard copy of the information stored in a worksheet.

- **Check Spelling**

MS-Excel 2007 offers the check spelling facility. This is very helpful in making the spreadsheet free from any kind of spelling mistakes. The utility scans the spreadsheet from starting to end and reports the errors in the spreadsheets.

To check spelling,

1. Open an existing worksheet DEMO1. xlsx and change TOTAL to TaTAL in it.
2. Click the *Review* tab.
3. Select the *Spelling* option from Proofing panel. (See figure 4.1)

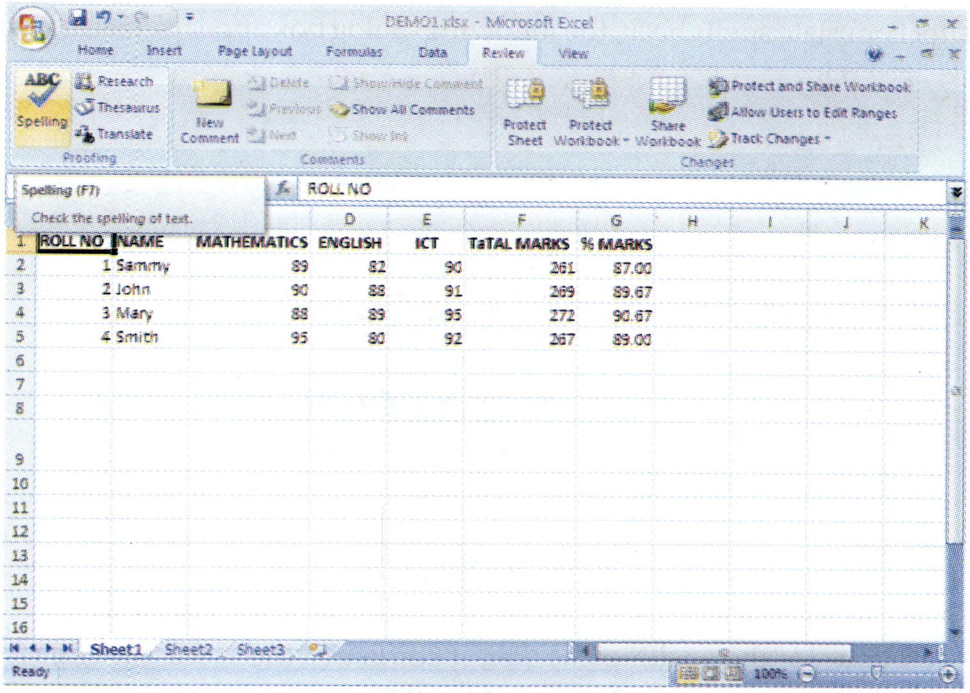

Figure 4.1 Spelling check

4. If some spelling mistake is there or any word not available in dictionary is found then a *Spelling* dialog box appears. Select the appropriate option. (See figure 4.2)

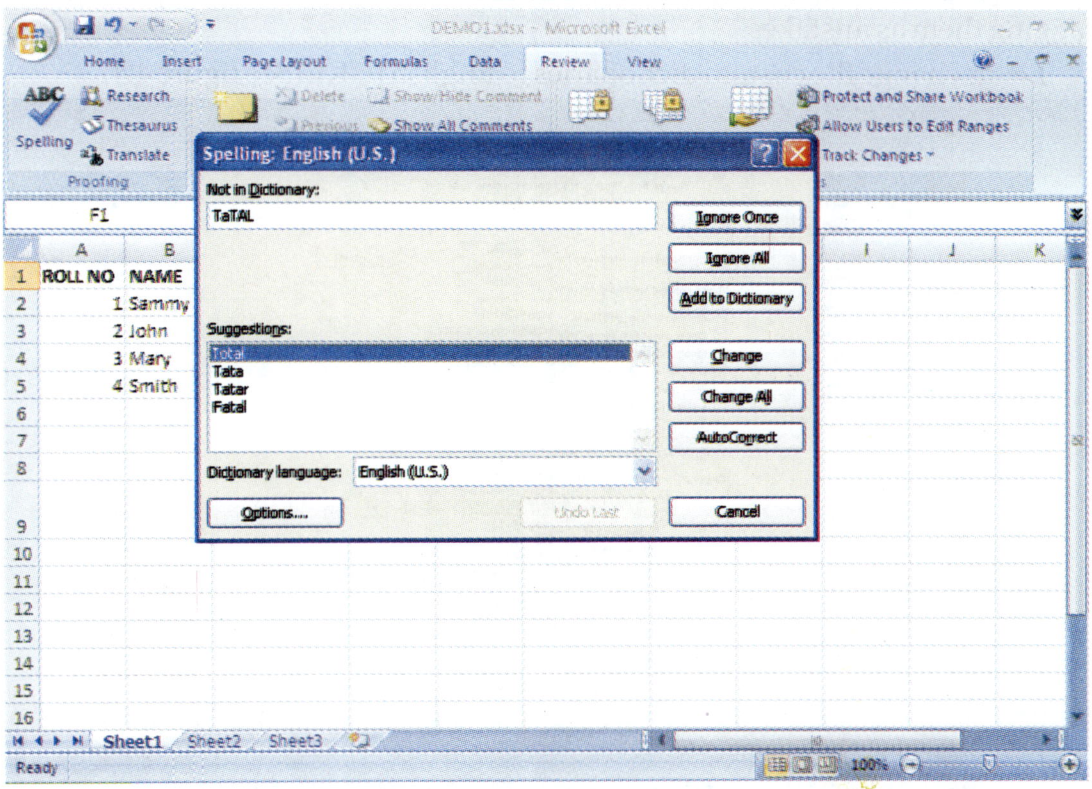

Figure 4.2 Spelling dialog box

5. After complete spell check, the following dialog box appears. (See figure 4.3)

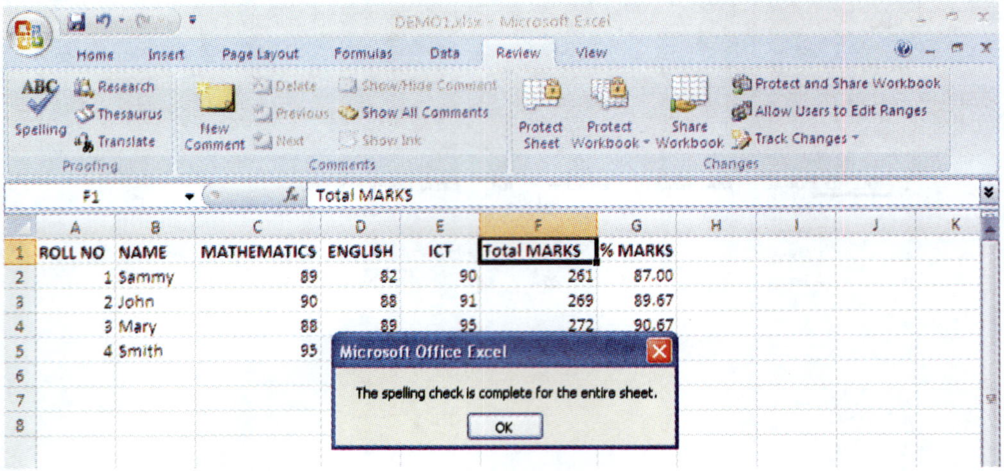

Figure 4.3 After spell checking

- **Use custom dictionaries to add words to the spelling checker**

When you use the spelling checker, it compares the words in your document with those in the tool's main dictionary. The main dictionary contains most common words, but it might not include proper names, technical terms, or acronyms. In addition, some words might be capitalised differently in the main dictionary than in your document. Adding such words or capitalisation to a custom dictionary prevents the spelling checker from flagging them as mistakes.

Let us change the custom dictionaries to English (UK). (See figure 4.4)

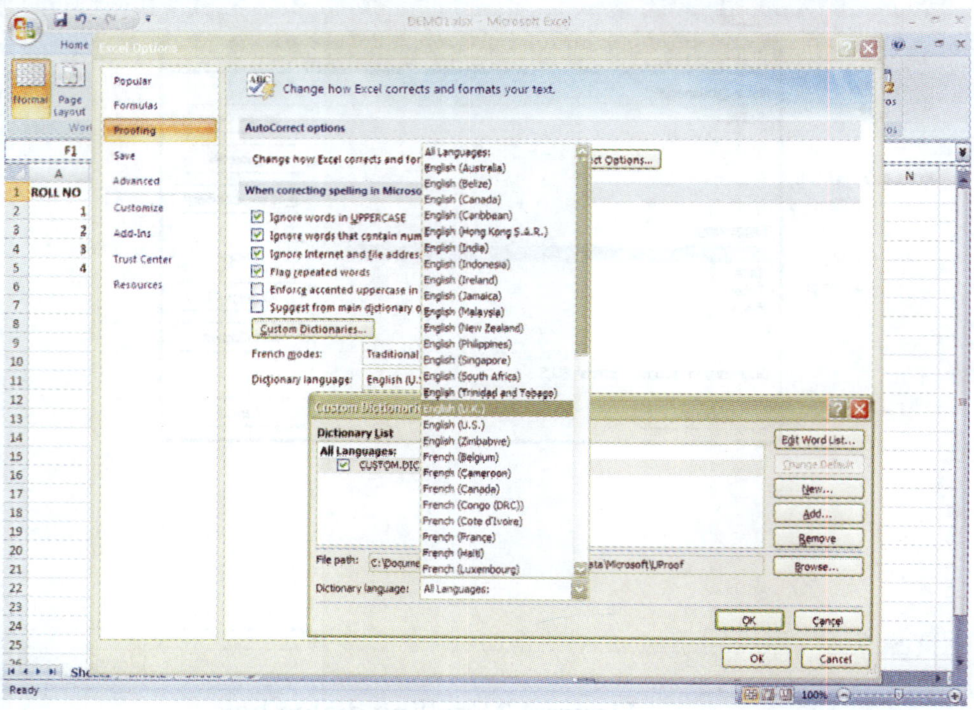

Figure 4.4 Customising dictionaries

Note

Any custom dictionary setting you change in one Microsoft Office program affects all the other programs.

6. Save your workbook.

- **Preview the Layout**

Print preview is one of the most important printing utilities offered by MS-Excel. Print preview displays the worksheet in exactly the same form, as it will look after printed on the paper. It is better to preview the worksheet before giving the print command.

To preview the layout,

1. Click the *Office Button*.
2. Select the *Print Preview* option from Print. (See figure 4.5)

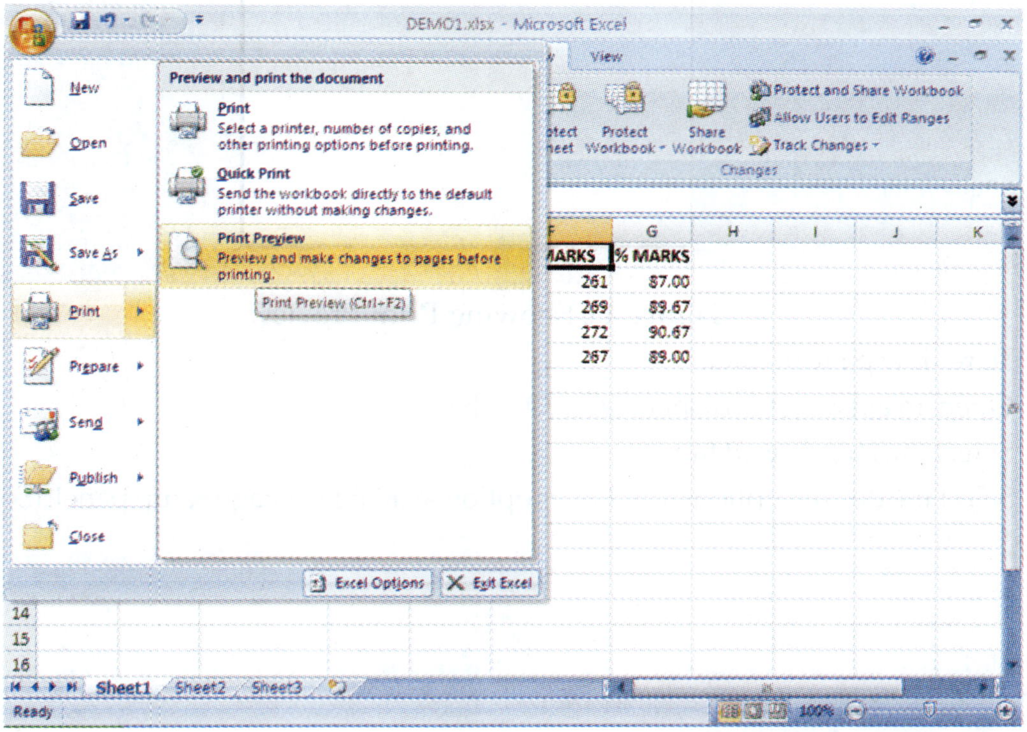

Figure 4.5 Selecting Print Preview

3. On clicking, the layout of the worksheet appears. (See figure 4.6)

- **Review Page Breaks**

To print the exact number of pages that you want, you can use *Page Break Preview* view to quickly adjust page breaks. In this view, manually inserted page breaks appear as solid lines. Dashed lines indicate where MS Excel will break pages automatically.

Using the page break preview, the entire worksheet can be displayed with page numbers and the boundaries of the pages. You can drag these boundaries to include or discard some information from a page.

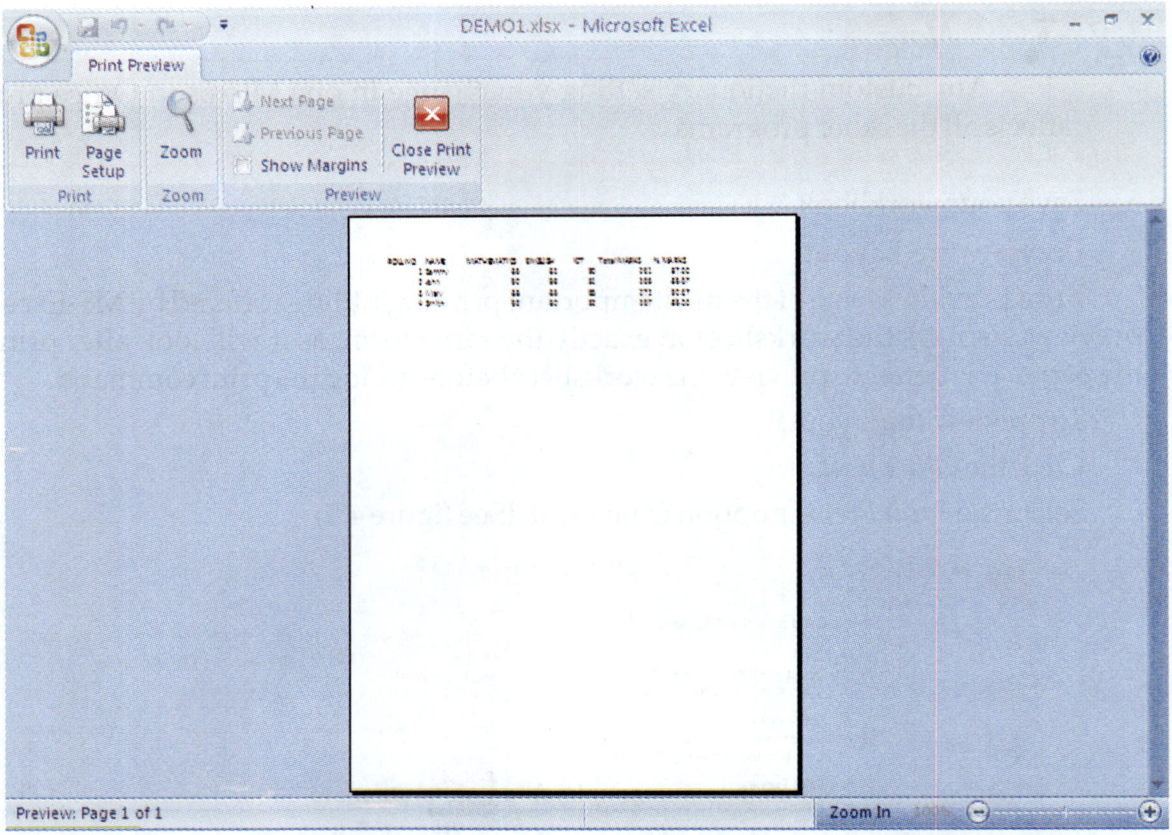

Figure 4.6 Showing Print Preview

To review page breaks,

1. Open an existing worksheet DEMO1. xlsx.
2. Select the *Page Layout* tab.
3. Select the desired option from *Breaks* option available in Page Setup panel. (See figure 4.7)

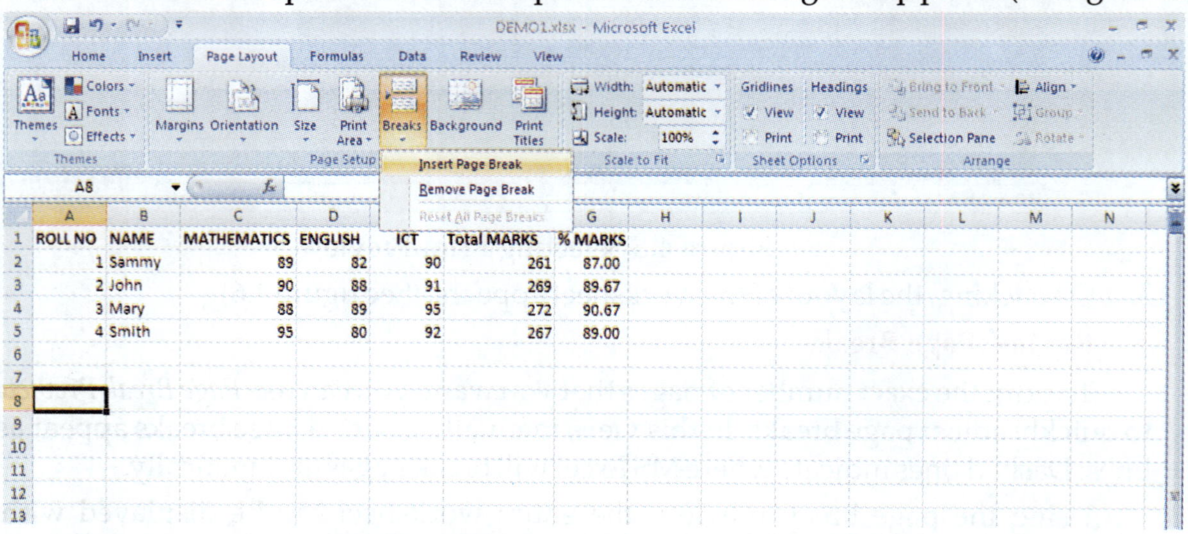

Figure 4.7 Selecting Insert Page Break

You can do one of the following:

- To move a page break, drag the page break to a new location.

Note

Moving an automatic page break changes it to a manual page break.

- To insert a vertical page break or a horizontal page break, select a row or column below or to the right of where you want to insert the page break, right-click, and then click *Insert Page Break* on the shortcut menu.
- To remove a manual page break, drag the page break outside the page break preview area.
- To remove all manual page breaks, right-click any cell on the worksheet, and then click *Reset All Page Breaks* on the shortcut menu.

4. On clicking, the selected option will be applied. (See figure 4.8)

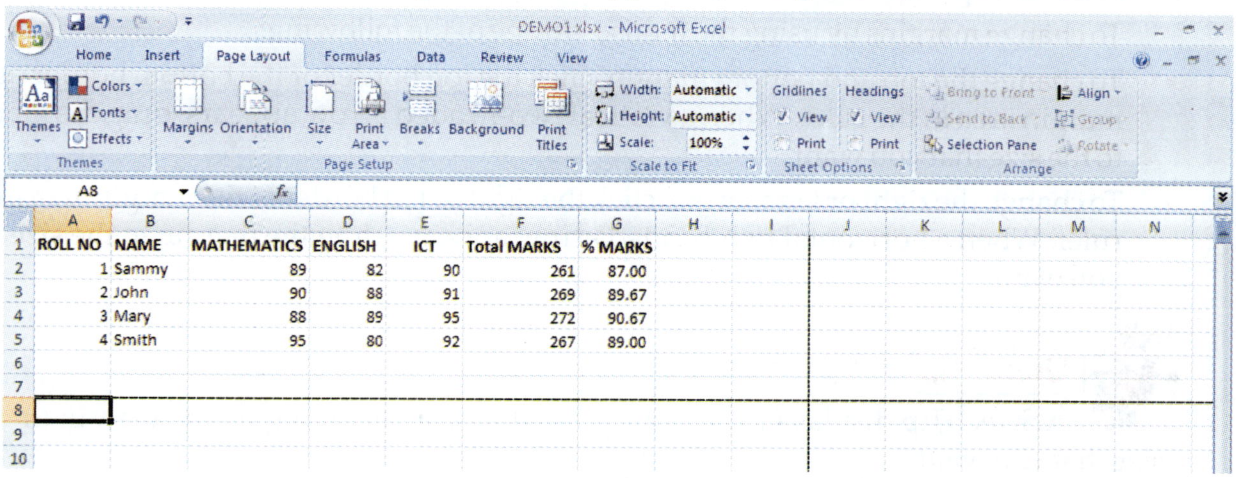

Figure 4.8 After applying Insert Page Break

5. To return to Normal view after you finish working with the page breaks, on the *View* tab in the *Workbook Views* group, click *Normal*.

Useful Tip

For returning to Normal view, you can also click *Normal* on the status bar.

- **Change Page Setup and Sheet Settings**

Before you print a MS Excel worksheet that contains large amount of data or charts, you can quickly fine-tune it in the new Page Layout view to achieve professional-looking results. In this view, you can change the layout and format of data the way that you can in Normal view. But you can also use the rulers to measure the width and height of the data, change the page orientation, add or change page headers and footers, set margins for printing, and hide or display row and column headers.

To change page setup and sheet settings,

1. Select the *Page Layout* tab. (See figure 4.9)

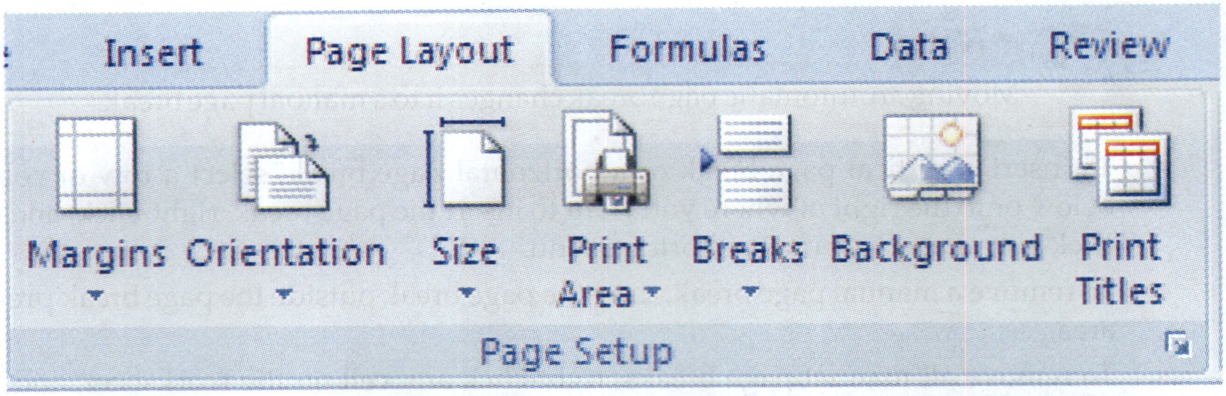

Figure 4.9 Page Setup options

2. Select the appropriate option(s) from the Page Setup panel.

   To change margins by using the mouse, do one of the following:

   - To change the top and bottom margin, click the top border or the bottom border of the margin area in the ruler. When a vertical two-headed arrow appears, drag the margin to the size that you want.
   - To change the right or left margin, click the right or left border of the margin area in the ruler. When a horizontal two-headed arrow appears, drag the margin to the size that you want.

Useful Tip

A ScreenTip displays the margin size while you are dragging the margin to the size that you want.

   To change orientation, click *Orientation*, and then click *Portrait* or *Landscape*.

   To apply a specific paper size to the current section, click *Size*.

   To mark a specific area of the sheet for printing, click *Print Area*.

   To specify where a new page will begin in the printed copy, click *Breaks*.

   To choose an image to display as the background of the sheet, click *Background*.

   To specify rows and columns to repeat on each printed page, click *Print Titles*.

3. On clicking, the selected option(s) will be applied.
4. Save your workbook.

Note

Page Layout view is useful to get your data ready for printing. Page breaks are more easily adjusted in Page Break Preview view. For an exact preview of how the data will be printed, you can preview the worksheet pages in Print Preview view.

OR

1. Select the *Page Layout* tab.
2. Select the button on Page Setup panel. (See figure 4.10)

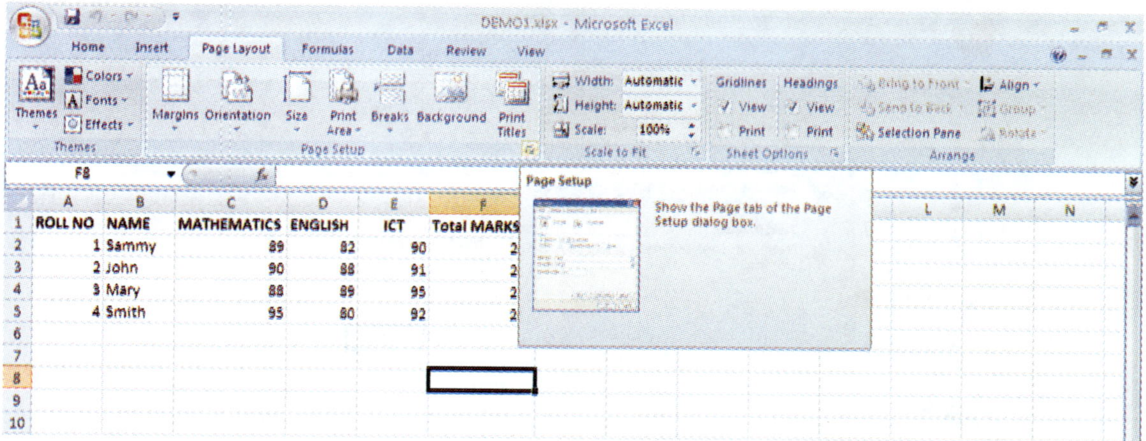

Figure 4.10 Changing Page Setup

3. A *Page Setup* dialog box appears. (See figure 4.11)

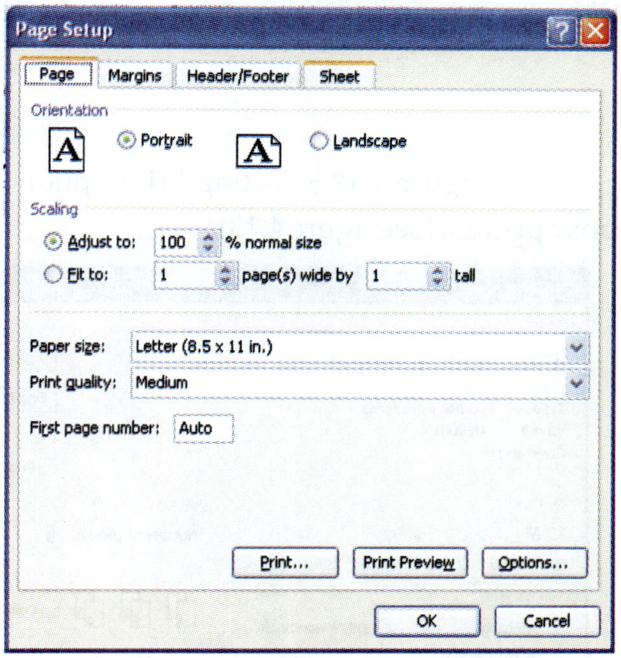

Figure 4.11 Page Setup dialog box

4. Make the appropriate changes.
5. Click OK button.
6. Save your workbook.

- **Set Print Options**

Print command is used to take the hard copy of the information stored in a worksheet. You can set print options and preview the worksheet before giving the print command.

To set print options,

1. Click *Office Button*.
2. Select the *Print* option from Print. (See figure 4.12)

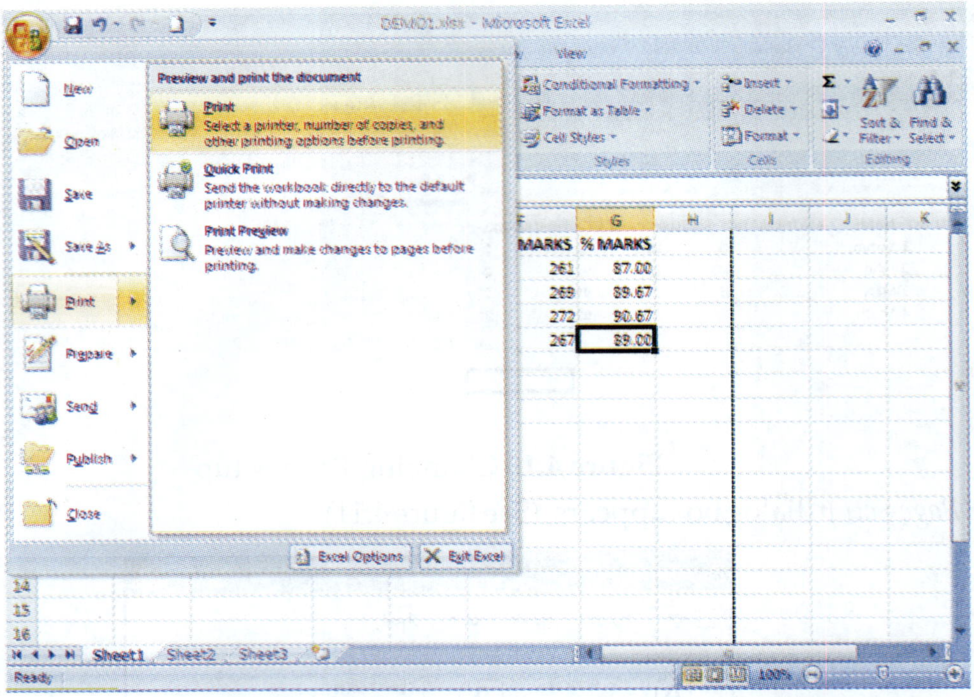

Figure 4.12 Selecting Print option

3. A *Print* dialog box appears. (See figure 4.13)

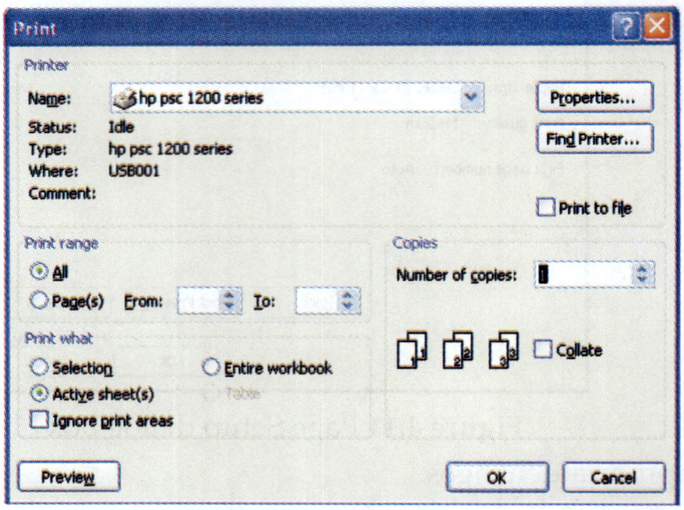

Figure 4.13 Print dialog box

4. Set the print options as per your requirement.
5. Click OK button.

You get the printout of your edited worksheet.

SUMMARY

- Editing consists of modifying, copying and moving data from a location to the other either in the same worksheet or different worksheets.
- Excel offers the check spelling facility. This is very helpful in making the spreadsheet free from any kind of spelling mistakes.
- Any custom dictionary setting you change in one Microsoft Office program affects all the other programs.
- By previewing the layout of the worksheet, you can see how it will look after being printed on the paper.
- Review page breaks allow you to see the worksheet with page numbers and the boundaries of the pages. You can drag these boundaries to include or discard some information from a page.
- Moving an automatic page break changes it to a manual page break.
- You can change page setup and sheet settings using Page Setup facility in MS-Excel.

REVIEW QUESTIONS

STATE WHETHER TRUE OR FALSE

1. Editing features do not allow you to change the contents in a worksheet.
2. It is better to preview the worksheet before giving the print command.
3. The *Breaks* option is available in *Page Setup* panel.
4. Moving an automatic page break changes it to a manual page break.

FILL IN THE BLANKS

1. You can spellcheck the text of your worksheet using .... option from Proofing panel.
2. Any .... dictionary setting you change in one Microsoft Office program affects all the other programs.
3. For returning to Normal View, you can click .... on the status bar.
4. The .... dialog box can be used to change page setup and sheet settings.

MULTIPLE CHOICE QUESTIONS

1. Before printing you can see the preview of the spreadsheet using the ....
   (*a*) Page Preview (*b*) Spelling
   (*c*) Print (*d*) None of these
2. By default, the print preview option will display .... worksheet(s).
   (*a*) Two (*b*) One
   (*c*) Three (*d*) Four

3. You can set print options from .... dialog box.
   (a) Print (b) Spelling
   (c) Insert Function (d) None of these

ANSWER THE FOLLOWING

1. Explain the editing and printing of worksheet in Excel.
2. How will you edit and print worksheet by
   (i) checking spelling
   (ii) reviewing layout
   (iii) reviewing page breaks
   (iv) changing page setup and sheet settings
3. What are the different printing options in MS-Excel? Discuss.

ASSIGNMENT

1. Create a spreadsheet to show the results of a survey to find out what pets are owned by pupils in your class. Edit the spreadsheet using the following features:
   - checking spelling
   - reviewing layout
   - reviewing page breaks
   - changing page setup and sheet settings.
   - save the spreadsheet with the name *PetSurvey*.
2. Create a database called *Marks List* that will contain the marks of 20 students in five subjects namely English, Language, Maths, Science and ICT and perform the following:
   - Create two columns, *Total* and *Percentage*. Calculate the total marks obtained by each student in the Total column. Calculate the percentage of marks obtained in the subjects Maths, Science and History and display it in the Percentage column.
   - Check the spelling of the text in the worksheet.
   - List the total and percentage in the last two columns of the marks list.
   - Highlight the marks of all the students who have obtained above 75 marks.
   - Review the layout of the worksheet.
   - Review page breaks.
   - Change page setup and sheet settings.
   - Save the workbook as Marks List.

UNIT 5

PRINTING WORKSHEET

Specific Objective

After reading this unit, the student will be able to:

1.5.1 demonstrate skills in previewing and printing a worksheet.

1.5.0 Introduction

Print preview is one of the most important printing utilities offered by MS-Excel. It allows you to see the preview of the page as it would look on paper, after printing. This option generally avoids most common printing errors due to margins, print areas etc. It is better to preview the worksheet before giving the print command.

Generally we do not print all the information stored in worksheet at a time. MS-Excel has very good printing features for helping us to print the selective cells from the worksheet. Excel has option for fitting the whole sheet into a page or number of pages specified by the user.

Printing options cover the options of page setup, setting print area, print previews and printing to a single or multiple pages etc. In this unit, we will discuss about previewing and changing print settings.

1.5.1 Previewing and Changing Print Setting

- **Previewing Worksheets**

You can view a worksheet before printing to adjust the margins or to make any final changes to the worksheet. You can see how the worksheet will look when it is printed, without actually printing it.

To preview a worksheet,

1. Open an existing worksheet DEMO1.xlsx.
2. Click the *Office Button.*
3. Choose the *Print Preview* option from Print. (See figure 5.1)
4. On clicking, the layout of the worksheet appears. (See figure 5.2)

You can make use of the following buttons in the preview window to make any changes to the final copy. (See figure 5.2)

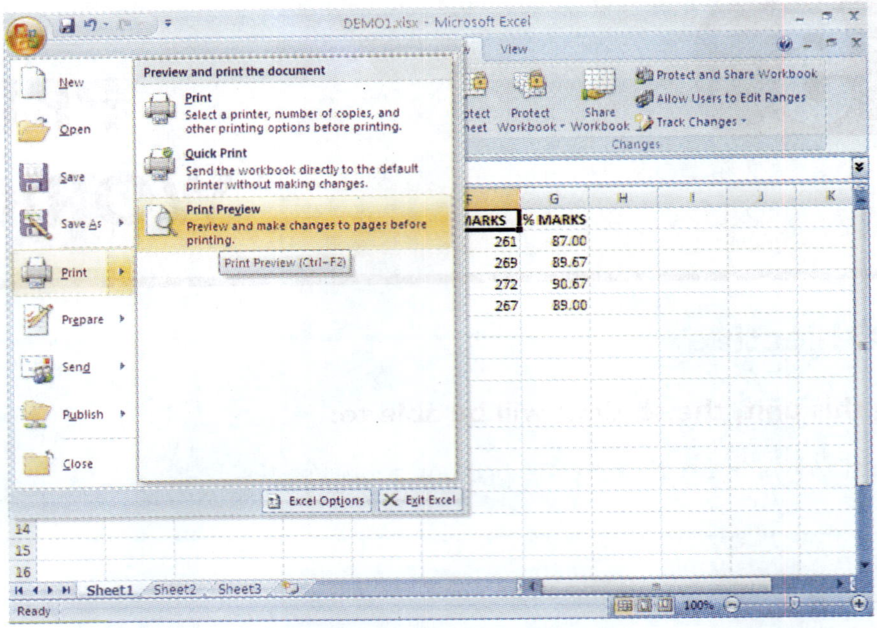

Figure 5.1 Selecting Print Preview

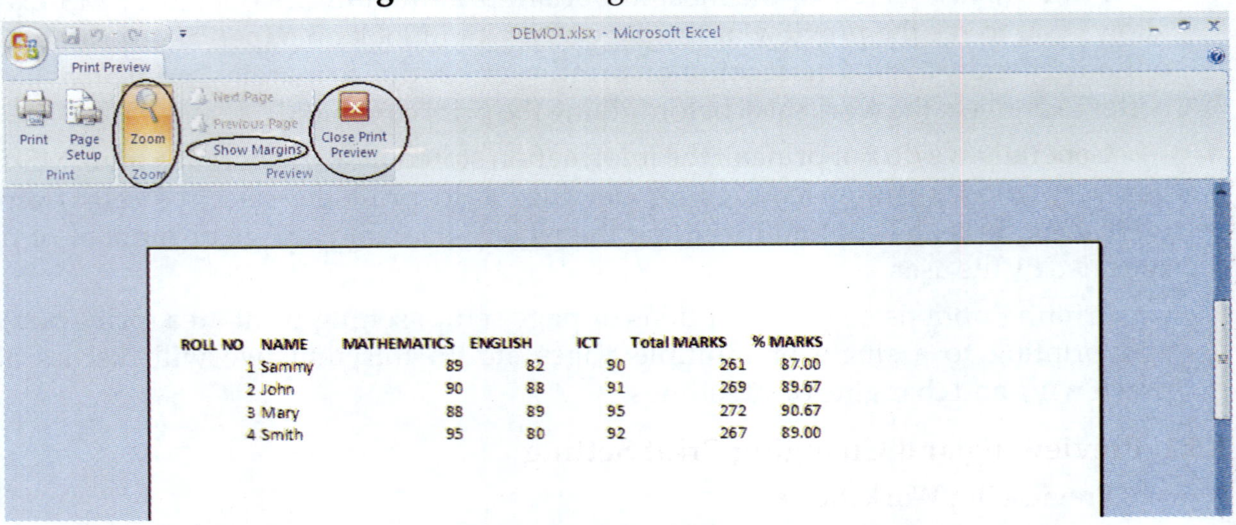

Figure 5.2 Print Preview of a worksheet after applying Zoom

Zoom button — To zoom into or out of the preview page

Margin — To adjust the margins of the worksheet.

Close button — To exit the preview and return to the Excel 2007 window.

By default, the print preview option displays a single worksheet. MS-Excel 2007 provides an easy way to preview multiple (maximum two) worksheets in the print preview screen.

- **Changing Print Settings**

Before printing a worksheet you can easily change the print settings according to your requirement. Before printing a worksheet, you can preview the worksheet using the print preview given earlier.

To change print settings,

1. Click the *Office Button.*
2. Select the *Print* option from Print. (See figure 5.3)

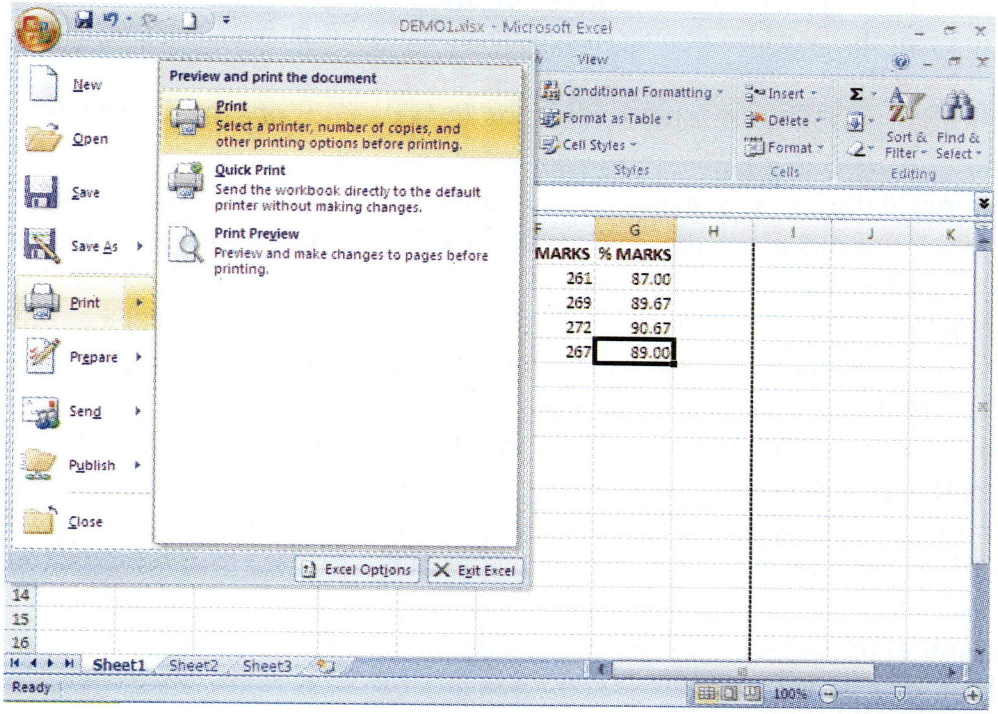

Figure 5.3 Selecting Print option

OR

As an alternative to above two steps, press Ctrl + P to open Print dialog box.

3. A *Print* dialog box appears. (See figure 5.4)

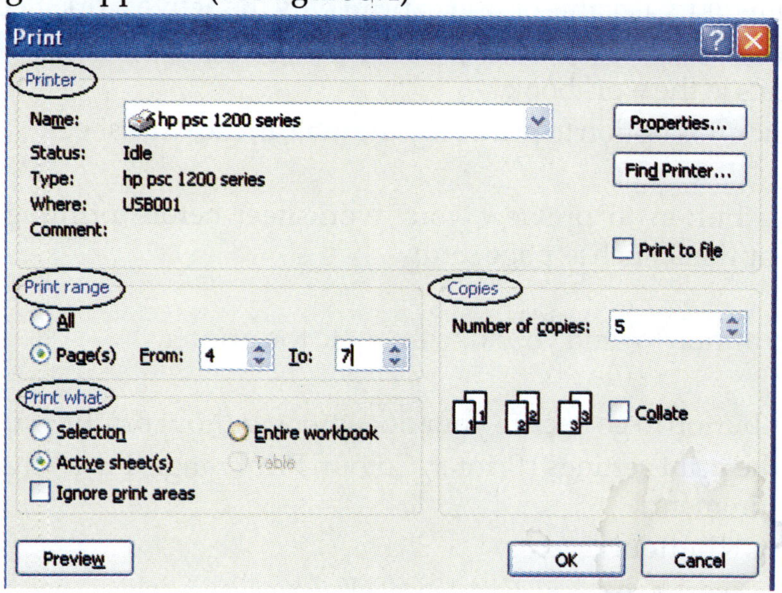

Figure 5.4 Print dialog box

You can print entire or partial worksheets and workbooks, one at a time, or several at once. If the data that you want to print is in an MS Excel table, you can just print the Excel table.

You can also print a workbook to a file instead of to a printer. This is useful when you need to print the workbook on a different type of printer from the one that you originally used to print it.

The following are some useful buttons and other options in the *Print* dialog box:

Printer

- **Name:** In the list, click a printer that you have installed and want to use.
- **Status:** For the selected printer, tells the status of the printer, such as idle, busy, or the number of files before your print job.
- **Type:** For the selected printer, tells the type of printer that you selected, such as laser.
- **Properties:** Click this button when you want to change the properties, such as paper type, for the printer you are using.
- **Find Printer:** Click this button to find a printer that you have access to.
- **Print to file:** Select this check box to create a file from the document instead of routing it directly to a printer. The file is saved with print formatting, such as font selection and colour specification, in a *.prn* file that can be printed to another printer.

Copies

- **Number of copies:** In this list, click the number of copies that you want to be printed.

Print range

- **All:** Click this option if you want to print all pages in your file.
- **Pages:** Click this option and add the page numbers or page ranges in the box.

Print what

- **Selection:** Click this option to print only what you have selected.
- **Active sheet(s):** Click this option to print only the active worksheets.
- **Entire workbook:** Click this option to print the entire workbook, including all the worksheets in the workbook.
- **Table:** Click this option to print only the table in the worksheet.

Preview

- Click this button to preview your worksheet before printing it and select other printing options, such as page setup.

OK

- Click this button to send your document to the printer.

Cancel

- Click this button to go back to your document without printing it.

4. Change the print settings (Printer, Colour, Print range, Print what and Copies) as per your requirement.
5. Click the OK button.
6. Save your workbook and Exit from MS Excel by clicking on ✕ on the upper right corner of the worksheet

SUMMARY

- Print preview is one of the most important printing utilities offered by MS-Excel 2007.
- Print Preview in Office Button allows you to see the preview of the page as it would look on paper, after printing.
- Print preview option generally avoids most common printing errors due to margins, print areas etc.
- It is better to preview the worksheet before giving the print command.
- Before printing a worksheet you can easily change the print settings according to your requirement.
- MS Excel 2007 provides an easy way to preview multiple (maximum two) worksheets in the print preview screen.
- To change the print settings (Printer, Colour, Print range, Print what and Copies) you can use the *Print* dialog box which can be opened by selecting the *Print* option from Print.

REVIEW QUESTIONS

STATE WHETHER TRUE OR FALSE

1. You cannot preview worksheets in Microsoft Excel 2007.
2. Before printing a worksheet you can easily change the print settings in it.
3. You can click the Table option in Print what to print only the table in the worksheet.

FILL IN THE BLANKS

1. Print preview allow you to see the .... of the page as it would look on paper, after printing.
2. You can also print a workbook to a .... instead of to a printer.
3. To change print settings, you can use the .... dialog box.

MULTIPLE CHOICE QUESTIONS

1. To see the preview of the spreadsheet you use the command
   (*a*) Print Preview (*b*) Print
   (*c*) Preview (*d*) None of these
2. Using Zoom you
   (*a*) can see the spreadsheet more closely
   (*b*) can see the spreadsheet more clearly
   (*c*) both (*a*) and (*b*) above
   (*d*) neither (*a*) nor (*b*) above

3. MS Excel 2007 provides an easy way to preview maximum .... worksheet(s) in the print preview screen.
   (a) One (b) Two
   (c) Three (d) Four

ANSWER THE FOLLOWING

1. What is previewing of a worksheet? Discuss.
2. How will you change the print settings of a worksheet? Discuss.

ASSIGNMENT

1. Create the Mark List workbook and perform the following:
   - Insert the header "Student Mark List".
   - Insert data of five students.
   - Change the print settings such that the worksheet gets printed vertically having three copies of it.
   - Save the workbook.
   - Finally, print the worksheet.
2. Create the Employee workbook and perform the following:
   - Insert the header "Employee Details" in the worksheet.
   - Insert data of ten employees.
   - Insert the page number.
   - Save the workbook.
   - Select the colour options.
   - Select a printer.
   - Finally, print the worksheet.

SECTION

TWO

TERM-THREE

PROJECT WORK

UNIT 1: Project Work—Research Report

General Objective

After reading this section, the student will be able to:

1. apply Internet and Word Processing skills to produce a document.

UNIT 1 PROJECT WORK—RESEARCH REPORT

Specific Objectives

After reading this unit, the student will be able to:

2.1.1 search for information on the Internet.

2.1.2 copy, paste and save information from the Web onto a Word Processing document.

2.1.3 format and edit the information using format and editing tools.

2.1.4 share the information by attaching it to e-mail message.

2.1.5 access attached information and print.

2.1.0 Introduction

The Internet is a giant network of computers all over the world. It has facilitated the speedy transfer of information across the globe. You can transfer and access information from one computer to other computers anywhere in the world.

The ability to effectively search and locate information on the Internet is an important skill for education and essential for success in the 21st century. The results from a single search task can produce a very large amount of information. Without the new literacy skills and strategies that the process of searching and locating information on the Internet requires, this can quickly become a difficult task. Therefore, searching on the Internet is not just a popular activity, but an important skill needed to obtain information.

2.1.1 Searching Information from the Internet

Computers have become an integral part of our culture. As technologies continue to move ahead, so too must the educational system. The information and technology skills are the 'new basics' and being able to find and use information more effectively is essential to the success of students of all ages. Information and Communication Technologies (ICTs) have infiltrated our daily lives. In order to provide the students with an adequate education, it is necessary to address these changes in the society through the education process. It must be clear that technology will remain a fundamental part of the education system and teachers are expected to incorporate the use of technology in classroom instruction.

As schools move to integrate technology into classroom curricula, students need to develop the new literacies required to prepare for a future in an increasingly digital society. "To become fully literate in today's world, students must become proficient in the new literacies of ICT". We can identify these now literacies in terms of five functions:

1. Identifying important question.
2. Locating information.
3. Critically evaluating the usefulness of information.
4. Synthesising information to answer questions.
5. Communicating answers to others.

Of these five functions, the ability to locate information is perhaps the most critical, as much of what we do on the Internet stems from our ability to properly search for specific information. Furthermore, as the size of the Internet increases, efficient access to information becomes increasingly more difficult. Obviously, information is worthless unless it can be efficiently located and retrieved.

Figure. 1.1 Internet Explorer symbol

To access the Internet, you need to double-click the Internet Explorer symbol displayed on the monitor. Move the mouse on the mouse pad until the mouse pointer is positioned over the Internet Explorer symbol as shown in figure 1.2.

Figure 1.2 The desktop icons/symbols

Double-click the left mouse button to start Internet Explorer.

To access a site of your choice, type the Website address in the space provided and press the Enter key.

Let us now collect and save information on some desired topics. In order to help locate information easily, there are a number of sites on the Internet that provide a search engine (a program that helps to locate information on the Internet). Let us have a look at a search engine and use it to locate information. First, let us go to the site *http://www.google.com/*, which offers a search engine. (See figure 1.3)

Now let us search the following two topics:

1. agriculture
2. what is ICT

In the space provided for the search, you need to enter the word or words that describe the item you wish to search. Let us search the topic 'agriculture'. First type it in the search box and then click the *Google Search* button. (See figure 1.3)

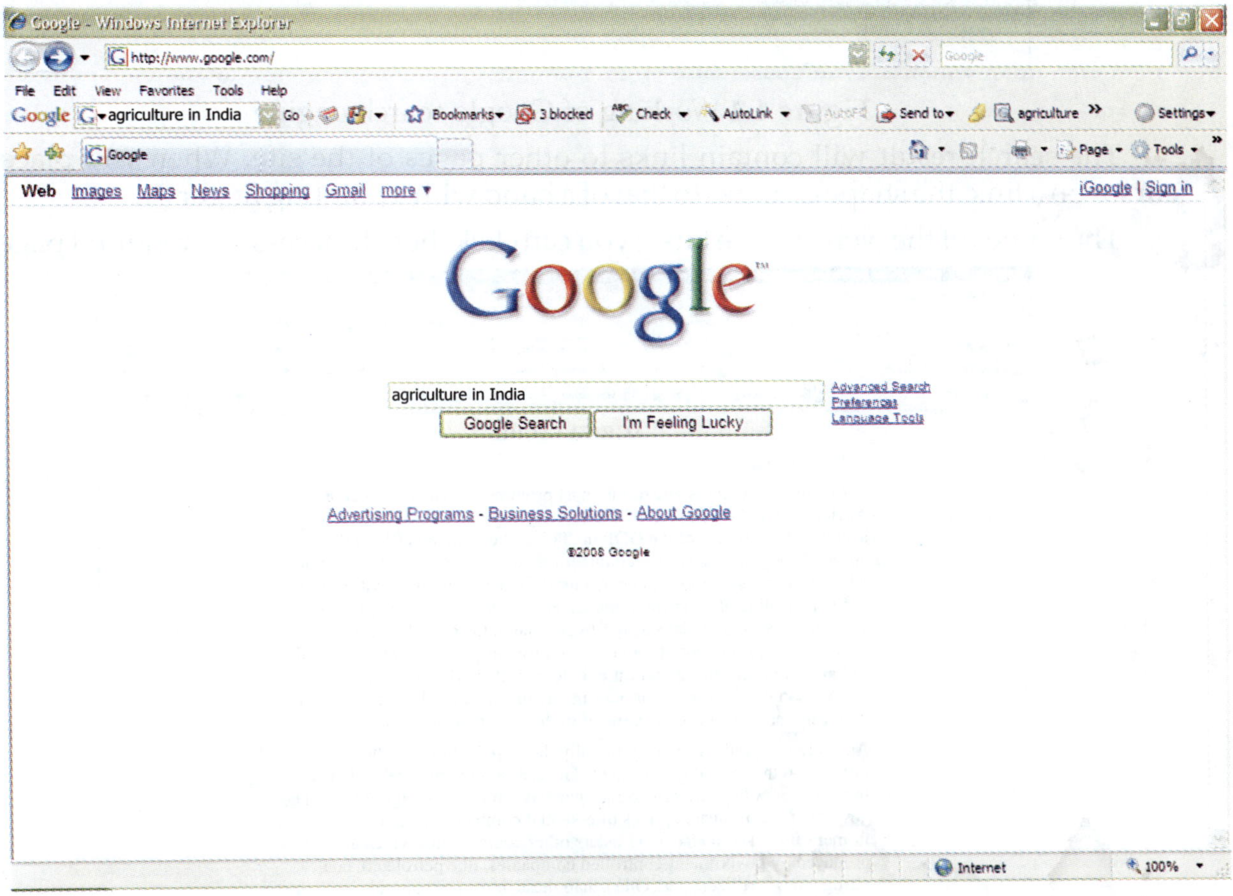

Figure 1.3 Searching on Google

The result of search will be displayed as a list that contains the required information with a short description of each site (See figure 1.4)

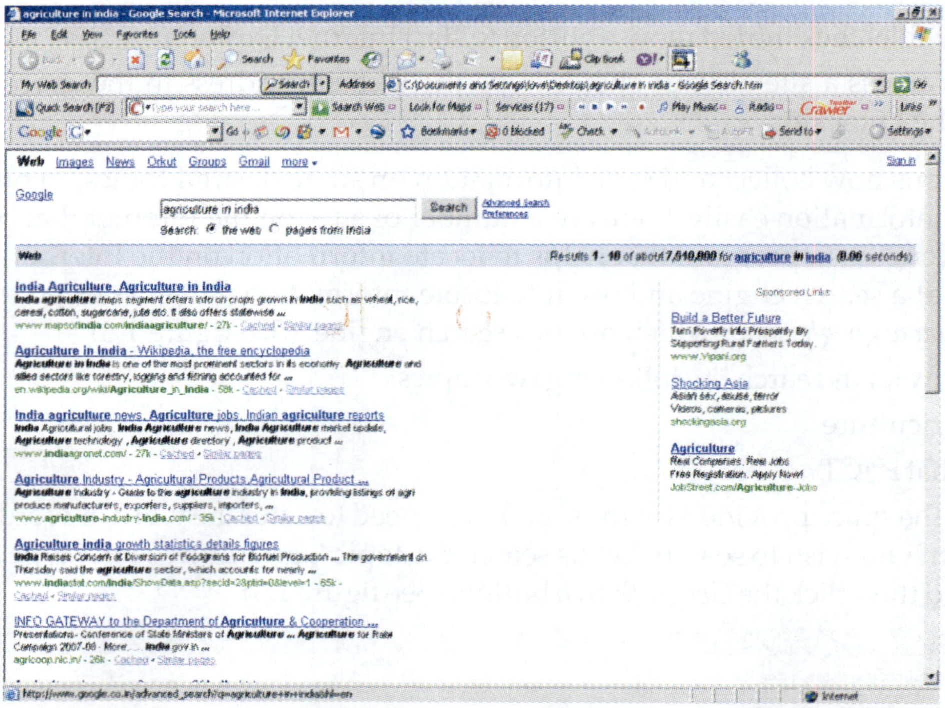

Figure 1.4 Working of Google search engine

The search result will contain links to other pages of the site. When you place the cursor on a link, the shape changes to that of a hand with a pointing finger.

The names of the websites are links; you can click them to access, the required page.

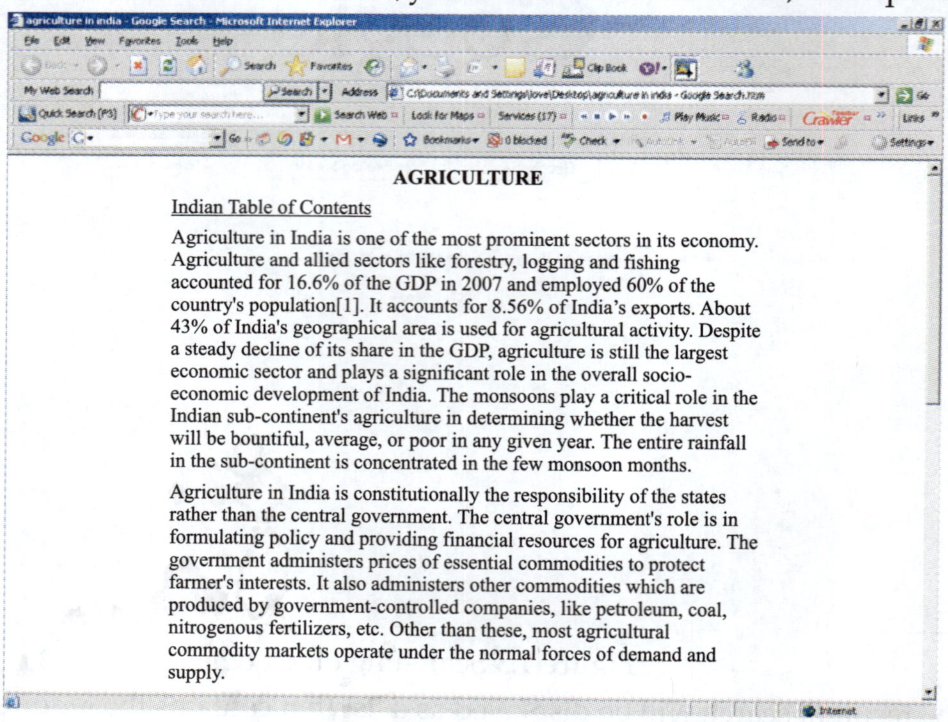

Figure 1.5 Searched information

Now let us search another topic 'what is ICT'. First type it in the search box and then click the *'Google Search'* button. (See figure 1.6)

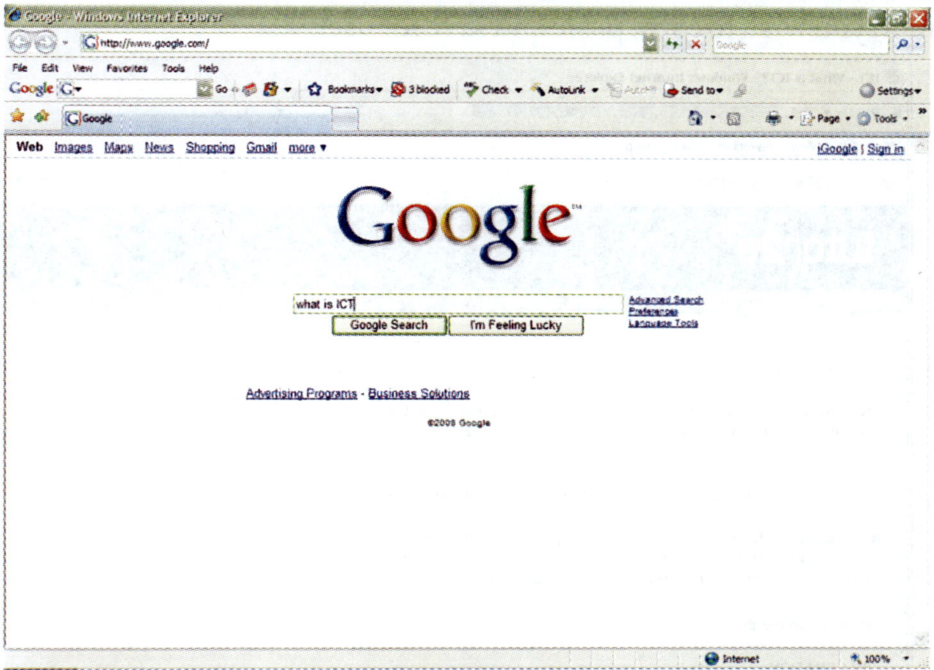

Figure 1.6 Searching on Google

The result of the search will be displayed as a list that contains the required information with a short description of each site. (See figure 1.7)

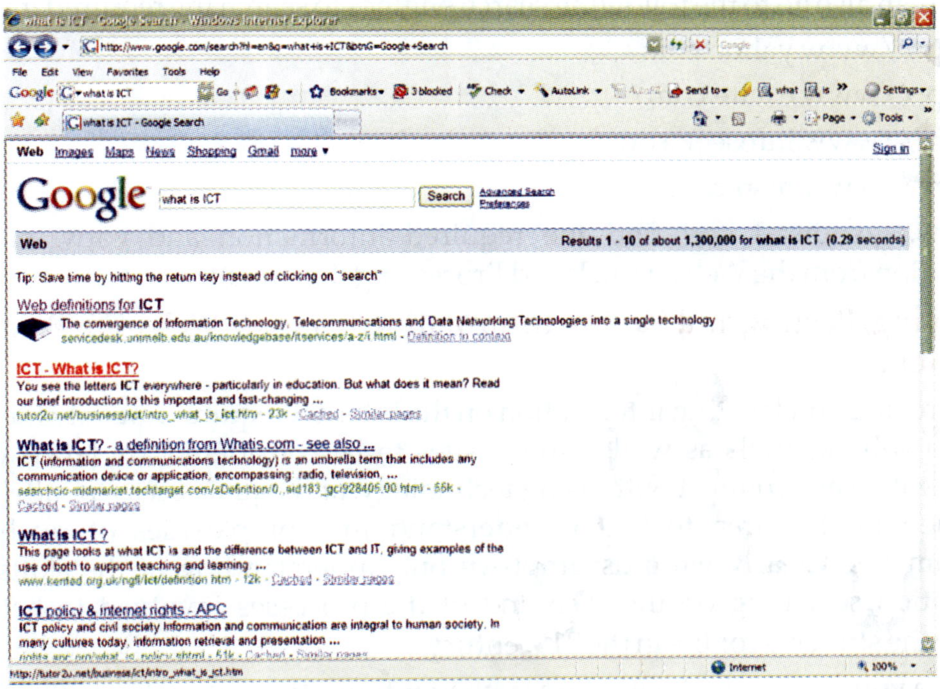

Figure 1.7 Working of Google search engine

The names of the Web sites are links; you can click them to access the required page.

From the search list, click on the desired site to open the document containing the information you wish to copy, paste and save for use.

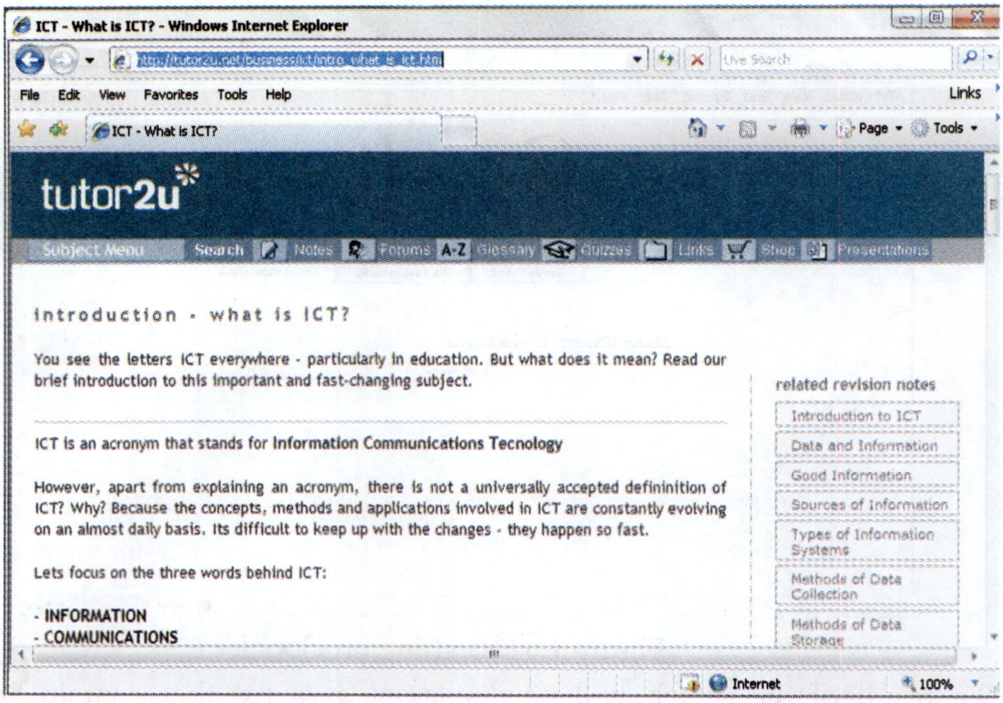

Figure 1.8 Searched information

You can also go to the following search engines to search the required information:

http://www.yahoo.com/

http://www.excite.com/

http://www.infoseek.com/

http://www.msn.com/

Now, go ahead and find the required information and copy, paste and save information from the Web on to a Word Processing document.

2.1.2 Copying, Pasting and Saving Information from the Web onto Word Processing Document

Searching and locating information on the Internet requires not only literacy skills but problem solving skills as well. Other issues to be considered are levels of technology attainment, user's comfort with using technology, and equal access for all. More research is needed in this area to better understand the complexities of reading in online environments. Clearly we must improve our understanding of the skills required for information searching on the Web and of the processes involved to help adequately prepare the students for life in the 21st century.

Once you are satisfied with the searched information, either the entire document or a part of it, select it.

On right clicking a pop-up menu appears. (See figure 1.9)

Select the *Copy* option.

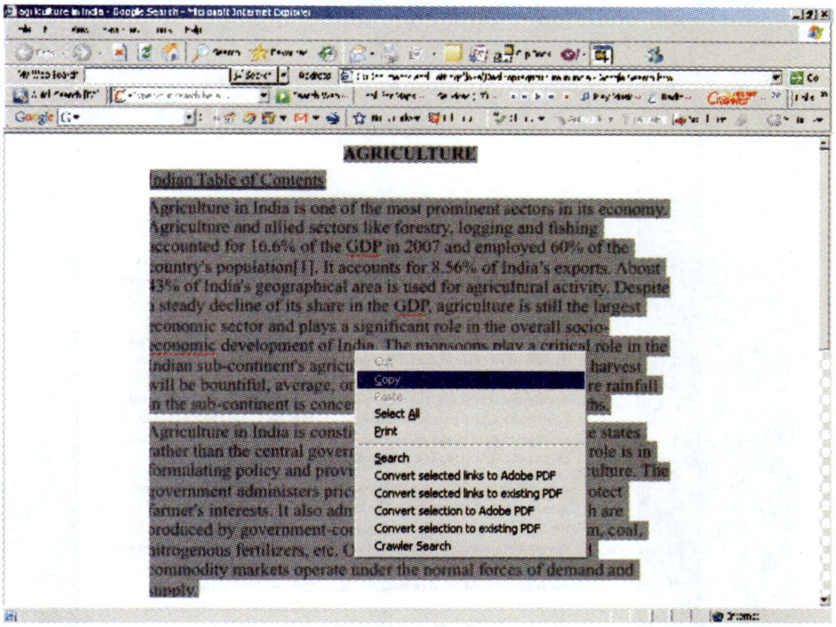

Figure 1.9 Selecting *Copy* option

For pasting, open the Microsoft Word 2007. Click the right mouse button. Select the *Paste* option. (See figure 1.10)

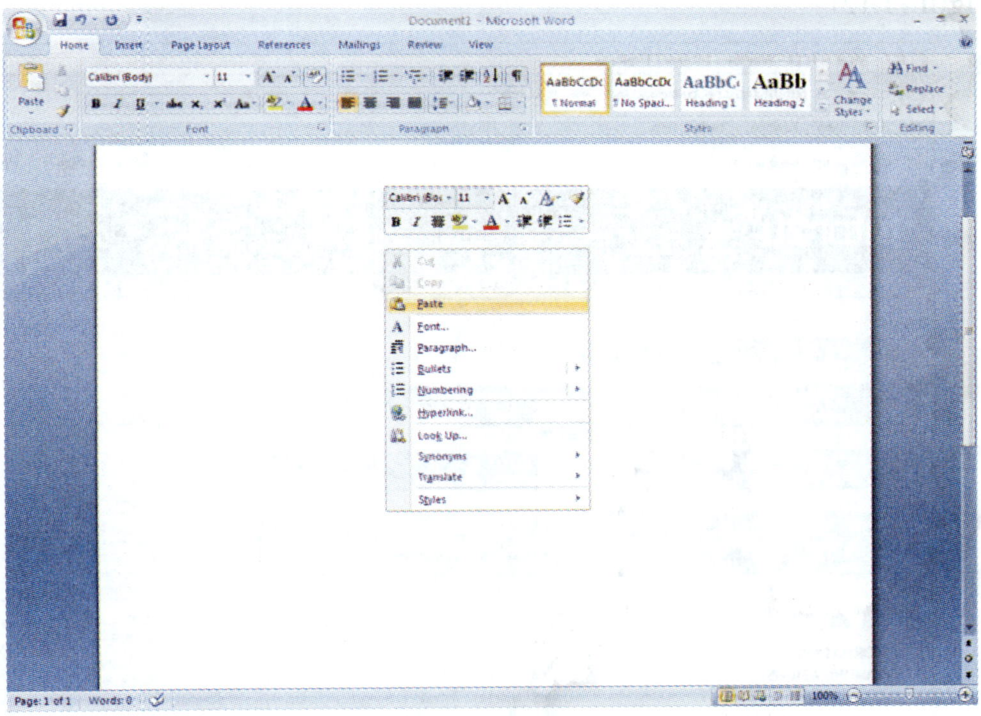

Figure 1.10 Selecting *Paste* option

On clicking the *Paste* option the selected document is pasted in Microsoft word. (See figure 1.11).

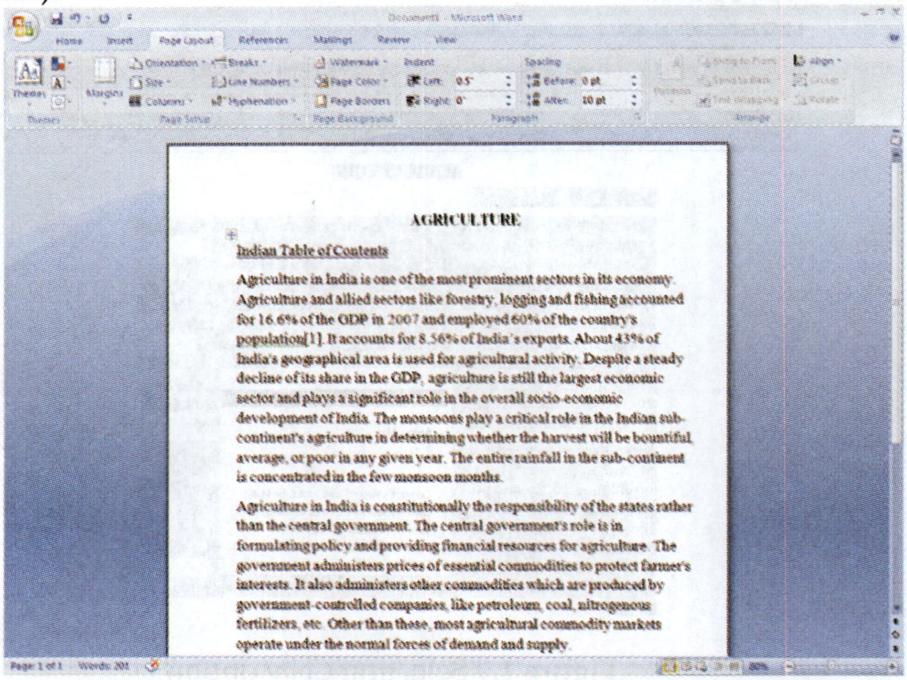

Figure 1.11 Pasting information into Word document

Similarly, you can copy and paste the information searched on the topic "what is ICT". (See figure 1.12)

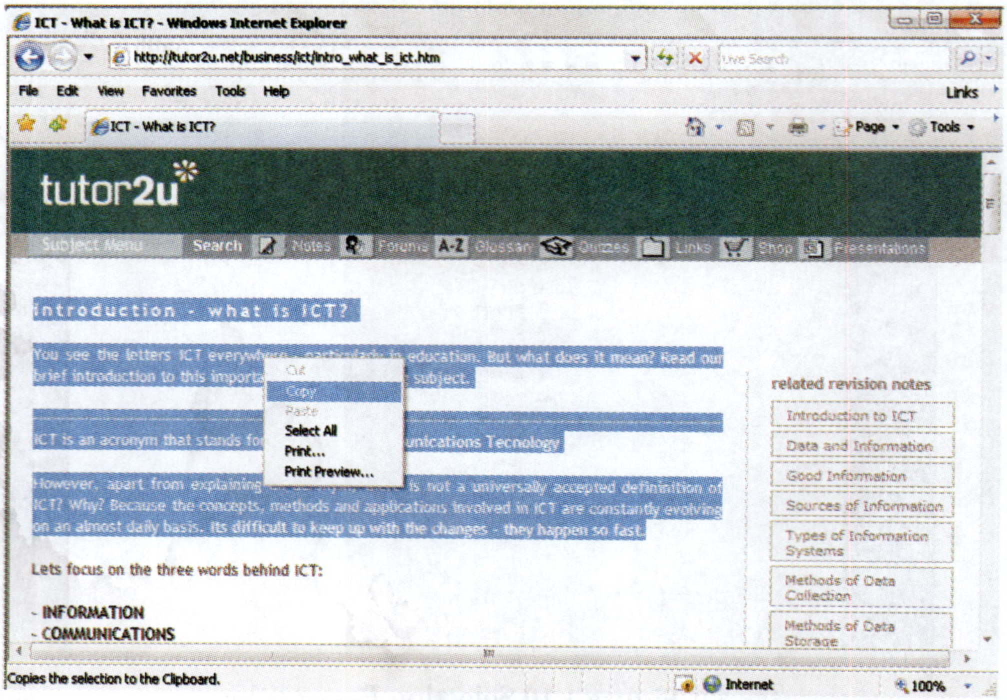

Figure 1.12 Selecting *Copy* option

Now open MS Word 2007 and use *Paste* option to paste the selected information in it. (See figure 1.13)

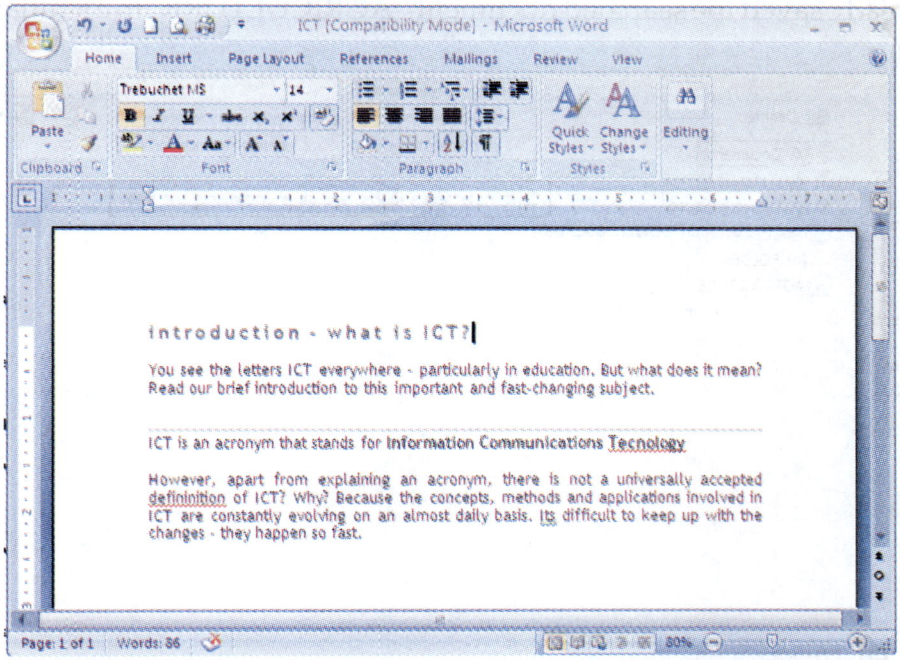

Figure 1.13 Pasting information into Word document

For saving the pasted document in Microsoft word, press the *Office Button* and select the *Save As* option. Now to save a copy of the document, choose the appropriate option available in *Save As*. (See figure 1.14)

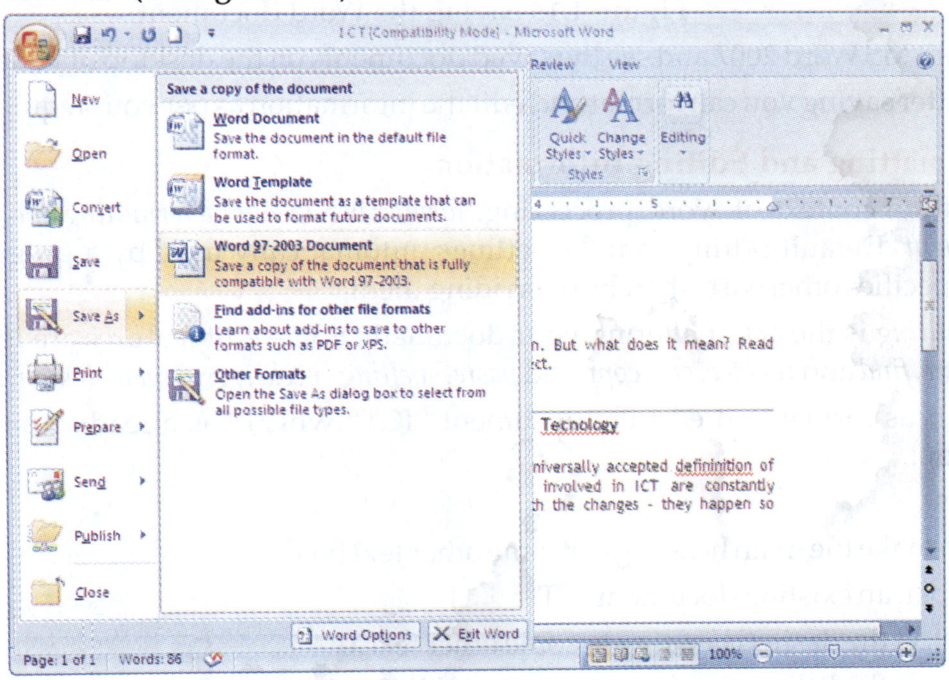

Figure 1.14 Saving information into Word document

You can save the document either on the desktop or in some other folder of your choice (See figure 1.15). Let us save the file on the desktop and name it "ICT", where we have already saved the searched document "AGRICULTURE" in a similar way'.

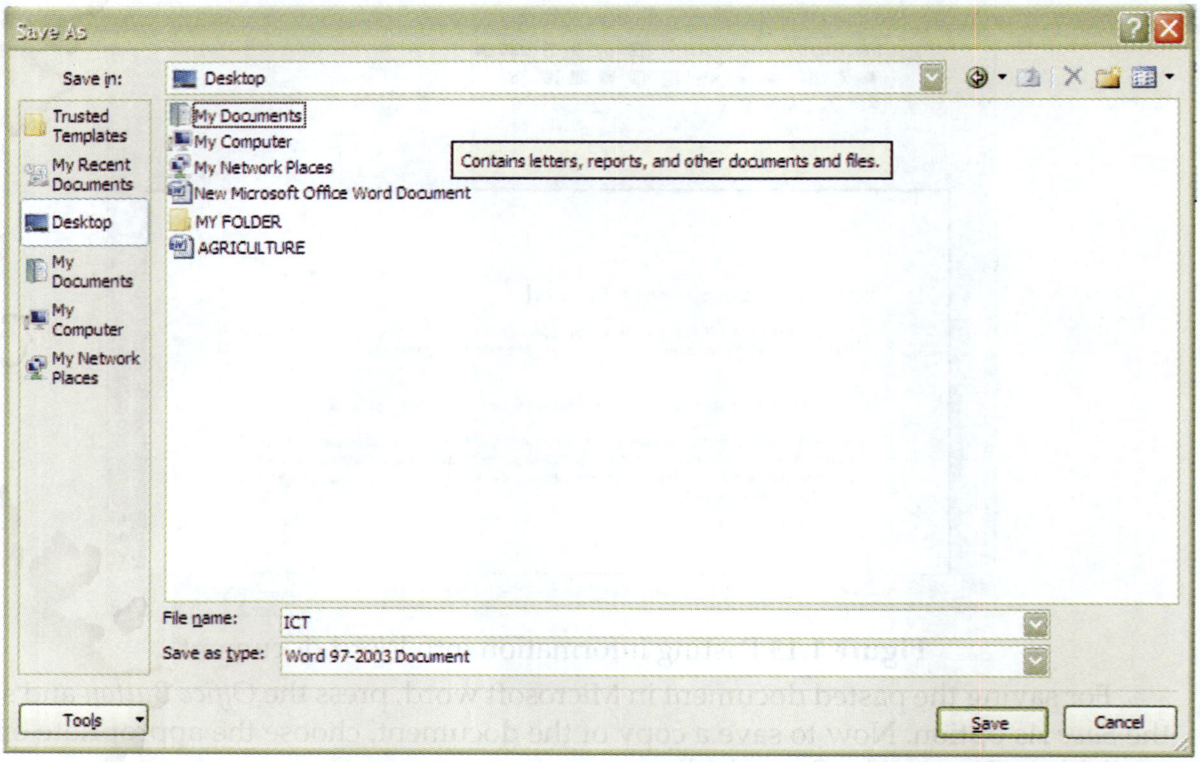

Figure 1.15 Saving the Word document

Exit MS Word 2007 and see the saved documents on the desktop of your computer.

After saving you can format and edit the information as per your requirement.

2.1.3 Formatting and Editing Information

In the context of word processing, *formatting means determining the appearance of a document.* Default settings are the settings automatically used by a program unless the user specifies otherwise, thereby overriding them.

Editing is the act of altering your document. Some edit features are *insert* and *delete, undelete, find* and *replace, cut, copy* and *paste, spelling checker, grammar checker,* and *thesaurus.*

Let us format and edit the document "ICT" which has already been saved on the desktop:

Bold

To make the main headings or some other text bold,

1. Open an existing document ICT.
2. Select the desired heading or some other text.
3. Select the *Bold* option from the *Font* panel. (See figure 1.16)

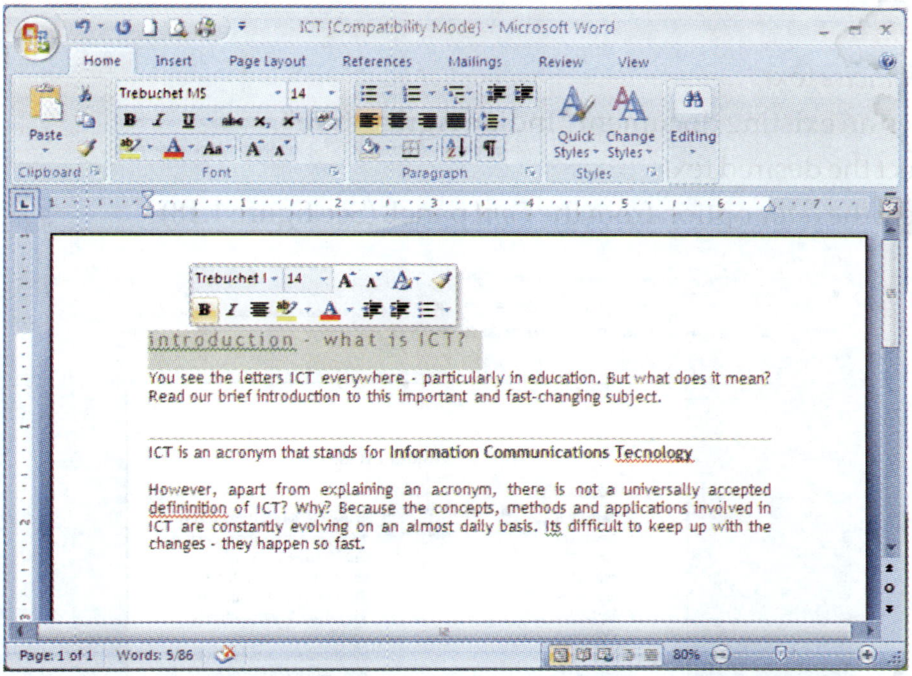

Figure 1.16 Applying **Bold** option

4. On applying the *Bold* option the selected text changes to bold. (See figure 1.17)

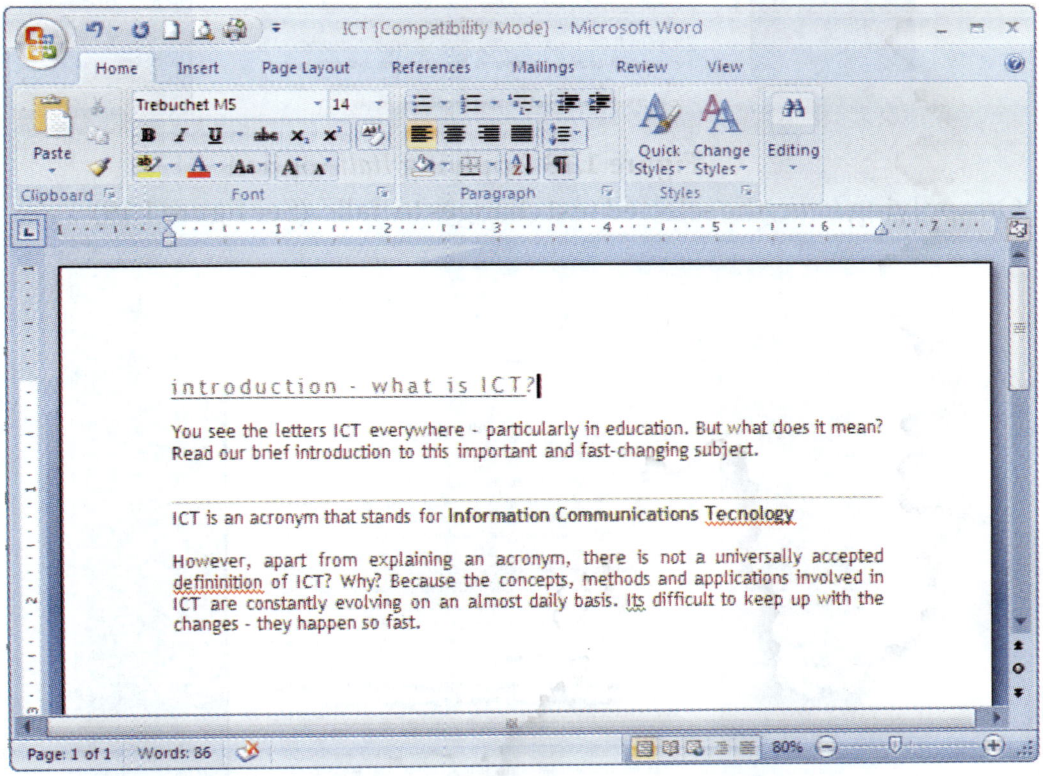

Figure 1.17 After applying the **Bold** option

5. Save your document.

Italic Text

To *italicise* text,

1. Open an existing document "Indian Agriculture".
2. Select the desired text.
3. Select the *Italic* option from the *Font* panel. (See figure 1.18)

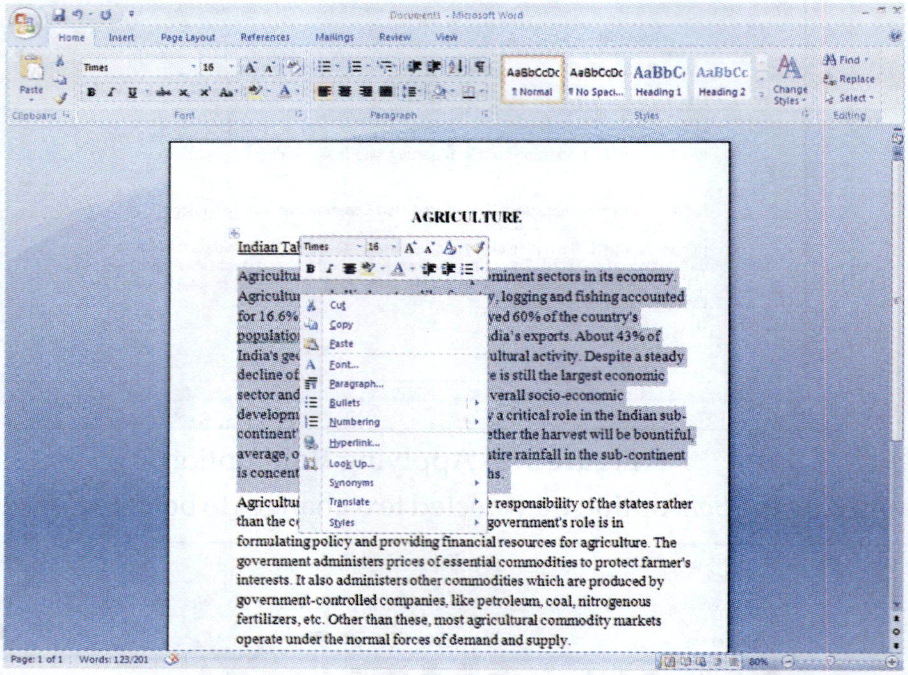

Figure 1.18 Applying *Italic* option

4. On applying *Italic*, the selected text changes to italic. (See figure 1.19)

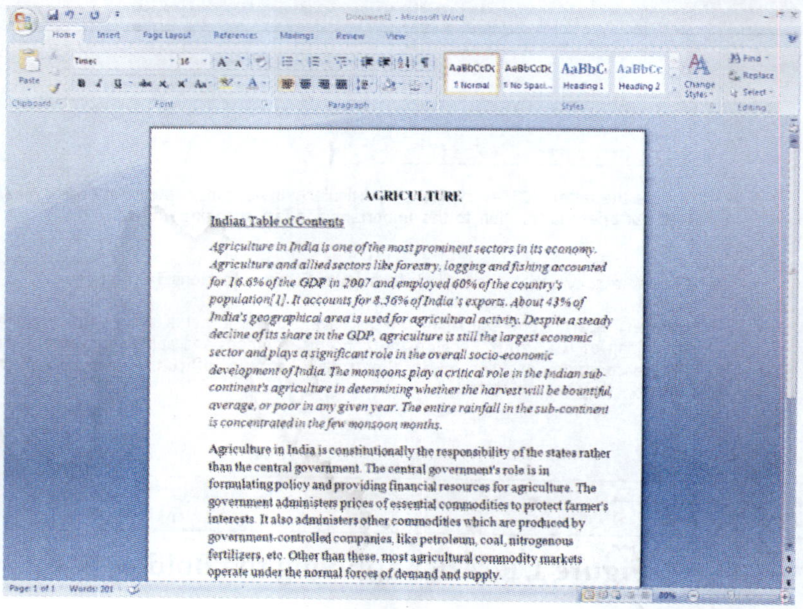

Figure 1.19 After applying *Italic* option

Underline Text

To underline text,

1. Select the desired text.
2. Select the *Underline* option from *Font* panel. (See figure 1.20)

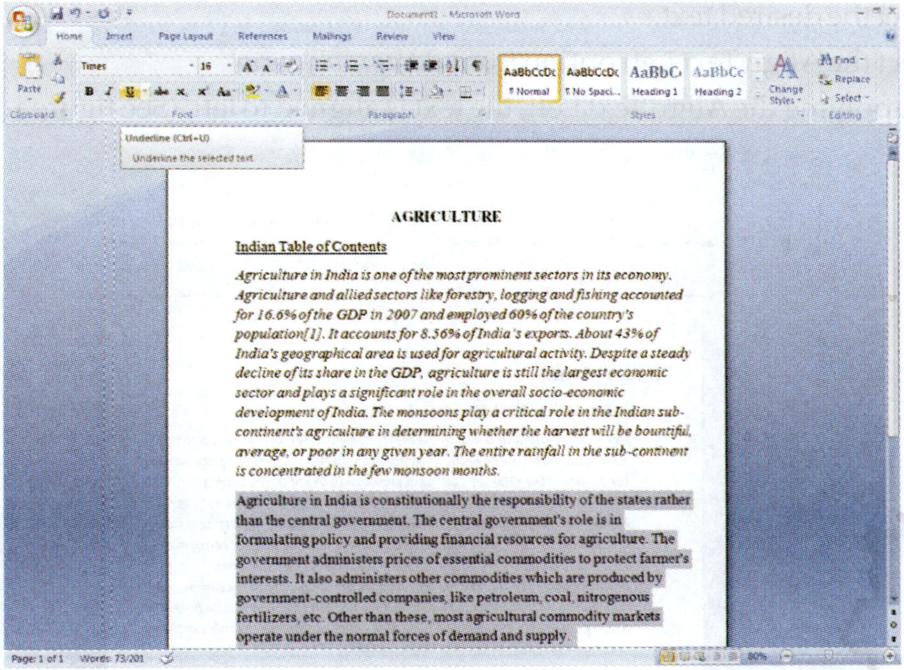

Figure 1.20 Applying <u>Underline</u> option

3. On applying *Underline*, the selected text is underlined. (See figure 1.21)

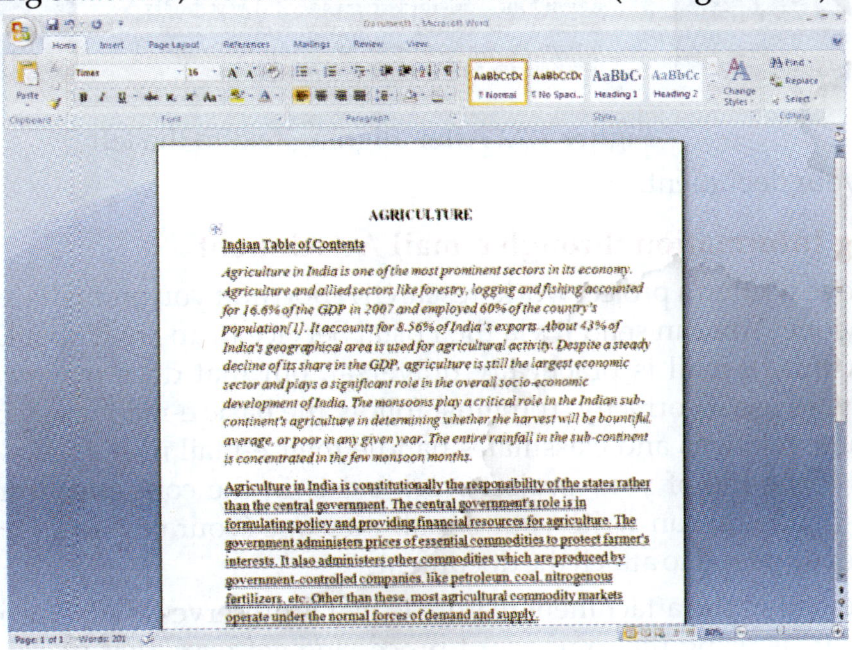

Figure 1.21 After applying <u>Underline</u> option

Aligning Text

You can align the text to left, center, right, or full justified. Generally, in documents texts are left aligned.

To align text left,

1. Select the desired text.
2. Select the Align Text Left option from *Paragraph* panel.
3. On applying the Align Text Left, the text is aligned to left. (See figure 1.22)

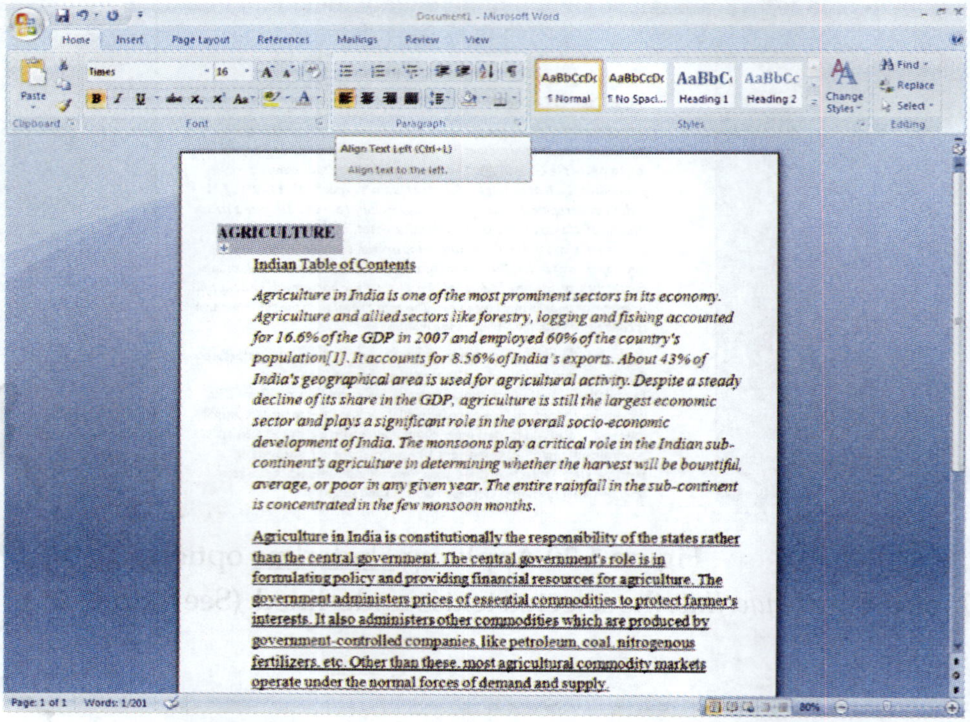

Figure 1.22 After aligning text to the left

4. Save your document.

2.1.4 Sharing Information through e-mail Attachment

You have written a project work–research report and you immediately want to show it off to someone. You can send it via the Postal Service in an envelope. E-mail has its own version of this. E-mail is practically universal, but that does not mean that everyone knows how to use it correctly. You must follow the basic e-mail usage guidelines to help your friends, relatives and classmates handle their e-mail responsibly and to safeguard everyone. If the file of your project work exists in the computer from which you are sending e-mail, you can write your e-mail message (your cover note) and then use the Attach File command to attach the document.

The benefit of the attachment feature is that it preserves all the formatting, provided the recipient is using the same word processing software that you used. You can also attach pictures, sounds, videos, and other files to your e-mail message.

Note

It is very important that the persons receiving the e-mail attachment have the exact same software that created the attached file, such as Microsoft Word 2007, or have software that can read and convert the attached file.

For sharing information,

1. Click *Start* at bottom left of the screen.
2. Click *All Programs.*
3. Click *Microsoft Office.*
4. Click *Microsoft Office Outlook 2007.* (See figure 1.23)

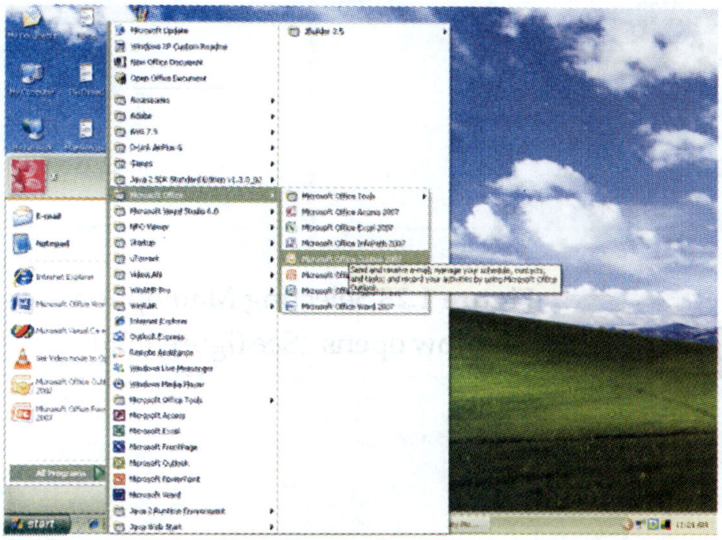

Figure 1.23 Opening Microsoft Outlook

5. On clicking, you will get *Outlook Today* window. (See figure 1.24)

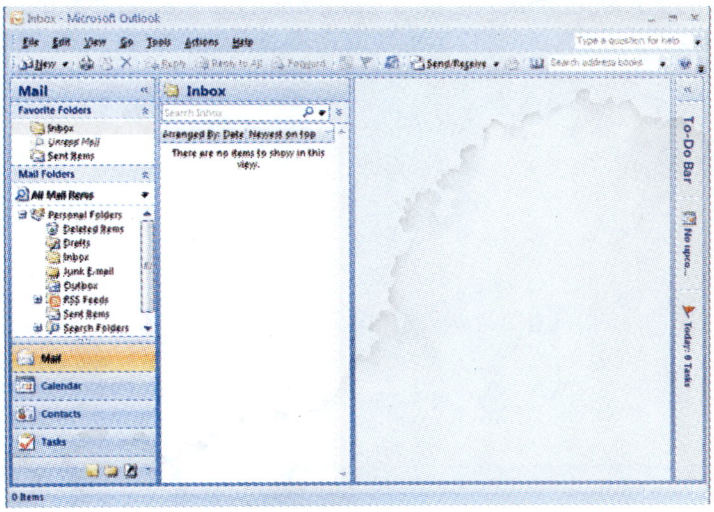

Figure 1.24 Preparing to share information using *Outlook Today*

6. Click on *Mail* option. (See figure 1.25)

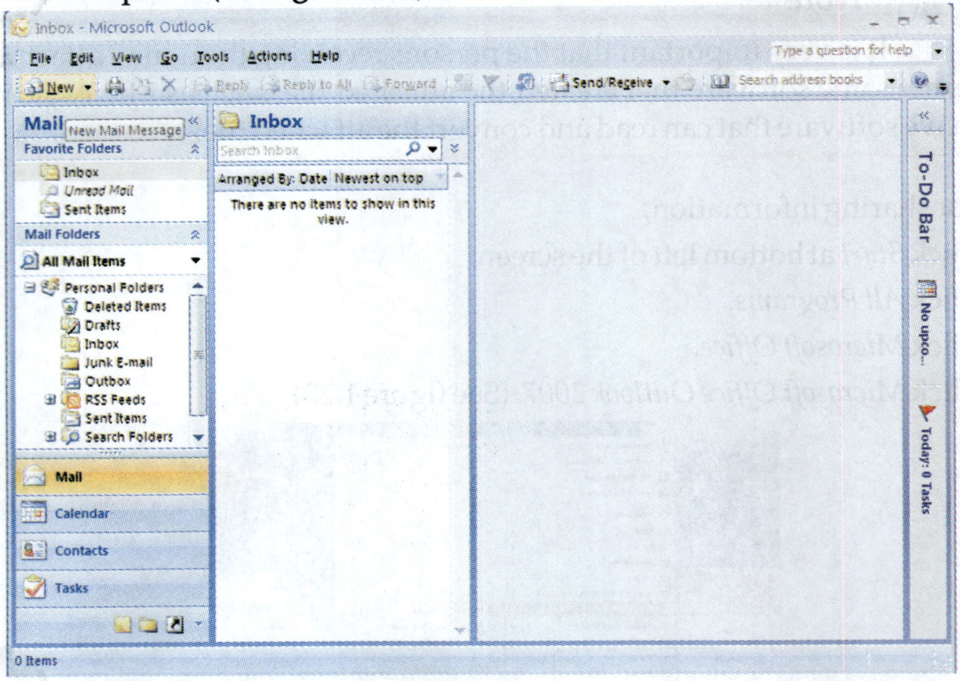

Figure 1.25 Selecting Mail option

7. On clicking, the *Message* window opens. (See figure 1.26)

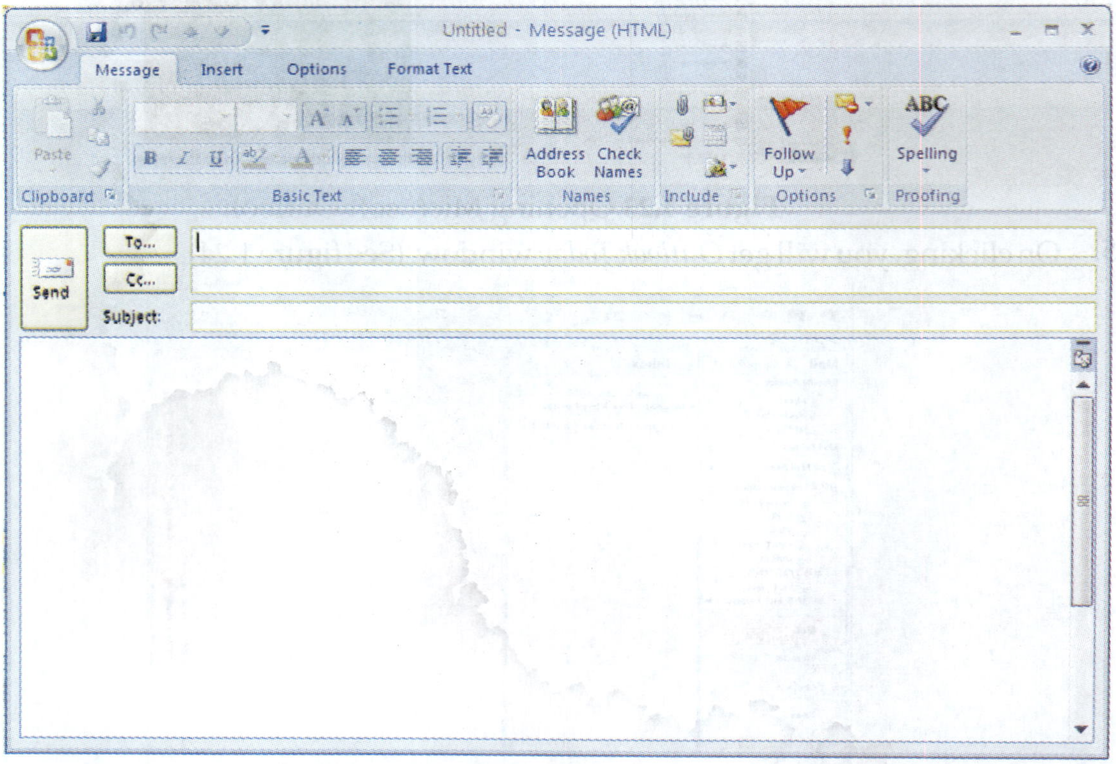

Figure 1.26 Message Window

8. Select the *Attach File* option available in *Include* panel. (See figure 1.27)

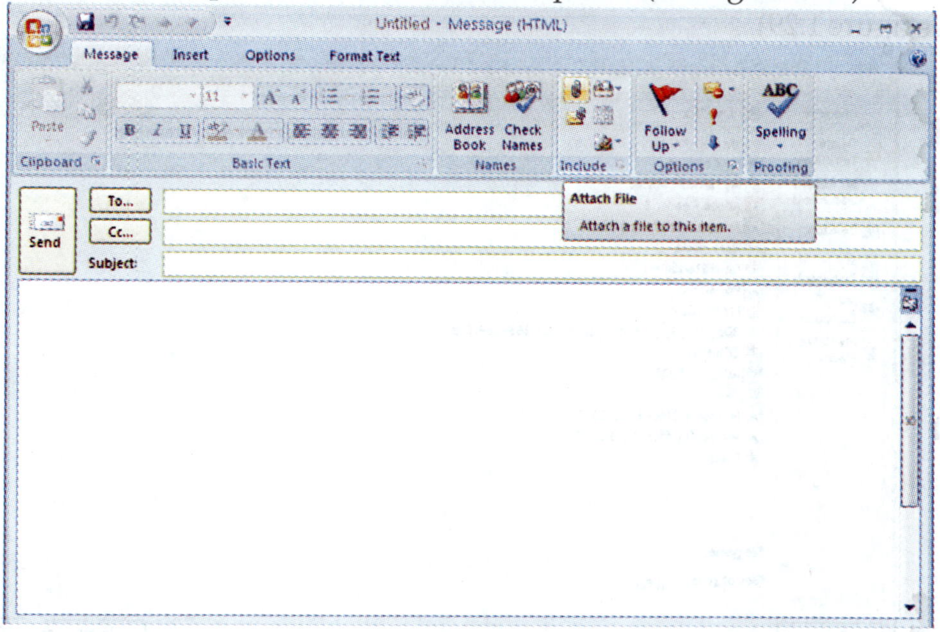

Figure 1.27 Selecting Attach File option

OR

You can also select the *Attach File* option available in *Insert*. (See figure 1.28)

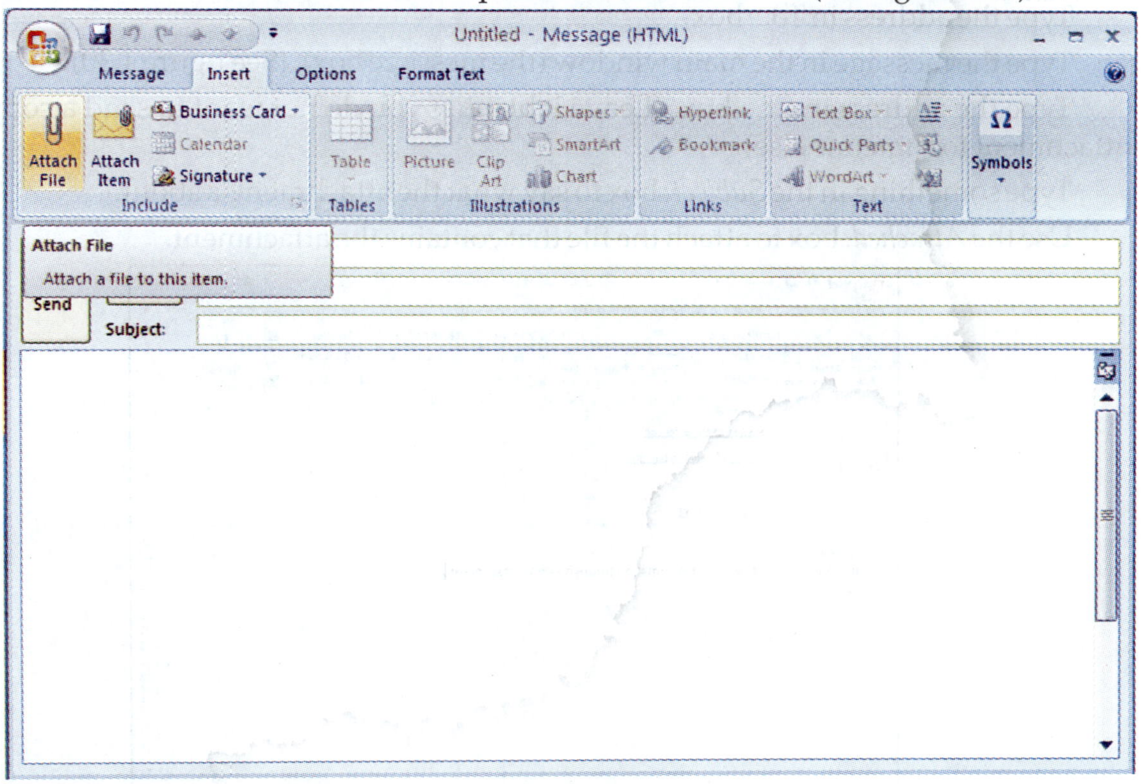

Figure 1.28 Alternate way of Attaching File

9. Now choose the file to be attached. Here, we have selected file ICT present at *desktop*. (See figure 1.29)

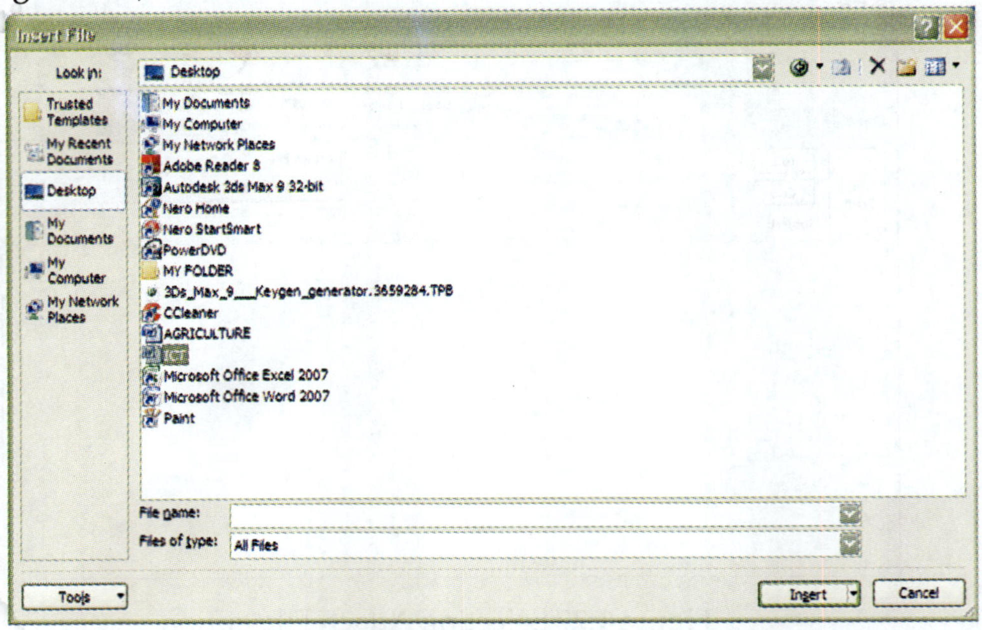

Figure 1.29 Choosing file for attachment

10. In the *Message* window,

Type the address in To... box

Type the message in the main window (the message box). (See figure 1.30).

Type the address in *Cc...* box. (Leave it blank if you do not want to send a copy of the attachment to someone else).

Type something in the *Subject:* box to say what the attachment is about.

Use the *Attached:* box to attach the file that contains the attachment.

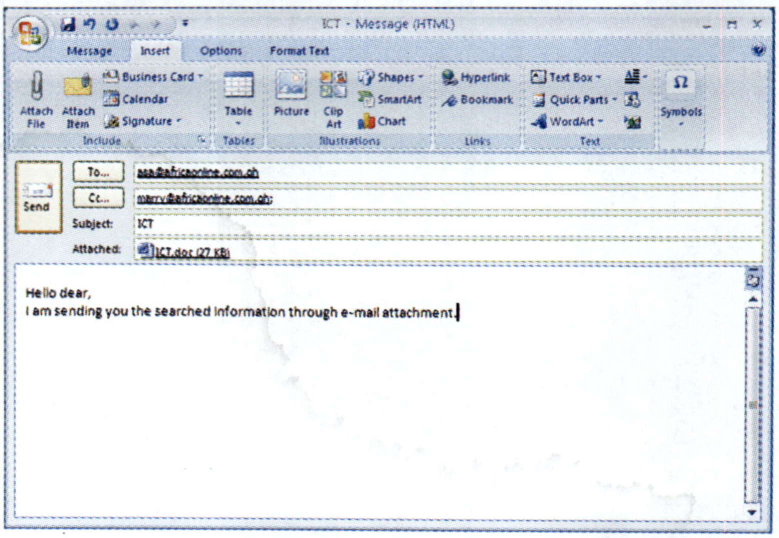

Figure 1.30 Sending an e-mail attachment

11. Click on *Send* to send the e-mail message and attachment.

In the same way your friends, relatives or classmates can send an e-mail with an attachment to you.

2.1.5 Accessing and Printing Attachment

Now you are familiar with sending an e-mail attachment. It can be accessed easily and printed.

To access and print your own documents,

1. Start Microsoft Word 2007.
2. Open the desired attachment.
3. Click on the *Microsoft Office Button*.
4. Select *Print* option from Print. (See figure 1.31)

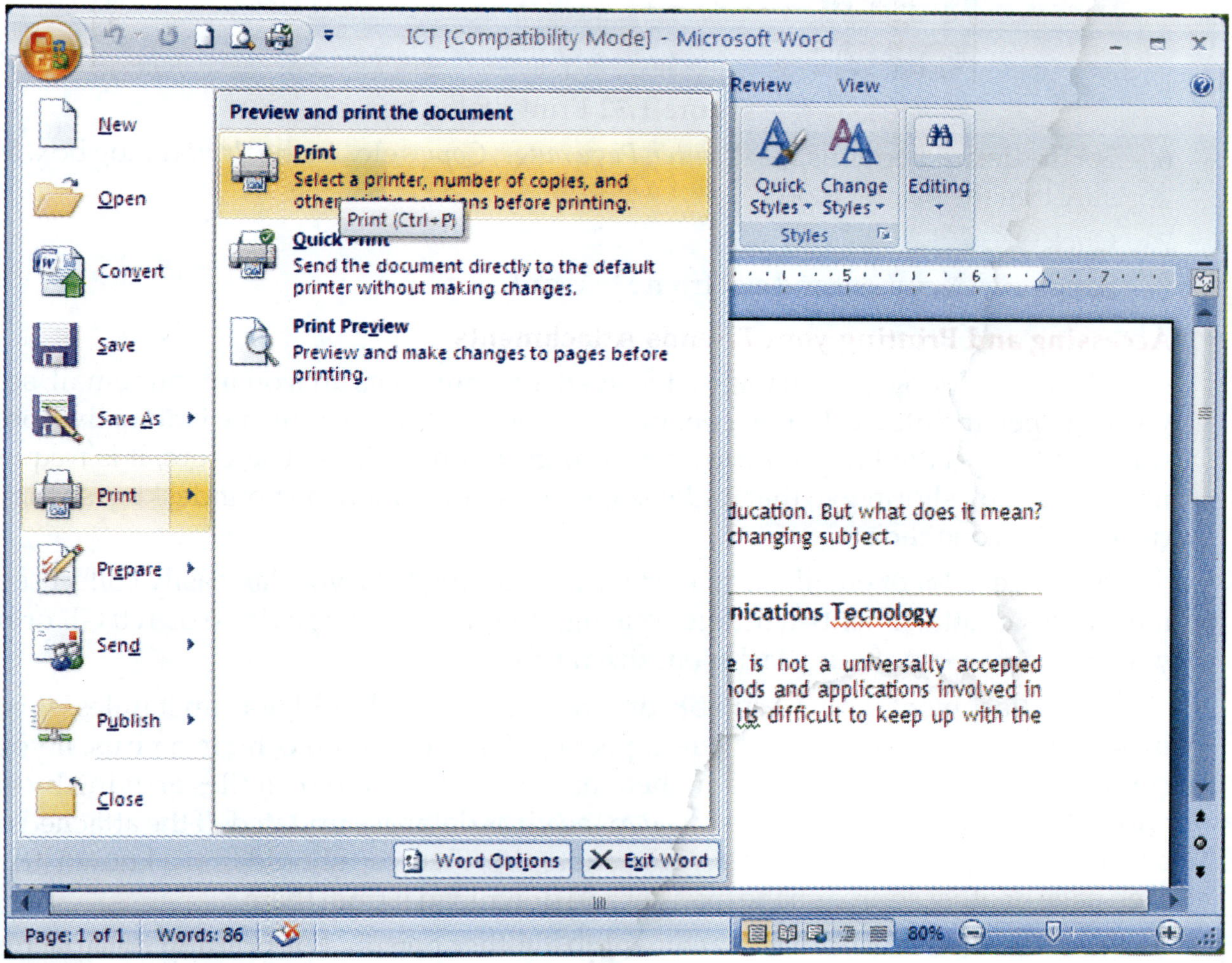

Figure 1.31 Preparing for printing a document

5. A *Print* dialog box is opened. (See figure 1.32)

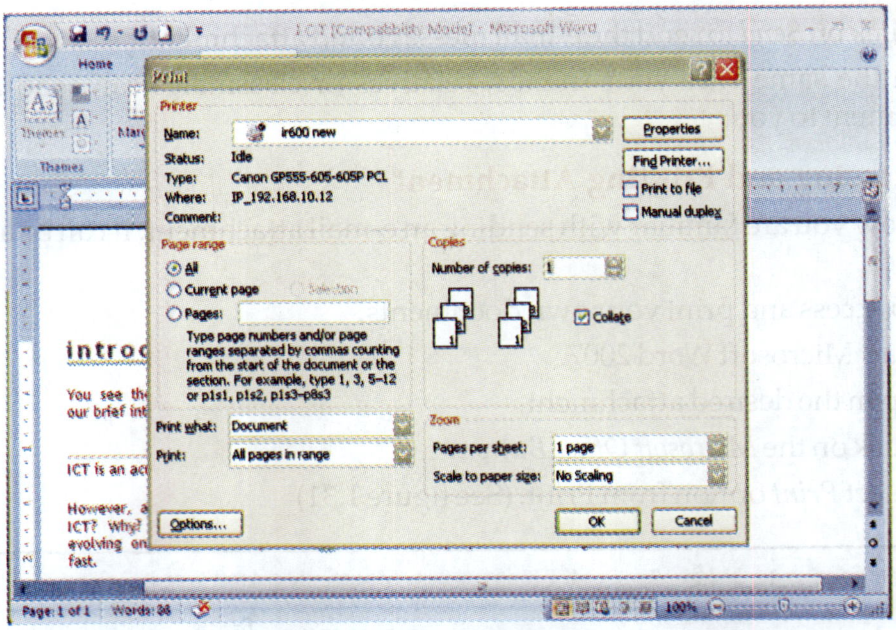

Figure 1.32 Print dialog box

6. Set the desired options, *i.e., Printer, Page range, Copies* etc., in the *Print* dialog box. Make sure that the printer is on.
7. Click OK.
8. Save your document and exit from MS Word.

Accessing and Printing your Friends Attachments

Most email programs display a received attachment as an icon in your email, so that you can open the file by double-clicking on the icon. However, the file is actually stored in some folder specified in your program configuration settings. Therefore, it is frequently useful to have a shortcut to that folder somewhere convenient on your desktop so that you can open it in one click.

If you get a lot of email, particularly from mailing lists, you can easily collect several megabytes of attachments without noticing. If you have a large drive of 160 GB or more you need not worry about attachment sizes at all.

If an attachment is an executable program, then you should not run it unless it is sent by someone you trust and you were expecting it, since it could contain a virus. If you are running a *virus protection* program, then make sure it is set to scan files arriving by email and it should keep you secure if you keep the virus database updated. If the attached file is a common program or utility that you want to use, then you should find a known, trusted Web page or other source on the Internet and download it from there.

You can also forward the attachment to another person. For printing the attachment follow the steps 1 to 8 as described above.

Close the *Microsoft Outlook* by clicking the button on the upper right corner of the Microsoft Outlook screen.

Disconnect from the Internet and shut down your computer properly.

ANSWERS TO REVIEW QUESTIONS

TERM-ONE

Section-I

UNIT 1: INFORMATION AND COMMUNICATIONS TECHNOLOGY (ICT)

STATE WHETHER TRUE OR FALSE

1. False	2. True	3. True	4. False	5. True
6. False	7. False	8. True	9. True	10. True

FILL IN THE BLANKS

1. Information and Communications Technology
2. Data
3. semistructured
4. Information Processing Cycle
5. e-learning
6. Web tutor
7. ICTs
8. Programmers
9. Database Administrator (DBA)
10. Network Administrator

MULTIPLE CHOICE QUESTIONS

1. (b)	2. (a)	3. (c)	4. (d)

UNIT 2: INTRODUCTION TO COMPUTERS

STATE WHETHER TRUE OR FALSE

1. True	2. True	3. True	4. False	5. True
6. False	7. True	8. False	9. True	10. True

FILL IN THE BLANKS

1. Computer

2. 'Father of Modern Digital Computers'
3. Operating System (OS)
4. Booting
5. icons
6. rebooting
7. Virus
8. Ergonomics
9. Ethics
10. Privacy

MULTIPLE CHOICE QUESTIONS

1. (d)	2. (b)	3. (a)	4. (d)	5. (b)
6. (b)	7. (b)			

Section-2

UNIT 1: HARDWARE

STATE WHETHER TRUE OR FALSE

1. True	2. True	3. False	4. False	5. True
6. True	7. True	8. True		

FILL IN THE BLANKS

1. CPU
2. Input devices, Output devices
3. impact, non-impact
4. CRT
5. impact

MULTIPLE CHOICE QUESTIONS

1. (b)	2. (c)	3. (a)	4. (b)	5. (d)

UNIT 2: SOFTWARE

STATE WHETHER TRUE OR FALSE

1. True	2. True	3. True	4. False	5. False	6. False

FILL IN THE BLANKS

1. System Software
2. proprietary
3. Windows Vista
4. proprietary
5. non proprietary
6. computer

MULTIPLE CHOICE QUESTIONS

1. (b) 2. (d) 3. (c) 4. (c) 5. (d) 6. (d)

Section-3

UNIT 1: KEYBOARDING AND MOUSE SKILLS REVIEW

STATE WHETHER TRUE OR FALSE

1. False 2. True 3. False

FILL IN THE BLANKS

1. User interface
2. typing software

MULTIPLE CHOICE QUESTIONS

1. (b) 2. (d)

TERM-TWO

Section-I

UNIT 1: WORD PROCESSING

STATE WHETHER TRUE OR FALSE

1. True 2. False 3. False 4. False 5. True
6. True 7. True 8. True 9. False 10. True

FILL IN THE BLANKS

1. application
2. reports
3. Word Wrap
4. Scrolling
5. New
6. name
7. Open
8. Text Editor/Star Word
9. Saving
10. Workspace

MULTIPLE CHOICE QUESTIONS

1. (d) 2. (a) 3. (b) 4. (a) 5. (a)

UNIT 2: EDITING TEXT IN WORD PROCESSING DOCUMENT

STATE WHETHER TRUE OR FALSE

1. True 2. True 3. True 4. False 5. False
6. True 7. False 8. False 9. True 10. False

FILL IN THE BLANKS

1. Copy
2. Cut
3. Paste
4. Undo
5. Redo
6. Find and Replace
7. OVR
8. Spell Check
9. Insertion
10. Editing

MULTIPLE CHOICE QUESTIONS

1. (b) 2. (d) 3. (a) 4. (b) 5. (d)

UNIT 3: FORMATTING WORD PROCESSING DOCUMENT

STATE WHETHER TRUE OR FALSE

1. True
2. False
3. True
4. False
5. False
6. True
7. True
8. False
9. False
10. True

FILL IN THE BLANKS

1. Formatting
2. Ctrl, I
3. Justify
4. numbers and bulleting
5. Line spacing
6. lowercase
7. Font size
8. centre
9. Left
10. underline

MULTIPLE CHOICE QUESTIONS

1. (c)
2. (b)
3. (a)
4. (a)
5. (d)

UNIT 4: INSERTING TABLES AND SYMBOLS IN WORD PROCESSING DOCUMENT

STATE WHETHER TRUE OR FALSE

1. False
2. False
3. True

FILL IN THE BLANKS

1. table
2. Symbols and Pictures

UNIT 5: PRINTING

STATE WHETHER TRUE OR FALSE

1. True
2. False
3. True
4. False
5. True

FILL IN THE BLANKS

1. Word Processing
2. Previewing
3. reduced
4. Two Pages
5. hard copy

MULTIPLE CHOICE QUESTIONS

1. (b) 2. (c) 3. (d)

Section-2

UNIT 1: THE INTERNET

STATE WHETHER TRUE OR FALSE

1. False 2. True 3. True 4. False 5. False

FILL IN THE BLANKS

1. ISP
2. browser
3. pornographic
4. Transmission Control Protocol
5. HTML

MULTIPLE CHOICE QUESTIONS

1. (d) 2. (b) 3. (c) 4. (a) 5. (d)

UNIT 2: USING THE INTERNET TO COMMUNICATE

STATE WHETHER TRUE OR FALSE

1. True 2. False 3. False

FILL IN THE BLANKS

1. E-mail
2. multiple
3. spell check
4. Chatting

MULTIPLE CHOICE QUESTIONS

1. (b) 2. (a)

UNIT 3: ACCESSING INFORMATION FROM THE INTERNET

STATE WHETHER TRUE OR FALSE

1. True 2. True 3. False 4. False

FILL IN THE BLANKS

1. useless
2. home page
3. URLs
4. Downloading

MULTIPLE CHOICE QUESTIONS

1. (d) 2. (c)

TERM-THREE

Section-I

UNIT 1: SPREADSHEET

STATE WHETHER TRUE OR FALSE

1. True 2. False 3. True 4. False
5. False 6. False 7. True

FILL IN THE BLANKS

1. Quattro Pro
2. row
3. navigation
4. create
5. currency, fraction
6. Save As
7. Formulae

MULTIPLE CHOICE QUESTIONS

1. (a) 2. (d) 3. (d)

UNIT 2: APPLICATION OF SELECTED FORMULA AND FUNCTIONS

STATE WHETHER TRUE OR FALSE

1. True 2. True 3. False 4. False

FILL IN THE BLANKS

1. =
2. syntax
3. Formula bar
4. MIN

MULTIPLE CHOICE QUESTIONS

1. (d) 2. (c) 3. (a)

UNIT 3: FORMATTING WORKSHEET

STATE WHETHER TRUE OR FALSE

1. False 2. True 3. False 4. True

FILL IN THE BLANKS

1. textual
2. deleting
3. columns
4. Merge cells

MULTIPLE CHOICE QUESTIONS

1. (a) 2. (a) 3. (c)

UNIT 4: EDITING WORKSHEET

STATE WHETHER TRUE OR FALSE

1. False 2. True 3. True 4. True

FILL IN THE BLANKS

1. Spelling
2. Custom
3. Normal
4. Page Setup

MULTIPLE CHOICE QUESTIONS

1. (a) 2. (b) 3. (a)

UNIT 5: PRINTING WORKSHEET

STATE WHETHER TRUE OR FALSE

1. False 2. True 3. True

FILL IN THE BLANKS

1. preview
2. file
3. Print

MULTIPLE CHOICE QUESTIONS

1. (a) 2. (c) 3. (b)

NOTES